Weekly Reader: 60 Years of News for Kids, 1928–1988

Introduction by Hugh Downs

WORLD ALMANAC
AN IMPRINT OF PHAROS BOOKS • A SCRIPPS HOWARD COMPANY
NEW YORK

Prepared by the staff of Weekly Reader,
Field Publications, Middletown, CT 06457

Library of Congress Cataloging-in-Publication Data

Weekly reader.

Includes index.
1. My weekly reader—History.   2. Children's
periodicals, American—History.   I. My weekly reader.
PN4878.W44   1988   071'.3   88-14214
ISBN 0-88687-373-8
ISBN 0-88687-365-7 (pbk.)

Library of Congress Catalog Number: 88-42609
Pharos ISBN Number: 0-88687-356-8

Printed in the United States of America.

World Almanac
An Imprint of Pharos Books
A Scripps Howard Company
200 Park Avenue
New York, NY 10166

10 9 8 7 6 5 4 3 2 1

Table of Contents

Introduction 5

Preface 7

1928–1929 9

1930–1939 16

1940–1949 56

1950–1959 96

1960–1969 136

1970–1979 176

1980–1988 216

Index 253

Remembrance of Times Past

A sight, a sound, a smell, a taste, a touch—any of these can call up memories of an earlier time. For a great many Americans, dipping into the pages of this book—and, thus, into our own past—will bring memories flooding back.

There is much here that we may have forgotten—or only half-remembered. Who would have thought that so many things that seem to have been around forever are really of such late vintage? The Empire State Building, the Mount Rushmore monument, the Cub Scouts, the Golden Gate Bridge, Fort Knox—the planet Pluto!—all of these were created or formed or built or discovered during the last 60 years.

There are stark images that remind us of hope and shattered hope and hope again. There is Neville Chamberlain, off to beard the German lion and save the world, side by side with a family wearing "monster masks" for protection from poison gas. There is a long line of refugees made homeless by war, trudging across a European landscape. There is a Russian tank on a street in Budapest and, 12 years later, another on a street in Prague. There is a cartoon soldier labeled "U.S. Guerrilla Aid" reaching down into a swamp to pull South Vietnam out of the muck. There is the image of Martin Luther King, Jr.—with his wife and child, and then at the Lincoln Memorial, and then on a motel balcony in Memphis—juxtaposed with firefighters at work on a street corner in riot-torn Milwaukee. How elusive has been our dream of peace, at home and abroad.

And then there are the children. An Indian child laughs in the arms of the Mahatma Gandhi. A group of blind children sit and listen as Helen Keller reads them a story. Shirley Temple helps build her new playhouse, made of glass block. An African child with a swollen belly gets something to eat at last. Children work and children play—and children learn. Even when you don't see their pictures, children are central in *Weekly Reader.* Because children, too, can do things. When the nation goes to war, children can help to make the difference between victory and defeat. American children can do their small part to feed that African child. And somehow hope is born again.

We were these children. These are our memories.

Hugh Downs
New York, NY
Spring, 1988

In the Beginning

Summer, 1928. It was still the Roaring '20s—a time of new ideas and unbounded energy, with little hint of the crash to come. Eleanor Johnson, a well-known reading expert, received a telegram from American Education Publications: "Ready to start your children's newspaper." A month later, the first issue was in the schools. For most of *Weekly Reader*'s life, Eleanor Johnson was to play a key role in guiding the little newspaper that set out to bring kids news that was "colorful but uncolored."

Circulation that first year rose to 100,000. Today *Weekly Reader* has 9 million subscribers—more than *Time* and *Newsweek* combined. Two-thirds of all adults in the country—about 150 million—used *Weekly Reader* when they were in school.

The secret of the paper's success is that it connects kids to the world outside the classroom, bringing to them life's most important and interesting information in a form they can read and understand. In the good times, it has cheered on economic recovery, victory, the wholesome life. In times of depression or defeat, it has tried to nourish and support as well as to explain.

Sometimes, looking back today, *Weekly Reader* does not seem to have adhered to its platform of fair and unbiased reporting. To avoid difficult or controversial discussions in the classroom, important events were sometimes omitted: the crash of 1929 was the first. And sometimes the prevailing bias of the age shines through clearly—most strikingly in the late '40s when the paper, like the country, was struggling to figure out whether the Russians were still the "friends" they had been during the war.

Gradually, as the country began to look more critically at itself in the '60s and '70s, so too did *Weekly Reader.* By the '80s, it was dealing with many more controversial topics than ever before, and doing so with a much more rigorous policy of unbiased journalism.

Weekly Reader: 60 Years of News for Kids, 1928–1988 captures the story of modern history, the story of our lives, as *Weekly Reader* told it to us in school. Four pages (selected from roughly 1,000) are devoted to each year. Most of the news in the first three pages is selected from the editions of *Weekly Reader* for grades four, five, and six. The fourth page also includes material from the kindergarten through third-grade editions. Because of space limitations, some articles have been edited or photographically reduced.

The last page of *Weekly Reader,* the "Skills Page"—the one we all remember so fondly—is represented only by its first appearance as the "Seatwork" page in Issue 1. This time you can read for pleasure only. There will be no quiz at the end of the period.

CURRENT EVENTS COMMUNITY LIFE

GEOGRAPHY BIOGRAPHY

HELPFUL SEATWORK

MY WEEKLY READER
Vol. I SEPTEMBER 21, 1928 No. I

HEALTH NATURE STUDY

Two Poor Boys Who Made Good Are Now Running for the Highest Office in the World!

A QUAKER BOY

A LITTLE boy sat in Quaker meeting. He had been there an hour. He began wiggling and wiggling, and whispered to his father, "Dost thou think meeting will be over soon?" After

church, he was punished, for Quakers were very, very strict.

That was in Iowa, about fifty years ago. The boy was Herbert Hoover. Today we are talking of making him President. Herbert was born in a small cottage. Next to it was his father's blacksmith shop.

Herbert had an older brother and a younger sister. They had lots of fun playing in the blacksmith shop. Being Quaker children, they never fought. To strike one another was a great sin.

When Herbert was six years old his father died. He did not leave much money, so Mrs. Hoover had to take in sewing. She was very religious. She even led Quaker services in the different churches. Once, while she was away,

Herbert went to Oklahoma to visit his Uncle Laban. His three were the only white children in town. All the rest were Indian boys and girls.

Such fun as he had playing with the Indian boys! They taught him how to build Indian fires; how to trap rabbits and squirrels, and how to catch fish.

When Herbert was nine, his mother took a very bad cold and died. The Hoover children were orphans now.

Herbert went to live on a nearby farm with his Uncle Allan. Here he fed the pigs, hoed the garden, and helped milk the cows. He went to the country school every day. Quakers were very strict about school, too. They thought that learning was next in importance to religion.

A LITTLE NEWSBOY

FIFTY-FIVE years ago, a baby boy was born in New York City. It was on the East Side, near the river, where many very poor people lived. He was named Alfred. He, too, is running for President this year.

Many of our Presidents have been born very poor. In America, everyone has a chance to become great. It does not matter where we are born, nor what we have. It all depends on what we are.

Alfred's mother and father were born in this part of New York, too. When Alfred was born, they lived in a flat. They had four small rooms on the top floor.

Alfred's father was a big, jolly Irishman. He had many friends, for he was always doing a good turn for them. One of his sayings was, "A man who cannot do a favor for a friend is not a man". He had a team of horses and made money by trucking. Alfred loved to sit on the high seat with his father and help drive through the crowded streets.

He was a very busy boy. He got up every morning between five and six o'clock. He was the priest's altar boy from the age of seven to fourteen. He had to be at church for early mass.

After school, Alfred sold newspapers and did anything he could to make money. All the Smiths worked, for the family was poor. Mrs. Smith made umbrellas to sell. She was a good mother. Alfred loved her dearly. She kept her children neat and her house clean.

Alfred worked, yet he had plenty of time to play. He loved most of all to give shows. There was an attic above

Where Al Smith Was Born

his house. It was a club-room for all his playmates. Alfred was a good actor. He could sing and knew lots of funny Irish songs. The boys liked him and he was their leader.

They loved to sit on the river bank and watch the workmen who were building a great bridge. It was to join Brooklyn with New York and was a mile long. That was the longest bridge of its kind in those days. It was started before Alfred was born and was finished when

he was ten. Alfred and his family were the first to cross. "I and the Brooklyn bridge grew up together", he says.

(Both stories will be continued next week.)

WINGS FOR SAFETY

Traffic police are at busy corners to make travel safe. Often they themselves are in danger of being run over.

In some of our cities, traffic policemen have new evening clothes. They are almost as pretty as the clothes God gave the night flying insects to wear. What is prettier than a white moth flying in the darkness? Policemen have lovely white capes to wear at night. When they stretch out their arms they look like great white moths. From far away,

drivers can see them. They are safe, and their white wings are pleasing to see.

Often man can do no better than copy old Mother Nature. He gets his best ideas from her.

MY WORD LIST

Qua-ker—a member of a very peace-loving church.
black-smith—a man who shoes horses.
al-tar—a place of worship.
mass—a church service
cur-rent—a body of air or water going one way.
af-fect—to make a change.
a-vi-a-tion—flying.
foil—to defeat.

Our little Buddy is robust and ruddy
   Disease germs he knows how to foil,
For just like a man, he takes all he can
   From a bottle of cod-liver oil.

The Wizard of Today

YOU have all heard of the wonderful wizards of long ago. The Wizard of Oz, with his magical powers, was able to help all the people of the forest. He fixed the tin soldier so he could walk. Of course, that story is only a fairy tale. But there really are great wizards today who do equally wonderful things.

A great wizard of today is Thomas A. Edison. Without his inventions, the world would be very different. Just fifty years ago he gave to the world the first **real** magic lamp, an electric light bulb. A great celebration is to be held this week in his honor. President Coolidge will send a message to him from the White House. He will speak over the radio and tell what Edison has done for the world.

What are some of the things he has done for us? Suppose we spend an evening together. We shall keep our eyes open and try to find out.

Let's turn on the phonograph and have some music. Turn on the lights, so we can dance. The telephone is ringing—it's a tele-

Edison Is a Kindly Wizard

gram from Dad. He is coming in on the 7:30 train and wants us to meet him. Good, it is Friday night, perhaps he will take us to the movies.

We drive to the electric railway station. We get father. It is Friday night, so he takes us to the movies to see "Peter Pan".

The theater is very beautiful. It gleams with hundreds of electric lights.

How many of these things could we have done tonight without Edison's help? Not one! We could not have turned on the phonograph nor the electric light, for Edison invented them. We would not have had father's message so surely, for Edison improved the telegraph and the telephone. We could not have started our car, nor would it have been lighted so well, for Edison made the batteries. He invented the electric train that father used. We could not have gone to the movies, if Edison had not invented the movie machine.

Edison is a wonderful man, 81 years old. He is still able to work in his shop in West Orange, New Jersey. This very month, Edison has put a new radio on the market. For a long time, he would have nothing to do with the radio because of static. Recently, his son Charles begged him to turn his magical powers to it. The result is a new Edison radio. It has two receivers. One is for local stations, the other for distant stations. It also contains a phonograph.

What do you know about Thomas A. Edison's life? Make a list of some of the wonderful things he has done for the world. Books from the library or a reference book will help you with these questions. You may decide who makes the best report to the class.

MR. GRUMPY AND MR. SPRIGHT

Mr. Grumpy went down the street,
A worse looking man 'twould be hard to meet.
With his head held low and his back so bent,
He cast dark gloom wherever he went.

Next down the street walks Mr. Spright,
He swings along with real delight.
Back straight as an arrow, and head held high
'Tis a joy to see Mr. Spright go by.

Mr. Grumpy   **Mr. Spright**

Now, children, which would you rather be,
Straight Mr. Spright or crooked Grumpy?
Now's the time to decide, for each day you grow
Like one or the other, be it ever so slow.

SEATWORK

THE dandelion is so common that we make fun of it. Yet there are lots of interesting things to learn about it.

1. Do you know how it got its name? It came from the French words "dent-de-lion", which mean "tooth of the lion". "Dent", meaning "tooth", gives the name dentist to the man who fixes teeth. The dandelion has teeth on its leaves.

2. It blooms longer than any other flower. Dandelions have been known to bloom for nine long months. They get so old that their hair turns white. Each hair has a seed in its root. When they are ripe the wind blows them off like kites.

3. The leaves make "greens", and the roots can be roasted for "coffee".

4. Do you know why there are so many? Dandelion roots are very long. No matter how dry the summer is, they get plenty of water to drink. Animals do not like to eat dandelions, for they taste bitter. There are other reasons. Can you think of them?

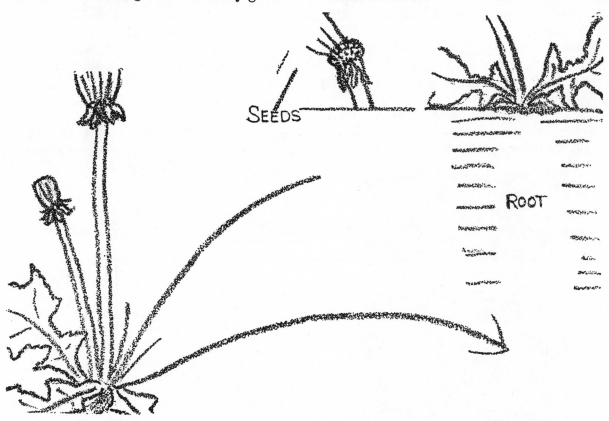

SEEDS

ROOT

SOMETHING TO DO

Dig up a dandelion plant, root and all. In the space above, finish the drawing with crayons. Draw the flower, the leaves, and the seed with its "sail". Draw a root in the space marked "root".

On page two:

Mark an x where Al Smith was born.
Mark an x where the Brooklyn Bridge is.
Make the policeman's cape blue.

CAN YOU ANSWER THESE?
(Draw a line around the right answer.)

1. Was Herbert Hoover born in a city? Yes....No
2. Did his father shoe horses? Yes....No
3. Was Al Smith a lazy boy? Yes....No
4. Were these two boys rich? Yes....No
5. Was the Brooklyn Bridge finished last year? Yes....No
6. Can you see the blue cape as clearly as you could the white one? Yes....No

The Little King of Rumania

YOUNG King Michael, on the tenth of May, will take up some of his royal duties. Dressed in the simple costume of Rumania, the seven-year-old king will ascend his throne. He will make a speech to his people. He will tell them that he is proud to be their king. He will promise them that he will do all he can to help make them happy.

The tenth of May was chosen for this ceremony because on that date, ten years ago, greater Rumania was formed. Many parts of the country were united under one flag. May 10 will be a holiday for the whole kingdom. New postage stamps and new coins have been made for this great day. Flags will wave throughout the land and church bells will ring.

Michael will be very busy on that day. He will open a special government meeting. He will lay the cornerstone for a wonderful new church, which Rumania is building. He will unveil (or uncover) three new statues.

There will be a large party in the palace. It will be gay with music and flowers. Many famous persons will be there, dressed in their best clothes. Many men will wear their soldier-clothes. Their boots will shine with polish. Golden swords will hang from their belts. The ladies will wear silks and satins. Everyone will bow to the boy king. The finest food that can be bought in the land will be served at this party.

People throughout Rumania will join in the celebration. It is said that 100,000 peasants will form a parade. They will wear brightly colored costumes. The celebration will last for more than a week.

King Michael has received many gifts from his people. One that pleases him most is a gift from the children of Rumania. It is a little guitar. The little king loves music. He likes to play and sing. He is so fond of his new guitar that he takes it to bed with him every night. On one side of his bed in the royal palace is his guitar. On the other side lies his dog, Mumbo.

The guitar is made of many pieces of the finest wood. It is trimmed with a tiny royal crown made of mother-of-pearl. The little king carries it about the palace and plays his favorite tunes on it.

Michael Takes a Walk With His Mother

Michael will not rule alone until he is grown up. His grandmother, Queen Marie, and men of the government do most of the ruling for King Michael.

Tell all you know about King Michael. What would you do if you were a king or a queen?

"Think before you speak; pronounce not imperfectly, nor bring out your words too hastily, but orderly and distinctly."—George Washington.

MEMORIAL DAY

April 26 is the day when many Southern States honor the men who died in the War Between the States. It is called Confederate Memorial Day. Northern States observe Memorial Day later— May 30.

CHINOOK'S LAST BIRTHDAY

CHINOOK, leader of Commander Byrd's dog teams at the South Pole, was 12 years old the last of January. On the morning of his birthday, he followed his master, Arthur T. Walden, from camp with the rest of the dogs. As they made their way over the ice and snow toward the ship, Chinook lagged behind. That was very unusual for Chinook. He, the leader of the dogs, was so well trained that when any dog was lazy he bit him on the ear. It was as much as to say, "Hurry along there, you lazy one".

Soon after leaving camp, Chinook disappeared. His master, who loved him as few men love a dog, searched for him. But Chinook could not be found. It is thought that he went out alone into the frozen Antarctic to die. He had not been feeling well. Perhaps he knew that he was growing too old to do his share of the work. Rather than disappoint his master whom he had never failed, he would go out alone and die. Being tired and sick, he must have lain down on the soft white snow and gone to sleep.

A Dog Team in the Antarctic

What Shall Be Our National Flower?

FOR many years, the bald eagle has been America's national bird. But America has never had a national flower. Ireland has the shamrock, Scotland the thistle, and England the rose. Americans have often talked of choosing a national flower but until recently nothing has been done.

The American Nature Association has asked everyone in America to vote for a national flower. For the first time, children will have a vote in a national election.

Thousands of votes, from all parts of the United States, have been received at Washington. Among these votes, the wild rose holds first place; the goldenrod second place; the columbine third place.

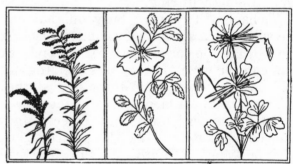

Goldenrod   Wild Rose   Columbine

SPRING STYLES IN MILK BOTTLES

For more than 40 years, Miss "City Milk" has come to our doors in the same dress. She has worn a thick, coarse coat of glass. So clothed, she was fat and noisy.

The New Sealcone   The Old Bottle   New Spring Style

This year, New York is starting a new fashion for milk. A new garment called the "sealcone" has been especially made for her. It is a dress cut with straight lines. In it Miss "City Milk" is slim, tall, and pale.

The new container for milk is made of heavy white paper coated with paraffin. It is air-tight, leak-proof, and germ-proof. It is not expensive and will be thrown away after it is used once. Glass milk bottles cost about $4\frac{1}{2}$ cents. Many of them get broken and are lost. The new sealcone costs only $\frac{3}{4}$ cents. It is hoped that this new container will lower the cost of milk.

Dear Children:

Here is a picture of a four-year-old boy who traveled as airmail. Around his neck was tied a large tag addressed to the postmaster. Air stamps were stuck to the tag to pay for his trip.

When the mail plane landed at the Ford airport in Detroit, the boy's father and mother were there to receive their "mail". But as long as he was "mail" they were not allowed to receive him until he went through the post office.

He was bundled into the mail wagon and taken to the main post office with the rest of the mail. There, his tag was stamped "Received, Detroit", with the date. Then, he was delivered to his father and mother, who had followed him to the post office.

JOAN OF ARC

Joan of Arc was born in April, 500 years ago. All of France is celebrating her birthday. Festivals are being given in her honor.

A great festival was held in Paris, April 12 and 13. It was called the Joan of Arc Pageant. More than 3,000 French people dressed in costume. They wore clothes that were worn in the time of Joan of Arc. Knights in shining armor rode through the streets on horseback.

Special French postage stamps have been printed in her honor. On them is the picture of the Maid of France. She rides a white horse and waves the French flag.

Why does the world remember this maid who lived so long ago? Why have stories

about this little French girl been written in all tongues?

The world remembers Joan of Arc because she was so brave. She gave courage to the soldiers of France and led them to victory. They drove the enemy away. Joan of Arc brought peace to France.

Tell all you can remember about Joan of Arc. Do you know anything about her which is not told here?

AMERICA'S SMALLEST PONY

The pony in the picture is the smallest one in America.

He is only 20 inches tall.

He weighs 28 pounds.

How much do you weigh?

The pony's name is "Mulligan".

The picture was taken

when he was one month old.

1930-1939

At home, millions stood in bread lines in sullen shabbiness. The federal government intervened as never before to soften the sharp edge of hard times. Huge, awe-inspiring public works of construction were created—the Golden Gate Bridge, the TVA power system, Hoover (now Boulder) Dam. And there came the promise of new technology—TV, glass-block houses, and blackboards that weren't black and, thus, were easier on the eyes.

Abroad, we saw the rise of Adolf Hitler and the Nazis, their lust for conquest, and their lethal persecution of Jews and others who ranked low in their crazed, racist view of life. And Japan became a potential threat to the U.S. as its militarists made a bloody grab for natural resources and *Lebensraum* in China and the Pacific.

The 1930s had more than its share of melancholy events, interspersed here and there with hints of brighter days ahead. *Weekly Reader*'s tone was one of determined optimism that "this too shall pass." During the Great Depression, the editors sought to make kids feel good about themselves and the nation's future. *Weekly Reader*'s treatment of the menace abroad was less sure, reflecting the uncertainty in the country itself. The sense is one of something very unpleasant happening "over there." In 1939, after World War II had begun, *Weekly Reader* published a supportive piece about Charles Lindbergh; in a nationwide radio address, the famous flyer had said that the U.S. should stay out of Europe's quarrels. Millions of Americans held this isolationist view throughout the '30s. Not until Japan's surprise bombing of Pearl Harbor late in 1941 would the nation become truly united in taking on the Axis powers.

A Great Speed Contest

SHIPS of the sea, land, and air are all trying to go faster, faster, faster. Each country wants its big ocean liners, trains, automobiles, and airplanes to go faster than those of any other country. Great Britain, France, Italy, Germany, and the United States have gone into a speed contest.

Squadron Leader A. H. Orlebar of England tells about this modern speed race. He flew an airplane 368 miles an hour, which is faster than man had ever traveled. He says that racing boats, automobiles and airplanes are planned very carefully for their speed. These racers are later used as models. Their motors and the shapes of their bodies are copied. These copies are put into the boats, automobiles, and airplanes which are used for fast travel.

Recently the ocean liner, Europa, crossed the

The New Europa, Fastest Ship in the World

Atlantic in 4 days, 17 hours, and 6 minutes. This ship belongs to the North German Lloyd Line. It beat its sister ship, the Bremen, by 18 minutes. It won the ocean race for speed, although it had to fight its way through heavy winds and heavy seas.

The Europa is built for speed. Her bow (front end of a ship) is rounded. Her propellers (which drive a ship forward) are small and turn very quickly. Two of them churn the water inward, and two churn it outward.

As the Europa sailed swiftly over the sea, a new fast train made its first trip between Boston and New York City. It made the trip in 4 hours and 45 minutes, for it traveled almost a mile a minute. This is said to be the fastest train schedule in the United States. Long ago it would have taken the pioneers in their covered wagons over a week to make the trip. Did it not take those pioneers two years to cross the plains and mountains to the Far West? Today you can go by train from New York to California in five days.

The new fast train belongs to the New Haven Railroad and is called the Yankee Clipper.

Each coach is named for one of the famous old Yankee clipper ships. They are called the Flying Cloud, Surprise, Northern Light, and other clipper ship names. They bring back the memory of those days of slower travel.

Yankee clipper ships sailed the seas 75 years ago. With many sails spread wide to the wind, their sharp bows clipped or slid swiftly through the water. They went faster than any other boats at that time. They were speed ships and were used to bring tea from China. On the slower ships, tea often spoiled during the long trip. Clipper ships were also used to carry passengers to California and Australia during the days of the gold rushes.

As the Yankee Clipper train started its fast trip and the Europa sailed over the sea, an automobile was being prepared for a speed test. At Daytona Beach, Fla., Kaye Don was tuning up the motor of the Silver Bullet. He wanted to break the record of 231 miles an hour which Major Segrave held.

In Germany, Dr. Hugo Eckener is making plans for an airship line across the Atlantic Ocean. Passengers, mail, and freight will then be carried between the United States and Europe in about two days. Do you know how long it took the Pilgrims to cross the Atlantic Ocean in the Mayflower? It took them more than two months.

An Old Clipper Ship

The race for speed has been going on for many, many years. Men will always dream of ships of the land, sea, and air that travel faster than any ship has ever traveled before. Do you want to build a racing car? Do you want to fly swiftly across the country in an airplane or would you rather travel in a covered wagon? You would see many interesting things on the wagon trip that you would miss in the airplane.

Those who go too fast miss many happy things. In the racers they can only feel the swift rush of the wind. They cannot see the beautiful things around them. At times let us go along more slowly as the pioneers did long ago. Let us stop to listen to a bird's cheery song. Let us watch the beautiful colors in the sunset.

World's Largest Dam Is Being Built

DID you ever pile up stones in a stream to keep back the water? If you did, you made a dam. Animals make dams, too. The beaver is known for being a good builder of dams. He cuts down small trees with his sharp teeth. Then he pulls branches through the

The Colorado River Flows Between High Cliffs

water to the place where he wishes to build his dam. He puts sticks, stones, and mud around his pile of trees. This dams up the stream and makes a lake. This lake is the winter home of beavers.

Perhaps man first learned to make dams by watching the beaver. He dammed up streams and made lakes. Then he had plenty of water after the streams had dried up.

The Largest Dam in the World

This month, men are starting work on the world's largest dam. It will take seven years to build the great dam. A thousand men will help with the work.

The dam is being built on the Colorado River. It will be called the Hoover Dam. A very high wall will be built between the banks of the river. It will be 727 feet high, or higher than the Washington Monument. It will hold back the water of the Colorado River and

form a large lake. This lake will be more than one hundred miles long.

The large dam will be a great help to the farmers. It will store up water for the dry valleys of the West. Canals will be built which will carry water from the lake. These canals will water more than seven million acres of land. Part of this land is desert land. It is dry and brown and of no use to man. After it is watered by the canals, it will become green and fertile. Groves of orange, lemon, and date trees will grow on land that was once brown and dry. Parts of seven western States will be changed into beautiful garden lands.

The water that falls over the dam will turn big wheels. The wheels will make electric power. This power will be used in large factories. It will be used for electric lights.

The early Spanish explorers were the first white men to go up the Colorado River. That was three hundred years ago. The roaring mountain river meant only one thing to the early explorers. It meant a way to travel inland by boat. At that time, rivers were used only for travel.

THE JAPANESE CHERRY TREES IN WASHINGTON

THE famous Japanese cherry trees in Washington, D. C., are in bloom. Every spring thousands of persons in their gay Easter clothes go to see the trees. Easter is very late this year. The trees are covered with their dainty pink blossoms long before the Easter parade.

The Japanese cherry trees were planted in 1909 by Mrs. Taft, while her husband was the President of the United States. When Japan heard that the Japanese trees had been planted, she was eager to show her friendship for the United States. The Japanese Government sent three thousand cherry trees to the United States as a mark of good will. Lincoln Memorial may be seen beyond the cherry trees.

A NEW WORLD

There have been many interesting discoveries in the evening sky, since the children of Greece watched the picture stories of the stars long ago. For some time, astronomers (men who study the sky) have known about eight planets (worlds that move around the sun). Now they think they have found a ninth planet, for last month a new one was seen. The earth is a planet and it is the only one on which we are sure there is life. The planets do not have any light of their own. They shine because the light of the sun is thrown upon them.

The new planet is the tiny spot marked with arrows. It is so far away that it can be seen only with the most powerful telescope.

Clyde Tombaugh, a boy who loves the stars, was the first person to discover the new planet. When Clyde was a small boy, he lived on a farm in Kansas. During the long cold winters, he read books about the stars. He even built a small telescope from a picture in one of these books. A telescope is a long tube with lenses which make the stars seem closer to the earth. Later Clyde went to Flagstaff, Arizona, to work in the Lowell Observatory (a building from which the sky is studied). There men had been searching for the new planet for about 16 years.

One evening while Clyde was taking pictures of the stars a flash of light appeared on one of the pictures. Clyde rubbed his eyes and looked again. The light was the new world. He had found the planet for which men had searched for years. His heart gave a leap of joy. He wanted to shout his great discovery to the world, but he had to wait. He studied the planet very carefully. Other men also studied it before the news was given to the world.

The New Boy Scout Cubs

SMALL boys have always wanted to follow their big brothers to Scout meetings. Often they have worked hard to learn flag signals. They have practiced building a fire without matches. They have learned the Scout oath of loyalty. Each one has waited eagerly, impatiently for his twelfth birthday, so that he could join the Boy Scouts of America. But no longer will they have to wait until they are twelve years old. A new branch of

The First Two Cubs of St. Louis

the Boy Scouts has been started for younger boys. These junior Boy Scouts will be called Boy Scout Cubs. There are in the United States 4,000,000 boys from nine to twelve years old, who may now join the new club.

The Cub groups will delight the heart of every small boy, because they are divided into "Dens" and "Packs". Each Den will meet in the basement or in the garage of some boy's home. About once every month all the Dens in one neighborhood will come together for a large group meeting. These large groups are the Packs, while the small groups are the Dens which make up the Packs.

Each member of the Cubs will be called "Wolf", "Bear", or "Lion". These names tell the rank of the members. The boys will change their names, as they become better and better in their work. At last, when they are twelve years old, they will become "Tenderfoot" members of the older Boy Scouts of America.

For their meetings the Cubs will have their own uniforms. They will wear dark green sweaters, navy blue breeches, green caps, and blue stockings trimmed in green. When the Dens meet, the boys will take the oath of loyalty to their country and their homes. They will learn to help others and to be kind to all animals. They will play new games. They will discuss their collections of stamps, bugs, or other things which small boys love to own. They will make things with their hands, as the American Indian made things long ago. At the Pack meetings there will be stunts and short plays.

All small boys like dens. They enjoy holding club meetings in basements or in garages. Small boys also like packs in which they may be called wolves, bears, or lions. The names take them into the thrilling land of the jungle, where Mowgli, a hero of the Jungle Books, lived.

Dear Boys and Girls,

Here I am safe and sound in China. I have so much to tell you that I don't know where to begin!

First of all, I shall tell you about my exciting trip across the Eastern Sea. We were in a very bad storm. The winds howled and the waves were like mountains. My ship was large but old. As the heavy waves dashed over it, I thought surely it would sink. In the midst of the storm, the fire alarm sounded. I put on my life belt and rushed out on deck. I tried not to be afraid, but I really was. I did not know which was worse, the fire or the water!

The fire broke out on the ship's lowest deck. It was soon put out. Can you guess what caused the fire? Pirates! We do not often hear of pirates outside of story books. But there are real pirates on this sea. A band of Chinese pirates dressed like coolies boarded our ship in Japan. They started a fire, thinking that in the excitement of putting it out they could take the boat. But the Japanese were too smart for them, and the pirates were soon put in chains.

As the boat neared China, I saw several war-ships. I saw more and more boats as we came nearer land. There were big flat-bottomed boats called junks. They have tall sails made of cane or bamboo matting. Crossbars on the matting make the sails look like the wings of great bats.

There were smaller boats called sampans.

These boats have three white sails on them. The sails look like large, white pillow cases. Each boat has a large eye painted on its bow (the front of a boat). I asked the captain why. He said that the people of China think that all boats must have eyes to find their way about. He said, "If boat no eye have, how can boat see go?"

Love to you all,

Uncle Ben

The White House Fire

Little Peggy Anne and Herbert Hoover, Jr., did not come to the White House for Christmas.

But President and Mrs. Hoover had a party for some other children on Christmas Eve.

The children played and sang Christmas songs in the White House. Then they all sat down to supper. They were eating ice cream and cake.

Suddenly the watchman came into the dining room. He went over to President Hoover and said something to him. President Hoover left the room. Soon all the other men left the room, too.

Cling-Clang!

The children went on eating their ice cream and cake. They heard fire engines. The fire engines came nearer and nearer. Cling—clang—cling—clang. They stopped in front of the White House. The White House was on fire.

Mrs. Hoover knew the White House was on fire but she was not afraid. She knew that if there was any danger someone would come and tell her.

The party went on. The children finished eating their ice cream and cake.

After the party was over they all went out on the porch. They watched the firemen fighting the fire. They saw the long ladders.

They saw the water coming out of the long hose.

The fire was in a part of the house far away from the dining room. It was in President Hoover's offices. The children were not in danger. They had all been quiet and calm. The firemen watched until the fire was out.

Miss Jane Addams Works Hard for Peace

EACH year, a magazine* gives a prize to the American woman who has done the most good for her country. This year, the prize was given to Miss Jane Addams. She was given the prize for her outstanding work for world peace and for helping the poor people of her city. The prize was five thousand dollars.

Miss Addams has worked all her life for the good of others. Her first work was among the poor people of Chicago. She bought a big house in an old part of the city, where persons from 36 countries lived. This country was strange to them. Some of them could not even speak our language. They did not know where to go to enjoy themselves when their hard day's work was over. Miss Addams opened her house to these people. She let them come in and read. She let them see her beautiful pictures. Then she began to teach them how to make things. Mothers learned to sew, while fathers read and studied. There were dances for the young people and races in the swimming pool for the children. There was a storytelling hour, too.

Miss Addams named her house Hull House in honor of the man who built it. She has kept Hull House open for many, many years. Thousands of persons in Chicago have learned much and have been very happy at Hull House.

Miss Jane Addams works not only for the happiness of the people in America, but also for the happiness of the people of other countries. She has always hated war. War makes every one unhappy. Miss Addams works hard to keep peace in the world. She has gone to many peace meetings in Europe. She has led many peace meetings in this country. She says that the countries of the world must never have another war.

*The Pictorial Review

The world's biggest war was ended 13 years ago. It was ended on November 11. That day in every year we call Armistice Day. We are all glad to talk about peace on Armistice Day. We are glad that this year's prize was given to one who is working so very hard for world peace.

Miss Jane Addams is now a fine old lady whom every one loves. This September, she

Miss Jane Addams with a Little Friend

was 71 years old. She says she is very proud of her prize. Someone asked her what she was going to do with the five thousand dollars. She said she was going to use it this winter to help men who are out of work. We are not surprised to hear Miss Addams say this. All her life, she has given her time and money to make others happy. That has made her happy, too.

The World's Highest Building Is Opened

JUST before noon on May 1, President Hoover pressed a button in Washington, which turned on the lights in a new building in New York City. At the same time, two little children broke the paper ribbons which tied shut

the main door of the building. This meant that the Empire State Building, the world's biggest building, was finished. Many people went inside, and a big party was held on the eighty-sixth floor. There were music and speeches, which were sent by radio to all parts of the country. Lunch was served to 200 people. From this high dining room, they could see into four States and the Atlantic Ocean.

The Empire State Building was built by a company of which Mr. Alfred E. Smith is head. "Al" Smith ran for President against Herbert Hoover in the last election. It was Mr. Smith's grandchildren who broke the ribbons at the front door. They are shown in the picture above. Mr. Smith is standing next to his little granddaughter.

The Empire State Building towers like a giant above the tall skyscrapers of New York City. Its top is nearly one-fourth of a mile above the street, and is often hidden by clouds and fog. Those who stand on the street and look up at the high tower often become dizzy. The main part of the building is 86 stories high. On top of this is a smaller tower of 16 stories, which looks like a large candle. Around the very top is a wide strip of bright metal, which shines in the sunlight. Strips of shining metal run straight to the top of the building from the ground and look like silver arrows.

This great building has many stores on the first floor, and the upper floors are used for offices. There are 63 elevators in this big 102-story building to carry the people to their offices. They go so fast that it takes less than a minute to reach the highest floors.

The Empire State Building is so big that 25,000 people can work there at one time. It is said that about 40,000 more people will visit it each day. So altogether there may be as many as 65,000 persons in this great building in one day. This is as many people as live in a big town. How many people live in your town?

The Giant Empire State Building

CONCERTS FOR BOYS AND GIRLS

ON OCTOBER 9, the Music Appreciation Hour began. That is a radio concert which Dr. Walter Damrosch gives every Friday morning at 11 o'clock. At that time, radios in schools and homes in all parts of the United States will tune into stations which are on the WEAF, WJZ, and NBC chains.

The concerts will help boys and girls to enjoy and understand music. They will make the study of music more interesting.

GANDHI USES LOVE FOR A SWORD

LAST month, Gandhi (gän'-dĭ) sailed from India to England. Like a knight of old, he was going forth to free his country. Only this modern knight did not wear armor and carry a shield and a sword. He was a little, brown man

He Prefers To Be Called "Bapu" or Daddy

in the homespun village dress of the poorest peasants of India. With love for a sword, he was going to win freedom for India.

Gandhi was on his way to a meeting at London, England. India is under the rule of that country. For many years, England has been teaching her to govern herself. Last year, a meeting called a Round Table was held to plan ways to give more freedom to India. This autumn, the Indian Round Table met again. To that meeting, Gandhi came. He knows more than anyone else in the world about the needs of the people who live in India.

He was sent to the meeting by the people of India. He is their leader. He is called the Mahatma (mä-hät'-mä) or "Great Soul" by 350 million people.

That great leader was born in India. His family had taken part in their home government for hundreds of years. His father was wealthy and gave him many things. Gandhi was sent to England to school and studied to be a lawyer. He knows much about the work of government. He is a leader by birth and training. He is using his leadership to help his people.

It was his great love for the poor people of India that made Gandhi their leader. He gave up his money and his lands. He went to live among the very poor peasants. He said that he could help them more by becoming one of them. He spins the thread and weaves the cloth to make his own clothes. He lives on goat's milk and fruit. He spends one day a week alone thinking and praying.

Now he is in England to tell the government about the needs of his people. He wants England to help him by giving freedom to India. He is not using force to win freedom and happiness for his people. He is using love, for he believes that love is the greatest thing in the world. If Gandhi wins freedom for India, it will be a great victory. It will be the first time that love and peace have ever won freedom for a country.

HELP FEED THE HUNGRY

A LITTLE girl five years old sent this letter to President Hoover. She printed it herself in big, uneven letters. It read:

"DEAR MR. HOOVER: HERE IS A BIG WHITE PENNY FROM MY BANK. WILL YOU PLEASE USE IT TO BUY SOME BREAD AND BUTTER AND MILK AND CANDY FOR THE LITTLE BOYS AND GIRLS WHO ARE HUNGRY?

FROM ROSEMARY."

The "big white penny" which she sent was a bright new fifty-cent piece. She had heard her mother and daddy read about children who were hungry. She felt sorry for them and took the biggest "penny" out of her bank. Then she sent it to President Hoover with her letter.

Many of our people are hungry this winter because crops did not grow well last summer. There was very little rain and the fields dried up. Others have no money because they are out of work. Some of them are hungry, too. The American Red Cross is asking each one of us to help feed the hungry. Do you belong to the Junior Red Cross? Can you help the Red Cross? Can you in some way help to feed the hungry children?

PLANE LANDS AT WHITE HOUSE

LAST month, an autogiro (au-to-gī'-rō) circled over the White House at Washington, D. C. Twice the strange plane flew overhead before its pilot brought it down on the south lawn.

The autogiro was invented by Mr. Juan de la Cierva (hoo-än' dā lä the-err'-väh). It has four

The President and the Pilot

whirling blades fastened to the top of it. It can land in a very small space because it can fly straight up and down, while the ordinary airplane must glide up on a slope after running along the ground. Airplanes that do not have to taxi a great distance after landing will be a very great improvement in the field of aviation. They can be used in many places where the ordinary airplane would not be practical.

After the plane landed at the White House, President Hoover gave the Collier Prize for "the greatest achievement in aviation in America" to the pilot and three other men who have done much work to prove the usefulness of the autogiro.

Pip, the very black mascot of the Hobby Club, is an old friend of the boys and girls who read My Weekly Reader. He has much fun with the members of the club, and wants to share his adventures with you. Each week he will write a letter telling you about the Hobby Club.

Dear Boys and Girls,

The boys and girls made some pictures of my adventures with the jellyfish at the seashore this summer. They just came back from the photographer. Here they are.

Next week I'll tell you about our trip home from the seashore.

THE WORLD STEPS INTO MY WEEKLY READER

Would you go exploring to the ends of the earth? Then follow these characters into the pages of My Weekly Reader, and go with them around the world.

Sometimes they will take you to the Far North or to hot jungle lands with famous aviators and explorers. Sometimes they will take you to countries where real princes and princesses live. They will take you wherever exciting and interesting things are happening.

Each week, boys and girls in all parts of the United States read and talk about the stories in My Weekly Reader. They like to read the same news that Dad and Mother are talking about. They think it is great fun to know what is happening in the world today.

A Wonderful Woman Who Cannot See or Hear

EACH year, a magazine gives a prize * to the American woman who has done the greatest good for others in the last ten years. The prize is five thousand dollars, and it was given last month.

Helen Keller Reading Stories to Blind Children While on a Visit to England This Summer

It was given to a woman who cannot see and cannot hear. Her name is Miss Helen Keller. Miss Keller is blind, and she is deaf. Yet she has done far more for others than many of us who can see and hear.

Helen Keller has helped many, many blind people. She has worked that they might have schools to go to. She has raised more than one million dollars for the blind and the deaf. When she was given the five thousand dollar prize, she did not think of the fun she could have with the money. She said slowly, "This will bring more joy to those in the silent dark. A Braille letter, a flower, a chat, a little walk, what priceless joy these little things bring to the loneliest people in all the world."

Helen Keller was born in the South 52 years ago. She was a well and a strong baby, but before she learned to walk, she became sick. The sickness hurt her eyes and ears and left her blind and deaf. She could not see her mother and father. She could not hear them talk, and for this reason, she could not learn to talk. She could not run and play with other children, for she could not see.

Close your eyes and stop up your ears tightly. Then you will have some idea of how dark and quiet everything was for Helen Keller.

Darkness Changed to Light

There were not many schools for the blind and deaf when Helen was a little girl. She stayed at home and was a very sad child. At last, her father heard of a teacher who could help her. He sent for the teacher, and she came to live with the Kellers. It was not long before Helen was a busy, happy child. She learned to talk by spelling words in her teacher's hand. Helen was quick to learn, and it was not long before she could write on the typewriter. In this way, she could tell her thoughts to others. She began learning to talk when she was ten years old. She did this by putting her fingers on her teacher's lips and throat. Helen was the first deaf and blind child to learn to talk. Today she talks before great crowds of people. She even talks over the radio.

Miss Keller spends all her time working for the blind and deaf. She does not stay at home because she cannot see or hear. She goes all over the world giving talks for the blind. Her teacher goes with her. Sometimes Helen Keller rides in airplanes. Sometimes she rides on big ocean ships. She has made friends in many lands. She writes stories and tells about all the interesting things she "sees". She has raised enough money to start hundreds of schools for blind children. Many of these little children would have nothing to do if it were not for Helen Keller's work.

Some little blind children sent this letter to My Weekly Reader. It was written on heavy paper on which there were raised dots. It is called Braille writing. Blind children read by feeling these dots with their fingers.

I am sure the Weekly Reader

gives other children as much

pleasure as it gives us.

* Pictorial Review Achievement Award.

Giants That Will Never Die!

HIGH on Mount Rushmore in the Black Hills of South Dakota stands a small log house. It is the workshop of the famous American sculptor, Gutzon Borglum (gut-zon bor'-glum), who has made the models for a giant monument. Under his direction, workmen are carving from the solid granite side of the mountain the figures of four Presidents of the United States and a five-hundred-word history of our country.

As you climb the steep road to the top of Mount Rushmore, you will see great rocks and a thick growth of pine and spruce trees. Then suddenly, you will come out upon the bare stone face of the mountain. There you will see workmen sitting on rope swings a thousand feet above the ground. Their tools are big drills and machines with which they cut into the hard granite. Chip, chip, chip, the sound echoes far down the mountain. Under skillful fingers, the granite becomes a face. Slowly the eyes, nose, and mouth appear. The top of the mountain forms the top of George Washington's head, which stands out against the dark

Can You Find the Face?

mountain. The men swinging from the side look very small against the giant piece of work which they are making.

The head of George Washington is now finished. It is 60 feet high from the chin to the top of the head and can be seen many miles away. The figure, which will be 420 feet high, has been chipped roughly from the stone as far as the waistline. This giant statue will be finished and dedicated next August as part of the celebration of the 200th birthday anniversary of George Washington. President Hoover hopes to take part in the ceremony.

On one side of Washington is the statue of Jefferson, on which Mr. Borglum and his helpers are working. It is to be finished and

Writing History on a Mountain

dedicated with the one of our First President. On the other side of Washington, there are two blank white spaces, which stand out against the dark granite. They are the spots where the figures of Lincoln and Roosevelt will be carved. Those two statues will be finished by the summer of 1935.

The four figures will show the important periods in the history of our country. Washington was the leader under whose direction America became a nation. Jefferson added new lands west of the Mississippi River. Lincoln helped to make our country a united land. Roosevelt was President when the Panama Canal was built. The Canal opened the route to Asia of which Columbus had once dreamed.

From the very heart of the United States, these giants of stone will look out across the country. Scientists say that they will last for one-half million years if the mountain stands that long.

OUR NEXT PRESIDENT LOOKS OVER HIS MAIL

A S THE winner of the race for President, Franklin Delano Roosevelt received thousands of notes and telegrams of congratulation. Among them was a message from President Hoover. Showing his good sportsmanship in defeat, he wrote, "I congratulate you on the opportunity that has come to you to be of service to the country and I wish for you a most successful administration. In the common purpose of all of us I shall dedicate myself to every possible helpful effort."

Mr. Roosevelt's mother is enjoying the friendly messages with him.

A FUTURE FIRST LADY OF THE LAND

M RS. FRANKLIN D. ROOSEVELT is off for school with her young granddaughter, Anna Eleanor Dall. She is teaching in a school in New York. But after March 4, Mrs. Roosevelt will probably be too busy as the mistress of the White House in Washington, D. C., to continue her work as a teacher.

A GOOD BOOK FOR YOUR SCHOOL LIBRARY

"Creating a World of Friendly Children, Suggestions for Children's Activities and Programs" (The Committee on World Friendship Among Children, New York, N. Y., $0.25). This book has in it children's messages of good will, games of many lands, menus of many lands, plays, pageants, and songs of world friendship. It tells you much about child life in other lands. Let's make friends with the boys and girls all around the world.

GREAT SCIENTIST TO STUDY STARS

W HEN Dr. Albert Einstein (īne'-stīne) landed in California the other day, he had his violin tucked under his arm. He is a famous scientist who has just come from his home in Germany to the United States to work on a new scientific theory.

Dr. Einstein has made many wonderful discoveries in the field of science. Now he is very much interested in the study of the sky. He says that by watching the stars he learns many things which will help him with his work.

Near Pasadena, California, is the great Mt. Wilson Observatory, which is perched high on the top of a mountain. There Dr. Einstein will watch the sky and study the stars through the largest reflecting telescope in the world.

Dr. Einstein works very hard. He spends many hours each day and night working on theories about time and space. When he is tired, he takes his violin and plays. That is restful for him after the long hours of hard work.

A PIGEON TAKES PICTURES

Did you ever hear of a pigeon taking pictures? This one does. He is a carrier pigeon and belongs to the German Army. A camera is strapped to his body. When the pigeon is

flying, the camera takes pictures of the country below him. It will take 200 pictures on one flight. The pigeon carries a tube for letters on one leg, too.

Carrier pigeons are very useful birds. In war time, they carry letters from one part of the army to another. They can fly over places where airplanes cannot fly. The pictures which they take show the soldiers what the country around them is like and where the enemy army is. In times of peace, carrier pigeons are used to carry news.

ARE YOU CURIOUS?

A boy asks Wise Owl this question: "How did the saying start, **he works like a dog?** I never saw a dog do much but lie in the sun and sleep."

Wise Owl answers: "Long ago, man made dogs tame so that they could help him with his work. He trained his dogs to turn wheels to grind grain; to carry packs on their backs; to pull heavy loads on sleds and wagons; to watch cows and sheep; and to do many other things. Early man worked his dogs hard."

If you wish to ask Wise Owl a good question, send it to:

Wise Owl, My Weekly Reader, Columbus, Ohio.

NEWSBOYS GO TO WASHINGTON

These boys are newsboys.
They make money by selling newspapers.

Newsboys from all parts of our country went to Washington, D. C., this winter.

Do you like to read the news?
What newspaper do you like to read?

GOOD-BYE, RIN-TIN-TIN!

I'll Miss You, Old Pal

THE world's most famous moving-picture dog, Rin-Tin-Tin, is gone. For many years, he took part in the movies and entertained people with his very clever acting.

President Roosevelt Finds Work for Many Men

MANY, many men all over the world cannot find work to do. They may be very fine workmen, but they are not needed today. Machines have taken their places. Many factories which make cloth used to hire hundreds of men. Today machines do much of the work. Only a few men are needed now at the factories. They take care of the machines.

The millions of men who are out of work have no money. They cannot buy the things which they need. This not only hurts them, but it also hurts the men who sell things. Much of our business stops and the whole country is hurt when thousands of men are out of work.

Finding Work for Idle Hands

President Roosevelt is trying hard in many ways to find work for men. One thing that he is doing is to start a building program. He will spend more than three billion dollars ($3,000,-000,000). This is our money, because it comes from taxes which we all pay. Since it is our money, President Roosevelt is using it to build things which all of us use. Roads, bridges, post offices, and schools are being built. This makes

Road Building Makes Work for Thousands of Men

work for many men. They are digging, digging, digging, making new roads. They are hammering, hammering, hammering, making new bridges and schools. This not only gives them work to do, but it also makes work for other men. The builders need lumber, steel, cement, and many other supplies. This gives work to men who furnish building supplies. All these men are happy to be at work again.

Besides such things as roads and bridges, many

houses are being built in big cities. This not only gives men work, but best of all, it makes better homes for poor people. Our Government lends money to build the houses. Then it lets the poor people live in them for very low rents. Rents have been high in big cities, and during these hard times, many poor people have been put out of their homes. With the new houses which our Government is building, we hope that this will not happen again. The new houses will be built in the most modern way. They will be made of steel, cement, and other things which will not burn. They will have many big windows which will let in plenty of sunshine all day. These houses will be easy to keep clean. Poor people who live in them will have better health. Our country has been very slow in building good homes for its poor. Countries across the sea have been building them for years.

Besides the building program, President Roosevelt is doing many other things to give work to more men. He has put thousands of men to work in our forests. He has asked the men who hire workers to hire them for less time. This will give work to other men. Under the blue eagle of the NRA, hundreds of thousands of men have gone back to work this fall.

The hard times, or depression, has been hard on all of us. But it has taught us many good things. It has taught us to think of others and to work together. It has taught many of us to enjoy our work and also to enjoy our free time.

FOLLOWING PRESIDENT ROOSEVELT

(Ability To Follow the News and Organize Material)

Use part of the blackboard and bulletin board space to help you follow the many things that President Roosevelt is doing to find work for men. You may wish to put the clippings, headlines, and pictures under these three headings: **The President's Building Program**; **Forest Camps**; **The NRA**. Perhaps a special committee can be appointed to look after the news for each column.

Perfect score is 15.   **My score is** ....

Shall We Be Friends With Russia?

DID YOU ever live next door to an old house into which new neighbors had just moved? Perhaps you climbed the fence to see what the strange little boy was doing. Perhaps you played football in your own back yard and paid no attention to him.

Sawing a Door in the Fence

The Soviet Union of Russia is very much like that new family next door. It is a new government living and working in an old land. At first, the nations of the world climbed their fences to see what the strange government was doing. Then they went back into their own yards and left the Soviet Union alone.

But the nations had a hard time pretending that Russia was not a next-door neighbor. After all, it is a large part of both Europe and Asia. It is nearly three times as large as the United States. Its important products are lumber, fur, wheat, fish, and minerals. It buys from other nations machinery, ships, tea, coffee, cocoa, cotton, rubber, and many other things.

Some of the nations wanted to trade with Russia. So they decided that perhaps the Soviet Union would make a good neighbor. One by one, they climbed their fences again and smiled at their new neighbor. When the Soviet Union smiled back, they said, "Let's shake hands and be friends." Today most of the great nations of the world speak to and trade with Russia. Only the United States has stayed in its own back yard and pretended that its new neighbor did not live in the old land of Russia.

Of course, the new Soviet neighbor is very different from the old Russian neighbor. For hundreds of years, Russia had been ruled over by a czar, or king. That ruler had much power over his people. The men who helped him govern Russia were rich and powerful nobles. They owned vast stretches of farming land which they rented to peasant farmers. Those nobles even owned whole villages in which the peasants lived. The peasants were very poor. Those who owned small farms had to pay heavy taxes on their lands. They worked from sunrise to sunset in the fields. Many of them could not read or write, because they had never gone to school.

At last toward the end of the World War, in 1917, the people of Russia revolted against the czar and his nobles. They overthrew the old government and set up a new one in its place. During the years that followed the revolt, many changes took place. The new government became the Soviet Union or the United States of Soviet Russia. That government took over all the property in the country. It took over the mills, mines, factories, and farms. Then the Soviet Union began to build up its new government. With the help of engineers and builders from our country and other countries, too, the government built railroads, bridges, giant dams, and power plants. It made great tractors and other machinery and taught the peasants to use them on their farms. The government built and ran automobile factories, shoe factories, cloth mills, and other industries. It has worked hard to build up a new nation.

That new nation is now on friendly terms with most of the great nations of the world. Even the United States is holding out its hand in friendship. President Roosevelt sent a friendly mes-

LUMBER FOR SALE!
Huge Logs Waiting in the Harbor of Leningrad To Be Loaded on Freighters for Shipment Across the Sea

sage to Mikhail Kalinin, the head of the Soviet Union. Kalinin answered the message and sent Maxim Litvinoff (lit-veen'-off) to the United States to talk with President Roosevelt. Perhaps our country will make friends with its neighbor across the ocean. Perhaps the United States will trade with Soviet Russia. Will trade with Russia help our country? No one really knows. But at least, the two nations will be friendly neighbors.

The Father of Wireless Comes to Our Country

THE little girl in the picture below is on a big ship. She is on her way to our country. Her home is across the sea in Italy. She has a pretty first name. She is called Elettra. Her whole Italian name is Elettra Marconi (mär-kō'-nē).

Elettra Shows Her Daddy How It Works

Elettra's father is a very great man. Mr. Marconi is the man who first sent wireless messages.

That is, he found a way to send messages through the air. We should not have radios today if it were not for the hard work of Mr. Marconi.

The first week in October was Radio Week at the Chicago Fair. Mr. Marconi and Elettra were asked to come to the Fair. They were treated like a king and a princess. Parties were given for them. Many people came to the Fair to see the famous Marconis.

Mr. Marconi went to the Travel and Transport Building. There he sent a message around the world by wireless. This was done almost as quickly as you can wink your eye. One evening, the lights of the Fair were turned on by a person in Italy. This was done by the wireless, too.

Mr. Marconi said that many wonderful things had been done by wireless. But many more wonderful things will be done. The next great step is to bring clear moving pictures with sound over the radio. This is called television (tĕl-e-vĭzh'-ŭn). Already television programs are being given in big cities. But the pictures are dim, or not clear. It will not be very long before we shall have a moving picture screen on our radios. Won't it be fun to see, as well as hear, what is going on in all parts of the world?

THE ART OF MAKING MONEY PLENTY
IN EVERY MAN'S POCKET; BY
Doctor Franklin

ARE you a good puzzle worker? Then you will have great fun trying to figure out this story. It is a clever little rebus by Benjamin Franklin. But what is a rebus? Are you wrinkling up your forehead and asking that question? Look back at My Weekly Reader for October 21, and you will find another rebus. But it is not so hard to solve as this one is. If your notebook file is not on hand, here is the meaning of a rebus. It is a puzzle in which pictures take the place of whole words. Pictures even take the place of parts of words. When you read the story, substitute the words which belong in it for the pictures.

Franklin's rebus begins, "At this **time when the general—**". Figure out the rest of this rebus, which the "Father of Thrift" wrote to tell you how to be thrifty. See if you can solve all or nearly all the rebus before the answer is given in the next issue of My Weekly Reader.

ARE YOU A STAMP COLLECTOR?

Here is a picture of the stamp from Uncle Ben's letter. It is a French air mail stamp. From time to time, we shall print other interesting stamps from our traveler's letters. Watch for them.

ANGIE, THE BOOKWORM, FINDS A NEW BOOK

Shall I tell you about a new book treasure which I have just found? It is "Discovering Christopher Columbus", by Charlotte Brewster Jordan (The Macmillan Co., N. Y., $3).

I felt as if I were sitting on top of the world when I opened that book and followed the traveling map-maker through Spain. I visited many old cities with him on his long quest for help. I even sailed away from Palos with the brave explorer to discover a New World across the sea. I learned many new and exciting things, too, which were in old letters and diaries, many of them written by Columbus himself. But best of all, I liked the pictures and maps in this new book. Many a bookworm will want to read "Discovering Christopher Columbus".

WILLIE WONDERS

He Is on the Way to the South Pole

THE STORY OF A BIRD

Look at the bird on the right.
It is the picture of an eagle.
It is blue and stands for the NRA.

The other picture is
an old Indian drawing of a bird.
It is an old picture of the thunder bird.

Today we put the picture of the eagle
in our store windows.
The blue eagle takes good care
of all those who use it.

The Heath Hen Joins the Dodo

NO, THE dodo is not a strange creature from the pages of "Alice in Wonderland". He was once a very much alive bird and a very homely, stupid one, too. But his race has long since vanished from this earth, so we need not shed real tears, only crocodile ones, for the departed dodo.

The Lone Heath Hen— Last of Its Race

But we should regret the passing of many other species from our fields and forests. Once passenger pigeons flew across our country in great flocks that darkened the sky like a cloud. Today not one of these birds survives. The great auk, that bird of black and white plumage, which once lived in the northern regions of the world, can be seen today only in museums. The Eskimo curlew, a small long legged, long billed bird with soft brownish feathers, has practically been wiped out by hunters during its migrations. The Labrador duck, another bird of our northlands, has vanished, too, and now still another species is following in their footsteps.

New Laws Help Children Who Have To Work

JANUARY 29 is Child Labor Day. Schools and churches and clubs all over our country are celebrating Child Labor Day. They are thinking about the poor children who work in factories and mills. They are doing much to shorten their hours and make their work more pleasant. They are trying to end all harmful child labor.

Many boys and girls in our country work until late at night. They work in cotton mills in the South and in factories in the North. Often children can get work when their mothers and fathers cannot. They are paid only a few cents each hour, but this helps to buy bread and butter for the family. The child workers grow pale and tired and sick. Some of them go to school part of the day, but they are too tired to learn much. Do any of your school friends work in mills after school?

Many of our boys and girls work on truck farms, too. Hour after hour, they pick peas and beans. Some work in sugar-beet fields, cotton fields, and tobacco fields. Some are doing work that no child should do.

Helping the Child Worker

Some kind men and women are trying to help these child workers. They belong to the National Child Labor Committee. This committee tries to see that children do not work too long at a time and that children are paid for their work. It also tries to see that very young children are not allowed to work. The committee has done much good work, but there is much that it cannot do.

The N.R.A. has done much to help child workers. The new N.R.A. codes have stopped the work of more than one hundred thousand children under the age of 16. Many of these children have gone back to school. The N.R.A. has also given thirty thousand children between the ages of 16 and 18 easier work to do. The hard work which they once did is now being done by grown men who need work. But there are still thousands of child workers under the age of 16 who are not helped by the N.R.A. Some are working 12 hours a day washing dishes in roadside restaurants. Some are working too many hours in

homes as servants. Many others are working until late at night at their own homes. They do home work for factories, such as cutting lace, making garters, and sewing on buttons. One family of six makes only 40 or 50 cents for an evening's work. New laws must be made to take care of these workers.

All Work and No Play

For this reason, the National Child Labor Committee and others are working hard to have a new law made for our country. Under this new law, our Government can say whether boys and girls under 18 years of age may work. It can also say how long and in what way they may work. It will be a national law and will take care of all children in all States.

Before this kind of law can be made for our whole country, three-fourths of all our States must vote **YES** for it. Twenty States have done this. Sixteen more must vote for it before it can become a law. Has your State voted **YES**, for the law which will help child workers? If not, you can help to have this law made. If you think it is a good law, tell others about it. Write letters to those who make the laws in your State. This will help them to know that you and many others want them to vote for the new Child Labor Law.

Face to Face With the Relief Problem

THE cold October winds make us turn up our collars and think about warm woolly coats and mittens. The crackle of dry leaves underfoot makes us think of Jack Frost and the first snow of winter. Everywhere people are busily getting ready for winter. Coal is rattling down narrow chutes. Heavy clothing and blankets are

What's the Answer?

being taken out of tar bags and cedar chests. Jars of newly canned fruits and vegetables line the cellar shelves. Four-fifths of our people will meet winter cheerfully and comfortably because they have food, clothing, and shelter or the money to buy them.

But the promise of winter just around the corner means a long struggle against cold and hunger for the other one-fifth of our people. Some of them will receive help from relatives or friends. Some will try to make both ends meet by part-time jobs. Many will have to depend on the Government for food, shelter, and clothing this winter. Uncle Sam must work out some plan of relief for about twenty-three million people.

Last winter, the Government worked out a way to solve the relief problem for the time being. Civil works and public works programs were organized, and several million men were put to work. Some helped build roads. Some worked on buildings, bridges, and other public projects. About three hundred sixty thousand entered the Civilian Conservation Camps and helped with the work of saving and replanting forests.

Then when spring came, the civil works program was dropped. During the warm spring and summer months, many families could take care of their own needs. Business and industry were picking up, and many who had been out of work

were again earning their own living. They no longer needed Government help. But the pick-up in business was not great enough to take care of all the unemployed. This winter, the relief rolls promise to be large. The Government says that billions of dollars may be needed for relief in the months to come.

Mr. Hopkins, who is in charge of Federal relief, says that the costs may be greater than those of last year. Of course, nearly four million unemployed persons have already gone back to work and been dropped from relief rolls. But at the same time, many of those who lost their crops and cattle during the summer drought have been added. Also, the funds allowed each family have been increased from $16 a month to $24 to meet the rising cost of living.

Mr. Hopkins points out that two-thirds of the persons needing relief are willing and able to work. Indeed, some of them are working part time, but their wages are too low to buy the necessities of life. He says that the remaining one-third on the relief rolls are housewives, old persons, and disabled persons. They may never be wage-earners even during the most prosperous times.

But in spite of those facts, not everyone approves of that vast amount being spent for relief. Some say that the Government is going too deeply into debt. Those persons point out that ruinous taxes will have to be collected to meet such a big debt. Others say that the Government relief program has been used to create political sentiment in favor of the Democratic party. They have even said that the Democratic victories in recent fall elections were due to that spending of relief funds. Those critics demand that relief funds be cut sharply.

How Can the Money for Relief Be Raised?

Very much like a real ghost, the problem of raising relief funds is now haunting the Treasury Building in Washington, D. C. The Treasury Department is at work on Uncle Sam's budget for next year. That budget will be presented to Congress when it meets in January. In the budget message last year, President Roosevelt predicted that the Government would not earn enough money to cover the Government expenses. In order to balance a budget, one cannot spend more than one makes. Uncle Sam was spending more than he made, but the President promised that by the following year, the budget would balance. He said that more men would be taken off relief and put back to work in the general pick-up in business and industry.

But Uncle Sam is still spending more than he is taking in. He is still trying to balance the budget. Some suggest new taxes. Others point out that more taxes would hold back recovery. Some suggest that the Government use for relief the food surpluses which the A.A.A. took over to help raise prices. They suggest that the unemployed be put to work raising their own food and making their own clothing and other necessities.

Cheap Electricity Will Be Made for Many People

NOT long ago, President Roosevelt made a trip to the South. On his way, he visited one of the biggest projects ever started by our Government. This big project is in the valley of the Tennessee River. Hundreds and hundreds of men are at work there building dams. By building dams in the river, cheap electric power will be made for the people who live in the valley.

President Roosevelt Visits the Joe Wheeler Dam on the Tennessee River

One of the big Government dams is called Norris Dam.

The electricity made at Norris Dam will be sold to the farmers of the Tennessee Valley. It will be very cheap, for our Government will sell the electricity at low rates. Electricity will help the farmers with their work. They will use it to run their farm machines. The cheaper the electricity, the more of it the farmers will be able to use. They will use it in their barns and in their homes. Electricity will help the farm women with their hard work. It will make the farmers' homes more pleasant, for it will run radios, give bright lights, heat, and many other pleasant things.

Courtesy New York Tribune

LITTLE AMERICA AWAKENS

With a shout of joy, the men at Little America welcomed the sun back to the Antarctic. They were tired of the close, cramped quarters in their snow-covered village, where they had spent the winter. They were eager to get ready for the spring and summer work. Besides, their leader, Admiral Byrd, would soon return to the camp.

At one time, Admiral Byrd was afraid that he would never return to Little America. He had spent four long winter months alone in a little hut 123 miles away. The bitter cold and the fumes from his oil stove had been very hard on him. But Dr. Poulter's rescue party arrived just in time.

As soon as the big tractor stopped near the hut, the men set to work. First of all, they made Admiral Byrd rest while they kept house and made weather records. Dr. Poulter also began a study of the stars and the aurora. From the world's southernmost station, he has taken many pictures of the aurora. At the same time, men at Little America were taking pictures of the aurora. Dr. Poulter hopes to learn much from a comparison of those pictures, when he returns to the base camp.

But the party will not start the journey over the ice until Admiral Byrd is stronger and the weather is warmer. Although spring has returned to the Antarctic, it is still bitterly cold there. Nevertheless, Little America has come to life again after its winter's nap, and the men are getting ready for their leader's return and the summer's work.

Mickey Mouse Joins the Parade

EARLY this month, if you had looked into one of the big airship hangars at Los Angeles, you would have seen not an airship but a giant mouse. It was a rubber one, too. A model of Mickey Mouse, famous in motion pictures, had been made to take part in the Thanksgiving Day parade which is held each year in New York City.

MICKEY MOUSE GROWS BIGGER

Walt Disney, standing between Mickey's huge feet, is very proud of his lively little movie stars, Mickey Mouse and Minnie. So famous are they that last spring, the League of Nations at Geneva, Switzerland, drew up an international treaty especially for them. By that treaty, films of Mickey Mouse will be allowed to enter any country in the League without the payment of a duty or tax.

That model will soon travel across our country to New York City, where it will take its place with other rubber figures in the Thanksgiving Day parade. Some of those other rubber men and animals have as famous a designer as Mickey Mouse has. Mr. Tony Sarg is the artist who has made many of them. He was born in Guatemala (gwä-ta-mä'-la), Central America. Once a soldier, he gave up that career to become an artist, and many a boy and girl have been enchanted by his puppets and puppet shows.

WINNIE THE POOH DIES AT AGE OF 20

Last month, Winnie the Pooh died at the London Zoo. She was a brown bear for whom Mr. A. A. Milne named his famous children's book. Perhaps no other book of poems is more loved by children in all parts of the world.

Winnie the Pooh was brought to London in 1914 from Canada. She was brought there by the Canadian regiment of soldiers known as the Princess Pats. They used the bear as their mascot and became very fond of her. The soldiers taught the bear to roll over on her back and do many tricks. She could say "pooh" in a high voice to make everyone laugh.

HERE ARE THE PRIZE WINNERS

Would you like to work out this prize-winning puzzle sent by the Beauty Hill School?

1. His first name
2. What he liked to do when a boy
3. His last name
4. What he once lived in
5. He once lived there
6. What he became
7. What is in Washington, D. C., now
8. He was ....
9. He was ....
10. He was ....
11. What his friends called him

WILLIE WONDERS WITH ADMIRAL BYRD

He Saves the Boat and Meets the Admiral

The Soil Takes to the Air

THE high March winds whipped up the dry powdery soil of the Great Plains and carried it in heavy black clouds eastward. Those sand clouds made a dark blanket far above the earth. The sun shone with a blue-gray light through the grayish yellow dust. The headlights on trains tried to pierce the thick cloud ahead. Automo-

WHERE DUST STORMS BEGIN
During the last three years, six feet of topsoil have been blown from this barren Kansas field by the winds. Only one lone "button" of earth, held fast by the roots of bushes, is left to show that the land was once higher than this man's head.

biles were stalled on the highways. Man and beast sought shelter before the stifling dust smothered them. A dust storm was sweeping across the country from the interior to the Atlantic Coast.

All through the month of March, one dust storm has followed on the heels of another. They start out on the Great Plains where the soil is dry and powdery from several years of drought (lack of rain). It is easily picked up by the wind. Higher and higher, it rises on the waves and eddies of the air currents. Mile on mile, it travels with the wind. Then suddenly the air currents drop sharply. Some of the flying soil falls to earth again. The rest moves on to sift down little by little or to be carried out to sea.

That flying soil from the Great Plains was once held firmly in place by buffalo grass, sagebrush, and other brush which grow in a semi-desert region. But during the World War, our country needed more space in which to raise wheat and other grain. Men were too busy fighting in Europe to raise their own crops. The countries across the Atlantic began to buy more wheat from the United States. Of course, to supply the big demand, new fields had to be found. Acres and acres of wheat were planted where the sagebrush once grew. A part of the Great Plains became a region of dry farming, when it should have been a grazing country for great herds of cattle.

Such dry semi-desert land could not withstand years of farming and years of drought. Without the sagebrush and buffalo grass to hold the topsoil, it was quickly swept away by the high winds of March and even the more gentle winds of the summer time.

Other fields in the Southwest and in parts of the West have given their share of soil to the dust storms, too. Those are the tired overworked fields. The humus in them is gone. Humus is that part of the soil which is made up of plant food and which helps to bind the soil together. It has been used up by long years of planting the same crops over and over again. That humus has not been put back into the soil by the use of fertilizer. The worn-out land has also been hit by drought. Without humus and without moisture, the worn-out soil is just as easily picked up and carried away as the semi-desert soil.

The dust storm is the high price that Uncle Sam must pay for years of poor planning and poor farming. It has already taken its toll of some two million acres of land, and it promises to do even greater damage in the future. So Uncle Sam must act quickly.

The ruined acres will be planted with grass and turned into grazing grounds. But that work will take many years. Perhaps one hundred years will pass before all that semi-desert region can be turned into the cattle country which it always should have been.

Another pet plan of Uncle Sam, which will take many years, is the great tree belt. That has already been started. It will run from Canada across the United States to Texas. Trees will be planted along that belt. They will help to hold the soil in place and the moisture in the ground.

THE FIRST OF FOUR MILLION
This little Austrian pine (in circle), planted in Oklahoma, is the first seedling in our national shelter belt.

The League Acts for Peace

MORE than two thousand years ago, Greece was a land of small city states. Each one was a little nation. It governed itself and made its own laws. But those little city states had many enemies.

Into the Jaws of Death

At last, some of the city states of Greece came together and formed a league. They had regular meetings to talk over and work out their problems. They set up a league army and a league fleet to act as policemen. The league had rules which each city must obey. The league did not say that a city could not go to war, but it did try to settle quarrels peacefully.

Down through the centuries, there have been many of these leagues. Even today there is a very modern one. Instead of having for members just a few cities, it boasts a membership of 59 nations or countries. That League was formed by nations which were very tired of fighting. They had just gone through the great World War, and they wanted peace more than anything else. So the nations set up the most complete peace machinery that could be put into force.

Just now, the League has a very hard problem to work out. Two of its members, Italy and Ethiopia, are at war. Italy needs more land. Her country is a small one, smaller than the State of New Mexico. Forty-two million people try to make a living in that long narrow land which is shaped much like a boot. Of course, people cannot live comfortably or well in such crowded quarters.

Italy is like the old woman who lived in a shoe. You remember, she had so many children that she did not know what to do. Italy has decided that something must be done. She must find more land for her people. If she had larger and better colonies in Africa, she could send some of her people over there to live. Italy looked longingly at Ethiopia, a free country. It is three times as large as Italy. Not many people live there. If Italy should take over Ethiopia, she could develop the country. She could send many of her people there to live. She would be able to raise raw materials and send them home for her own factories to use. She could sell goods to her new colony.

Ethiopia, on the other hand, is a free country. The Ethiopians enjoy their freedom. Since Bible times, these people have had their own rulers. Every army that has ever tried to conquer Ethiopia has been driven out. The Ethiopians are proud of their freedom and will fight fiercely for it.

When Ethiopia found that her freedom was in danger, she sent an SOS call to the League of Nations. She is a member of the League and needed its protection. The League set to work at once studying the problem and working out a peace plan. At last, a plan was drawn up and set before Italy and Ethiopia. Ethiopia accepted it. Italy turned it down and, a short time later, marched into Ethiopia.

The League of Nations declared that Italy had broken its rules. A member of the League may not go to war within three months after a peace plan has been offered. Italy has not waited three months. The League said that Italy had started the fighting and that she must be punished. The League decided to cut off trade with Italy. Its members voted not to have any dealings with that nation at all. Only Austria, Hungary, and little Albania refused to break off their trade with Italy.

TRYING TO HEAD OFF A WAR
The Council of the League of Nations meets around a table, shaped like a horseshoe, to work out a plan to stop the war between Italy and Ethiopia.

Will the League of Nations prove that it is a powerful peace machine with all its members pulling together for world peace? For centuries, the world has been divided into nations. These nations have often made war against each other. Sometimes they have joined together in leagues to protect themselves. But they have never been able to stop wars. Will the League of Nations be able to bring peace and order to a troubled world?

One of World's Biggest Bridges Will Span Golden Gate

The Golden Gate is in California. It is a strip of deep water between the Pacific Ocean and the San Francisco Bay. All boats going to San Francisco go through the Golden Gate. The Golden Gate is about two miles wide. Could the Golden Gate ever be spanned by a bridge? Many people said, "No." Such a long bridge in one span across such deep water had never been built. The bridge would have to be stretched across the Golden Gate in one long span, because the water is too deep for pillars to be built in it. Pillars would also be in the way of big boats that must pass through the Golden Gate. Could the bridge builders of today build such a long bridge?

The biggest engineers in our country studied the problem. At last they said, "Yes, it can be done." Work on the Golden Gate Bridge was started in January, 1933. Thousands of men who were out of work joyfully picked up their picks and shovels and went to work. They built two great towers on each side of the Golden Gate. These towers are the highest and largest bridge towers in the world. They are 740 feet high.

Big steel ropes, or cables, will swing from one tower to the other. This work might be likened to a spider spinning its web between two posts. So much wire is put into the cables that the wire would go around the world three times at the Equator. So much cement has been used in the bridge that the cement would make a sidewalk

Starting Work on World's Highest Bridge Towers

five feet wide all the way from New York to San Francisco.

The big bridge is expected to be finished in 1936. It will be the longest single clear span bridge in the world. It will be 700 feet longer than the main span of the George Washington Bridge across the Hudson River. The Golden Gate Bridge will be so high above the water that the highest mast of any ship will go under it. It will be the world's first bridge ever built over the outer mouth of a big ocean harbor.

LAWRENCE THE MODERN HERO

Back in the days of the World War, an Englishman led the wandering desert tribes of Arabia against the Turks. The Englishman had fair hair and blue eyes, but he wore the long white robes

Lawrence of Arabia

of a desert prince. In his belt was a short gold sword. He was Colonel T. E. Lawrence, who had as many adventures as any prince in the "Arabian Nights".

Lawrence and his desert tribes had few supplies to carry on a war. They traveled and fought in a region where no food could be raised. Even the water holes were five days apart by slow moving camels. By day, the hot sun shone on the men and baked their skin. At night, the icy winds from the highlands blew through their thin robes and made them shiver with cold. But in spite of these hardships, Lawrence and his tribes helped to win the World War in the East. This Englishman had been able to do what no chieftain could ever do. He made the tribes forget the bitter quarrels which had raged among them for more than six hundred years. He united all the Arabs and made them trust him. At the end of the war, he led his men into Damascus, where later Feisal, a young Arab prince, was crowned king of a new kingdom, Iraq. But Lawrence refused all honors for himself.

All during the rest of his short life, he tried to keep out of the public eye. He even changed his name so that people would not know him. Then quietly he set to work as an airplane mechanic and designer and as a writer. In his books, he told about his life and adventures in Arabia.

Meet Miss Sea Cow

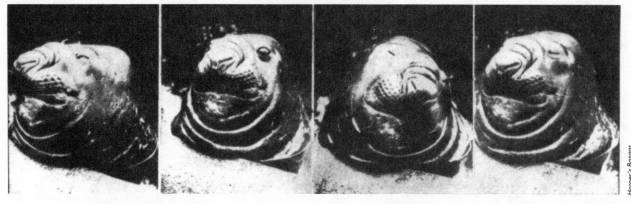

Harper's Bazaar

Her home is a big pool at the zoo in Berlin, Germany. And from her happy expression, she must be having a very good time. Can you put her thoughts into four titles (one for each picture) with lots of snap to them? For the best titles, My Weekly Reader will give as prizes books for your home libraries.

SHE DID IT!

Amelia Earhart Putnam made the first non-stop flight alone from Hawaii to California. She did it in spite of the fact that people in Hawaii did not want her to try the long flight. Now the famous flyer has added another record to her long list of "firsts". She was the first woman passenger to fly the Atlantic, then the first woman to fly it solo. She was the first woman to fly an autogiro, first woman to make a non-stop flight all the way across our country, and first woman to receive the Distinguished Flying Cross.

A Little Girl Welcomes Amelia Earhart Putnam to Hawaii

Dear Wise Owl,

When Admiral Byrd crossed the Equator, he put his penguins into a cool part of the ship so they would live. But how will they live when they are put into a zoo? Our room would like to know. Will you please tell us?

Yours truly,
Florence Levion, Grade 4, Corning, Ohio.

Dear Florence,

Your question is a good one, but I'm afraid no one can answer it. Zoos have tried in many ways to keep Antarctic penguins alive. They have spent thousands of dollars giving penguins the right kind of food and trying to keep them cool and happy. But in spite of everything, the penguins have grown lonely and sad and then they have died. Even before Byrd's ship left Dunedin (dŭn-ē'dĭn), he sent word that 12 "lady" penguins in a flock of 20 "lady" penguins had fretted themselves to death in the ice box.

DANNY DOO AND RANGER BILL   By Ray Evans, Jr.

Dan and Ranger Bill see many tents in the valley. It is a camp of the Civilian Conservation Corps.

Dan meets the C.C.C. boys. "How are you, buddy?" says one boy. "Did you come to see our camp?"

Dan and Bill plant many trees on the hillside. Trees keep the soil from slipping.

When water washes the soil from the hillsides, it is called erosion. Dan helps build dams to stop erosion.

Men Along the Rhine

The Market Place in Frankfort, Germany, Into Which Soldiers Marched as They Once Again Occupied the Rhineland

EARLY in March, along the border between France and Germany, were heard the heavy tramp of marching feet and the deep rumble of army trucks. Airplanes roared overhead. French soldiers in steel helmets or berets and blue uniforms were taking up their quarters in the French forts and towns on the Rhine River. German soldiers in gray uniforms and steel helmets had marched into the towns on the German side of the Rhine. They were once again occupying the Rhineland.

The Rhine has marked part of the boundary line between France and Germany for hundreds of years. Over this river, men have fought since the time of Julius Caesar. In those long ago days, France was called Gaul and Roman soldiers guarded the west bank of the Rhine. Tall Germans with blue eyes and light hair lived on the east bank of the river. Once they even crossed the Rhine and started to settle in Gaul. They liked the rich valleys and the deep forests of that land. But Caesar was afraid of these strong blond men and helped the Gauls drive them back into their own country. During four hundred years, the Rhine River marked the border between the Roman Empire and the Germans to the east.

As the years passed, the Roman camps and settlements and the villages of the Gauls and Germans grew into cities. Men learned to mine the rich veins of iron and coal in the Rhineland. The powerful noblemen of the region built strong castles along the banks of the river. They forced every boat which sailed by to pay a heavy toll. Those noblemen became very wealthy, for the Rhine was one of the chief waterways of early times.

Even today the Rhine is one of the most important rivers in all Europe. It rises in Switzerland where it is fed by mountain torrents. It flows for about 850 miles, marking the boundaries between Switzerland and Austria, Switzerland and Germany, and France and Germany, until it comes at last to Holland and empties into the North Sea. On its long journey through Europe, the Rhine changes from a swift mountain stream into a wide green river. It touches land rich in forests and minerals. It is a shipping outlet to the sea for Germany, Belgium, and Holland.

So important is the Rhine River as a trading route and boundary line that special plans were made for it after the World War. Germany was not to build forts in the Rhineland or to bring any soldiers there. The Rhineland was to be a peaceful province where thousands of German people lived and worked.

But the Rhineland belongs to Germany. For hundreds of years, her troops have guarded the border along the Rhine. Across the river, France has strong, well-armed forts. Germany does not like to be told that she cannot send troops into the Rhineland. She wants to guard her own land. So, early in March, her leader, Adolf Hitler, ordered his soldiers to march into the Rhineland and take over the old forts. The people of

The Beautiful Old City of Cologne
on the East Bank of the Rhine River

the Rhineland were glad to see the German soldiers. Crowds gathered in the streets of the towns. Men and women leaned out of windows to watch the troops. There were cheers and shouts of welcome.

On the other side of the Rhine River, the people of France watched anxiously. The French Government said that Germany had broken her promise. She was once again occupying the Rhineland. France was afraid that the German soldiers might even come across the river into her land. Twice within one hundred years, German soldiers had crossed the border and marched into France. The French Government quickly ordered more troops to the Rhine.

All through the night, these French soldiers were on the march. They came by train, in trucks, and on foot. Dusty from their long journey, they arrived at the border to take up their watch across the river from the German soldiers.

A New King Rules One-Fourth the Earth

KING GEORGE V had five boys and one girl. He named his oldest son Edward Albert Christian George Andrew Patrick David of Windsor. That was a long name for a little boy, and his father and mother called him David for

Edward VIII, the New King of England

short. The rest of the world called him the Prince of Wales. Since the year 1301, the oldest son of the King of Great Britain has been called the Prince of Wales. Wales is a part of Great Britain.

Last month, after the death of King George V, the Prince of Wales became King of Great Britain. He is now called King Edward VIII, by the Grace of God, King of the United Kingdom of Great Britain and Ireland and the British Dominions Beyond the Seas, Defender of the Faith, Emperor of India. That is a long title for a king, isn't it? But the title has to be long, because the King rules over so many countries. King Edward rules over nearly five hundred million (450,000,000) people. Of these, 350,000,000 live in India.

When Edward was made King, his little curly-haired niece, Margaret Rose, said to him, "Uncle David, must I now call you King?" Her older sister Elizabeth said, "Uncle, you will have to work hard now, won't you?" King Edward said to his little nieces, "I shall try as best I can to carry on the work of my father."

The people of England loved King George V very much. When he died last month, the people knew that they had lost a real friend. King George was very kind to his people and did everything he could to help them. Will Edward VIII be as good a king as his father was? Many think that Edward will be a very good king and will do much for the people of his country.

King Edward Is Known and Loved Throughout the Empire

King Edward knows his people well. He has traveled among them and has learned to know the common people. Once, while in India, he surprised everyone by talking with the lowest class of people, the untouchables. Those poor people are so hated in India that some people will not go near them or speak to them. The untouchables could hardly believe their eyes when Edward, who was then Prince of Wales, not only looked at them but talked with them.

When Edward was a soldier in the World War, he was a good friend of the Tommies, as the English private soldiers are called. He played cards with them in the trenches and did not want them to know that he was a Prince.

After the war, Edward visited the homes of many coal miners. He saw how the poor people lived and then went to work to help them. Last year, he visited the poorest parts of London and saw the tumbled-down houses in which many people had to live. He started work on tearing down the old houses and building new ones.

King Edward owns a large ranch in Alberta, Canada. There are four thousand acres in the ranch, and the fields stretch for miles and miles. King Edward has visited the ranch several times. The last time was nine years ago when he spent long summer days pitching hay with the hired men. He wore cowboy clothes. After round-ups, he led the cowboys in their singing by playing the ukulele. Old Gropper, a chestnut-colored pony that the Prince liked best to ride, is still at the ranch.

But just now King Edward is very busy in the British Isles. There he is trying to work out the hard problems of the British Empire. The British Empire covers many different countries and races. They must all be governed wisely and well. The new King Edward VIII is doing his best to make his people happy.

The Drought Takes Its Toll

This summer, dry weather and great heat swept across our country from the Rocky Mountains to the Atlantic Coast. Crops in the Middle West were ruined. Some four hundred million bushels of corn were destroyed by the drought in Missouri, Kansas, Iowa, Nebraska, Oklahoma, and South Dakota.

Cattle and sheep could find neither food nor water in the dried-up pasture lands. But the tiny prairie dogs, rabbits, ground-squirrels, owls, hawks, and snakes all were able to find food and water. These small wild animals got along better than the larger woodland creatures or the farm animals.

Uncle Sam Builds a New Treasure House

The Burglar-Proof Entrance to Uncle Sam's Treasure House

AT FORT KNOX in the Kentucky hills, Uncle Sam has just built a real treasure house for his wealth. It looks like a very old fort. It is made of rough granite with strong inner walls of steel and concrete. Far beneath the building are huge vaults, and around the treasure house are two moats or ditches filled with water.

If anyone tries to break into this treasure house, a guard can press a button and the water will flood the underground vaults. If anyone tries to make a hole in the walls with blow-torches, a deadly gas will escape from the walls and overcome the person. The treasure house is bomb-proof, and its glass windows are bullet-proof. It is also guarded by hundreds of soldiers.

The United States Government is guarding this treasure house with such care because it will hold most of the Nation's gold. Our total supply of gold is more than ten billion dollars' worth. Ten billion dollars, when written as a number, looks like an endless row of round zeros. But let's change the number into gold bricks or bars. Suppose that each solid gold brick is the size of an ordinary building brick. Ten billion dollars' worth of gold would make enough of these bricks to fill an eight-room house from cellar to attic.

Just last year, some of this great wealth was moved from San Francisco, California, to Denver, Colorado. It was hidden away in the big mint in that inland city. Now the gold which has been stored in the vaults of Philadelphia and New York is being moved from the Atlantic coast six hundred miles inland to Fort Knox, Kentucky. The gold is being taken there this month in 50 armored trains which are guarded by soldiers and guns.

Uncle Sam thinks that the gold will be safer stored far inside our country. If our coasts should be attacked by an enemy, the gold might be taken. Of course, no one really expects this to happen. But our Government is just "playing safe".

For Your Science Scrapbook

This is a music typewriter. Of course, it does not sing or play tunes. But its keys are music notes just as the keys of a regular typewriter are the letters of the alphabet.

The new typewriter was invented by a musician of Dresden, Germany. It will be a great help to the composers of music. Instead of writing their music by hand, they will type it. For over one hundred years, composers have dreamed of such a machine as they slowly and carefully put down music notes on paper. Now composers can type their music, tap, tap, tapping out the notes quickly on the typewriter.

Making a 10,000-Mile Hop

Late this summer, two flyers from Soviet Russia set out for a long hop across the top of the world. At San Pedro, California, they filled the fuel tanks of their giant airplane and loaded the storage space with supplies. Then the daring flyers took off and flew to Seattle, Washington. From there, they hopped to Juneau, Alaska. They are flying from our country to Soviet Russia by way of the Arctic Region.

Join the George Washington Puzzle Contest—This scene at Mount Vernon shows some things that were not there at the time of George Washington. Can you find them?

A Treasure Ship May Be Raised from the Sea

Eleanor Goes Overboard in Search of Gold

A man has found a sunken ship near New York City. He thinks that it is an old British ship, the Hussar (hoo-zär'). That ship was sunk near New York in 1780. It was bringing gold to America to pay British soldiers who were here fighting in the Revolutionary War. The Hussar was sunk when the British were driven from New York.

The sunken ship was found a short time ago by Mr. Simon Lake. He has been searching for the old Hussar for 50 years. Last month on his 70th birthday, he found what he thinks is the gold-filled Hussar. He says, "Within six weeks, I expect to step inside the sunken ship. If I were a betting man, I would bet 100 to 1 that the Hussar has been found at last."

Mr. Lake builds submarines and knows a great deal about deep-sea diving. He has made a submarine to use in searching for sunken gold. He has made a diving suit which he calls "Eleanor". Instead of hands, Eleanor has two long claws made of steel. A diver inside Eleanor can make the long claws reach far out in all directions. The strong steel "fingers" can break into any strongbox. Two strong searchlights make the dark water as light as day. Mr. Lake is shown in the picture pulling ropes to lower Eleanor into the water. The steel claws of Eleanor may be the first to break into the gold room of H. M. S. Hussar.

Tie a Knot on Your Nose for Safety!

This funny sign hangs in a park in Moscow, Russia. It shows a man with a long nose on which a knot is tied. On the knot hangs this sign: "Tie a knot to remember by." This is another

way of saying, "Remember to look out for traffic before you cross Moscow's busy streets. Stop, look, and listen."

Many people have been killed on the streets of Moscow. They would not have been killed if they had paid attention to the safety rules. To make more Russians read

—Sovfoto rules of safety, funny signs teaching safety are being put up in the city.

In the News

Old Mother Nature will have a show.

On June 19, the sun will be dark for a little time.

Many men have gone to Siberia to take pictures of the eclipse.

Airplanes of War Roar Over China

Japanese Boys Loading a Hospital Truck With Supplies for Wounded Soldiers

MANY little boys and girls are being driven from their homes in China. Their mothers and fathers are trying to find safe places for them. Airplanes are roaring, and shells are bursting around them. Many persons are sick and need help. Japanese children have lost their fathers in the fighting, and everywhere they hear talk about war. All this is because of the fighting which is going on in China between Japanese and Chinese soldiers.

Much of Shanghai (shăng'-hī'), the greatest city in China, has been blown up by Japanese airplanes. Billions of dollars have already been lost, and many more will be lost. It will take years to build up the beautiful city of Shanghai again.

The fighting in China is thousands of miles away, and some of us may not be thinking much about it. But all of us may have to think about it. All parts of our world have been brought close together by radio, fast-moving airplanes, and ships. Trouble in one place is soon felt in other places many miles away.

If the fighting in China keeps on, the people in our country will feel it. It will stop much of our trade with China and Japan. Last year, our trade with these two countries amounted to nearly five hundred million dollars. Japan has already blocked China's coast.

Why Japan Is Fighting China

Japan is one of the most crowded countries in the world. Our country has eleven times as much land. But Japan has about half as many people as has the United States. Only about one-sixth of Japan's land can grow crops. Japan cannot even raise enough rice to feed all her people. She must buy food from other countries. Besides food, Japan must buy from other countries such things as cotton, wool, oil, coal, and machines.

Japan needs more land for her many people. It seems as if Japan is trying to take the land she needs from China. Because of Japan, China has lost much of her rich land in Manchuria (măn-chōor'-ĭ-à). Now Japan is starting a war in North China, and people think that she will try to make China give up even more land. But this time, China is trying to fight back.

No one knows how long the fighting in China will last. Some say that Japan does not have enough money to fight for more than three months. Nothing else costs so much as war. It takes countries many, many years to pay for war. None of the countries have yet paid all it cost them to take part in the last World War.

The people of the world hope that the fighting in China will soon stop. Everyone wants the trouble to be settled in a peaceful way. Some countries have asked Japan and China to stop hurting women, little children, and others who are taking no part in the fighting. The United States has asked Japan and China not to fight any more.

The Rising Sun

The Japanese like their country to be called Nippon. The word "Nippon" means "Land of the Rising Sun". The cartoon above shows a Chinese family looking toward the rising sun. Instead of brightness and warmth, they see airplanes of war coming from the sun's rays.

Television Steps Out of the Workshop

"WHO INVENTED television? What is it? How does it work?" are the questions which pop into our minds as we hear about television tests and programs in our own country and abroad.

WHERE PICTURES ARE BROADCAST

The top of this tall radio mast on Alexandra Palace is used to send pictures through space. The lower part is for sound broadcasts.

We cannot name one man and say that he is the inventor of this new wonder of science, as Bell is the inventor of the telephone or Morse of the telegraph. Dozens of inventors have worked on television, and each one has added something to it. Each one has carried it a step farther toward the practical sets which you and I can use and enjoy. But two men who are working hard on television are Dr. Zworykin of RCA-Victor and Mr. Philo Farnsworth. They have both made television scanners. These scanners are somewhat like cameras. They change the light which comes from a picture or scene into radio waves which can be broadcast. With the help of these two inventors, television has now come out of the workshop and is being tested on the air.

Suppose we hop across the ocean to London, England, and visit a studio where television is in use. The studio is inside Alexandra Palace, the home of the British Broadcasting Company. On the palace is a giant radio mast. Its top is used to broadcast the pictures, while the lower part is used to broadcast the sound. Inside the studios are the television cameras, or scanners, and the microphones. With these, a moving picture of a person is sent through space at the same time that his voice is broadcast. Voice and picture can be picked up by television receiving sets which are tuned into the station for several miles around.

Suppose you live somewhere within fifty miles of Alexandra Palace and have a television receiving set. At the hour when a program is to be broadcast, you turn on your receiving set. It looks very much like a radio set, but it has a little picture screen in the top. On one side are the three knobs for sound. These you turn to make the voices and music come in clear and soft or loud. On the other side are three knobs for the pictures. These you turn to make the pictures come in bright and clear.

Of course, the television pictures will not be so clear or so steady as our modern motion pictures. The light will flicker on the screen. Sometimes persons will even look as if they were swimming under water. But the television pictures will be better than the very first motion pictures were. Like those early "movies", television is still in the testing stage. It has just come out of the inventors' workshop.

ACTION! CAMERA!

A television scene is being "shot" in this studio at Alexandra Palace in London, England. The television camera is picking up the picture. The microphone above the musician is picking up the sound. Both picture and music are being sent through space at the same time.

Getting "Sunshine" from Lamps

Child Health Day

May Day is Child Health Day. Each year, the President of the United States makes a proclamation about Child Health Day. He says that the children of today are those who will run our Government of tomorrow. To do this well, they must have health.

A King's Farewell to His People

A KING AND HIS FAMILY
The new King and Queen of England with their little daughters, Princess Margaret Rose and Princess Elizabeth.

hours before, he had been King Edward VIII, the ruler of the world's greatest empire. Now he had given up his throne.

For the first time in more than one thousand years, a British King has given up the throne of his own free will. He has handed the crown and all the duties which go with it to his oldest brother, the Duke of York. He will rule as George VI and his pretty Scotch wife will be Queen of England. Their older daughter, ten-year-old Princess Elizabeth, is now the heir to the throne. Some day, she may be Queen of England and rule over the great Empire.

"I NOW quit altogether public affairs, and I lay down my burden. It may be some time before I return to my native land, but I shall always follow the fortunes of the British race and Empire with profound interest and if at any time in the future I can be found of service to His Majesty in a private station, I shall not fail.

"And now, we all have a new King. I wish him and you, his people, happiness and prosperity with all my heart. God bless you all! God save the King!"

These words circled the globe by radio as Edward said farewell to the people of his Empire. A few

A KING AT PLAY
King George VI goes for a ride with Princess Elizabeth.

Dogs That See for Their Masters

NEARLY ten years ago, Buddy, a German shepherd dog, came to our country from Switzerland. If she could talk, she would tell newspaper re-

Walking Along Quickly and Surely With a Seeing Eye Dog for a Guide

Courtesy The Seeing Eye, Morristown, NJ

porters that she is a pioneer. Buddy was one of the first Seeing Eye dogs. She went to school and learned to be the eyes for her blind master, Morris S. Frank.

Mr. Frank and Buddy visited many eastern cities in the United States. Together they made their way in and out of traffic on the busy streets. Mr. Frank walked along quickly, as if he could see the automobiles and the people. No one would have guessed that he was blind. But Mr. Frank really had a very good pair of eyes. In his hand was the strap on Buddy's harness. Beside him walked the great shepherd dog to guide him safely through the traffic.

Out of those visits grew the Seeing Eye School at Morristown, New Jersey. Mr. Frank had tested his dog in our busy cities. He had found that she was a good guide for a person who could not see. Why should not other German shepherd dogs be trained to be the eyes for blind masters?

Today there are 250 German shepherd dogs who have gone to school. These Seeing Eye dogs are the friends and constant companions of blind men and women in 27 States. Some of them are the eyes for boys and girls who cannot see. These faithful dogs help their masters work and play like other people.

Bertha's Balloon Bursts

The time between the boom of the bursting balloon and Bertha's reaction was about three-tenths of a second. That much time was needed for the sound to reach her brain and for her to react.

Glass Houses To Live and Work In

Did you ever try to study at a desk which was in a dark corner of the room? Did you ever try to study under a light which was too bright? Do you remember how uncomfortable you were both times? You really could not study.

SHIRLEY'S NEW PLAYHOUSE

She had a hand in building it, too. Shirley spread some of the mortar on the glass block.

If you lived in a glass house, there would be no dark corners or light that was too bright. Glass block scatter the light so that it enters every corner of a room. Glass block also act as a screen, making the light soft.

Houses of glass have many good points. Glass block are both warm and cool. They keep out the heat of summer and the cold of winter. They keep out the noises of the street. They will not burn, and they are very strong. So the old saying, "Those who live in glass houses should not throw stones", is not true of the modern glass house. You could huff, you could puff, you could kick, but you could not blow the modern glass house down. Glass block are, indeed, very strong.

All these good points are making glass houses and buildings very popular. Everywhere schools, stores, libraries, churches, factories, and homes are being made of glass. Shirley Temple, the famous little "movie" star, has a new playhouse made of glass. My Weekly Reader is being printed in a new glass building. Oh, many a glass wall is now rising in the United States. Are builders in your town using glass block?

Sue is in the trailer.
Pee Wee is in the trailer.
Boots is in the trailer.

Tom is in the trailer.
Dick pulls the trailer.
They go for a ride.

New Homes Needed for Families Leaving Germany

HOW would you feel if you were told that you could not go to school, to church, or to the movies? How would you like to have someone tell your father to give up his work and much of his money? Many Jewish, Catholic, and Protestant people in Ger-

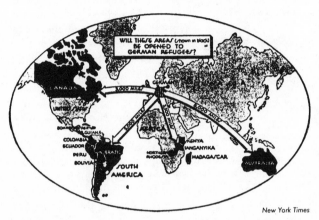

New York Times

The countries shown in black on the map have large sections in which few people live. Some of these countries have already said that they are willing to take a certain number of homeless people from Germany. But the question of how to raise the $600,000,000 needed to move thousands of homeless people has not been answered.

many have been told those things. Life is so hard for them that they want to leave Germany. Their friends in England, America, and other countries are trying to help them find new homes.

Where can those persons from Germany go and how can they make their living? Many of them are doctors, lawyers, and merchants who have been good citizens of Germany. Adolf Hitler, leader of the Germans, does not want them any longer in Germany.

The map above shows countries in black to which some of the suffering people of Germany may be allowed to go. As you see, those lands are far from Germany. It would cost many millions of dollars for so many people to go to such faraway places. Friends in America and other countries are planning to raise the money.

A Shot That Made Things Worse

Last month, a 17-year-old boy fired a shot in Paris. He was a young Jew who had lived in Germany. He went to Paris, France, to find work, but that was not easy to do. One day in November, he got a letter from his mother and father in Germany. The letter said that they were being sent out of Germany, that they had no place to go and would lose everything they had.

The bad news made the boy lose his head. He could think of nothing else to do but to harm some German. So he went to a Paris building in which men were working for the German Government. He fired some shots which killed one of the men.

The news of the man's death made more trouble for Jews living in Germany. Early the next morning, German crowds set fire to Jewish churches and shops throughout Germany. The crowds also harmed some buildings of Catholics and of members of other churches. They smashed windows, burned buildings, and drove Jews from their homes. Thousands of Jews had no place to go. The news of the suffering he had caused made the boy in Paris feel very sad. He was sorry that his act had made matters worse.

People in many parts of the world have held meetings and have sent messages to Hitler asking him to stop harming the Jews. President Roosevelt said that he could hardly believe that such things could happen in the world today.* Messages did little good. Mr. Hitler gave more orders which made it even harder for the Jews. He ordered the Jews to pay the German Government four hundred million dollars. This money is a "fine" which the Jews must pay for the shot that was fired by the boy in Paris.

Those who leave Germany will have to leave most of their money behind. Many of them would rather give up their money and go to live in some other country. They would rather be in a land in which people of all religions may live in peace and say what they think.

Many Germans know that the things that have been happening in their country are wrong. They are sorry. As one German saw windows being smashed and buildings burned, he whispered to an American, "Don't look—this is not the real Germany." The man could have been sent to jail for saying this. Germany does not have free speech as we have in America. Her people are not allowed to say what they think. That is one reason why the German people themselves can do so little to stop the suffering of so many people in Germany.

---

* "The news of the past few days from Germany has deeply shocked public opinion in the United States. . . . I myself could scarcely believe that such things could occur in a twentieth-century civilization." The President said that he was speaking of Nazi persecution of Catholics, Protestants, and other Germans as well as Jews.

The World Wants Peace Yet Spends Millions for War

THOUSANDS of men in Europe have been digging under the ground like moles. The men are getting ready for war. They fear their neighbors and try to keep them away by building underground forts of concrete and steel. The forts are joined together by tunnels. They are for the use of soldiers in time of war.

Half a million German workmen are now building a long line of forts under the ground. The forts are along the German border from Belgium to Switzerland. The Germans call their line the Limes (lī'mēz). That is a Latin word meaning wall. The Romans used the word long ago for walls which they built to keep enemies out of their country.

The French have a line of underground forts along their border next to Germany. They call it the Maginot (mäzh'-ĭ-nō) Line. France has spent 400 million dollars on her Maginot Line. It is named for Mr. Maginot, the French War Minister, who began the work in 1925. He started something which has been copied all over Europe. Czechoslovakia, Poland, Russia, Belgium, and Switzerland have built such underground forts.

The picture above shows how easy it is to spend millions of dollars for underground forts. Some of them are like big cities that can house thousands of soldiers. These forts have electric light plants, water pipes, sewers, large storehouses for food and war supplies, bakeries, libraries, and even streetcars. In time of war, armies can live for months in those underground cities without going outside.

French soldiers used such an underground city during the World War. It was far below ground at Verdun (vĕr-dûn') and was so strong that the Germans could not break through. The writer visited the underground city at Verdun soon after the Armistice was

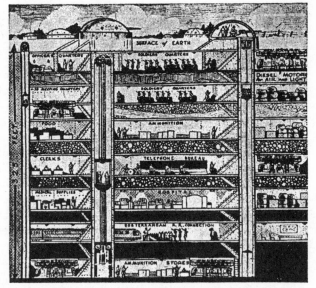

A SECTION OF THE MAGINOT LINE

Here you see a building below the ground instead of above. How many layers of rooms or stories are there in this part of the Maginot Line? In which story is the hospital? Where is the food stored? What use is made of the other rooms? How do the men go up and down?

signed in 1918. It was interesting to see that city of no sunlight in which so many soldiers had lived like rats.

Long ago, many cities were built with strong walls around them. In the Far East, Chinese workmen spent years building the Great Wall of China. They hoped it would keep out wild men from the North. Some of the early American settlements had wooden stockades or walls to keep out the Indians. As time went on, men became more civilized. Many thought the World War was the last great war that would ever be fought, but they were wrong. Today the world has more walls and forts than it has ever had. The walls that used to be above the ground are now built under it.

After the World War, leaders of many nations met and agreed to spend less money getting ready for war. Most of those nations are now spending more money than ever before. Next year, 60 nations are planning to spend twenty-five billion dollars ($25,000,000,000). If some of that money could be spent for food, clothing, and hospitals, there would not be so many people in the world today who are hungry and sick.

Our country has been watching closely what is going on in Europe. A study has been made to see if the United States is ready if war should come. Roosevelt says that a report will be made to Congress in January.

Friday, November 11, is Armistice (är'-mĭ-stĭs) Day. It is a day on which we give thanks for the peace that ended the World War. This year on Armistice Day, many parts of the world are far from being at peace. Wars are going on in Spain, China, and even in the Holy Land. How happy the world would be if those fighters would lay down their arms as the soldiers did on November 11, 1918.

Will You Be a Winner in the Great Work of Conservation?

About 25 acres of land have been set aside for the birds near Cape Girardeau in southeastern Missouri. Many tired flyers are finding rest, safety, and food in the Springdale Bird Sanctuary this spring. The people of Cape Girardeau are proud of their sanctuary. More than that, both children and adults are finding many ways of helping the birds in their own yards.

Are the people of your community hearing about the important subject of conservation of birds, wild animals, and plants? My Weekly Reader will give many ways in which you can begin this important work in your neighborhood.

Austria Becomes Part of German Empire

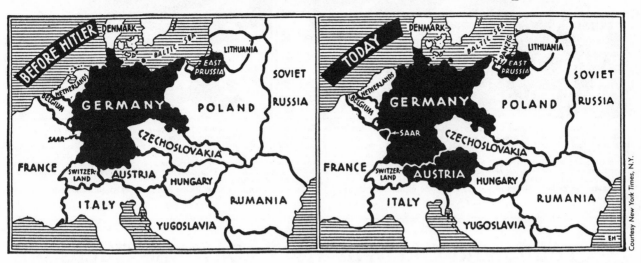

Courtesy New York Times, N.Y.

Science Works for Peace

Last month, it looked as if there would be war in Czechoslovakia (chĕk-ō-slō-vä′-kĭ-à). If there had been, science would have played a big part in the war. The latest inventions would have been used to kill thousands of men and to destroy buildings.

THE BRITISH PRIME MINISTER

Mr. Neville Chamberlain knew there was no time to lose so he flew to Germany for a talk with Hitler.

There was no big war, and science helped to stop it. This shows that science can be used for peace as well as for war. Without the airplane, radio, and long-distance telephone, the leaders of the nations could not have worked so quickly for peace.

When war comes, it often breaks out in a hurry. To stop war, men must act quickly. Last month, when Mr. Hitler said the German army would begin fighting on October 1, the radio carried the news to all parts of the world. Almost at once, messages asking for peace were sent to Germany from far and near.

The airplane, which has become such a deadly thing in time of war, was also put to use for peace. Mr. Chamberlain, the Prime Minister of Great Britain, rushed in an airplane to Germany. Like a dove of peace his airplane flew over countries getting ready for war. Mr. Chamberlain tried to stop war from coming. He talked with Mr. Hitler of Germany about

peace. This talk might have come too late if it had not been for the airplane.

A few days later, it looked as if the peace talk had failed. Hitler said that his big army was ready to start fighting. Then the wires hummed with messages for peace, and Hitler was made to know how much the world hates war. At last, he said he would have a talk with the leaders of England, France, and Italy. They came together quickly. There was no time to be lost. Then it was that the great inventions of science, such as airplanes, automobiles, fast trains, radios, and telephones, played such a big part.

Even a Gasproof Baby Carriage

Children in many countries of Europe were given gas masks this fall. Many of them needed new shoes, instead. Great Britain has spent millions of dollars so that each person will have a mask to take poison gas

WAR WEARS AN UGLY FACE

If you lived in some of the countries of Europe, you would have gas mask drills as well as fire drills at school.

from the air he breathes. Even babies in carriages have been fitted with gas masks. One of the newest things is a gasproof baby carriage.

DOG TALES— Dogs of the Saint Bernard Monastery in the Swiss Alps
By Paul Burchfield

We Saint Bernards are naturally sad-looking, but now we have something to look sad about. Not long ago, a Paris newspaperman wrote a story telling how we killed a little girl and were in such disgrace that we were sent to faraway Tibet. Well, now, only part of that is true. Some of my brothers did bite a little girl who died later. But we were not banished, because our kind masters know that we mistook her for a wolf in the snow. Why, we are the world's kindest dogs. We all love children.

Humans can make mistakes as well as dogs. One of my brothers named

Barry had saved forty lives. One of them was a little girl. Barry licked her face and arms until she came to. Then he carried her to safety on his strong back. One day, not long afterward, he was going to save his forty-first person, but the man mistook him for a wolf and shot him. So please do not think we are bad because our mistake was as natural as the man's. Over Barry's grave are the words, "BARRY THE HEROIC—SAVED 40 TRAVELERS AND WAS KILLED BY THE 41ST."

We are big dogs, stand 36 inches high, and weigh up to 250 pounds.

Young and Old Will Try To Save the Circus

THOUSANDS of boys and girls have signed a letter to be sent this month to President Roosevelt. The letter asks the President to do what he can to help save the circus.

For a long time, things have not been going well with the circus. This summer was the worst time of all, when hard times, rain, and labor troubles kept circuses from making money.

By the middle of this summer, most circuses had either gone back to their winter quarters or had sold out and quit. The Ringling Brothers and Barnum and Bailey Circus, the largest of all our shows, ended its tour in June. Downie Brothers and Sells-Sterling closed in July. The Cole Brothers-Clyde Beatty Circus lasted until the first of August. Many smaller circuses have given up and quit.

"Save the circus" is now the cry of many children and grownups in America. Circus lovers old and young want to keep the circus from dying out.

New Legs for Charlie McCarthy

Courtesy The Eagle Magazine

Charlie McCarthy has learned to walk. Carpenters in Hollywood have made a new set of legs and arms for Charlie. The new legs are only of wood, but Charlie walks along with a lively step. Now that he can walk across the stage, perky Charlie McCarthy expects to become a great actor.

Courtesy Parma, Ohio, Police Dept.

Safety Sallies help the children.

War Comes to Europe

French children are leaving their homes and going to the country.

ARMIES are marching against one another in Europe. Cannons are booming. Tanks are rumbling across fields. Fighting airplanes are roaring overhead by day and by night. War has broken out.

Poland's Past Troubles

The trouble arose in Poland, a small country in the northern part of Europe. Poland is both an old and a new country. Poland was a country nearly 1,000 years ago. It was much bigger long ago than it is now. It changed its size many times. Parts of its land were taken by other countries. About 150 years ago, all that was left of Poland was divided among other countries. Poland disappeared from the map of Europe.

Poland came into being again, twenty years ago, after the World War. Nearly one-third of the new Poland was made up of land that had been in Germany. This is one reason for the trouble which has brought on war.

Men thought the new Poland should have a seaport, so that it could send out goods and bring in goods by boat. So when the new Poland was made, it was given a narrow strip of land to the Baltic Sea. At the end of this strip of land was the great seaport of Danzig (dän'tsik). Danzig did not become a part of Poland, but was left as a free, self-ruling city. Poland had the right to use it for shipping. There were many Germans in Danzig.

Poland's narrow strip of land to the Baltic Sea

split Germany into two parts. Polish land separated East Prussia, a part of Germany, from the rest of Germany. Germany had the right to use a railroad connecting the two parts.

Almost from the time the new Poland came into being, there has been trouble between Poland and Germany over Danzig and Germany's rights in Poland. Poland thought Germany was getting too strong in Danzig. Last April, Hitler, the leader of Germany, asked Poland for a strip of land to join the two parts of Germany. Poland refused to give up any land.

The Beginning of War

Time passed. Poland and Germany became more and more unfriendly. Hitler said that Danzig belonged to Germany. He asked Poland to give up all land that had once been part of Germany. He threatened to send soldiers into Poland. Poland would not give in to him.

Then German leaders in Danzig said they would put Danzig under Germany's control. A few hours later, German soldiers moved against Poland from Germany and East Prussia. Poland asked England and France for help. These two countries asked Hitler to take German soldiers out of Poland, while the trouble was being settled. When he refused, England and France declared war upon Germany.

And so, within a few days, four countries were at war—Germany, Poland, France, and England. Children were hurried from the big cities of France and England into the country, where there was not so much danger of airplane raids.

EUROPE'S TROUBLE SPOT Find the Baltic Sea, Danzig, East Prussia, Germany, and Poland. The arrows show where German soldiers attacked Poland.

Uncle Sam Works To Keep Out of War

Workmen have placed the hatch covers of an American ship on the pier and are busily painting American Flags on them. When the liner sails across the Atlantic, its captain wants nations at war to know that his ship belongs to a neutral nation.

THESE are busy days in Washington, D. C., our Nation's capital. The desks of President Roosevelt and Secretary of State Hull are piled high with important papers. Their telephones ring often as our ambassadors in European countries call them to get advice and to make reports. Telegrams, cable messages, and radio reports pour in.

President Roosevelt, Mr. Hull, and others in our Government are working hard to keep us out of the war in Europe.

As soon as war was declared on Germany by Great Britain and France, President Roosevelt proclaimed our neutrality. That is, he told the whole world that we are neutral (not taking sides). By international law (rules among nations), every neutral nation makes such a proclamation when war is declared in any part of the world.

President Roosevelt also put our Neutrality Act into force. By that Act, Americans are not allowed to sell guns or ammunition to any nation at war.

President Roosevelt does not approve of our Neutrality Act. He says that it does not make us neutral, because Germany does not count on us for her war supplies, but Great Britain and France do. He wants a new Neutrality Act to be written. The new one would allow any nation to buy war supplies as well as other goods from us. But the buyers would have to pay cash for the supplies and would have to come and get them.

During the weeks to come, you will hear much talk about the Neutrality Act. You will find that some persons approve of it and want it kept in force. Others do not like it and want a new law, such as the President's "cash and carry" one, passed. The members of Congress were called back to Washington last week to discuss and perhaps change our Neutrality Act.

Other steps are being taken to keep us out of war, too. American citizens who are abroad are being brought back to our country as soon as possible. Mr. Hull and the State Department are also trying to keep American citizens at home. Mr. Hull has called in all American passports now in use. He will not issue new ones unless the persons have very good reasons for being abroad. Even then the new passports will be good only for six months and must be returned to the State Department in Washington at the end of that time for safekeeping.

Ships To Be Marked

Every American ship that sails the seas has been very carefully marked so that nations at war will know it belongs to a neutral nation. Huge American Flags are painted on the hatches and can be plainly seen by airplanes from above. Huge American Flags are painted on the hulls and can be plainly seen by submarines.

Ships To Guard Our Coasts

Warships have been stationed on the Atlantic and Pacific coasts and at the Panama Canal. More than one hundred old destroyers have been put into good condition and may be used to guard our coasts or to protect our ships.

In fact, our Government is doing everything in its power to keep us out of war. President Roosevelt thinks that we cannot be too careful. He said in his radio speech to the Nation a few weeks ago, "When peace has been broken anywhere, peace of all countries everywhere is in danger."

Meet the People in the News
A Famous Flyer Speaks Over the Radio

Colonel Charles Lindbergh made a speech over the radio several weeks ago. His pleasant voice was carried over the big networks and into hundreds of homes throughout the country.

If you were listening, you heard Colonel Lindbergh express his views about our country and the war in Europe. He feels that the United States should keep out of Europe's quarrels.

Blackboards in Color

When you sit at the side or in the back of the classroom, do you sometimes have a hard time seeing the writing on the blackboard?

Experiments are now being made with colored blackboards on which writing is easier to read. High schools in New York City are trying out white and green blackboards, or chalkboards, which are made of bullet-proof glass. The University of Illinois has been working on different colored boards and colored chalk for the past two years.

A Zoo Is Moved

Until a few days ago, one of the world's biggest zoos was in London, England. There were animals in it from all parts of the world. There were two giant pandas that looked like big teddy bears. There was a baby elephant. There were monkeys that had a tea party every afternoon.

Now the London Zoo has been moved. Men were afraid enemy airplanes might drop bombs on London and the animals in the zoo might get out. The most valuable animals were sent to a zoo in the country. They will stay there until all danger is past.

Pandas come from western China. There are only a few of them in our part of the world. The pandas of the London Zoo have been moved to the country.

My Weekly Reader tries to present several points of view on all important questions. It is not our purpose to try to settle any issue but to get boys and girls to think about the vital problems of today.

Meet a Man of Science

This picture of Dr. George Washington Carver was taken by one of our own editors.

This story has 191 words in it. You should read it silently in about one minute. Your teacher will time you. Read as fast as you can, but be sure to understand what you read. Then do Test C.

Dr. George Washington Carver has been in the news this autumn. He has just won a medal for his work with peanuts and sweet potatoes. Out of these two familiar foods, he has made many new products.

Dr. Carver was born about 75 years ago in Missouri. His mother and father were Negro slaves. But Dr. Carver worked his way through school and college. Then he became a teacher.

As a teacher, he was especially interested in chemistry and farming in the South. He made a careful study of peanuts and sweet potatoes, two crops of the small southern farmer. He has made nearly three hundred useful products out of peanuts alone. Face powder, cheese, axle grease, and oils used in medicines were just a few of these products. He has made more than one hundred different products from the sweet potato. Flour, printer's ink, library paste, and lard are some of his sweet-potato products.

Today Dr. Carver is Director of the Department of Agricultural Research at Tuskegee Institute in Alabama. He is also one of the world's famous chemists, and he is going on with his work and his experiments.

Triceratops

What's in a Name?

We'd like you to meet these dinosaurs under their correct names, and we're sorry the artist mixed them up. But we're also very proud of our bright-eyed readers who caught this mistake.

Tyrannosaurus

1940-1949

The 1940s found America engaged in a world war for the second time in less than 25 years. How would *Weekly Reader* handle this starkest of human conflicts? The answer came in a notice to teachers headlined "*Weekly Reader* in Wartime." The editors announced their policy in a sentence: "We will reflect the changes in wartime America and the world without stressing the horrors of war."

Weekly Reader focused on the home front. Cover stories pictured the nation as the chief arsenal and granary of the Allied war effort. "The making of automobiles has stopped," young readers learned in 1942. "We need airplanes and tanks now more than we need automobiles." The farm belt went to work to feed the U.S. and allies like the British, whose food supplies were gravely threatened by submarine wolf packs.

To bring students into the war effort, *Weekly Reader* published "work-for-victory" features. Readers were exhorted to avoid food waste, to walk to school to save the rubber tires on the family auto, and to save their pennies for war bonds.

Victory finally came in 1945. Immediately, and dramatically, *Weekly Reader*'s editorial focus changed. In the postwar '40s, young readers learned about an explosion of new technology. There was a new magic called plastics; radio phones that carried voices across the ocean; and a revolutionary camera that made its own prints in a minute. But there was also news of far-off threats to peace—the Iron Curtain dividing Communist from non-Communist Europe, and bitter enmity between Jew and Arab in the Middle East.

More Airplanes and More Airships

The workers shown here are finishing the fuselages of airplanes.

NEWSPAPERS tell us that the Government has ordered 12,000 new airplanes for the Army and 48 new airships for the Navy. Do you know the difference between an airship and an airplane? There is much news about both now, so you should know how one is different from the other.

We know more about airplanes because more of them have been built. An airplane depends upon its engine to lift it into the air and to hold it in the air. When an airplane's engine stops, the airplane must come down.

An airship is really just a large balloon. The kind of airship ordered for the Navy is known as a dirigible (dĭr′ĭ-jĭ-b′l) or blimp. "Dirigible" means "steerable." A dirigible is a balloon that can be steered where the pilot wants it to go.

A dirigible or blimp has a long bag filled with gas that is lighter than air. Below the bag is a cabin which holds the crew and the engines. The engines drive the dirigible where the pilot wants it to go. If the dirigible had no engines, it could go only where the wind blew it. The dirigible's engines make it move, but they do not hold it up in the air any more than a boat's engine holds it up in the water. The dirigible floats in the air because its bag is filled with gas that is lighter than air.

When the bag is full, the dirigible must be held down with ropes until its crew is ready to take off. Once in the air, the dirigible can stay there even though its engines may stop. To make the airship come down, some of the gas is let out of the bag.

The Government wants more airplanes and airships. Airplane factories are working night and day, but they are behind in their orders. Other companies are making airplane parts to help the airplane makers finish their airplanes more quickly. One company that has made nothing but automobile bodies for years is beginning to make airplane wings. Some automobile companies will soon start making airplane engines.

To speed up the work, airplanes are made in three sections—the fuselage (fū′zĕ-lĭj) or body, the wings, and the engine. When the three sections are finished, they are put together.

Airplanes are harder to make than most other kinds of machines because airplanes have so many parts. The fuselage and wings of a Curtiss pursuit plane have 15,000 parts, not counting 78,000 rivets. The engine of this airplane has 6,000 parts. The propeller alone has 190 parts. No wonder airplane makers need help!

Akron, Ohio, is the center of airship building in this country. Only a few small blimps have been built there in the last few years. Now the workers are starting on the first six of the new blimps for the Navy. They will cost about $8,000,000.

Our Navy will soon have more airships like this one.

"Made in the United States"

HAS your family bought a new rug in the last few months? Has your family bought new furniture, dishes, glassware, or a mirror? Whether or not there are new things of these kinds at your house, take a look at the bottom or back of them. You will probably find a label there. The label will tell you where the thing was made.

If you have new things of the kinds mentioned, the chances are very good that the label will read, "Made in the United States" or "Made in U. S. A." Many more of these things are now being made in this country than were being made here a few years ago. Just two years ago, more than half our glassware and many of our dishes came from other countries. Many of the counters in ten-cent stores were covered with things made in other countries. Many of the dishes and much of the glassware in stores selling only high-priced things came from other countries, too.

Now you will find that our stores have very few things made in other countries. Many of the workers in Europe are making things needed for war. Ships no longer go regularly between this country and Europe. Storekeepers here are not ordering things from Europe.

All this has led American workers to try making the things that once came from other countries. Our workers are finding that they can make such things just as well and often better.

Our ten-cent stores now have no buyers in Europe. Instead, glassware and dishes that are cheap but good are coming from factories in Ohio and West Virginia. Cheap knives are coming from factories in New England.

In Vermont, women are making the kinds of cloth that once came only from Scotland and England. In New York, workers are making hand-hooked rugs like those that once came only from China, Japan, and countries in northern Europe. Our workers are now turning out as fine things as ever came from another country.

Fostoria Glass Co.

Artists are busy working out new designs for tumblers.

Meet Elektro and Sparko

Boys and girls, meet Elektro and Sparko. Elektro and Sparko are at the New York World's Fair, which has just opened for this year. Elektro is an electrical man. Sparko is an electrical dog. In the picture, they look like something you might have seen in a nightmare, but they are really very friendly. They are welcoming fair visitors for a big electric company.

Elektro can talk and walk. He can shake hands, chop wood, carry heavy loads, and do many other kinds of work. Sparko can bark, wag his tail, walk, sit up, and beg. It's hard to think what he might beg for, because he never eats anything. Maybe he is begging for an electrical cat to chase up an electric light pole.

Electricity has a big share in both our world's fairs this year—the New York World's Fair and the Golden Gate Fair in California.

Electricity is making both places fairylands at night. At the New York fair, great fountains of water rise and fall and change color as music plays. The fountains and the colors are controlled by electricity. The Golden Gate Fair is already well-known for its beautiful lighting at night. The walls of the buildings glow and sparkle under hidden lights. Electrical tubes filled with gas make long lines of colored light—green, pink, blue, and amber. They look like lightning that has been trapped and tamed. The Golden Gate Fair has giant lanterns of light 86 feet high.

International

Sparko will have to "speak" again as Elektro doesn't seem to understand the meaning of his bark.

Radio's Twenty Years

Columbia Broadcasting System

BACK in 1920, there were just a few radio sets in this country. All of them were homemade. There were no real radio stations. A few men and older boys "played with radio" as a hobby. They built their own receiving sets and sending sets and talked with one another through the air.

One of the men whose hobby was radio was Dr. Frank Conrad. Dr. Conrad was a young scientist who worked for the Westinghouse Company, a company that made electrical machinery and supplies.

One day Dr. Conrad received this letter: "My Aunt Franny is coming to visit me next week and she does not believe music can be sent through the air. Will you please play a phonograph record for her next Friday night at ten o'clock?" Dr. Conrad played a record over his sending set for his friend's aunt, proving to her that music could be sent through the air.

A few days ago, Dr. Conrad spoke on a program broadcast by the Westinghouse Company. This program was the beginning of radio's twentieth birthday party. Regular broadcasting began in 1920.

Broadcasting, like most big businesses, had a small beginning. Dr. Conrad first talked over the station he made in his garage to friends who had receiving sets. When he grew tired of talking, he played phonograph records. The owner of a near-by music store agreed to lend Dr. Conrad the latest records if Dr. Conrad would mention the store once in awhile in his broadcasts. The owner of the store soon noticed that he was selling more records—especially the records Dr. Conrad played over his station. That was the beginning of radio advertising.

In November, 1920, something happened that made more people want radio sets so that they could hear broadcasts. November, 1920, was the time of a presidential election. Leaders of the Westinghouse Company had decided to go into the radio business. To make more people interested in radio and broadcasting, the Westinghouse men decided to try sending out election news. Dr. Conrad's station was moved to the roof of the Westinghouse Company. The station became station KDKA. Only a few people had radio sets, so the Westinghouse Company loaned sets to some of its workers and their friends. On election night, these radio listeners were the first to know that Warren G. Harding had been elected President.

From that time on, the radio business grew fast. About the time KDKA started in Pittsburgh, WWJ started in Detroit. Soon WJZ was started in Newark, New Jersey. It was later moved to New York. In 1922 there were more than 600 little broadcasting stations all over the United States. By 1924 there were 1,400—so many that the Government had to make rules for broadcasters.

The first broadcasting stations had just one or two rooms and four or five workers. Now the studios of KDKA take up a whole floor in a downtown skyscraper and the station has a large building in the country, from which the broadcasts go into the air.

There are more than 800 regular broadcasting stations in the United States now. If all the receiving sets in use now were divided equally among the people, there would be one set for every two persons. If all the radio workers were gathered in one place, they would make a large city the size of Cleveland or Detroit.

We must remember that radio has not stopped growing and improving. Broadcasting is getting better. Television is being improved, too. Do you suppose Aunt Franny has a television set yet?

National Broadcasting Company

Here you see a radio program as it is being put on in a large radio studio. The words and music go by wire to a building in the country. In this building is the transmitter, which sends words and music into the air. The tower of a transmitter is shown in the upper left corner of this page.

CCC Boys Work for the Government

CCC Boys at Work

U.S. Forest Service

Many big boys in this country work for the Government. They are called CCC boys.

The boys come from all over the country. They come from cities and towns. Many CCC boys come from farms.

The boys live in big camps. There are CCC camps all over the country.

CCC boys learn to work in the CCC camps. The boys do many kinds of work. They work all day.

The CCC boys plant trees on land that is not good land. They plant trees in woods where trees have been cut down.

CCC boys help people who come to the parks. The boys show people how to make fires. The boys show people how to put out fires. The boys help to keep the woods safe from fires.

When work is over, the boys go to the camp. They read and write. They play games. The boys go to school. They learn things that help with their work.

The Government pays the boys for the work they do. The Government gives the boys a home in the CCC camp. The Government gives every CCC boy $30 a month.

Safety at School

The children go to school.
•
The children work for safety.

The children drink.
•
The children work for safety.

Tomorrow's Railroads

PERHAPS you have ridden on one of the fast streamlined trains of today. Perhaps you have watched a long freight train go puffing and steaming down the tracks. Perhaps you have visited a railroad station and seen both old engines with smokestacks and sleek new streamlined engines. This month, one of the world's fastest freight trains went thundering down the tracks of the Santa Fe Railroad. This new train is the first freight train to use a Diesel (dē′zĕl)-electric locomotive. It can pull as big a load as could fifty-four hundred horses. It can pull about one hundred loaded freight cars at a speed of about 75 miles an hour on level tracks.

Such a locomotive can be used to pull cars loaded with fruits and vegetables quickly from place to place. The Diesel-electric locomotive does not have to stop and be serviced as often as do the steam locomotives.

Along the tracks of the Illinois Central Railroad thunders another fast long-distance freight train. It is the MS-1. It carries goods through the Mississippi River valley between Chicago and New Orleans. For more than five hundred miles straight, this fast freight train goes at an average speed of nearly 40 miles an hour.

That speed may not seem very fast to you. You hear so much about passenger planes that travel 185 and 190 miles an hour. You hear about passenger trains that have an average speed of more than 50 miles an hour. You are probably thinking that the family automobile can do much better than 40 miles an hour on the open road. But for freight trains today, an average speed of 40 miles an hour for hundreds of miles at a stretch is good time.

Of course, many of the fast streamlined passenger trains travel at an average speed of 84 miles an hour. They are easy riding and comfortable. They are clean, warm in the winter, and cool in the summer.

The railroads have made great strides ahead in the past few years, but they are not standing still. They are making even greater plans for the future.

By 1950, most of the freight trains on the important railroads of the Nation will be traveling at an average speed of about 50 miles an hour. To reach this average speed, the tracks will have to be made smoother and stronger. Engines will have to be made stronger with better balanced wheels. Freight cars will have to be built to stand greater strain. They will also have to be built with more evenly balanced wheels.

Within the next ten years, the new freight cars

The Santa Fe Railroad boasts the world's first Diesel-electric locomotive to pull a freight train. As you know, a powerful Diesel engine is run with a cheap crude oil. In a Diesel-electric locomotive, the electric generator is driven by a Diesel engine.

may be quite different from the great boxlike ones you see today. Plans are being made for a new style in freight cars.

The freight car of tomorrow may be built like a flatcar with containers that fit neatly into the floor. These containers will divide the car into quarters or halves. There will be large containers to fit over entire cars. There will be special containers cooled by dry ice to carry quick-frozen foods quickly from place to place. Today these frozen foods must be sent by express, and express is more expensive than freight.

By 1950, trains on the important railroads may be covering a greater distance in a day than automobiles could cover. Then drivers who are in a hurry will take their automobiles by train. The automobiles will be driven onto a special flatcar and parked. They will be well-protected from the weather and jolting. They will be carried from place to place quicker than they could be driven. The owners will travel comfortably and quickly on the train but will have their automobiles to drive at the end of the trip.

The builders of new passenger and freight trains have special laboratories just as the automobile and airplane companies do. In these laboratories, models of new trains are built and tested. Streamlined models are tested for speed in wind tunnels. Tests are made for wear and tear on trains and engines.

As you grow up in the next ten years, the railroads will be growing, too. By 1950, passenger and freight trains will be giving better service than ever before. How old will you be in 1950? Will you still be in school? Will you be working? Whatever you are doing, the future improvements in the railroads may play an important part in the life of your community.

Blind Children Can Read *My Weekly Reader*

If you were to visit the Perkins Institution at Watertown, Massachusetts, you would find the children enjoying MY WEEKLY READER just as you do. A great many blind children read MY WEEKLY READER now, for Editions No. 3, No. 4, and No. 5 of MY WEEKLY READER are printed in Braille.

Advance page proofs of MY WEEKLY READER are mailed each week to the American Printing House for the Blind. There Braille copies of your newspaper are printed for children who cannot see.

A special Braille issue of MY WEEKLY READER is printed each year for those who can see. In this special issue, the words are printed above the Braille letters.

If you would like to see a copy of MY WEEKLY READER in Braille, send fifteen cents to the American Printing

House for the Blind, 1839 Frankfort Avenue, Louisville, Kentucky, and ask for the special Braille issue. Be sure to give your complete address, so there need be no delay in sending the Braille issue to you.

Gabriel Farrell, Perkins Institution

Flying Over the Roof of the World

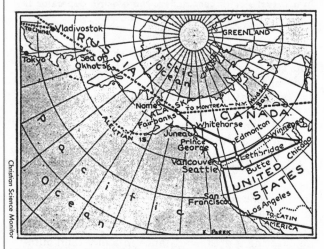

Christian Science Monitor

Solid black lines show air routes already in use. The broken lines are planned air routes.

SUPPOSE you wanted to visit your neighbor who lives in the third or fourth house down the street. How would you go from your house to his? You would probably go out your front door and down your front walk to the sidewalk. You would turn and walk along the sidewalk until you came to your neighbor's walk. Then you would turn and go up his walk to his front door.

A bird would take a much easier way than that. It would simply fly in a straight line from your roof to your neighbor's roof.

Aviators and explorers have known for a long time that the shortest way between certain lands is over "the roof of the world." If you could look straight down upon the top of our world, you would see that Russia, Alaska, Canada, and Greenland are neighbors around the Arctic Ocean. The map shows this.

You can see how easily Alaska could be a steppingstone for travelers between Russia and the United States. In the same way, Greenland

can be a steppingstone between North America and Europe.

Of course, travel over the roof of the world is easy in only one way—by air. Winters in the Far North are long and hard. In many places, the land is buried under deep drifts of snow. Some of the land is never free of ice and snow. Part of the Arctic Ocean is never open to ships because of ice. In winter, ocean ice creeps farther south.

None of those difficulties which make land travel hard is much of a hindrance to travel by air. An airplane can fly just as easily over ice fields as it can over green pastures.

You can easily see why airplanes have been a great help in the Far North, especially in winter. Airplanes fly winter and summer all through northern Canada and Alaska. Fish from Alaska are flown to Chicago overnight. The trappers are sending out more and more of their furs by airplane. Airplanes bring out precious cargoes of gold, silver, and radium in a few hours.

Plans are being made now to join the air routes of Canada and Alaska with air routes in Russia. There have been weather stations along the planned air routes for several years. The weather information gathered by these stations will make flying over the roof of the world as safe as flying from New York to Chicago. Landing fields are being cleared as the neighbors of the North come to agreements about the new air routes.

Airways are already more common than highways in many parts of the Far North. Even some of the Eskimos are beginning to use airplanes instead of dog sledges.

Some days ago, two airplanes from Russia landed at Seattle, Washington, with some Russian aviation experts. In a few years, there will be much more travel between the neighbors of the North. The roof of the world may soon need a traffic light.

Men Learn To Cook and Sew

Almost all army kitchens have potato peeling machines like this one.

HOW many men do you know who can cook or sew? Probably not very many. Thousands of American men are learning to cook and sew, however. You probably know someone who has gone into the Army in the last few months. If you do, you can be sure that he has learned to sew or that he is learning. And he may be one of the many men learning to be army cooks or bakers.

Thousands of men are learning to be good cooks and bakers in the Army. In each camp, there is usually one cook and one baker for every 100 soldiers. There is also one man in nearly every small group of soldiers who knows a little about cooking.

Our soldiers get good food and food that is good for them. In fact, our soldiers are probably the best-fed soldiers in the world. The food in army camps is often better than the food many families have at home.

For breakfast, a soldier in camp may choose from these things: fresh fruit juice, dry cereal, oatmeal, eggs, bacon, pancakes, coffee, milk, bread, butter, and muffins. A common Sunday dinner is: chicken, mashed potatoes, gravy, peas, cake, and ice cream. There is plenty of everything—even pie and cake.

Of course, the camps cannot have good food unless they have good cooks. The heads of the Army are making sure there are plenty of good cooks and bakers, however. The Army has nine schools in which cooks and bakers are taught.

Army cooks and bakers must go to school for at least two months. Since there is so much to learn, a man must decide whether he wants to be a cook or a baker. He cannot be both.

Cooks learn to plan meals, to cook different foods in the best ways, and to cook foods without waste. Bakers learn many of the same things in connection with bread, pies, and cakes. You can be sure that the men in school learn to cook or bake as well as they can. They have to eat the things they make, even while they are in school!

Cooks and bakers learn to use many kitchen machines. In army kitchens, there are electrical mixers, choppers, and washers. There are even electrical potato peelers.

One of the baker's biggest jobs is baking bread for each camp. Just one camp may need 25,000 loaves of bread every day. One interesting fact about army pies is that they are not round. Army pie pans are about three feet long and not quite so wide. The pies are cut in squares.

Of course, not every soldier may learn to be a cook or baker. Every soldier must know how to do some kinds of sewing, however.

Every soldier must keep his clothes in good condition. He must darn his own socks, sew on his own buttons, and sew up small tears and rips in his clothes. The new soldier learns to do these things soon after he joins the Army.

Soldiers have small sewing kits called "housewives." The kit can be carried fastened to the soldier's belt. Each kit has thread in three colors—black, white, and olive drab. Olive drab is the color of the soldier's uniform. The kit also has needles, pins, buttons, and a pair of small scissors.

Soldiers in our Army get good food and good clothes. They soon know how to "take care" of both.

This soldier learns that sewing on a button is not so hard as he thought. His "housewife" is on the table in front of him.

Trailer Homes

There are big shipyards at Wilmington, North Carolina. The Government is building ships there.

Many workers are needed to build the ships. Men from other cities are going to Wilmington. They are helping to build the ships.

Wilmington is growing. New houses are being built. But many men cannot find houses for their families.

The Government is buying trailers. The men and their families will live in trailers. When the men find houses, they will move out of the trailers.

Many men are finding work in big cities. Men are going to towns to work.

The trailers are in Washington, D. C. Soon they will be taken to Wilmington and workmen will live in them.

Cities and towns are growing.

Workers cannot find homes in some cities and towns. Some people are living in trailers. Some workers and their families are living in tents.

Science News Bits
Meet Dr. Carrot

Dr. Carrot, whom you see in the picture, was made by Walt Disney for the people of England. Dr. Carrot's job is to get people to eat more carrots. Carrots are good for people and do not cost very much. Scientists have found that eating carrots helps people to see better at night. Carrots are especially good for night flyers.

• Dr. Carrot wants to help people see better at night. Long ago, English women raised carrots only for their leaves, which were used as decorations on hats. "Queen Anne's lace" is really a wild carrot. •

DR. CARROT

DANNY DOO AND LOKI — Loki Gives You Another Drawing Lesson   By Ray Evans, Jr.

Here's another drawing lesson. Try your hand and send your pictures to Loki. We'll print the best ones.

The fourth grade girls and boys in the following schools sent in lists of clever names for Loki's goat: Randolph School, Asheville, N. C.; Miss

Grace Clinker's Pupils, Lodi, Ohio; Lovett School, Chicago, Ill.; Walls School, Pitman, N. J.; Trawtwein School, Racine, Wisc.; Vernon City School, Vernon, Calif.; Laning Ave. School, Verona, N. J.; Crawford School, Terre Haute, Ind.; Stevens School, Omak, Wash.; Miss Reba Hayes's Pupils, Stuttgart, Ark.; Horace Mann School, Oklahoma City, Oklahoma.

America Shows What It Can Do

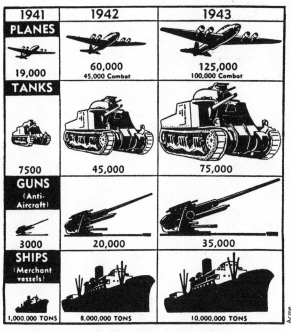

1941	1942	1943
PLANES 19,000	60,000 45,000 Combat	125,000 100,000 Combat
TANKS 7500	45,000	75,000
GUNS (Anti-Aircraft) 3000	20,000	35,000
SHIPS (Merchant vessels) 1,000,000 TONS	8,000,000 TONS	10,000,000 TONS

This chart outlines part of America's work for the next two years.

THINK of some place that is about 120 miles from where you live. Then imagine a giant airport as long as that distance and one mile wide. An airport that big would be needed to hold all the warplanes that America will build during the year 1942. The airplanes would have to be placed as close together as possible.

An airport to hold the warplanes America will build next year (1943) would have to be more than 250 miles long. During 1942 and 1943, 185,000 warplanes will be built. That many of anything can hardly be imagined.

This year and next, America will build swarms of warplanes. Building warplanes is only a small part of the work America will do, however. The chart shows how many tanks, antiaircraft guns, and ships will be built. America will build a warplane every four minutes, a tank every seven minutes, and two ships a day. The time you spend reading this story is enough to finish several airplanes or a large part of a ship.

Even the work shown on the chart is only a small part of the war work America will do. Thousands of army trucks must be made. There must be tons of ammunition. There must be food and clothing for the soldiers. There must be medicines and bandages. You can think of many other kinds of work that must be done by America at war.

Work in the amount planned has never before been done by any nation. America has never done so much before, but all Americans know that they can do what has been asked.

In order to do this work, we must make changes in our way of living and in our way of doing things. For years, America has been a peaceful nation, living in peaceful ways. It cannot change to a nation at war without making changes in Americans' ways of living.

Some of these changes have already come. More will follow. The making of automobiles has stopped. We need airplanes and tanks now more than we need new automobiles. Automobile factories are being changed to airplane and tank factories.

In a short time, the making of new radios for home use will be cut almost in half. Our fighters need more radio equipment. Some of the materials used in ordinary radios are needed as war materials. Rubber, tin, and aluminum have become almost precious. They are being saved for only the most important uses. Men's suits will be made with less material. Eleven suits will be made of the same amount of material now being used for ten. We must all be more saving of everything.

One man is in charge of all America's war work. You can see how important his job is. He is Donald Marr Nelson. The President placed Mr. Nelson in charge of the Nation's war work a few weeks ago. Mr. Nelson's job is to speed up our war work and to keep it going.

Mr. Nelson is a good man for this job. He has had years of experience in getting things done in the quickest and best way. When Mr. Nelson was a young man, he wanted to take some special training in college. He needed money to do this. He decided to go to work "for a while" with a company in Chicago. He stayed with the company and became one of its heads. When he left the company to work for the Government, he was in charge of buying the thousands of different things his company sells.

Mr. Nelson helped to plan America's war work. He knows that America can do it. His rule of life has always been to plan what must be done and then to keep working. "We have not planned too much for America," Mr. Nelson says. "America can do this and more." Americans think so, too.

Meet Donald M. Nelson. He is "boss" of America's war work. He works hard, too—from early in the morning until late at night. His home is near Chicago.

———— BUY DEFENSE STAMPS ————

Japan's Fight To Rule the Far East

JAPAN has been at war longer than any of the other nations that are now fighting. In 1931, a Japanese army went into China. This army brought part of China under the control of Japan.

Soon afterward, Japan told the world that, from then on, Japan would be guardian of the Far East. All other countries were supposed to let Japan do what it thought was right. Japan tried to get more power over China. In 1937, Japan went to war with China, expecting China to give up quickly. The war has gone on and on. Now Japan is also at war with Great Britain, Australia, the Netherlands Indies, and the United States.

The map shows that Japan itself is not very large. In fact, Japan is not much larger than California. Think of California as an island separated a little from the United States. Then imagine California trying to get control of North and South America. Now you have some idea of the job Japan has set for itself in the Far East. You can also see why Japan is in trouble with other nations in the Far East and with nations that have land there.

Let's take a quick look at Japan, to see what kind of nation it is. Japan could be called "a nation with growing pains."

Japan itself is a string of islands that stretch along the coast of Asia for about 3,000 miles—the distance across the United States. In these islands, there is just a little more land than there is in California. There are 14 times as many people as there are in California, however.

This big population is one reason for Japan's "growing pains." Japan is using force to get more land and other things it needs. Getting control over the Far East would give Japan much of what it needs.

Japan has become one of the world's greatest manufacturing countries. It did not have room for farms for all its people. More and more of them had to go to the cities to earn a living in factories and business. Japan must make and sell things to support its people. Japan wants to control the Far East in order to sell things to the countries there and to get the raw materials Japan needs to keep its factories running.

Japan has some coal, but it would like to get much more at low cost from China. Japan would like to have control of China's big iron supply. Japan needs oil. Other countries of the Far East can supply it.

Japan would like to control its neighbors in order to get food for the big Japanese population. Japan raises some of its own food, but it needs more. Much of Japan is mountainous, so that much of the land is not fit for farming.

About one-sixth of the land in Japan is farm land. As you might expect from the large number of people, most of the farms are small. In Japan,

Japan is a string of islands near the coast of Asia. Korea and Manchukuo are under Japan's control.

a big farm is one of more than three acres. A farm as big as a city block seems huge beside most Japanese farms.

The chief crop is rice, which is the main food of the Japanese people. Rice is raised on about half the farm land, but still there is not enough rice for all the Japanese people. Japan gets much rice from China.

Most Japanese farmers have been raising silkworms to help make a living. Until recently, the United States bought almost all Japan's silk. Now we no longer buy it. Losing this market for silk has cut off one of Japan's most important ways of getting money.

Japan thinks it must rule the Far East in order to get what it needs. Its great needs are materials with which to make things and buyers for those things. It is true that Japan has "growing pains." However, the way in which Japan is trying to cure these pains has gotten that nation into serious trouble with other nations.

——————— 8 25c WAR STAMPS BUY 1 MESS KIT ———————

It is fun to share good things. Be sure to take MY WEEKLY READER home this week and share the stories and pictures with your parents. You will enjoy reading and discussing the stories with your parents.

The Fudge Maker

Madame Chiang Kai-shek (chė-äng′ kī-shĕk) is the wife of the general of the Chinese army. He says that she is worth more than a million soldiers to China. She is in charge of all the war work of Chinese women. She is also the "mother" of the thousands of Chinese war orphans.

Madame Chiang Kai-shek has just sent two pandas as a gift to the children of the United States. The pandas are part of her thanks for the help American children have sent to China.

Madame Chiang Kai-shek went to school in this country. While here, she learned to make fudge, chocolate cake, and fried chicken. Her friends say that these are still the only things that she can cook.

International

General Chiang Kai-shek (above) is leader of the Chinese army. **Madame Chiang Kai-shek** is his best helper.

International

— BUY WAR SAVINGS STAMPS —

New Disney Designs

Walt Disney Productions

Walt Disney's artists designed the flying squirrel for the Jacksonville Air Base and the fighting bulldog for the 62d Pursuit Squadron.

Three years ago, a letter came to Walt Disney from a navy flyer. That letter started something that has grown into a full-time job for five of Mr. Disney's artists. The letter asked Mr. Disney to draw a design that could be painted on the airplanes of the carrier *Wasp*. One of Mr. Disney's artists then drew a design showing a very angry wasp.

Since that first design was made, hundreds of other groups have asked for Disney designs. Now five artists do nothing but make these designs. There are Disney animals in all branches of the fighting forces.

— BUY DEFENSE STAMPS —

Work for Victory

Help your parents to save their automobile tires by walking to school. Save your own bicycle tires, too, by walking to school. We all must work to save rubber. Do your part. Walk more and ride less.

— $10 WILL BUY 1 ARMY "PUP" TENT —

DANNY DOO AND LOKI—How To Spot Airplanes

To Teachers: My Weekly Reader in Wartime

The Wartime Commission of the U. S. Office of Education proposes for all children during wartime *adequate protection, intelligent participation,* and *balanced perspective.* MY WEEKLY READER has been called upon to interpret this policy to schools. The editorial staff accepts this grave responsibility.

MY WEEKLY READER will continue, as in the past, to dedicate itself to the promotion of child growth. We promise to do our share in guarding America's children from the hazards of fear, tensions, and frustration and to contribute to emotional stability through the inspiration and reassurance which the carefully selected current content of MY WEEKLY READER brings to children. Ours shall be a positive philosophy of optimism.

Participation. Reports from Great Britain and China show that children of those countries suffer less from the impact of war when they are actively engaged in contributing to present war needs and participating to the limit of their capacities. Thrilling stories of how useful children can be are now coming to America.

MY WEEKLY READER will carry some of these stories of children at work in the United Nations in wartime. In addition, MY WEEKLY READER will suggest a program of *participation* for American children. Watch for these suggestions under the head "Work for Victory" which will deal with problems about which *children can do something.*

Balanced Perspective. MY WEEKLY READER will give children a *balanced* perspective which is realistic, but sane, as it portrays real people and events, and relates the children's lives to current developments. Selected news content which represents all aspects of life which are important, interesting, intelligible, appealing, and valuable to children at the various maturity levels will be featured.

The following areas will be covered during the year appropriate to each grade level:

Our American Neighbors
Racial Minority Groups in U. S.
Geography in the News—Strategic Areas in the World
Children of the United Nations
Resources of U. S. in the News
Science and Aviation News
Current Biographies

Eleanor M. Johnson

Managing   Editor

Science News Bits

Press Association

This woman easily lifts a bale of Bubblfil to show how light it is. Bubblfil may take the place of kapok, sponge, rubber, and cork.

Air wrapped in cellophane is a new invention that will help to save many lives. The new invention is made by making threads of cellophane that are really strings of air bubbles packed closely together. This material is called "Bubblfil."

Bubblfil is already being tested for navy life jackets. It seems to work as well as any material used in life jackets to keep men afloat. It may also be packed into the sides and ends of lifeboats so that they will be hard to sink.

Oscar, the Sailor Cat

Oscar is a black sailor cat. He has had adventures enough to use up all his nine lives.

He first went to sea on the German battleship *Bismarck.* The *Bismarck* was sunk and Oscar was taken on board the British destroyer *Cossack.* Then he became the pet of the aircraft carrier *Ark Royal.*

Later, both the *Cossack* and the *Ark Royal* were sunk. Oscar was rescued from a floating board and taken to land. Now he is waiting for the British navy to give him another ship.

--------WALK AND CARRY--------

DANNY DOO AND LOKI—Loki Drives the Colonel's "Jeep" for a While

Roy Evans, Jr.

U. S. Navy Fights Packs of Sea Wolves

From a German seaport, a submarine quietly slips out to sea. The "sub" captain has 25 trained men with him. They have food and fuel to last for several weeks, for they will be at sea until they have used their eight deadly torpedoes.

The submarine is run by a Diesel (dē′zĕl) engine, which uses oil as fuel. This is the engine which the sub uses on the surface of the sea. When the captain thinks that an enemy ship has seen him, he will quickly dive 250 or 300 feet below the surface. Then the sub will be driven by electric batteries.

The sub travels for days, looking for ships of the United Nations. When the captain sees such a ship, he orders the sub to dive. He puts his periscope up through the water and takes aim.

"Fire!" he orders.

A torpedo glides through the water. The torpedo may rip a hole in the side of the ship, or it may explode near the ship and wreck it. Then the United Nations have lost another ship and many lives and goods.

Hitler's submarines work in packs. They are the wolves of the sea. Hitler is said to be building from 15 to 30 submarines a month. This spring, these wolves of the sea will be busier than ever.

The United Nations must kill off more and more of these wolves or we will lose the war. We cannot win the war unless our men, guns, and planes get across the seas. They cannot do this if submarines sink our ships.

One way to protect our ships is to send warships across the sea with them. A group of 50 or 100 ships, loaded and ready to cross the sea, gather in one of our ports. Several destroyers wait outside. Airplanes are ready on shore.

When all the ships are ready, they leave port together. Destroyers steam ahead and follow close behind. Airplanes will fly overhead until the ships are far out to sea, then the planes will go back. This system of protecting ships is called the convoy system.

The airplanes are the eyes of the convoy. They can see a submarine from afar, often when it is below the surface. The airplanes radio messages to the warships below. The destroyers are the killers. They dash toward the sub and drop their "ash cans" over it. When these explode, they may wreck the submarine.

We are having several difficulties with the convoy system. The speed of the whole convoy has to be the speed of the slowest ship. This wastes the time of the faster ships. We do not have enough destroyers to protect all our ships. We do not have enough aircraft carriers to take planes all the way across the sea.

There is another way to fight submarines. When you cannot find the wolf in the forest, you may try to destroy his den. So our airplanes bomb the

The rolls are the "ash cans" to be dropped over submarines. The arrow shows the man who will drop them overboard.

ports in Germany where the subs are built. We cannot destroy the subs there, but we can destroy factories, supplies, railways bringing up supplies, and warehouses.

Right now, the United States is building four or five ships a day. But the submarines are sinking about the same number a day. We must find a way to destroy the subs or we cannot win the war.

———————————————— SAVE TIRES ————————————————

IMPORTANT!!!

In previous years, we have sent present subscribers a bundle of copies of the first issue of MY WEEKLY READER. Due to the WPB restriction of paper, this practice will not be followed this fall.

Please get renewals to MY WEEKLY READER in early. Subscriptions cannot be started next fall until the order has been received.

War Inventions May Come to Your Home

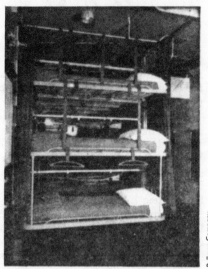

Left—a "walky-talky"; *center*—uniforms for hot climates, for a ski trooper, for a snowshoe trooper, for a paratrooper; *right*—sleeping car.

SOLDIERS on the fighting fronts are now using inventions that you and your family cannot buy. The Army worked hard to make these changes to meet the needs of our fighting men. After the war, some of these inventions may find their way into your home.

Today, soldiers in cold climates wear suits that are only half as heavy as the sheepskin suits they used to wear. These suits are of windproof cloth on the outside and of soft, light material on the inside. Soldiers who fight in the jungles or in the mountains wear uniforms of special tough cloth. These uniforms may tear, but the holes do not get bigger as holes in most cloth do. Shoes to go with these uniforms last four times as long as your shoes do. The shoes have nylon laces that will not break.

Would you like a warm, light suit for winter? Would your mother like to buy you a suit that would not tear and shoes that last four times as long as those you have now?

Today, soldiers in strange lands purify their drinking water by dropping a tablet into it. They make coffee in plastic canteens, light as paper but so strong that a 200-pound man can step on them without breaking them. When this canteen is on the fire, it does not burn a man's hand as a metal canteen does.

The soldier carries a one-pound stove to cook meals in the open and to heat his tent. He carries a tiny can opener on a chain. He has waterproof matches to light his fire. He has a sleeping bag that weighs less than six pounds.

Would you like to have these things on a scout trip? How many of these things would be useful at home?

The Army has also found new ways of keeping food. For hot climates, there is butter that will not get soft or spoil. There is cheese spread that will not sour. Cake flavoring comes from a tablet.

The Army uses dried soups and vegetables. The Army may serve these in dishes that bounce when they are dropped and that do not break. These things might be good for home use, too.

New sleeping cars to carry soldiers across the country have been made. Berths, or beds, in these cars are in threes, one above the other. The berths come as "upper," "middle," and "lower." They are roomy and comfortable. The cars will be useful after the war.

The Army now gets weather reports direct from enemy countries. Instruments have been dropped by plane in lonely spots. By radio, these instruments send facts about the weather until their batteries are dead. In peacetime, these instruments can send weather reports from Alaska, Greenland, Iceland, and other places that are far away.

With the "walky-talky," soldiers talk with each other from different parts of a fighting front. The "walky-talky" is a simple two-way radio. Can you think of peacetime uses for it?

Inventions needed by our Army have brought great progress. These inventions would have come more slowly without the war. Some persons say we are "living in 1963" right now.

Will these inventions really come to your home after the war? We cannot be sure. First, the factories need to get ready to make such goods in large amounts. Then, people need to have enough money to buy the new things. If these things cost too much, people may not want them. People will have to learn to use these new inventions.

Which of these things do you want after the war?

——————I WILL TAKE GOOD CARE OF ALL MY CLOTHES——————

Take MY WEEKLY READER home. Read and discuss the stories with your parents. If you have soldier relatives in the Mediterranean region, your family will be especially interested in the front-page story.

Work for Victory

Take care of your overshoes and galoshes. Do not wear them with shoes that are too big for them. Bring them into the house instead of leaving them outside in cold weather. Wear them only in wet weather, to make them last as long as you can. Holes in overshoes can be repaired at shoe-repair shops.

Oscar's Victory Hints

I do not want to fool you; I am not really a cook. I eat all my meals "out." I just want to remind you to remind your family that Uncle Sam needs kitchen grease. He needs it to make gunpowder and dynamite.

A tablespoon of grease a day adds up to a pound in a month. Uncle Sam wants that much from every family. Think how much grease you could save if you fried fish for me every day.

OSCAR, *The Cook's Best Friend*

Farming for Victory

SOON American farmers will be plowing their fields. This spring, plowing will be different from plowing in other years. It will be more than just getting the ground ready for another year's crops. Farmers will be planting more than seeds. Farmers will be planting victory.

The work our farmers do this year is as important as the work done in any war factory. From American farms will come what is as necessary as guns to win the war. From American farms must come food for victory.

In time of peace, each American farm worker helped to raise enough food for 15 people. Now American farm workers must raise food for at least twice that many people.

More food is needed now than ever before. All our fighting men must be fed. They do not have time to help raise food. Our fighting men eat more than people doing most other things. Our fighting men eat twice as much meat as most other people.

Our farmers must raise food for more people than just Americans at home and in other countries. Our farmers must raise food for people of other countries, too. England cannot raise all the food it needs. Neither can Russia. Some of Russia's best farm land has been taken or spoiled. Food from American farms is going to England, Russia, China, and other countries.

Our farmers will raise more of certain foods and less of others. Certain foods are needed more than others. What our farmers should raise has been carefully planned. Our farmers will raise more meat animals, such as pigs and cows. Raising more meat animals means that more food for them must also be raised. Farmers will raise more corn and oats. Farmers will raise more chickens, vegetables, peanuts, cotton, potatoes, and beans. More milk and eggs are needed. Not so much wheat is needed.

Some of our farmers are learning about new crops. One of them is soybeans. They came from China. Some have been raised here for years, but now they are becoming an important crop. Rice will be raised in more parts of the South. In some places, sunflowers and castor beans are being planted. Oil from sunflower seeds and castor beans is useful in many ways. Soybeans, sunflower seeds, and castor beans must help to supply oils we once bought from other countries.

Farming for victory is not easy. Farmers must do more work with fewer helpers. Many farm workers have joined our fighting forces. Many have gone to work in war factories. We now have almost nine million farm workers, but we need three million more.

About twelve million workers are needed to harvest crops in a good year. Farmers must have more help this year. Last year, boys and girls from cities helped farmers to harvest their crops. Boy Scouts helped. So did workers from factories.

Farmers in all parts of the country are getting ready for one of America's greatest battles. It is the "green battle" of food.

This ship is being loaded with food for England. Our farmers must help to feed many nations.

Negroes Help Uncle Sam

These young Negroes are getting their "wings." Soon they will be fighting for Uncle Sam in all parts of the world.

Hugh Mulzak (left) is the captain of one of Uncle Sam's ships.

Marian Anderson, the great singer, gives money from her concerts to help Uncle Sam and his soldiers.

16 25c WAR STAMPS BUY 1 STEEL HELMET

Little Friends in Russia

(Above) Russians like to dance at Easter.
(Right) Russian children like music.

Children in Russia like to dance at Easter.
This year, they may not want to dance.
The war is very near the children of Russia.

TAKE THE PENNIES OUT OF YOUR BANK FOR UNCLE SAM

Four-Footed Soldiers

Dogs are being used in many ways by our Army, Navy, and Coast Guard. They help to guard beaches, war factories, camps, and airfields. Dogs carry messages. Dogs find wounded men on battlefields. Dogs carry first-aid kits. Dogs pull heavy loads. The newest job of all for dogs is listening for airplanes. The keen hearing of some dogs helps them to hear coming airplanes long before men can.

Max has won his silver wings as a "parachute pup" at Fort Benning, Georgia.

Back to the Philippine Islands

GENERAL MacARTHUR is keeping his promise. He is going back to the Philippine Islands. When he left there, more than two years ago, he said, "I shall return." He left secretly with a few other persons in a small boat. He is going back with airplanes, warships, and thousands of men. The whole world knows he is going back. American bombing plans are attacking the Japanese in the Philippines almost every day.

The Japanese have held these islands for more than two years. The Americans and Filipinos in the Fort of Corregidor (kôr-rä-hê-dôr') surrendered May 6, 1942. For two years, Japanese warships have sailed out of the big harbors of Manila and Davao (dä'-vou). Japanese airplanes have flown from the airfields of the islands. Soon we shall be using those harbors and airfields for ships and planes to fight the Japanese.

We wonder what General MacArthur remembers best about the Philippine Islands. He must remember the capital city of Manila, where he lived. Maybe he remembers Manila's palm trees and old stone churches. Maybe he remembers the warm days and cool nights of the islands. He is sure to remember the rice fields built up like stairsteps on the sides of mountains. Best of all, he must remember the small, slender, brown-skinned Filipino people. He lived and worked with them for years. He helped to train the "Joe Philippines," as the American soldiers call the Filipino army.

Maybe General MacArthur has been teaching his men lessons about the Philippine Islands. Most Americans do not know much about them. They are a large group of islands, almost as large as Japan. There are more than 7,000 islands in the Philippine group.

The two biggest islands are Luzon (lōo-zŏn) and Mindanao (mĭn-dä-nä'ō). Luzon is about the size of Ohio. Mindanao is about the size of Indiana. The city of Manila is on Luzon. About two-thirds of the land area

Christian Science Monitor

of the Philippines is in these two islands. Many of the islands are no bigger than a city block.

The Philippine Islands are not so far south as we usually think. If they were moved straight across the Pacific Ocean, their northern end would be in the middle of Mexico. They would extend a little into South America.

Not all the people are Filipinos. The Filipinos are just the largest group of people living there. They came from other islands hundreds of years ago. There are many Chinese. There are some wild tribes who were there before the Filipinos came. These wild tribes live in the mountains and forests. Before the war, many Japanese had settled in the islands, especially around Davao on the southeastern coast of Mindanao.

The Japanese have not had much of a "vacation" in the Philippine Islands during the past two years. Many Filipinos have kept on fighting, attacking the Japanese from secret hiding places. Many of the Filipinos have refused to work with the Japanese. Many of the mines and sugar mills are closed. Filipino farmers have raised only what they needed for themselves.

Many "Joe Philippines" and their friends have been getting ready for General MacArthur's return.

Getting the Philippine Islands back will be a big help to us in fighting Japan. These islands are right in Japan's path to islands farther south, such as the Netherlands Indies. Japan took those places at the beginning of the war. By holding the Philippines, we can keep Japan from getting the oil and other things she needs from those islands.

The Philippine Islands are important in another way. Their harbors and airfields are close to China. We can use them to attack Japan's biggest armies which are now fighting in China. When General MacArthur goes back to the Philippine Islands, he goes a long way toward victory over Japan.

How To Be Two Places at Once

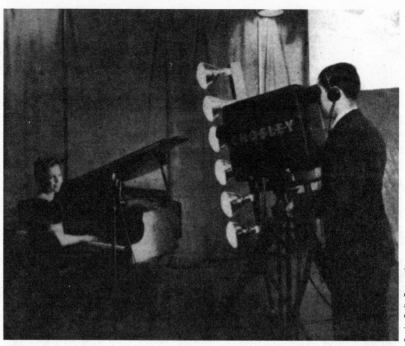

Right—Broadcasting both the sight and sound of a piano concert in a television studio. *Above*—In your home, the concert may be heard by means of this receiving set. The pianist will then appear on the small screen at the top of the cabinet.

TODAY, you and your parents can sit at home and, by radio, *hear* news of a baseball game, a fire, or the building of a new airplane. By radio, you can hear a play, a famous singer, or a speech by the President.

After the war, you may sit at home and *see* the baseball game while it is going on. You may watch the fire or see the plane as it takes off. As you listen to a radio play, you may see the actors on the stage. You may see the famous singer. You may see the President as he talks.

You will be able to do these things by television. *Tele* means distant. By telephone, you can talk at a distance. By television, you will see at a distance. With television, you will feel as if you were two places at once.

To do this, you will need to have a television set in your home. A television set will look much like a radio cabinet. In fact, it is likely to be a cabinet with radio, phonograph, and television combined. On the front of the television cabinet will be the screen upon which the pictures will appear.

Far away from you, the television broadcasting company will prepare the broadcasts for you. The company will produce a play on its stage. As the play goes on, men will take pictures and send them out to you. At the same time, the voices of the players will also be sent to you. You will get the pictures and the voices as the play goes on.

The television company will also have their machines on trucks. Trucks will drive to the ball field to show you the game. Men will be able to drive to a fire and show you the firemen at work.

Radio was just a baby at the time of the last war. Television is just a baby now. Television, like radio, is sure to grow up. Then it will be able to do more and more things.

Television will be able to show you all sorts of news events. It will show you football games, parades, airplanes in flight, ships at sea, floods, streamlined trains, and so on.

The television screen will probably have advertising. But a voice will not only *tell* you what a bicycle looks like or how to lay out a garden. A picture will *show* you the bicycle. A picture will *show* a family planting a garden.

Television may be used in schools to show you how to do many things. It may show you how to do first aid. It may show you how to use new tools or how to make your school safe.

Television was made possible by the invention of the radio tube. Television may use an underground cable, or it may use wireless apparatus, just as radio does. The wireless method is the cheaper. This is how most television pictures will be sent after the war. Television is hard to understand. To most persons, television is still a puzzle.

There are now about a dozen television broadcasting stations in this country. About 5,000 television sets have been sold to homes near New York City. The owners of these sets now get television programs for only a few hours each week.

Several years after the war, it is thought that television sets will be sold for $150 to $200. These sets may come to most of the homes that now have radio. Then you will know what it is like to be in two places at once.

——— FOOD FIGHTS FOR FREEDOM ———

WACS in Other Lands

Acme Photo by Bert Brandt

These WACS in England gave a party for English children.

A FEW weeks ago, a soldier in Africa was given a medal for bravery. This soldier is a woman. She is one of the WACS who have gone to Africa. Her name is Margaret Maloney.

Private Maloney saved a soldier who fell into some burning gasoline. She was badly burned herself, but she put out the fire in the other soldier's clothes.

There are about 800 WACS in Africa now. There are others in England and Italy.

General Eisenhower says that the WACS are some of his best soldiers. The men with our Air Forces in England praise the WACS there. These men say that their attacks on Germany depend upon the good work of the WACS.

The WACS in Africa do many kinds of work. They do not fight, of course. Their work is a great help to the fighting men, however. The women do office work and work in the army post offices. The women send messages, write news, and take pictures for the Army. WACS run telephone switchboards. To do this, the telephone workers must know many different languages.

One WAC is General Eisenhower's secretary. Two others drive automobiles for General Eisenhower's officers. These women also take care of the automobiles.

The WACS in Africa like to go shopping in their free time. From the African people the WACS buy shoes, rugs, and jewelry. They buy more jewelry than anything else.

The women do not have much free time. Besides doing their work, they must clean their own rooms, and wash and iron their own clothes. The WACS are usually in bed by ten o'clock.

In England, most of the WACS work with the Air Forces. The women work as "weathermen." They work in the radio stations of the Air Forces. Many of the WACS work at telephone switchboards. The women go to a special school to learn English telephone ways. Our women learn that "You are through" does not mean that you must stop talking. It means that you may start talking.

The WACS in England get up at 6:30 a.m. They work 12 hours a day. They keep their own rooms clean and they must take care of their own clothes.

In their free time, the WACS in England like to travel. Some of them take trips on bicycles. They visit churches and other buildings that are hundreds of years old.

Our WACS make friends with the English people. The English people invite the WACS to their homes.

Some of the WACS live in big cities. Others live in their own camps out in the country. Most of the WAC camps are near camps of English or American soldiers.

These WACS in Italy stopped to look at a fountain.

———STRAIN ALL WASTE FATS INTO A TIN CONTAINER———

See Oscar in the foxhole hide.
With a walkie-talkie by his side.
As a soldier, brave and true,
Oscar sends this call to you:

"Boys and girls, give much more!
Buy bonds and stamps to win the war.
Stamps buy trucks, ships, and tanks,
And walkie-talkies for the Yanks."

The children bought tanks.

Official Army Photo

School War Bond News

School children buy war bonds.
The war bonds buy big airplanes.
The war bonds buy trucks and jeeps.
The war bonds buy tanks and gliders.

Last year, school children
bought 13,500 airplanes.
The children bought 44,700 jeeps.
The jeeps helped the soldiers.
The airplanes helped the soldiers.

Milkweed Helps the Soldiers

Uncle Sam needs milkweed floss.
He needs the milkweed floss
for the soldiers.
Children are picking milkweed floss.

The milkweed floss is used
in making life jackets.
The life jackets are for the soldiers.
The milkweed floss is used
in making suits.
The suits are for the soldiers.

The boys are picking milkweed.

Soil Conservation Service

Peek, the Brownie

Peek and the brownies make snow animals.

Franklin D. Roosevelt

"THE only thing we have to fear is fear itself," Franklin D. Roosevelt said 12 years ago, when he first became President of the United States.

All his life, President Roosevelt never let himself be afraid of fear.

But Mr. Roosevelt's courage was given its greatest test in 1921, when he was 39 years old. That summer he and his family went to their summer home on the seacoast. There he was stricken with infantile paralysis. He became paralyzed from the waist down.

However, he built up the rest of his body. He even found a way to strengthen his crippled legs. He discovered that they felt better when he exercised them under water. The best place for these exercises was in the waters of Warm Springs, Georgia. Mr. Roosevelt set up a hospital there for infantile paralysis victims, including himself. Twice a year, he went there for treatment. It was there he died, April 12, 1945.

When Mr. Roosevelt realized that he would never be able to walk, he showed how great his courage really was. He took up his political life once more. He became Governor of New York. After a second term as Governor, he was elected President of the United States in 1932.

When war came, he had new problems to solve. These problems dealt with the relations between our country and the rest of the world. In dealing with these problems, he made many journeys which were dangerous and especially difficult for a man who could not walk.

These journeys took him to Casablanca, Cairo, Teheran, Quebec, Hawaii, the Aleutians, and Yalta. In some of these places, he met with the leaders of other great countries.

Together, these men made plans to keep all the peoples of the world living together in peace after the war. President Roosevelt thought it was possible for nations to stop fearing one another and to make world-wide peace. He still believed that the only thing we have to fear is fear itself.

Harry S. Truman

"I KNEW that boy would amount to something from the time he was nine years old. He could plow the straightest row of corn in the county. He could sow wheat so there wasn't a bare spot in the whole field." Thus spoke the mother of Harry S. Truman, new President of the United States.

President Truman is proud of having grown up on a Missouri farm. When he was elected to the United States Senate in 1934, he made a promise to the people who voted for him. He said, "Here is one farm boy who is going to keep his feet on the ground."

When Mr. Truman went into politics, his first job was as overseer for the county highway department. Soon he was elected a county judge.

His next step carried him to the Senate. He always had been a studious man. Now he began to study the affairs of the Nation. He became alarmed that large amounts of the taxpayers' money were being wasted in the building of army camps. So he climbed into his Chevrolet coupe and, paying his own way, made a 30,000-mile trip.

He found a great deal of waste in government planning and construction. He made a report to the Senate. He became chairman of the Truman Committee. This committee has done a number of good jobs for the country. It has saved government money. It has forced changes to speed up and improve the building of ships and airplanes. It has helped to do away with shortages in aluminum, rubber, zinc, lead, steel, and manpower.

As a farm boy, Harry Truman plowed his corn straight and sowed his wheat carefully, so that none would be wasted.

As President of the United States, this man will believe in running this country well, both at home and on the two war fronts. He has promised he will try to carry on as he believes President Roosevelt would have done.

——— DOING HOME CHORES SAVES MANPOWER ———

After V-E Day--W Day

Harold M. Lambert

"VICTORY in Europe is won—on to Tokyo!" was America's slogan on V-E Day. Most people did not even stop work to celebrate the end of the European war. Soldiers, civilians, and children all seemed to realize that after V-E Day will come days of hard work.

President Truman said to the people of our country, "If I could give you a watchword for the coming months, that word is—work, work, work."

Farmers know that V-E Day does not mean their labor will be lessened. Victory will not solve food shortages. In fact, the United States will have to produce more food than ever. The countries we have freed will now look to us for food.

More than 250,000,000 Europeans are to receive a portion of their food from America in the months ahead. Almost every nation on the Continent is in

need. This all adds up to a gigantic grocery order. As far as possible, this food will be grown in Europe. But some food will have to be imported until the hungry nations can plant and harvest their own crops again. Much of this imported food will have to come from American farms.

Hard work lies ahead of our country's transportation system, too. Soldiers, equipment, and supplies are being moved to west coast ports. But most of our factories are east of the Mississippi River. Supplies for the European war had to be hauled only a fairly short distance to the Atlantic ports. Now, everything must travel the far greater distance to the Pacific ports. Some of the cargoes will be shipped by boat. But the railroads still will

International

have to haul even greater loads than they have carried during the last four busy years.

Months of hard work lie ahead of industry, too. V-E Day meant W Day for war plants. Paul V. McNutt, chairman of the War Manpower Commission, said, "While the lives of our men in the Pacific are at stake, the workers on the home front will not let them down."

However, factories gradually will begin the difficult job of shifting from war work to peace production.

It probably will be at least a year before factories can produce large quantities of civilian goods once more. Until then, shoes still will be rationed. The supply of woolen goods will not be plentiful. Cotton goods will be even more scarce, because more cotton will be needed to clothe our armies in the tropics.

There will be no new automobiles, very little more gasoline, and perhaps even less meat. V-E Day will not make much difference to most of us. Every day will be W Day until Victory-Over-Japan Day, or V-J Day.

Southern Pacific Bureau of News

Railroads already are moving loads of tanks to the west coast. As the upper picture shows, farm boys are busier than ever raising food. The picture on the right shows workers turning out metal for planes needed in the Pacific.

———— TAKE A SHOPPING BAG TO THE STORE ————

UNRRA* on the March

CHRISTMAS in the United States will be a happy one. Many families will be together for the first time since the war began. Christmas trees, gifts, happy songs, and fine dinners will help to make the day bright.

But what will the people in Europe do? Some of them will have a happy Christmas. They are glad the war is over. They are glad that their men are back from the war. There may not be many Christmas goodies. There will be few Christmas gifts. Families will be glad to be together again.

But many people in Europe have no homes. Some of them are far from home. There is not enough food in Europe to go around. Most people are in need of warm clothes. Little children are lucky to have food and warm clothes even though they do not have toys. Christmas will not be a very happy day for thousands of people in Europe.

Friends and relatives in this country are doing what they can to help those needy people. Groups of people, such as the Red Cross, are helping. Another group is working hard to help the people of Europe. This group is UNRRA.

UNRRA is a group of people from 44 different governments of the world. UNRRA's job is to help the people who are in great need because of the war. UNRRA is helping people in Europe and the Far East.

UNRRA provides food, fuel, clothing, and medi-cines for these people. UNRRA takes care of the sick. It helps people to get back to their homes. UNRRA finds lost members of families and brings them home.

Farms in many European countries were turned into battlegrounds. Bombs and tanks tore up the land. It must be made ready for farming again. UNRRA is sending farm machines to Europe. Seeds and fertilizers are being sent to the farmers. Scientists are going to Europe to help put the land to work. They will show the farmers how to take care of the land. They will show the farmers better ways of planting and growing crops. Soon, Europe will be able to help feed her hungry millions again.

Thousands of people in Europe had to leave their homes and their countries during the war. Now they are on their way back. They do not know what they will find when they come to the end of the long journey.

Many cities and towns are in ruins. The people have to travel on foot. There are no lights. The drinking water is not pure. UNRRA is putting power plants to work. It is helping the people to get lights and pure water. UNRRA is helping to clean up the cities. It is helping cities and towns to rebuild the houses, stores, and streets.

Hundreds of people are working for UNRRA. People in the 44 countries that belong to UNRRA are doing the work in European countries and the Far East. They take care of supplies. Doctors and nurses take care of the people who are ill. Workers help to rebuild cities and towns.

Where does UNRRA get its money to carry on its work? The governments that belong to UNRRA give the money. The United States has given millions of dollars. UNRRA needs more money. Our Government has been asked to give much more money.

*United Nations Relief and Rehabilitation Administration

79

Our Soldiers Are Coming Home

International

Our soldiers are happy to be home.

The war is over.
Our soldiers are coming home.

Many soldiers have been away
for a long time.

Some soldiers have been in Europe.
Some soldiers have been on islands
in the Pacific Ocean.

———— SAVE WATER ————

———— LET HONEY KEEP YOUR SWEET TOOTH HAPPY ————

We Are Proud of This Reader

We don't know if Fritz Fischer of the 4th Grade at Rosedale Garden School, Plymouth, Mich., is an airplane artist, but we do know that he has sharp eyes. Fritz calls our attention to the fact that the plane on page 74 is an autogiro, not a helicopter. Thank you, Fritz. Please cross out "helicopter" in the caption and write "autogiro."

———— SAVE SHOES ————

Oscar

People say, "The early bird gets the worm." I know the early cat gets that bird! I am an early cat, but I am not after birds. I am too busy packing boxes for my soldier friends overseas. A box on time will make a soldier happy on Christmas. Boxes must be off by October 15.

———— SAVE PAPER ————

General Wainwright Has Come Home

Many people were at the airport
in Washington, D. C.
They came to see a great general.
They came to see General Wainwright.

For a long time, the General was
in a Japanese prison.
He did not have good care.
He did not have good food.

"What do you want most?"
said some people.
"I want some ham and eggs,"
said the General.

The people were happy to see the General.

80

People Need Homes

More homes of every kind are needed for people in all parts of the country who do not have places to live.

MILLIONS of homes are needed in the United States. Very few houses were built during the war. Building materials were needed for new factories, army barracks, and navy yards. There were few workmen and very little material to repair old houses. Many houses are in need of repair. Many other old houses are so run down that they must be torn down.

Millions of people in the United States are living in one or two rooms, in trailers, or in some other makeshift way. As more and more men come home from the Army and Navy, more and more homes are needed. Finding homes for all these people is one of the big problems of today.

Many returned soldiers are not making enough money to pay high rents. Many soldiers cannot pay thousands of dollars for new homes. Low-cost homes must be found for returning soldiers because they must borrow much of the money with which to buy them.

Congress is helping with this big housing problem. Since families are in need of houses at once, something must be done in a hurry. So Congress has voted a great sum of money to help hundreds of homeless families right away.

Army barracks are being turned into homes. Army huts and small houses built for warworkers are being moved to places where they are most needed. These homes are not permanent. As permanent homes are found, the families will move into them.

Another sum of money was voted by Congress for the building of permanent homes for returned soldiers. Many of these homes will be ready-built. They can be set up in a day. The price of these homes will be low. Soldiers will be able to borrow money to build or buy these homes.

Congress has also made plans for a ten-year building program. Thousands of homes and housing units, or apartment houses, will be put up in cities and towns. Slums in big cities will be torn down. New apartments will take their places.

The Federal Government will work with the states and cities. The homes and apartments will be built with government money. The homes and apartments will be for people who cannot pay high rents.

The new houses will be made from many different kinds of materials. Some houses will be made of wood. Many others will be built of plywood. There will be houses with steel walls and roofs. Some houses may be made of aluminum. Many houses will be made of concrete.

The Government plans to put up "as many homes as can be built" within the next year. But building materials are still scarce. Many workmen are needed. By next year there may be 400,000 new homes and housing units ready for soldiers' families.

President Truman has asked Wilson W. Wyatt to take charge of the housing problem in the United States. Mr. Wyatt has a big job. He is working hard. He not only plans the building program, but he also sees that materials are sent where they are most needed. He has sent out orders saying that buildings well under way may be finished. Persons wishing to start new homes or buildings must get new permits. This order will stop the building of theaters, stores, and public buildings for the time being.

New Highways for U. S.

The picture shows an air view of a highway of the future.

WITH the end of the war came the end of the gasoline rationing. Hundreds of automobiles were taken from storage. They are now traveling over our highways. More trucks are traveling from city to city. Much more traffic is speeding over the highways since the war ended.

The work of thousands of American people depends upon automobiles and trucks. Automobiles carry thousands of people to work every day. In Detroit, Michigan, seven out of every ten people ride to work in automobiles. Trucks carry goods and supplies through our city streets and over our highways.

Good automobiles and good roads go hand in hand. They make travel safe, fast, and comfortable. Our roadways have not been improved so fast as our automobiles.

Highway experts have planned expressways to help traffic problems. The expressways will speed up traffic on country highways. The expressways will speed traffic to the centers of cities.

Over the new expressways, an automobile may travel safely at 70 miles an hour. An automobile may travel through the city at 45 miles an hour. An expressway does not have stop lights. Other highways do not cross it. They go over it or under it.

The Government has set aside a great sum of money for building the new expressways. Highway experts have been working on the plans for three years. The Government plans to build a network of express highways over the United States.

The Government will also help cities to build highways. Expressways are needed in cities more than any other place. About seven cars out of every ten on country roads are coming from or going to a city. More than half the miles driven every year are over city streets. Crowded city streets slow up traffic. They cause accidents.

Years will be needed to build these expressways. But tomorrow's roads will be as modern as tomorrow's automobiles. Then good automobiles and good roads will go hand in hand. They will make travel safe, fast, and comfortable.

Piney Woods School

Piney Woods School is a Negro school. It is 25 miles south of Jacksonville, Mississippi. Piney Woods is a self-made school. From the very beginning, teachers and pupils built the school buildings with their own hands.

"The Little Professor" started the school. He is

The girls are learning to sew in school.

Laurence Clifton Jones. He started the school with three pupils and $1.65. Today the school is worth thousands of dollars. It owns 1,700 acres of land. The school has 440 pupils.

"Teach boys and girls what they need" is the aim of the school. The pupils learn by doing. They learn to be farmers and carpenters. They become cooks, office workers, and teachers. The pupils learn to make a living at the school.

The boys take care of the farm and the gardens. The boys milk the cows and take care of the farm animals. The girls can the fruit and vegetables. The girls plan and cook all the meals at the school. They learn to be good housekeepers.

The pupils of Piney Woods are proud of their school. They leave the school ready to make a good living. They never forget that the Little Professor made it possible for them to go to school.

A New Kind of Magic

WHEN the Fairy Godmother turned the pumpkin into a coach, she used magic. Nowadays, there is a new kind of magic. This magic is called "plastics." By using plastics, a factory can turn coal into toy trains, toothbrushes, nylon stockings, and dozens of other things.

What is this magic stuff called plastics? The word "plastic" means moldable. A plastic is a material which can be molded, or worked into different shapes.

Plastics are made of many things besides coal. Soybeans, corn, peanuts, and other vegetables go into plastics. Lime and other minerals are used to make plastics, too. Many chemicals are also needed in making plastics.

A chemist mixes some of these things together in a great kettle, or vat. He uses a recipe, just as your mother does when she is making candy or cookies. The chemist's "batch" of plastic sometimes looks like cooky dough, too. Sometimes, it is a liquid. It may also look like powder or like soap flakes. This "batch" is called "raw" plastic.

The raw plastics are sold to "fabricating" (făb′-rĭ-kāt-ĭng) factories. There, some of the plastics are spun into fine thread or stiff bristles. Other plastics are turned into sticky sirup. Still others are made into rods and tubes, or rolled out into sheets like cooky dough.

The fabricating factory sells its products to the plastic manufacturing plants. These plants buy the raw plastics on spools, in chunks, sheets, rods and tubes, or by the tank carload.

There are hundreds of small plastic manufacturing plants all over our country. In these factories, workers weave the plastic thread into nylon hose or material for raincoats, aprons, and chair covers. The sticky plastics are spread on glass or wood, making "sandwiches." These sandwiches, when pressed in great machines, become strong, tough building materials.

In some factories, sheets of clear plastic are cut for use in place of glass in houses, automobiles, and planes. In other factories, colors are added to the plastics. The plastics are put into machines which press them into shape and bake them in ovens. Then, *presto!* The lump of coal has been changed into a toy train for you, earrings for your mother, or a fountain pen for your father. That is how magic works in 1946.

In the top picture, a worker is cooking a batch of plastic. The center picture shows plastic being rolled out into sheets. In the bottom picture, you see a table and chairs of clear plastic.

Dupont Publicity Dept.

Monsanto Chemical Co.

Dupont Publicity Dept.

Who Is Kilroy?

The other day, a sixth grade boy came home from school to find that someone had been writing on his front steps. He read the words. Then he ran excitedly into the house.

"Did you see Kilroy?" he shouted. "It says on the front steps that Kilroy was here."

The boy's big brother Bill laughed. "Take it easy, Dick," he said. "Kilroy has been *everywhere*. When I was in the Army Air Forces, Kilroy made all the pilots mad. We would land a plane in some far-off corner of China or India. We would feel mighty proud, thinking we were the first Americans there. And the first thing we'd find after we landed would be a sign saying, 'Kilroy was here.'"

"Pilots were not the only ones annoyed by Kilroy," Bill went on. "Sometimes, our infantry would march into some German town and find signs left by Kilroy."

"And now," said Dick, "Kilroy is here."

"Kilroy was here long before the war," Bill said. "Tramps used to find his name on boxcars and bridges and barns all over the country."

"Who *is* Kilroy?" Dick asked.

"Kilroy is anybody. Anybody who leaves one of those signs is Kilroy."

"But why don't we ever see a Kilroy?"

"People take great care not to be seen when they write, 'Kilroy was here.' This mystery about Kilroy is what has kept the good old joke going for so many years."

"Kilroy is in the comics now," Dick said.

"Didn't I tell you Kilroy is everywhere?" Bill laughed.

Why Is Sugar Rationed?

Sugar is still rationed. There is a sugar shortage. Sugar is still very scarce. It will be scarce until 1947.

Uncle Sam needed sugar to fight the war. He needed both sugar and candy for his men. He needed sugar for making rubber, gunpowder, and plastics.

The war is over. Uncle Sam does not need so much sugar. There are more ships to carry sugar now. Why is there not enough sugar to go around?

Months are needed to grow a sugar crop. The Philippines will need time to get its plantations ready for planting. Hawaii is still a big base for both Army and Navy. Many plantations are needed for other things.

Office of Emergency Management

Sugar cane grows tall in Louisiana.

Uncle Funny Bunny and Chumpy

By Dorothy

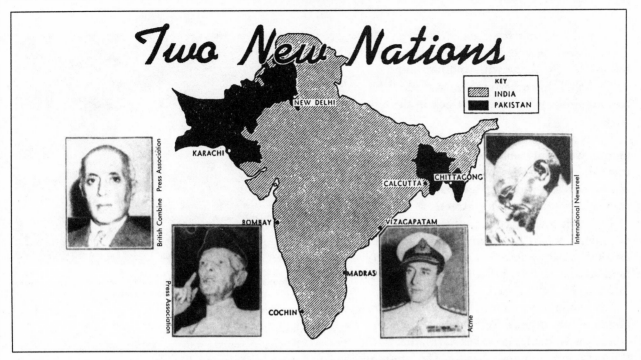

Two New Nations

Leaders of these two nations are: *left to right,* **Nehru, Jinnah, Mountbatten, and Gandhi.**

AUGUST 15 was Independence Day in India. The people rejoiced with songs and special prayers. The streets were gay with flags. At night, even the poorest people burned many candles and oil lamps to brighten their homes. In their celebrating the people remembered Mahatma Gandhi (mȧ-hät′mȧ gän′dė). This man, more than any other, won them their independence.

After 200 years, Great Britain granted India self-government. At first, Britain planned for all the people of India to live under the same government. But the Moslems and the Hindus felt that they could not live peaceably together. So India was divided into two countries.

The larger of these countries is the Dominion of India. This is the Hindu section.

The new flag of India has three wide stripes running lengthwise. One stripe is green. One is white. The third is yellow. In the center of the flag is a wheel design.

The Dominion of India kept the old Indian capital of New Delhi (děl′hī). The native ruler of the Dominion is the Prime Minister, Nehru (nā′rōō). Great Britain's representative is the Governor General, Earl Mountbatten.

Pakistan (päk′ĭ-stän) is the Moslem section of India. As the map shows, this country is cut in two.

Pakistan's capital is Karachi (kȧ-rä′chė). This city is a busy port about the size of Denver, Colorado. The Governor General, Ali Jinnah (ä-lė jĭn′ȧ) has his offices there.

The flag of this new nation is green with a white stripe along one edge. In the center of the green background are a white star and crescent.

Soon, the people of these two new nations will realize that being free means that they must solve their own problems. Some of these problems will grow out of their need for food and industrial products. As the following table shows, India has more industries than Pakistan. But Pakistan, for its size, raises more food.

Industrial Resources

	India	Pakistan
Cotton mills	380	9
Jute mills	108	0
Sugar mills	156	10
Iron and steel works	18	0
Paper mills	16	0
Glassworks	77	2

Agricultural Resources (in acres)

	India	Pakistan
Jute	984,000	1,404,000
Cotton	13,770,000	1,630,000
Tea	641,000	97,000
Rice	17,229,000	5,376,000
Wheat	4,200,000	2,785,000
Sugar	2,631,000	517,000

India also has all the country's iron ore and copper. It has most of the coal and oil. Pakistan has the greater supply of water power. But it has no money to build great dams and buy great engines to turn the water power into electrical power.

India and Pakistan must work together to become strong, independent nations.

Telephoning and Writing Across Oceans

"IT IS almost time for lunch. What are you going to have?" A man in an office in New York was talking by telephone with another man.

"Lunch?" the other man answered. "I haven't had breakfast yet! It's five o'clock in the morning here."

The second man was in Honolulu, Hawaii. The man in New York and the man in Honolulu were more than 5,000 miles from each other. They were talking across a wide land and part of a wide ocean as neighbors talk across a street.

That talk took place the other day. It was part of a birthday party. "Ocean radiophone" was celebrating its 20th year of regular use. The party was held in the Overseas Room of a big telephone building in New York.

Telephone and radio both help people to telephone across oceans. Telephone wires carry the words on land. Radio waves carry the words on the long jumps across oceans. The word *radiophone* stands for "radio and telephone."

The first regular overseas radiophone "line" was between New York and London. For years, this line has been the busiest of the overseas lines. Now it carries more than a thousand calls a day. On the day of the radiophone birthday party, a call between New York and London cost $12 for three minutes. Regular calls in 1927 cost $75.

Radiophone has made neighbors of about 60 different countries in all parts of the world. You can talk with people in any of these countries on your

Machines such as this send written words thousands of miles—even across oceans.

telephone at home.

Written words can be sent across oceans, too. A man in New York writes words on a machine like a typewriter. This machine is connected with another one in London. These machines are called "teleprinters." The machines are connected by a wire. It runs along the bottom of the Atlantic.

The machine in London writes the same words as the one in New York. The Mayor of New York wrote a message to the Mayor of London on a teleprinter just a few days ago. An answer came back in a few minutes.

Radiophone and teleprinter are making words travel farther and faster than ever before.

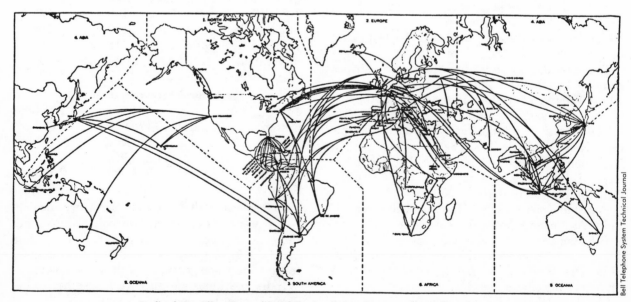

Radiophone "lines" are like threads sewing faraway lands together.

Tom Visits the Freedom Train

Hi there, girls and boys,

Has the big red, white, and blue Freedom Train been to your town? When it comes, be sure to pay it a visit. Wee B. and I went through the Train at Roanoke (rō′à-nōk), Virginia, the other day. We had the big thrill of our lives.

Brucie was thrilled because he helped to guard the Train. That is, he *thought* he was guarding it. He stood with the U. S. Marines lined up outside the Train. (He did not guess that I left him there on purpose. Dogs are not allowed on the Train.)

I was thrilled by the Freedom Train because I saw there the books and papers which made our country great. Ever since I started to school, I have heard about the Declaration of Independence and the Magna Carta. When I saw these documents on the Freedom Train, I suddenly realized that they had been written by *real people*. Long ago, people just like *us* carefully thought out what

rights a free man should have. Those people wrote down their thoughts. They worked, fought, and even gave their lives to get those rights for themselves and for us.

One of these rights is freedom of speech. Another is freedom to choose which church we shall go to. These are only two of the many freedoms promised the people of our country in the documents on the Freedom Train. People visiting the Train should remember these freedoms.

All our precious freedoms were won for us by our fellow men of long ago. You will find the whole story of that long struggle in the documents and the battle flags on the Freedom Train.

These things are in showcases along the walls of the cars. Wherever the Train stops, thousands of children and grownups pass through those cars. I asked one boy about your age what he thought of the Freedom Train. "It's wonderful, mister," he said. "It's history on *wheels!*"

Your big brother, *Tom Trott*

These officers of the U. S. Marines are inspecting the marine squad guarding the Freedom Train. The Train is seven cars long. It is making a 33,000-mile trip around our country. In the picture at the right, government workers are putting plastic cases on the documents for the Freedom Train.

Mr. Baseball

April 27 will be celebrated as "Babe Ruth Day" in cities and towns all over our country. Hardly anybody old enough to tell a baseball from a tomato needs to ask, "Who is Babe Ruth?" Asking that is like asking, "What is baseball?"

Babe Ruth was in the hospital a few weeks ago for a neck operation. He received letters from all over the United States and from other countries. Most of the letters were from girls and boys. Some of the letters were addressed to "Mr. Baseball." Mailmen had no trouble figuring out who "Mr. Baseball" was.

Most people think of Babe Ruth as the "home run king" of baseball. He became famous for hitting home runs. As a big-league player, he hit 730 home runs. In just one season, he hit more than 60.

Babe Ruth set many other records in baseball. He took the most bases on balls—2,056. Pitchers

Babe Ruth did much to make baseball the favorite sport of the United States. People who had never seen a baseball game went to see him play. He is 51 years old now.

"gave" him bases to keep him from hitting home runs.

He was a good pitcher as well as a good batter. In fact, he started in baseball as a pitcher. He set a pitching record in World Series games. He pitched 29 innings without letting the other team score.

Babe Ruth always liked girls and boys. He stopped anywhere to talk with them and to sign baseballs for them. He visited girls and boys in hospitals. Once he learned that a boy was not getting well after an operation. Babe Ruth went to the hospital the next morning. He sat beside the boy's bed and talked with him. Babe Ruth said, "This afternoon I'm going to hit a home run just for you." He did. Soon the boy was well and watching the "home run king."

Babe Ruth is too old to play baseball now. He will not soon be forgotten, however. He goes on playing in people's memories and hearts.

Elsie Travels With Her Calf

Elsie, the cow, has a new calf.
The little calf travels with Elsie.
They travel all over the country.
They travel in planes and trains.
Many people go to see Elsie and her calf.

Here is a drawing of Elsie and her baby.

Elsie and her calf are clean and healthy.

School Children in War Countries

These children help to build their teacher's house.

In some countries, school buildings were damaged in the war. Many school children could not go to school.

Today, the children are back in school. Some children go to school in people's homes.
Other children go to school in churches.
Some children go to school in damaged school buildings.

A Movie With No Ups and Downs

How often have you stayed seated all the way through a movie? Probably about as often as you have ice skated in your bathtub. You nearly always have to stand up several times to let people pass.

In a movie theater just built, you can stay seated during the whole show. This theater has a new kind of seat. It can be moved back and forth. To let a person pass, you just push your seat back.

The girl at the end of the row has pushed her seat back to let the standing girl pass. Pushing a seat back leaves plenty of room between it and the seat in front.

Problem of Palestine Comes Before the U. N.

TEL AVIV was built by the Jews as their chief city. It has many beautiful modern buildings.

THE United Nations has many serious problems to talk over this fall, during its meeting in Paris. One of these problems—the Russian blockade of Berlin—we have already discussed in WEEKLY READER. Another serious question for the U. N. is "What shall be done about Palestine?"

U. N. delegates have spent many months working on the problem of Palestine. They have pored over maps of the country. They have studied its geography and history. They must understand Palestine's geography, especially, before they can work out a satisfactory answer to the problem.

The Geography of Palestine

Palestine lies in Asia, at the eastern end of the Mediterranean Sea. It is a very small country, only about as big as our state of Vermont.

Compared to the United States, Palestine is poor in resources. Most of the country is barren, with little rainfall. Rocky hills run north and south through the center of Palestine. In the south is a great desert called the Negeb (nĕg'ĕb).

Along the coast is a narrow strip of fertile land. In Galilee (găl'ĭ-lē), in the north, are a few fertile river valleys.

The Struggle for Palestine

This poor little country is being fought over bitterly by the Jews and the Arabs. Already, many people on each side have been killed.

The Arabs claim Palestine because they have lived there for many hundreds of years. The Jews, on the other hand, say that Palestine was *their* homeland, as far back as Bible times. Later the Jews were scattered in many countries, on several continents. During World War I, the British freed Palestine from the rule of Turkey. The British favored the setting up in Palestine of a national home for the Jewish people. Thousands of Jews from Europe and other continents began immigrating to Palestine. Today, about one-third of the population are Jews. Thirty years ago, only one-tenth were Jews.

The Arabs became alarmed at this great flood of immigration. They were afraid that, before long, they would be outnumbered and the Jews would control the whole country. The Arabs demanded that Jewish immigration into Palestine should stop.

The U. N.'s "Jigsaw Puzzle"

In April, 1947, the problem of little Palestine was turned over to the United Nations. A commission was appointed to study the problem. The commission suggested that Palestine be divided into two independent states.

The commission tried hard to be fair to both Jews and Arabs. They tried to divide the most fertile land —Galilee and the coastal strip— between the two states. The commission also assigned to the Jewish state the parts of Palestine in which the Jews had settled most widely.

The smallest map on the front page shows how the U. N. commission divided Palestine. The map of the two states looks much like a jigsaw puzzle!

The commission's plan was approved by the U. N. General Assembly. The Jews consented to the plan, but the Arabs would not agree to it. The angry Arabs insisted that all Palestine should stay one country.

Last May, the Jews set up their own government in their part of the "jigsaw puzzle." They called their new state "Israel" (ĭz'rā-ĕl).

The Murder of Count Bernadotte

Jews and Arabs began fighting each other. The Arabs who lived in the neighboring countries of Trans-Jordan and Egypt supported the Arabs of Palestine.

The U. N. still tried to settle the problem peaceably. A U. N. mediator was sent to Palestine to work out a plan to which both sides could agree. The mediator was a Swedish nobleman, Count Bernadotte (bûr'nà-dŏt).

Last month, Count Bernadotte

was killed as he was driving through the city of Jerusalem in Palestine. His killers were members of the "Stern Gang," a group of Jews who believe in using force to seize Palestine. The government of Israel was shocked by the murder. The government outlawed the Stern Gang and tried to track down the killers.

The Bernadotte Plan

Before Count Bernadotte died, he worked out a new plan for Palestine. His plan is being presented to the General Assembly for consideration.

Count Bernadotte suggested a new division for Palestine. The large map on the front page shows how the country would look under the Bernadotte Plan. Count Bernadotte tried to avoid making a "jigsaw puzzle." He assigned to the Jewish state all of Galilee. He gave to the Arab state all of the Negeb.

Neither Jews nor Arabs are pleased with this new plan. The Jews feel that it does not give them a fair division of the land. The Arabs still insist that all of the country belongs to them.

The U. N. will try hard to work out a fair compromise. However, it may be a long time before the problem of Palestine is settled at last.

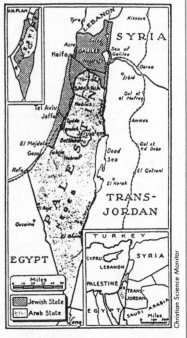

PALESTINE—Large map shows how the country would be divided under the Bernadotte Plan.

Iron Curtain Stretches Across The Danube River

AN IDLE BOAT *becomes a hotel at Regensburg, Germany, on the Danube.*

THE town of Regensburg (rä'gĕnsbōork) lies in southern Germany, on the banks of the great Danube River. Before World War II, Regensburg was a busy river port. Its docks were thick with cargo boats and puffing steamers.

Tankers brought oil from the big oil fields of Romania. Barges and cargo boats brought wheat from Hungary and copper from the mines of Yugoslavia.

The boats were loaded again with German manufactured products and sent down river toward the Black Sea, about 1,500 miles away. The Danube River was a great highway for trade between Germany and the countries of southeastern Europe.

Idle Boats and Men

If you were to visit Regensburg today, you would notice a big change. A few small boats still go up the river a hundred miles or so. Some coal from the Ruhr is shipped 125 miles down the river to Linz (lïnts), Austria.

Many of the larger boats at Regensburg, however, ride quietly at anchor. The crews of the ships loaf along the docks. One fine, big boat has been made into a hotel and restaurant!

What has happened to Regensburg? If you started sailing down the Danube on a cargo boat, you would soon find out.

A few miles below Regensburg, your boat would cross the border into Austria. Just below the town of Linz, you would be stopped by guards. "You cannot go any farther," they would tell you sternly. "You do not have the proper papers." Then you would know that you had reached the Iron Curtain.

The Iron Curtain on the Danube

In WEEKLY READER for October 11-15, we talked about how an imaginary Iron Curtain divided Germany into two parts—a Russian zone and the western zones. This same Iron Curtain stretches down through Europe to the Adriatic Sea.

Disagreement on the Danube

Who shall control the Danube River? The countries lying east of the Iron Curtain cannot agree with the western European countries on this question.

The western European powers and the United States want the river to be under international control, as it was before World War II. Then, all nations had equal rights to use the Danube for trade.

The countries which touch the Danube east of the Iron Curtain have a different idea. They insist on complete control of the river. Since Russia controls all of these countries, therefore Russia rules the Danube. No boats can sail on the Danube east of the Iron Curtain without Russian permission. And Russian permission is almost impossible to get.

Last August, a conference was held in Yugoslavia between the western powers and the Danube countries east of the Iron Curtain. The two groups could not come to an agreement on the use of the river highway.

Until they can agree, the Danube River will continue to be cut in two. Boats will not be able to carry cargoes past the Iron Curtain. The boatmen at Regensburg will have no work to do.

★ ★ Rounding Up the News ★ ★

New Senator

MARGARET CHASE SMITH is famous as the first woman to be elected "on her own" to a full term in the U. S. Senate. Up to now, our few women senators have been appointed or have been elected to fill their husbands' places as senators.

Mrs. Smith's husband once served in the House of Representatives. When he died in 1940, she was elected to take his place in the House. She made a good record. Last winter, she decided to run for senator.

"You'll never win!" her friends warned her. "Being elected senator is much harder than becoming a representative. Look who is running against you for the Republican nomination! Your two chief opponents are the Governor of Maine and a former Governor."

Mrs. Smith ran anyway. She made speeches all over the state. She visited tiny towns as well as big cities. In zero weather, she drove her car from town to town over snowy country roads.

One February day, on her way to make a speech, she fell and broke her right arm. She took time to have the arm put in a cast—then she went ahead with her speech! She didn't miss a day of campaigning, although for a while, she had to let someone else do her driving for her.

Everywhere she went, she made friends. She won the nomination. Last September, she won the election with the biggest majority in Maine history.

Mrs. Smith has been a telephone operator, a teacher in a one-room school, and a business woman. She loves to cook!

AMERICANS ARE READERS

More Americans can now read and write than ever before. This announcement was made recently by the U. S. Census Bureau. The Bureau has been making a study of the number of Americans who still cannot read a book or write a letter. Today, 2,800,000 Americans 14 years old or over can neither read nor write, the Bureau reports. The number is about 2.7 per cent of the Americans who are 14 or over. In other words, more than 97 out of every hundred Americans can read and write. However, 8,200,000 Americans 14 or over have had less than five years of schooling.

America's record is much better today than it was in 1870. Then, 20 out of every 100 people in the country could not read and write. By 1930, the number of "non-readers" had dropped to less than 5 out of every 100.

Boys' Friend

Father E. J. Flanagan of Boys Town, Nebr., is off on another trip. Last summer, he went to Japan to work out plans for helping the children of Japan. This spring, he has gone to Vienna, Austria, to work on the American program for Austrian youth.

Father Flanagan is famous as the founder of Boys Town, home of 500 boys who were once homeless or friendless. Today, people from all over America ask his advice on how to help boys to become good citizens.

He began befriending boys in 1917. Two of his first five boys had been in juvenile court. The other three, Father Flanagan had picked up off the street. He rented a house in Omaha, Nebr., for his five boys. He borrowed $90 to pay the first month's rent. Within two weeks, his "family" had grown to 25 boys.

Before long, Father Flanagan needed more room. He bought a farm 10 miles west of Omaha, where he built Boys Town. Many people who were interested in his work sent him money to help pay for the dormitories and other buildings.

The "citizens" of Boys Town run their own government. They elect one of the boys as mayor. If a boy breaks any rule, he is brought before a court of judges who are Boys Town citizens, too. The boys receive a good education and learn good trades. Many go on to college.

Father Flanagan was born in Ireland. He still has an Irish twinkle. The children of Vienna will find he is their friend, too.

Candy Drops from the Sky

The girls and boys of Berlin watch for Lieutenant Gail Halvorsen's plane. He flies food and coal into Berlin.

To the girls and boys, food and coal are not the important part of Lieutenant Halvorsen's load. The girls and boys watch for little parachutes floating down from the plane. The parachutes are handkerchiefs. Fastened to them are candy bars and lollipops.

Berlin children wait for the "candy pilot."

Lieutenant Halvorsen has dropped candy on more than 100 flights. The idea came to him one afternoon. He gave some chewing gum to two children. Near-by children looked very sad. The flyer did not have enough for all. He tried to figure out a way to give candy and gum to more children.

He thought of dropping candy from his plane. He talked with members of his crew. They liked the idea. All were soon buying candy and handkerchiefs to use as parachutes.

Now, many other people are helping the "candy pilot." A clothing company sends handkerchiefs. A candy company sends chocolate bars. Friends of the flyer sent 1,000 handkerchiefs and 400 pounds of candy.

Lieutenant Halvorsen has been saving the colored handkerchiefs. He will use them this winter. They can be found on snow more easily than white ones.

Rubber Is in the News

More and more uses are being found for rubber. People are riding across it, sitting on it, and wearing it.

In Akron, Ohio, a street has just been paved with rubber. Powdered rubber was mixed with hot asphalt. This pavement should stand cold weather well and be safer against skidding.

Cushions for autos and furniture are being made of "foam rubber." It is rubber filled with tiny bubbles of air.

Flyers are testing rubber suits. A flyer forced down in water can float in one of these suits. It keeps him up and keeps him warm.

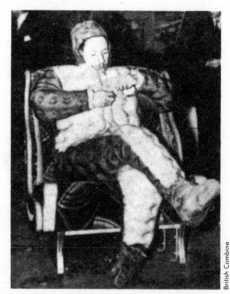

A flyer tries on a rubber suit. He can blow it up with his mouth in a few minutes. The suit weighs a little more than two pounds.

Uncle Sam Makes Plans To Help the Navajos

CIRCLE—Two Navajo children stand beside their mother. LEFT—A Navajo home is called a hogan. It is a round hut built of logs and earth. In front is the family's flock of sheep and goats.

Press Association

THE United States is getting ready to pay a very old debt. It is a debt owed to some of the earliest Americans—the Navajo (năv'à-hō) Indians.

Last month, Congress began studying a 10-year plan for helping the Navajos. The plan is in a bill presented to Congress by Secretary of the Interior Julius A. Krug. The Department of the Interior has the responsibility for looking after Indian affairs (WEEKLY READER, Feb. 28).

In recent years, the Navajos have had a hard struggle. Many of them have been poor, hungry, and sick. Many of the Navajo children have not had a chance for an education. Only one out of every five Navajos can read and write.

Last winter, blizzards hit the unlucky Navajos. Some of their sheep starved to death on the snow-covered land. This spring, the Navajos have only a little more than half the usual number of lambs in their flocks. They will have fewer lambs to sell.

Why are the Navajos having so much trouble — and why do we feel that we owe a debt to them?

The Story of the Navajos

The Navajos are the largest tribe of Indians in the United States. Most of them live on a great tract of land called a reservation. The reservation covers parts of four states—Arizona, Utah, Colorado, and New Mexico. It is larger than our state of West Virginia.

Before the white man came to America, the Navajos and the other Indian tribes roamed wherever they liked, over the western plains and deserts. When the white man conquered the Indians, they lost this freedom of movement. The white conquerors marked off certain regions as reservations where the Indians were to live.

At first, the Navajos managed to live very comfortably on their reservation. The Navajo families raised big flocks of sheep which grazed over the desert.

The Indians earned money by selling sheep and wool. Their flocks gave them plenty of meat for their own use. They wove some of their wool into colorful blankets. The blankets found a ready sale outside the reservation.

Of course, the dry land of the desert did not grow much vegetation for the sheep to eat. But the Navajos did not need to worry. The sheep owners could spread out over a wide territory. Then, each owner would have many acres on which his sheep could graze.

Trouble Begins

Gradually the situation changed for the Navajos. Many children were born. The children grew up and had families of their own. As the number of families increased, the number of sheep grew, too.

The vegetation on the desert was too scanty to feed the larger flocks of sheep. The hungry sheep nibbled every blade of grass and pulled up the roots of the grass. The vegetation did not have a chance to grow. Rain began washing away the bare, unprotected soil. The land became more barren than ever.

The U. S. Government tried to help. Government agents told the Navajos to cut down on the size of their flocks.

"Each family should average only about 60 sheep," the Indians were told. "Then there will be enough grazing land for all the sheep."

The Navajos obeyed. When they cut down their flocks, they were poorer than ever. Each family needed at least 250 sheep to make a decent living. With only 60 sheep, the Navajos could not make ends meet.

The Indians tried to make a living in other ways. Some of the men left their homes and went outside the reservation to work on the railroads. Some Navajos gathered piñon nuts from the pine trees to sell.

Many of the Indians found earning a living very hard. They had had no chance for an education. Living on the reservation, they had had little chance to learn the ways of the white man.

A year ago, American newspapers and magazines printed many stories about the hardships of the Navajos. Organizations sent food, clothing, and money to the Indians. Congress voted two million dollars for temporary help until a permanent plan could be worked out.

Uncle Sam's Plan

What is the 10-year plan of the Department of the Interior? In the first place, it provides more schools and hospitals for the Navajos. New roads will be built through the reservation so that the Indians can more easily reach schools, health centers, and stores.

The Government will try to make it possible for each Navajo family to earn a decent living. About one-fifth of the families will still raise sheep. The rest will be given a chance at other kinds of jobs.

Almost one-half of the families will go into farming. Some irrigation projects have already been started; others are being planned. When the land has water, the Indians can raise good crops.

Some Navajos will go into the lumbering and mining industries. The reservation has forests and mineral resources to be developed.

Some Navajos will work in stores, filling stations, and other small businesses on the reservation. Some will make beautiful Navajo jewelry for sale. Others will be helped to find jobs outside the reservation.

The Navajos are eagerly waiting to see what Congress will do about their problems. They say they do not want charity. They are a proud and intelligent people. Many Navajo men fought bravely in the American Army and Navy during World War II. The Navajos are asking only for a chance to take care of themselves.

JAPANESE VOTERS HOLD BIG ELECTION

They Are Learning About Democracy

LEFT—A newsstand in Tokyo, the capital of Japan. Note the election poster at the right.

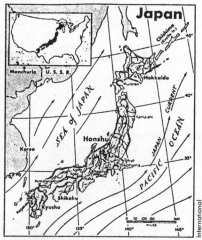

MAP—Japan's railroads run chiefly along the coast and through the mountain valleys.

Japan, the Warmaker

Why are the Americans in Japan today, and why is Japan changing its government?

For many years, Japan was a war-maker and a troublemaker. The powerful rulers of the nation wanted to conquer other countries of Asia. In 1931, Japan began invading China. In 1941, it started to gobble up the East Indies, Malaya, and other parts of southeastern Asia. Without warning, Japan attacked our naval base at Pearl Harbor in the Hawaiian Islands.

We had to fight a terrible war with the Japanese. In August, 1945, we and our Allies forced them to surrender. American soldiers moved in to keep order in the land. SCAP headquarters were set up to rule the country until the Japanese were ready to take over.

How SCAP Is Helping

Today, SCAP has two big jobs. The first job is to help Japan in becoming a democratic, peace-loving nation.

The second big job is to help Japan with its problems in farming and industry. Japan was "broke" and badly in debt by the end of the war. For many years, Japan had been spending most of its money on guns, battleships, and other weapons for warmaking. Besides rebuilding their own country, the Japanese must pay for damage they did to nations they invaded.

RECENTLY the people of Japan had an election. They chose members of their Diet, which is much like our Congress.

Such an exciting time they had! Candidates tried many ways to interest the voters. One candidate set up his headquarters on a life raft in a canal. Another rode through his district on the back of a cow.

On election day, the people cast one of the biggest votes in Japanese history. Nearly three-quarters of the eligible voters cast ballots. In fact, the Japanese made a better record than our American voters did in our presidential election last fall. In the United States, only a little more than half of the eligible voters took the trouble to cast their ballots.

Japan's New Democracy

The right to vote is a brand new right for many Japanese. Until three years ago, the people had very little to say about their government. The country was ruled by a small group of powerful leaders. At the head of the government was the emperor, who was worshiped as a god by the Japanese.

Today, the emperor and the little group of rulers have lost their power. The Japanese are learning how to have a democracy.

Americans now stationed in Japan are helping the Japanese to set up their democracy. The leader of the Americans is General Douglas MacArthur. His title is Supreme Commander for the Allied Powers He and his staff are called "SCAP" for short.

Worker for Peace

Dr. Ralph J. Bunche has been one of the busiest men in the United Nations since last fall. His title has been Acting Mediator for the U. N. on the Palestine problem .

Recently Dr. Bunche has been holding conferences between Jews and Arabs, on the island of Rhodes in the eastern Mediterranean Sea. When the United Nations met last fall in Paris, France, he had his headquarters in Paris. His job has made him one of the most outstanding Negroes in the world.

Dr. Bunche was born in Detroit, Mich., 44 years ago. He became an orphan when he was only 14.

He won an athletic scholarship to the University of California at Los Angeles. He helped earn his way by working as a janitor. During the summer, he worked on ships.

After graduating from U. C. L. A., he wanted to keep on learning things. He won scholarships which gave him the chance to study in Europe, Asia, and Africa. He earned his degree of Doctor of Philosophy. He became a college professor.

During World War II, he worked for the State Department. Later, he worked for the United Nations.

Dr. Bunche is a very hard worker. He has plenty of patience and he can keep his temper. He is fair. He has needed all these qualities in his big job.

A Picture in a Minute!

This month, a new kind of camera is going on sale at the stores. This amazing invention makes its own prints of the pictures it takes. The print is finished one minute after the camera snaps the picture.

The new camera is loaded with two rolls instead of the one roll used in old-fashioned cameras. In

Dr. Edwin H. Land (left) shows a friend the picture snapped of him a minute before.

the Land camera, one of these rolls is negative film. The other roll is a special kind of paper.

A picture is taken on the negative film. Then, a flap is pulled. Inside the back of the camera, the negative and the paper are pressed together through tiny rollers. The rollers squeeze a tiny pod fastened to the paper. The pod holds a special jelly. This jelly "prints" the picture from the negative onto the paper.

Then, the back of the camera is opened. The cameraman lifts out the print. The print is a little damp and sticky from the jelly in the pod. But the paper dries in a few minutes, leaving a good picture.

Hay for Your Gum

Farmers in the Northwest are planning to raise more hay for you this year. This hay is peppermint hay.

Peppermint grows like hay in big fields. The plants become three or four feet tall. They are cut like hay with machines. Then, they are dried and cooked.

The peppermint flavor comes from oil in the stems and leaves.

The man tramps peppermint hay in a big kettle.

A pound of peppermint oil flavors thousands of sticks of chewing gum. About half of our peppermint is used in that way. The rest is used in medicine, tooth paste, and candy.

Willy Quack

Dear Girls and Boys,
The little ducks see a turtle.
It lives in our pond.

The little ducks tease the turtle.
I scold the little ducks.
Love, Willy Quack

WEEKLY READER®
NEWS OF THE WORLD

1950-1959

In this mid-century decade, children learned through the pages of *Weekly Reader* about the growth of the U.S.; about high-tech marvels in travel and communications; about a first, timid reach toward the stars. The decade opened with the Korean War, but news of this bloody, seesaw conflict was muted in *Weekly Reader*.

The prefix *super* summed up the confident, expansive tone of the times. Two superpowers piled up their superbombs. Supermarkets popped up everywhere in supersuburbia. Superhighways spread like spider webs. In 1956, *Weekly Reader* marveled that motorists could now speed 800 miles from New York to Chicago without braking for a single stoplight.

TV images, including the first in color, brought the world into the sanctum of the living room. Viewers by the millions became transfixed by "the tube." And commercial air travel, soon to be enhanced by speedy jetliners, became the nation's choice for long journeys.

A landmark—or rather *sky*mark—year was 1957. In October of that year, the Soviets orbited a 23-inch sphere called *Sputnik*—the first-ever artificial satellite. The U.S. was impressed—and shocked. The supposedly plodding Soviet tortoise had gotten the jump on the American high-tech hare. U.S. educators declared a post-*Sputnik* age and called for curriculum reform. *Weekly Reader* did its part by increasing its emphasis on science.

ROCKETS
Are Flying High

Wide World

LEFT—An "Aerobee" rocket is shot from a metal launching tower in New Mexico. ABOVE—The sketch shows how Dr. Tsien's rocket ship would look.

HOW would you like to travel from New York to San Francisco by rocket ship—in one hour?

Of course, you won't be able to take the trip this year, or perhaps for many years. No one has yet built a rocket airplane which could make such a flight. However, a well-known rocket expert says that it could be done. He believes that our scientists already have the technical knowledge they would need to build such a rocket ship.

The rocket expert is Professor Tsien, who was born in China. He now teaches at the California Institute of Technology. Recently at a meeting of engineers, he described just what his rocket ship would look like.

Dr. Tsien drew sketches of his rocket airplane. The rocket ship in the drawing above is based on Dr. Tsien's sketch.

His rocket plane would be about 80 feet long and almost nine feet wide. It would have a ram-jet engine in addition to its rocket power. It would go 9,140 miles an hour—over 2½ miles a second.

When the rocket ship left New York, it would make a very steep climb. It would go up and up and up. Finally, it would climb so high that it would be above the blanket of air which surrounds the earth. We call this blanket of air the atmosphere.

Then the rocket would start curving down. When it reached the earth's atmosphere again, it would no longer need any power. At a height of 27 miles above the earth, the rocket liner would become a glider. It would coast down toward the earth during the final 1,800 miles of its 3,000-mile trip.

By the time the rocket ship had reached San Francisco, it would have lost most of its speed. When it landed, it would be traveling only 150 miles an hour.

The total time needed for the trip from New York to San Francisco would be less than one hour!

What's Ahead for Television?

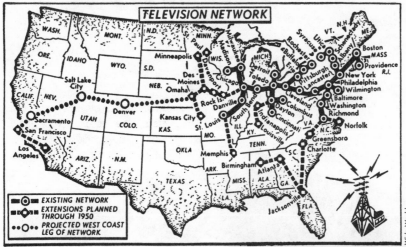

TELEVISION NETWORK

◉ EXISTING NETWORK
◈ EXTENSIONS PLANNED THROUGH 1950
○ PROJECTED WEST COAST LEG OF NETWORK

Wide World

Magnavox Co.

CBS Television

MAP—What cities will join the television network in 1950? At present, how far west does the network extend? TOP—Children enjoy television programs. BOTTOM—Television cameras move from one set to another in a modern television studio.

ANNOUNCER: Good evening, friends. We now bring you an interview with Mr. Ralph Samson, a leading television expert.

Just three years ago, there were only about 17,000 television sets in the whole United States. Today, there are close to four million sets in use!

Mr. Samson, how many television sets do you think we will have in the United States five years from now?

MR. SAMSON: The head of one big radio and television broadcasting company made a prediction on this subject recently. He said that, within five years, Americans would probably have 20 million sets in use. More than half the people of the United States will be able to watch television!

ANNOUNCER: Whew! Television is growing so fast it makes me dizzy. I understand the network of television stations is growing fast, too.

MR. S: It is, indeed. (He points to a map of the United States which is hanging on a wall.) The solid red line on this map shows how far the network extends today. It connects 25 or more cities. By the end of 1950, it will be extended to take in 43 cities.

ANNOUNCER: Mr. Samson, many people wonder why we need to build a television network. Why can't I tune in my television set to get broadcasts from Seattle or Dallas?

MR. S: The sound waves which carry radio programs and the waves which carry television programs are quite different from each other. Radio waves curve, following the curve of the earth. Therefore, radio waves from Seattle can easily be picked up here in New York City.

Television waves are pretty straight — like a beam of light. After traveling a few miles, they leave the curved earth and shoot out into space.

Ordinarily, you can't count on getting a direct television broadcast from a station which is more than 50 miles away from you.

So, you see, we have to find ways to give television waves a boost— to get them past that 50-mile limit.

ANNOUNCER: How have you solved this problem?

MR. S: We have worked out two ways to "boost" television waves. The first way is to send the waves from city to city over coaxial cables. These cables are buried underground. We are also building radio relay towers 30 miles apart, on hills, if possible. The tower catches the television waves, strengthens them, and passes them to the next station 30 miles away.

ANNOUNCER: I see. Mr. Samson, how soon will we have a television network from coast to coast?

MR. S: It will probably be two to four years yet. We will have to build a line of relay towers across the Rocky Mountains.

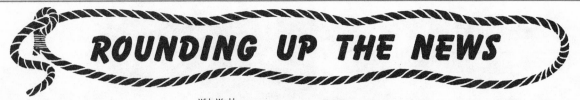

ROUNDING UP THE NEWS

New Jobs for the Walkie-Talkies

Science in the News

Recently, a Sioux Indian named Plain Feather was helping to make a movie. The movie, "Warpath," tells the famous story of General Custer, who was killed 75 years ago in a great battle between the Indians and the white men.

Plain Feather was giving directions to the Indians who were taking part in the battle scenes. He wore a war bonnet and rode on a swift horse. But he had one piece of equipment which looked very odd with his Indian costume. Plain Feather gave orders to his Indians with a walkie-talkie!

The walkie-talkie is a radio sending and receiving set which is so small and handy that you can

Wide World

carry it about with you. It first became popular in World War II. By using walkie-talkies, patrols of soldiers could keep in touch with each other without having to shout their orders.

Today, walkie-talkies and other small portable broadcasting sets

have many uses. They have been used by forest rangers in fighting forest fires. Firemen and policemen have found them valuable. Geologists use them to keep in touch with each other when they are hunting new mineral deposits.

Movie directors often use portable broadcasting sets in the studio, as well as in directing big scenes out of doors. When actors are speaking their lines, the director cannot shout orders to them because his voice would be recorded on the sound track, too.

When necessary, the director can talk to his actors by radio. Each actor will wear a little radio receiver hidden in his clothing or his hair. A wire antenna goes around his neck. The sound is carried to his tiny ear piece through flesh-colored plastic tubing.

THE TWO MacARTHURS

Wide World

General MacArthur

GENERAL Douglas MacArthur is commander of the U.N. forces in Korea. Since the end of World War II, he has also been head of the allied forces occupying Japan.

General MacArthur has been in the Army all his life! His father was a general, too. Douglas was born in 1880 at an Army post in Little Rock, Arkansas. He was only three years old when he first heard the sound of enemy gunfire. The Army post was attacked by a band of Indians.

Douglas went to West Point. He was manager of the football team and won his letter in baseball. His team was the first Army team ever

to beat the Navy in baseball. He graduated at the head of his class.

General MacArthur's 12-year-old son is named Arthur. Arthur was four years old when he was first "under fire"—almost as young as his father had been. In 1942, General MacArthur was in command of the U. S. forces in the Philippine Islands. The Japanese invaded the Philippines. Arthur had to escape with his mother and father to Australia.

Two years later, General MacArthur came back with a great Army and Navy to reconquer the Philippines. Arthur came back to the Philippines, too. He could hear the big guns of his father's forces thundering away at the Japanese lines.

After the Japanese were defeated, Arthur went to Tokyo,

Japan, where his father's headquarters were set up. He has lived in Tokyo ever since.

He is a baseball fan and a Boy Scout. But he has to imagine for himself what the United States is like. He gets his ideas of America by reading books and going to the movies!

Arthur MacArthur on a Navy Destroyer

International

"Jets" in the News

The tanker plane (left) is ready to "feed" the smaller jet plane.

A big plane and two small planes are in the news. All three planes have jet engines. Jet engines have no propellers. Jet engines suck in air at the front and push it out the back. Pushing the air backward makes the plane move forward.

The big plane has just made its first flight. It is a real sky giant. It is the world's biggest bomber. If it stood on its tail, its nose would reach to the roof of a 16-story building.

This giant has two kinds of engines. It has four jet engines and six propeller engines. The jet engines give the plane greater speed and help it in take-offs. The plane can fly about 500 miles an hour. It can climb to almost ten miles in the air.

Everybody Is Doing It!

Dear Children:

I shined my teakettle this morning. I put it on the stove. Soon it was singing a happy song.

"You are singing because you are shining clean," I said.

Lucky sat on the floor in the sun. He was washing his paws.

Mrs. Muff sat on the window sill. She was washing her fur coat.

Melody was taking a shower. She flipped water over herself with her tail and wings.

Judy came in. "What's doing around here?" she asked.

"Everybody is cleaning up. Look around," I answered.

Just then, Cuckoo came from the clock. "Clean, too," he called.

"Oh, oh!" cried Judy. "See my dirty hands. May I wash them, Aunt Em? I want to be clean, too."

"Keeping clean is like the measles. It is catching," I laughed.

Aunt Em

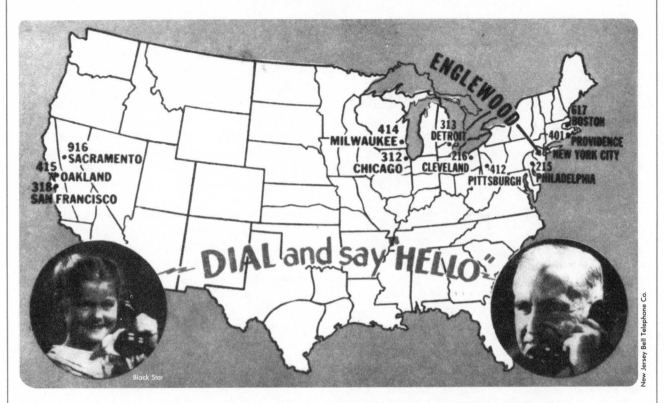

The map shows all of the cities which can be dialed directly from Englewood, New Jersey.

DIAL and say "HELLO"

"HELLO, Nancy. You sound as if you were right here in New Jersey."

"I can hear you well, too, Granddad. Did you have any trouble getting the call through?"

"None at all. I just dialed 916 for Sacramento, California, and then your number. Before I could say, 'Where's Nancy?' you were on the line."

Many telephone conversations such as that will be going on in the next few days. On November 10, a new long-distance dialing system will be used for the first time. People in Englewood, New Jersey, will be able to call people in 12 other large cities across the country. They will just dial the number and say "Hello." The system will work only one way at first. People in the other cities will not be able to dial Englewood. They will have to call a long-distance operator.

Machines take the place of operators in making these calls. Even the bills are made out by machines. A machine types on paper the two phone numbers, the time of day, and how long the persons talked. People making the new long-distance calls will have to keep one eye on their watches. There will be no operator to say, "Sorry, your time is up."

Seventy-five years ago, the first long-distance telephone call went only 8 miles. Now, telephone calls are sent by wire, cable, and radio to all parts of the world.

Nearly everyone needs to know how to use the telephone wisely. Good telephone manners win friends. In the box below are five "winning ways." Try them the next time you answer the phone or make a telephone call.

1. Answer by saying, "Nancy Jones speaking."
2. Speak clearly. Don't have "lazy lips."
3. Speak close to the mouthpiece and you will not need to shout.
4. Plan what you are going to say. Don't "hem and haw."
5. Be brief. Let others use the line.

The World's Best Neighbor--the U. N.

New shoes for Italian children.

United Nations

(A Radio Play for U. N. Week)

ANNOUNCER: The United Nations will celebrate its sixth birthday on October 24. Here in the studio are six boys and girls whose parents work for the U. N. in New York City. These girls and boys come from different countries. They are here to tell you what the U. N. is doing for children.

SANTHA *(from India):* In my country, there are so many people that we often do not have enough food for everyone. The U. N. sent dried milk from America to the Indian children. The people of Thailand had more rice than they needed. So these people sent some of their rice to us.

LEON *(from Greece):* The U. N. workers are not choosy about their jobs. They will do anything from packing food to spraying for mosquitoes. Moquitoes spread malaria. So the U. N. has been using its DDT spray guns in Greece and Italy.

GLORIA *(from Ecuador):* My country had an earthquake a few months ago. In some places, everything was destroyed. But the U. N. came to the rescue. I wish you could have seen the happy children when they first tasted United States milk! They even liked the cod-liver oil!

SYNG *(from Korea):* I guess everyone knows that my country is the place where the U. N. is fighting against communism. Many Korean boys and girls need food and clothing. Some of America's big cotton crop will soon be on its way to Korea. It will be made into children's clothes.

JOVAN *(from Yugoslavia):* Our U. N. help comes from Newfoundland. Hundreds of tons of dried Newfoundland fish have been sent to Yugoslavia.

CAROL *(from the U. S.):* My dad works on many U. N. committees. He says that the U. N. is the world's best neighbor. Some nations need food and clothing. So the nations across the seas share with them. Many countries need to learn how to use their farms and factories in a better way. The U. N. sends men to show them how.

Dad says that sharing makes good neighbors. It helps to make peace, too. Who wants to fight with a good neighbor?

Flight to the Moon: FIRST STOP

MAN-MADE MOON. *Spaceships of the future may take off from the earth for a "filling station" in space.*

Science in the News

Attention, please! The Lunaria, interplanetary flight number 17, takes off in 30 minutes. Destination: the moon; first stop: earth satellite vehicle.

This loud-speaker message seems very strange to us today. We might even have trouble understanding the words. The *Lunaria* is the name of a spaceship. Interplanetary flight means travel through space to the moon or to a planet such as Mars. Earth satellite vehicle means a platform out in space, traveling around the earth in the same way as the moon.

Scientists today agree that an earth satellite is the first step in space travel. Last month, in London, the British Interplanetary Society met to discuss a man-made moon.

An earth satellite might be set up outside the earth's atmosphere, beyond the pull of gravity. Once started in its orbit (route) around the earth, it would travel without fuel, as the moon travels.

Such a sky platform would have great value even before flights to the moon are possible. From this spot, our Government could watch what was going on down on the earth. The movement of enemy armies could be followed, or possibly stopped.

In addition, such a sky platform could serve as a refueling station for spaceships. It takes a tremendous amount of fuel to send a rocket into the earth's "upper air." It will take even more fuel to send a spaceship beyond the earth's layers of air. Therefore, the first stop on a flight to the moon would probably be a "filling station" on the earth satellite.

ROUNDING UP THE NEWS

The sleek-looking car in the picture is called the Sabre, named for the Air Force's jet plane. In spite of its long, fast lines, you couldn't get very far in this Sabre. It is only a full-sized model made of plaster. It was built by General Motors engineers to try out ideas which may be used in cars five or ten years from now. Its extra-powerful engine might drive the Sabre at speeds up to 150 miles an hour say the engineers.

The dashboard has 34 different controls and gauges. When you push one control, the headlights come out from behind the front grille where they are hidden when not in use. When you push another control, the leather seats will be

RIGHT — The high, sharp rear fenders on the Sabre are fuel tanks. One tank contains gasoline; the other carries methyl alcohol for the high-powered engine.

Wide World

warmed electrically to make them more comfortable in cold weather. A flashing light on your dashboard will warn you when your gas supply is low or the hand brake is on.

The car's top is stored in back and rises automatically when you

are ready for it. If you leave the car parked with the top down, you won't need to worry when a rain comes up. The top will rise as soon as raindrops start to spatter on the car seats.

KUKLA'S FRIENDS: FRAN and BURR

NBC Television

Kukla (at the left) poses with his friends, Oliver J. Dragon, Burr, and Fran.

Kukla has many friends on the *Kukla, Fran, and Ollie* television show. One friend, of course, is Ollie. Others are Beulah Witch, Madam Ooglepuss, Fletcher Rabbit, Cecil Bill, and Colonel Crackie.

Most of Kukla's friends are puppets, like himself, but he has two real-life friends: Fran Allison and Burr Tillstrom. Fran (who talks with Kukla on the show) used to teach school. Burr (who talks for Kukla) used to play with Teddy bears.

When he was a little boy, Burr liked to make his Teddy bears come to life. Using the bears and borrowed dolls, he gave puppet shows for his playmates. When he grew up, his "talking dolls" made him famous. ("Kukla" is the Russian word for "doll.")

Fran left teaching for a full-time radio job in Iowa. From Iowa, she went to Chicago and became well known as "Aunt Fanny" on radio's Breakfast Club.

Fran and Burr got together for their present show in 1947. Burr had been asked to put on a puppet show for television. He needed someone to talk to his puppets

while he worked backstage. "What I need," he said, "is a girl who can talk to a dragon." He thought of Fran. The girl who taught school and the boy who liked Teddy bears teamed up for one of TV's top shows.

Good-by, Penny Post Card

The penny post card will soon be a thing of the past! Starting January 1, 1952, government postal cards will sell for two cents. The penny card with its green picture of Thomas Jefferson will be replaced by a new card. This new card will carry a picture of Benjamin Franklin stamped in red.

Stamp collectors got a look at the new card last month. The Post Office Department hurried up printings of the cards so that they could be sold at the national postage stamp show in New York City.

Welcome, New Americans

Many families have had no country since World War II. They don't belong anywhere. They are called Displaced Persons.

The United States is helping some of these DP's. We ask some of them to come to our country.

"Come to America," we say. "We have a home for your family. We have work for you to do."

American ships bring the DP's to the United States. A train or bus takes them on the last part of their long trip.

Then they are met by American friends. "Welcome to America! We are glad you could come. We hope you will be happy here."

They have just come to America!

Uncle Ben's Gang Has Television Rules

DEAR PALS,
The gang was over Saturday afternoon. "May we turn on your TV?" Steve asked.

I said, "Help yourself. Get any program you want."

Steve, Tom, and Nancy wanted to watch a football game. Joe said, "Aw—I want to see the Hopalong Cassidy movie!"

"Rule three!" said Nancy. Joe grinned. The gang watched the football game.

Maybe you'd like to know our TV rules. We made them up together.

1. When we're at somebody else's house, the people who live there pick the programs.

2. If we don't like a program, we don't bother people who are enjoying it.

3. If we don't all want to see the same program, we look at what the most want.

4. We sit so everybody has a good view of the screen.

5. Bruno is the only member of the gang who can sit on top of the TV set. He likes to do that in winter because it's warm.

Your chum, *Uncle Ben*

The World Watches Southeast Asia

OMMUNISM is somewhat like a giant jack-in-the-box with dozens of lids. As soon as you close one lid, another may spring open.

In Korea, we are fighting to keep communism "in its box." What will happen, however, if the war ends in Korea? Will the communists then attack another country? This is the question facing free nations today. The leaders of these nations fear that the communists may next try to gain control of Southeast Asia.

A Rich Prize

Southeast Asia is a treasure house of important resources. It would be a rich prize if it fell under the control of the communists in China and Russia.

China needs rice. The "rice bowl" of Burma, Thailand, and Indo-China is one of the world's greatest rice-producing regions.

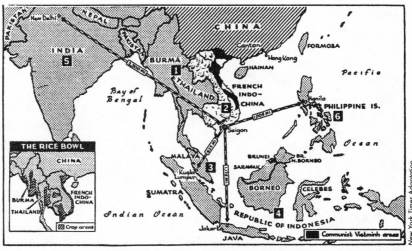

Communist control of French Indo-China would threaten Burma and Thailand (1); put important rice fields (2) in communist hands; open the gateway to Malaya (3), Indonesia (4), India (5), and the Philippines (6).

Russia needs oil, rubber, and tin. On the islands of Indonesia lie valuable deposits of oil. Over 90 per cent of the world's natural rubber comes from Southeast Asia. In 1949, Malaya, Indonesia, and Thailand together produced about 55 per cent of the world's tin.

•

HOW WELL CAN YOU READ A CARTOON?

Who are the firemen? What "hot spot" are they watching? Where else have the firemen had to fight a fire? What do you think the cartoonist wants the fire to represent? If you don't know, read the story to find out.

•

Indo-China Is the Key

Because of its position, French Indo-China is the key to Southeast Asia. A successful invasion of this country would unlock doors to the riches of other countries. Next to Indo-China lies Thailand, and beyond that are Burma and India. Southward lies the Malay peninsula, pointing into the islands of Indonesia. To the east lie the Philippine Islands.

A civil war is raging today in Indo-China. This "little war" could turn into a "big war" if the Chinese communists, with equipment from Russia, attacked Indo-China.

We know that the Chinese communists have brought together many of their soldiers near the Indo-China border. Military men guess that as many as 250,000 troops have gathered in southern China.

Does this mean that China is getting ready to fight in Southeast Asia? No one really knows. The story of Indo-China, however, may be an important one in 1952.

"Next hot spot?"

International

Long Live the Queen!

PEOPLE in Great Britain are smiling today. They are smiling even though their hearts are still sad because of the death of their king. A beautiful new queen now leads the British people. She is Queen Elizabeth the Second.

Queen Elizabeth has been learning to be queen since she was ten years old. She knows a great deal about the history and government of the British Empire. When she was 21 years old, she promised to spend her life serving her people.

A list of the queen's duties would fill up a dozen MY WEEKLY READERS. Nearly every day, Elizabeth must christen a ship, visit a hospital, go to a fair, or make a speech.

The queen's husband, Prince Philip, will not be king. However, he will help Elizabeth with her work. He will also help to take care of their little boy, Prince Charlie. He says he wants Charlie to be a "man's man." He has already bought Charlie a cricket bat.

When he gets older, Prince Charlie will have to study hard. He will have a private teacher to teach him history, good English, and fine manners. The little prince will stand up while he studies some of his lessons. He must get used to standing still for many hours. Some day, Charlie may take his mother's place. He may be Britain's next king.

Charlie and his baby sister, Princess Anne, will have fun playing in the big Buckingham Palace. At least two nurses will take care of them.

Queen Elizabeth will not wear a crown until the coronation, several months from now. Then, she will wear it only at very special celebrations. Whenever she appears, the people will shout, "Long live the queen!"

NEWS OF THE WEEK

Shoveling snow may be *soft* work but it is not easy. Many gadgets such as electric mats and heated cables have been invented to get rid of snow. Now a new machine called the Electric Sno-Blo has been invented. The steel machine scoops up snow from walks and driveways and blows it into a pile. Even steps and stone walls do not bother this machine. You just move it up to the wall and turn a switch. The snow is blown into a pile on the other side.

The Snow-Blo piles snow up to 20 feet on either side.

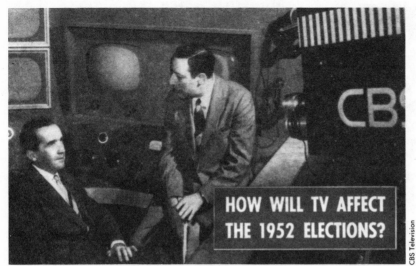

"See It Now" with Edward R. Murrow (left) is one of the TV shows that keep a nation-wide audience up to date on news.

GOOD-BY TO THE YANKEE CLIPPER

JOE DiMAGGIO, the great "Yankee Clipper," has played his last game of baseball. After 13 seasons with the New York Yankees, he says he is through as a player.

Joe's decision to quit is the decision of a true sportsman. "I feel," he said, "that I have reached a stage where I can no longer produce for my ball club, my manager, my teammates, and my fans the sort of baseball their loyalty to me deserves."

The star outfielder and slugger made up his mind last spring that he would not go on. He's getting older (37 now) and has had several injuries in recent years. His right knee and both shoulders have bothered him for a long time.

DiMaggio leaves baseball at the height of a great career. To him, the biggest thrill of that career was the 56-game hitting streak in 1941, when he batted an average of .408.

DOES YOUR TOWN have a television station? If it doesn't, you were probably caught in the "big freeze." For three and a half years, the number of TV stations has been limited, or "frozen."

Now, at last, the Government has given a "go ahead" signal for about 2,000 new TV stations. It will be some time before all of these new stations begin working, but television is on the march!

Television and Politics

This year, for the first time, television will play a big part in a Presidential election. Four years ago, there were just 900,000 television sets in American homes. Most of these were in the East. This year, there are over 15 million sets on a nation-wide hookup.

This summer, both the Democratic and Republican conventions will meet (three weeks apart) in the same building in Chicago. This will save the television companies the trouble of setting up costly equipment in two different places.

Television will probably change the pattern of political conventions. In the past, delegates have taken a lot of time for noisy parades around the convention hall. With drums and whistles, bands and singing, they called attention to favorite candidates.

This year, there will be fewer parades. Delegates will be asked to say what they have to say and then sit down. Neither political party wants to waste television time. Both parties want to please their nation-wide audience.

The political parties know the growing power of television. One of the parties is planning to spend around $1,000,000 for TV time. In 1948, this same party spent only $15,000 on television.

The Candidate and His Public

Candidates appearing on television are given this advice: "Remember you're a guest in the house. Don't be a smart aleck."

Yes, the candidate for office has now become a "guest in the house" of the voter who owns a TV set. The candidate must learn how to behave. He must develop a "TV personality."

The listener at home likes to feel that the candidate is talking directly to him. Television audiences enjoy natural speeches and want to hear facts. They aren't interested in long, windy speeches.

Television cameras are like detectives. They catch any "phonies" who try to bluff their way into office. Most people think television will have a good effect on politics.

Joe DiMaggio, Jr., whispers a word of advice to his famous father in the dressing room of Yankee Stadium.

Twenty years have passed since Joe, the son of an Italian immigrant, started with the San Francisco Seals, a minor league team. He joined the Yankees in 1936, and feels it was a great privilege to play with them.

"But it has been an even greater privilege to be able to play baseball at all. It has added much to my life."

Would you like a skunk for a pet? You may borrow one from an animal lending library.

Most libraries lend books. This library lends animals. The library is in Sacramento, California.

Boys and girls play with many animals at the library. There are rabbits, foxes, and others. The children may choose an animal to take home.

Each child promises to take good care of his pet. He must feed it.

The boys and girls keep their pets for one week. Then they may choose another pet to take home.

What animal would you choose?

Science News

PEOPLE have been searching for nests of the whooping crane for more than 50 years. This summer, two flyers in northern Canada found some nests of this bashful bird.

The whooping crane is one of our rarest birds. (We call it ours because it spends its winters in Texas.) Only about 30 whooping cranes are left.

The whooping crane is a tall bird. It stands almost as tall as a person. In the air, its wings spread farther than a man's outstretched arms. This bird gets its name from its loud call. It can be heard as far as two miles.

Whooping cranes play games in the air. One of their favorite games is to form two lines and fly toward each other.

Be a Good Visitor. Here are four things to remember when you visit.

THE WORLD WAITS FOR NEWS FROM RUSSIA

Russia (the U. S. S. R.) controls one-fourth of all the land on earth. The new premier of the world's largest country is G. M. Malenkov (upper left).

Marching soldiers are a common sight in Russia's capital city of Moscow.

IN AN American news office, the telephone jangled. By long distance from Russia, a reporter asked, "Have you heard the news?"

Suddenly the phone went dead. The world was waiting for important news. But all telephone communication between Moscow and the outside world had been cut off.

The news, of course, was that Premier Stalin had died. For more than a month, the world has watched Russia, waiting for more news.

In most countries, newspaper reporters and radio commentators are free to travel. They can interview anyone they like. They can send their stories around the world by telephone, telegraph, or radio.

In communist Russia, the government decides what news can be printed. Only six reporters from the outside world now work in Moscow. They are not permitted to travel to other parts of Russia. Unless the Russian Government approves what the reporters write, they cannot send their stories out of Moscow.

What Is the News?

Shortly after Stalin's death, Russia was ready to announce one bit of news. Georgi Malenkov* had become the new premier of Russia. Four other communists, who had worked with Stalin, would help the new premier.

How did Malenkov become the new ruler of Russia? What part will other leaders play in this new government? What is happening

---

*Gā-ôr'jĕ Mà-lĕn-kŏff'. In the United States, Malenkov is often pronounced with the accent on the second or first syllable.

inside Russia today? We do not really know.

We do know that Russia's 200 million people did not vote for their new leaders. Malenkov may have been chosen by Stalin. Like Stalin, Russia's new ruler must use force to stay in power. He must use police and soldiers to make the people obey.

Who Is Malenkov?

The outside world knows very little about Malenkov. His pictures show him to be a short, fat man. Malenkov spends most of his time at his office. He does not like to go to parties or talk with strangers. His wife and two children live in a house outside Moscow.

How long will Malenkov be able to control Russia? Will he be like Stalin? We must wait to see.

Will Hawaii Be Our 49th State?

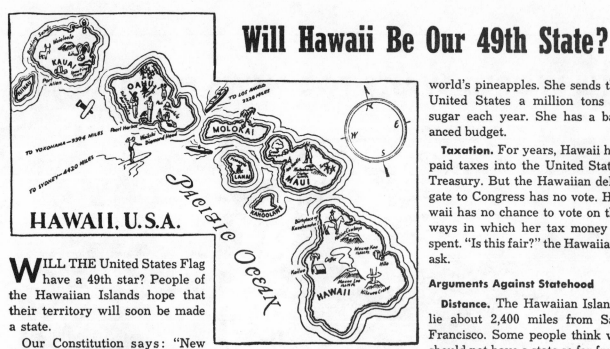

HAWAII, U.S.A.

WILL THE United States Flag have a 49th star? People of the Hawaiian Islands hope that their territory will soon be made a state.

Our Constitution says: "New States may be admitted by the Congress into this Union." Since 1900, when Hawaii became a United States territory, she has asked for statehood 17 times.

In recent weeks, the question of statehood for Hawaii has been discussed in Congress. Pretend you are a member of the Senate. Here are some of the arguments you would hear for and against admitting the Hawaiian Islands.

Arguments for Statehood

Fitness. Hawaii was promised statehood whenever she was ready for it. Hawaiians have been ready for a long time. Almost all Hawaiian people can read and write. For many years, their schools have taught the American way of life.

Wealth. Hawaii's big industries are sugar, pineapples, and tourists. She cans three-fourths of the world's pineapples. She sends the United States a million tons of sugar each year. She has a balanced budget.

Taxation. For years, Hawaii has paid taxes into the United States Treasury. But the Hawaiian delegate to Congress has no vote. Hawaii has no chance to vote on the ways in which her tax money is spent. "Is this fair?" the Hawaiians ask.

Arguments Against Statehood

Distance. The Hawaiian Islands lie about 2,400 miles from San Francisco. Some people think we should not have a state so far from our mainland.

Representation. Hawaii has a population of about 500,000 people. As a state, the Islands would have two Senators and one Representative in the United States Congress. Some people ask why Hawaii's half a million people should have the same Senate vote as Ohio's eight million people or Wisconsin's three million.

Boy Kings

Earlier this year, you read about the "boy kings," Feisal and Hussein (WEEKLY READER for September 22, p. 11). This month, the two boys, who are cousins, were officially enthroned.

King Feisal II of Iraq took the throne in Baghdad, a city famous in *Arabian Nights* legend. After the King took his oath of office, a 101-gun salute was fired in his honor. At night, a huge fireworks display went off over the Tigris River.

The little kingdom of Jordan welcomed its new king at Amman. King Hussein I began his reign by taking an oath before Jordan's Parliament. Amman's streets were gaily decorated. Crowds of people gathered on balconies and roofs cheered and shouted Hussein's praises.

King Feisal II   **King Hussein I**

News Around the World

In the Air:

"Taxi, sir?"

"No, thanks. I'm waiting for a helicopter."

That conversation takes place nearly every day at several New York and New Jersey airports. Helicopters are now carrying passengers as well as mail. The "sky buses" can fly from La Guardia Field to the International Airport in about ten minutes. Sometimes it takes a taxi two hours.

Helicopters may someday carry nearly all air passengers going less than 200 miles. Bigger two-engine 'copters will haul 30 to 40 passengers.

The chimpanzee looks glum about wearing his old dark suit. • • • Other TV workers will wear bright clothes for color TV.

California Academy of Science

Color TV Arrives

COLOR TV is here! Many test programs have been made. The "Kukla, Fran, and Ollie" show was one of those tested in color recently. Kukla's nose and cheeks looked as red as the audience had hoped.

A few months ago, TV colors were too bright. Now, they are beginning to look more real. Strawberry ice cream in TV ads looks so good that you can almost taste it. Color TV pictures taken outdoors are not so clear as pictures taken inside. However, plans are being made to telecast California's Tournament of Roses Parade in color.

Now that tests have been made, TV men are waiting for the government O. K. Any day, they hope to be told to go ahead. The rush to make color programs and color sets will then begin. Color TV sets may be on sale by next fall.

It may be several years before most Americans have color TV sets. The first sets will cost $700 to $1,000.

Persons with black-and-white sets can be happy about one thing. Their old sets will be able to receive color programs in black and white. No special attachments will be needed.

Color TV will not come overnight. Programs cost too much. For several years, there may be more black-and-white than color shows.

Headaches for TV Stations

Color TV is wonderful, but it makes many problems. Four to six times as much light will be needed for color TV. Planning costume and scenery colors that go well together is another problem. An actor cannot change his suit at the last minute. He might spoil the whole color plan.

Actors will have to use different make-up for color TV. If their make-up is not just right, their faces may look green or red.

Cameramen will have to learn some new tricks, too. Color cameras must be used differently. These cameras are almost twice as large as older TV cameras. They are hard to move around.

Color TV is coming. Keep that old red shirt. You may need it for a TV quiz program—in COLOR!

Rounding Up This Week's News

These men are the first to stand on top of the earth's tallest mountain. This summer, they climbed to the top of Mount Everest. It is far across the Pacific Ocean. Mount Everest stands on the border between the lands of Nepal (nĕ-pâl′) and Tibet (tĭ-bĕt′).

The man with the flags is Edmund Hillary. He lives in New Zealand. It is a large island near Australia. Mr. Hillary is a beekeeper. He ate some of his bees' honey as he climbed Mount Everest.

The other man is Tensing Norkay. His home is in India. He has been a guide for mountain climbers for 20 years. As a boy, Tensing herded yaks on the sides of mountains. Yaks look like cows with long hair.

They have climbed higher than any other person.

Associated Press

Science News: Plants

Leaves

Stem

Seed

Roots

H. Armstrong Roberts

Sally takes care of her plants.
She gives the plants water.

Plants have roots and stems.
They have leaves.

ESCAPE TO FREEDOM

This woman escaped from Czechoslovakia in this tank.

A HUGE passenger plane landed in New York City the other day. Inside the plane were 84 joyful people. Some of them had waited years for this day. They were all refugees who had escaped from countries controlled by Russia.

This group is one of the largest groups of refugees to fly to the United States. However, it is not the first or the last. Congress passed a special law last summer. This law allows 209,000 refugees to come to the U. S. during the next three years.

Life in Communist countries is miserable for people who do not belong to the Communist party. Communist leaders tell the people what to believe and where they should work. Communist teachers teach the people what the government tells them—whether it is true or not. The police watch everyone day and night.

Thousands of people who love freedom try to run away. Many are caught, but a few escape. Here are three true stories of people who risked death to win their freedom.

► For four years, a Czechoslovakian man and three friends worked quietly at night. They were building a make-believe tank on an old truck body. Finally, they were ready. One night, the four men, two women, and two children hid inside the homemade tank. Quietly, they drove toward the West German border. Communist soldiers who saw the tank thought that it was real. They did not stop it. By morning, the Czechs had driven into West Germany. Today, those eight brave people are living in the United States.

► A Polish pilot saw his chance one day. He was flying his MiG with some other planes on a practice flight. Suddenly, he ducked his plane away from the others. He flew to an island near Denmark. He had to crash-land in a grove of trees. He did not care. The Polish pilot was alive and free at last.

► Last fall, a Czech family hid themselves in a railroad car filled with lumber. For two days, they lay there. They thought they would die of thirst. Finally, the train rolled into the U. S. zone of Austria. The family was free.

Americans sing of the "land of the free and the home of the brave." But we often forget how wonderful freedom is. People living in Communist countries risk their lives for that freedom!

"It's wonderful to walk on free land," these refugees to the U. S. seem to say.

BACKGROUND TO THE NEWS · Indo-China War

AT GENEVA, the stage is set for peace talks on Asia. (See the front-page story.) The "hottest" war in Asia is now being fought in Indo-China. Let's turn the spotlight on this section of the world to see what is happening there.

Indo-China is made up of three states: Viet-Nam (vĕt'näm'), Cambodia (kăm-bō'dĭ-a), and Laos (lä'ōz). These three states are associated with France in the French Union. As "Associated States," they have some freedom but they do not have complete independence.

The desire for independence is strong among the people of Indo-China. The communists have taken advantage of this feeling to turn many thousands of Indo-Chinese against the French. For eight years, the country has been torn by civil war.

Fighting on one side are French soldiers and loyal Indo-Chinese troops. On the other side are followers of the communists, many of whom have been trained and equipped by Red (Communist) China.

War goods made in Czechoslovakia have been shipped through Russia and China to the communists in Indo-China. On the other side, the United States has sent guns, ammunition, and planes to aid the French.

Key to Southeast Asia

To the United States, and to all free nations, the defense of Indo-China is of the greatest importance. Because of its location, Indo-China is a gateway to all of southeast Asia — to Thailand, Burma, Malaya, India, Indonesia, and the Philippines.

Control of Indo-China would lead the communists to a treasure in natural resources. Southeast Asia is rich in such raw materials as tin, rubber, oil, and iron ore. The "rice bowl" of Burma, Thailand, and Indo-China is one of the world's greatest rice-producing regions.

The Long, Long War

During eight years of war, neither side has been able to win complete victory. The French have

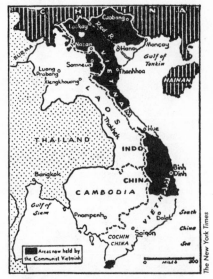

BATTLEGROUND. In what part of Indo-China do the communists control the most territory?

many good soldiers, modern equipment, and control of the skies over Indo-China. But the communists are wise in the ways of fighting in jungles and rice paddies. They attack by night, bombing bridges and destroying outposts.

About 30 million Indo-Chinese hope the day will soon come when they will be self-governing. Can they win independence and still remain free from communist control? We must wait and see.

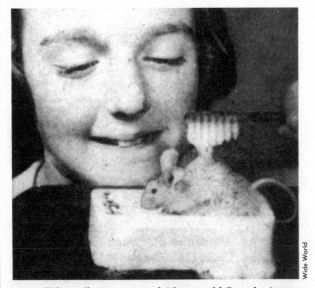

"Simon," pet mouse of 12-year-old Pamela Anson, doesn't seem to mind taking a bath. His mistress uses a toothbrush, a toy tub, and plenty of suds to give Simon his weekly bath. Pamela lives in England.

Animal Oddities

▶ A LARGE RED ANT upset the schedule of a train in Texas. It crawled into a semaphore and blocked the signal mechanism.

▶ OTTERS in the Philadelphia zoo have been seen picking up paper cups and boxes dropped by visitors and putting them in a neat pile.

▶ A DOG in Detroit has lived with a flock of chickens so long that she adds her howls to the roosters' crowing at dawn.

▶ BROWN-BANDED COCKROACHES, it is found, aren't too harmful inside a television set. All they do is eat some of the excess glue.

▶ A SEA LION at the Cincinnati zoo was operated on for removal of her four tonsils.

▶ THE BROLGA, an Australian crane, loves to dance. About 100 brolgas have been seen in a circle, imitating the steps of a leader in the center.

Power for Progress

Compare Edison's first electric power plant (left) with the atomic power plant of the future (above). The model of the atomic plant shows an atomic "furnace" (left), a water boiler (center), generator, and power lines.

ATOMIC POWER WILL LIGHT YOUR HOME

WHAT GOOD is an electric light bulb without electricity? This was the problem facing Thomas A. Edison 75 years ago. He had just made the first successful electric light—one of the greatest inventions of all time. But his job had only begun.

Edison had to find some way to make (generate) large amounts of electricity. He also had to learn how to distribute this electricity. He had to find some way to send the electricity into homes and offices.

Edison Solves His Problems

Edison set to work improving and developing the electric generator. The important parts of this machine are coils of wire and magnets. Electricity is made when the coils are kept turning inside a magnetic field.

Some kind of power is needed to turn the coils of wire. Edison's generators were run by steam from coal-heated water boilers. Many electric power plants today use this same kind of power. Others use the power of water falling over a dam.

Edison's second problem was distributing electricity. He designed such things as light sockets, safety fuses, and meters. He worked and slept in the ditches where his men were laying underground wires.

Three years after inventing the electric light, Edison opened the first electric power plant. This plant was the beginning of a great new business. Today, the electric business has over 50 million customers in the United States alone.

Taming the Atomic Giant

Edison captured and tamed the giant power of electricity. Today, scientists are working with another giant—atomic power.

If you live in or near Pittsburgh, Pennsylvania, you may be lighting your home in two or three years with electricity generated by atomic power. A Pittsburgh electric company is working with the United States Government in building a new atomic power plant.

The generators in the new plant will run by steam, much as Edison's did. The big **difference is that** this steam is made with heat from an atomic furnace.

The new plant will cost about $85,000,000. In building the plant, the Government and businessmen hope to learn how to build other plants at less cost. Later, atomic power plants will be built in other parts of the country. Perhaps one of these plants will serve your

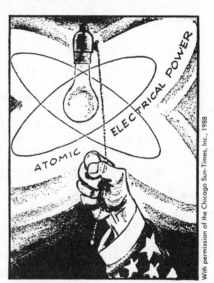

What do a light bulb and Uncle Sam's sleeve tell about a use for atomic power?

town. That mighty giant, atomic power, will then become your servant.

Atomic Power Around the World

Great Britain is one step ahead of the United States in building an atomic power plant. Work has already started on such a plant in England. This plant will be finished by 1956.

Much of what we read tells of the use of atomic power for war. But the two new atomic power plants show how this force can be used in peacetime.

In many parts of the world, there is neither coal nor water power to produce electricity. In these places, atomic power can work miracles.

Our Pledge to the Flag Is Changed

Did you see the Flag today? Did you say the pledge to the Flag?

This summer, the words of the pledge were changed. Two more words are in the new pledge. The two new words are *under God*.

The leaders of our country changed the pledge. They sent the new pledge to President Eisenhower. He liked it.

Now everyone is learning to say the new pledge.

Pledge of Allegiance to the Flag

I pledge allegiance to the flag of the United States of America and to the republic for which it stands, one nation, under God, indivisible, with liberty and justice for all.

"Greek" to Us. A British architect has solved a puzzle archaeologists have been working on for many years. After long and careful study, the man translated writing on an ancient clay tablet that was dug up years ago in Greece. He found that the writing was really a very early Greek language. This seems to prove that the Greeks knew how to write 1400 to 1500 years before the birth of Christ.

To make it easier to read, the writing has been copied onto a drawing of the tablet (pictured left). It says: "Kerowos, a shepherd of the place, A-Si-Ja-Ti-Ja, looking after the animals of Thalamatis, one man." Greek students must have had pretty good memories!

Hops said, "I'll get Frisky to play."

Hops said, "You have mumps."

Frisky said, "I don't have mumps."

New Cars + Old Cars = More Traffic + More Repairs

Fred Eldean Organization, Inc.

Ford Motor Co.

SPARKLING NEW. *Notice the long, low body design, the wire wheels, and the front grill on this 1956 car.* **WATCH OUT FOR FENDERS!** *The ever-growing lines of traffic in our cities are a real problem. This year, more than ever, the car-repair business is booming.*

SUPPOSE a modern Rip Van Winkle awoke today after sleeping for 20 years. Suppose he wandered into the town where you live. You find him staring at a new 1956 car.

He is surprised by many things —push-button windows, air conditioning. . . . "Where is the clutch for shifting gears?" Rip Van Winkle asks.

"Oh," you answer, "we've had the automatic shift on cars for several years. But look what's new this year—four buttons on this car control all the shifting. And, see,

it has a record player as well as a radio. There are safety seat belts and safety door latches. The seat belts keep passengers from being suddenly pushed forward. The latches keep the doors from popping open if there's an accident."

Not quite believing what he sees, our modern Rip rubs his eyes and looks around. On the street before him, he sees a solid stream of traffic. Something else has changed since Rip went to sleep 20 years ago.

More Cars, More Traffic

In 1935, there were about 26 million cars, buses, and trucks in the United States. Today, there are nearly 60 million. By 1965, there will be 81 million.

In 1935, motorists drove 230 billion miles. In 1955, they will drive about one *trillion* miles — almost four times as far as they drove in 1935. One trillion miles equals more than 200,000 round trips to the moon.

What explains our growing fleet of cars? For one thing, our growing population needs more trucks, more school buses, more taxis. People have more money and

more leisure time to spend on cars today. There are more "two-car" families. Housewives do more shopping in stores on the edges of towns.

More Cars, More Repairs

As the number of cars rises, so does the age of the average car. About 23 million Americans drive cars that are from four to nine years old.

Americans now spend over seven billion dollars a year for car repairs. Automobile repair shops and service stations are swamped with business. There are more cars to handle, and each job is harder to do.

One garage man explains it this way. "When they take a V-8 engine and start hanging air conditioners, power steering, power brakes, and other gadgets on it, it becomes a major operation just to clean the spark plugs. Sometimes, we can't even see the part we want to work on."

Yes, Rip Van Winkle, things have changed since you went to sleep 20 years ago. Would you care to trade in your 1935 "buggy" for a '56 model?

GOOD-BY TO CHURCHILL

Britain's Prime Minister Resigns

LOYAL SERVANT. Sir Winston Churchill's service to the British Government began during the reign of Queen Elizabeth's great-great-grandmother, Queen Victoria.

AT THE age of nine, Winston Churchill had double pneumonia. At 18, he fell 30 feet from a tree. At 24, he rode in a cavalry charge against 3,000 riflemen. At 45, he lived through two plane crashes. At 47, he fell off a camel. At 57, he was knocked flat by a New York taxi. And at the age of 79, he almost died as a result of a stroke.

None of these things stopped Sir Winston. But now old age has slowed his steps. One day this month, he walked into Buckingham Palace. He bowed to Queen Elizabeth and kissed her hand. He told her he wished to resign as Prime Minister of the United Kingdom.

The Queen did as the "grand old man" wished. She accepted his resignation and asked Sir Anthony Eden to become the new Prime Minister. A great chapter in history was ended.

Master of English

Today, Sir Winston is world famous for his brilliant mind, his wit, and his wisdom. Yet, as a boy, he nearly failed at school. "The cleverer boys," he said, "all went on to learn Latin and Greek. . . .

But we were considered such dunces that we could learn only English."

That schoolboy grew up to be one of the great masters of the English language. His stirring speeches gave hope to the British during World War II. His writing won for Sir Winston the Nobel Prize for literature. This award is one of the highest honors that can come to a writer.

A Stormy Career

As a young man, Churchill was a war correspondent for a London newspaper. Having been trained as a soldier, he often took part in the wars of which he wrote. He was captured once, during the Boer War in Africa. But he escaped and hiked 300 miles to freedom.

After this adventure, Churchill returned to England and was elected to Parliament. Since 1900, his life has centered around the House of Commons.

Few men in politics have had as many setbacks as Sir Winston. He was defeated five times when running for office. At times, when he lost government jobs, it looked as if his career were ended. But after more than 40 years' hard work, he became Prime Minister. He will go down in history as one of Britain's heroes.

Rounding Up the News

More than one million Volkswagens have rolled off this assembly line during the last ten years.

Here Comes the *Volkswagen!*

Can you identify the foreign cars you see on the highways today? Can you identify one of Germany's most popular automobiles? It is the "people's car" or *Volkswagen* (fōlks'vä-gĕn.)

This beetlelike, road-hugging car holds five people. It has a top speed of 65 miles an hour and goes 30 miles on a gallon of gasoline.

The main Volkswagen factory is in Wolfsburg, Germany. Plans are now being made for a Volkswagen factory in Brunswick, New Jersey. Here, the German cars would be assembled for the American market.

After World War II, many of Germany's cities and most of her factories lay in ruins. Wolfsburg had been bombed three times.

Today, thanks to the popularity of the Volkswagen, the town has been rebuilt. This car is one of the things that has helped West Germany's amazing industrial recovery.

Where East Meets West

Germany's old capital, Berlin, lies in East Germany. But only part of the city is under the control of the Communists. West Berlin is a free city.

It is not easy for Germans to cross the heavily guarded East German border. But, inside Berlin, they can find less dangerous ways to pass into the free part of the city. From there, they can be flown to West Germany.

West Berlin is crowded with refugees. Where have they come from? Where are they going to live?

Today, about 15,000 East Germans are escaping to West Germany every month. These refugees all have stories to tell. Some have come west to escape arrest by the Communists. Others want to be free to work or worship as they please.

It is not easy for West Germany to find jobs and homes for hundreds of thousands of refugees. Some have found homes in the United States and other countries. But many are still living in refugee camps.

Russia Makes Some Changes

RUSSIA's leaders act almost as if they were playing the game of musical chairs. The last time the music stopped, Georgi Malenkov lost his seat in the government of Russia.

Malenkov (mŭ-lyĕn′kŭf) had been Russia's Premier for two years. He was one of a small group of Communists who took charge of Russia after Joseph Stalin (stä′lĕn) died. This group decided who should be Premier. Russia's 215 million people had no chance to choose their leader in a free election.

Now Malenkov has lost his job the way he won it—by the decision of a few men. This small group of men has picked a new Premier. He is Nikolai Bulganin (bŏŏl-gà′-nyĭn).

"I See My Guilt"

Malenkov said that he decided to resign for the good of the country. He stated, "I see clearly my guilt for the unsatisfactory state of affairs in agriculture."

Russia has not been able to hide the fact that many things have gone wrong with the country's farming. Grain, potato, and cotton crops are poor. As much as one-fourth of a grain crop is sometimes lost because of late harvesting. Other grain has rotted for lack of storage space.

This hard-working woman hitches a horse to a wagon on a state farm in Russia.

Russia has less livestock today than it had in 1928. In 1953, nearly half of Russia's farm machines were reported to be broken down and in need of repair.

What Causes the Trouble?

Russia is the world's largest country. It is as big as all of North America. However, nearly half of Russia is covered by permafrost (permanently frozen ground). Deserts fill another million square miles of Russia.

More than three-fourths of Russia is too cold or too dry for farming. Even where temperature and rainfall are right, the soil is often poor.

To raise enough crops, Russia needs hard-working farmers, the best farming methods, modern machines, plenty of fertilizer, and

good seeds. Does Russia have these things? We do not know for sure. But we guess that the answer is "no" or "not enough."

Under Communist rule, the farmers have had to give up their own land. Today's farmer lives on a *kolkhoz* (kŏl-ĸôz′), or "collective farm," owned by the state. Following is one Russian's report on his family's life on a *kolkhoz*:

"We had meat three or four times a year. During most of the year we ate boiled potatoes. We lived in a one-room house and slept on the floor. For 27 villages there were just four tractors—often out of repair."

Can Russia solve her farm problems by substituting one Communist leader for another? What do you think?

Dr. Salk worked many hours in his laboratory.

International

Science News:

A Great Doctor

This month, many girls and boys are getting polio "shots." Then, these children will not get sick with polio. For the first time, there is a way to stop polio.

Dr. Jonas Salk found the way to make polio shots. He worked for about six years to find the best things to use. He tried many things that didn't work. But he kept trying.

Disneyland: Picture Story

Walt Disney Productions, Inc.

"Look!" says Walt Disney. "My big, new park is open. We call it Disneyland. It is in California.

"There are wonderful things to see. Let's ride around the park. We can go in the old-time train.

"Here we are in the world of make-believe. Look at the castle! Sleeping Beauty is inside."

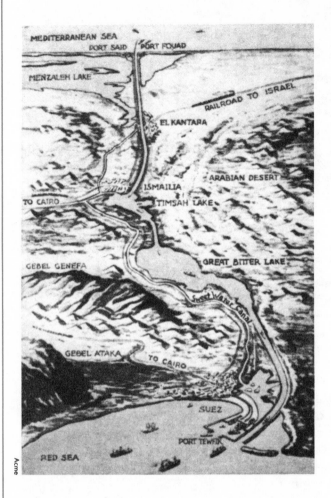

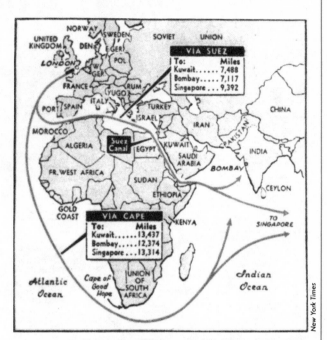

From London to Bombay, India, is it shorter to go by way of the Suez Canal or by way of the Cape of Good Hope?

◄ *Here is a close-up map of the famous Suez Canal. Moving ships may pass each other in the wider lake sections of the Canal, but not where the channel is narrow.*

STORM OVER SUEZ

A STORM broke over the Suez Canal this summer. Like many storms, this one started with a sudden flash of lightning and a big clap of thunder.

Surprise Flash

The "lightning" was a news flash from the country of Egypt. Egypt's leader, Gamal Abdel Nasser (nà'sĕr), reported that his country was taking over the Suez Canal.

Linking the Mediterranean with the Red Sea, the Suez Canal is a short cut from Europe to India and the East. This famous waterway does run through Egypt. For 81 years, however, it had been operated by the Suez Canal Company. This company was owned for the greatest part by French businessmen and the government of Great Britain.

Thunder Follows Lightning

"Thunder" of the Suez storm echoed from Great Britain and France. These countries were alarmed by Egypt's move. The Suez Canal, they said, is too important to be controlled by Egypt alone. It is used by ships of many different countries, carrying goods to all parts of the world.

Some 22 of these countries sent men to a meeting in London to study the puzzle of Suez. Could Egypt, by herself, keep the Canal in good working condition? Would Egypt let all ships pass freely, as in the past? Would Egypt be able to protect the Suez Canal in case of war?

Storm Clouds

It was agreed at London that the Canal does belong to Egypt. But there was disagreement as to who should operate the waterway. Of 22 countries, 18 thought the Canal should be run by a group of nations. India said that other nations should give only advice, and permit Egypt to run the Canal by herself.

Egypt did not take part in the London meeting. Rather, she called for still another meeting and more talks. So the storm clouds linger over Suez. Keep watching for more news from this part of the world.

🎥 World Parade

800 Miles Without a Stop Light on New York-Chicago Superhighway

The Indiana Turnpike cuts through lovely farm country. *Left:* Four turnpikes make up the New York-Chicago superhighway.

The last link in an 800-mile stretch of superhighway will be finished next week. Road builders in Indiana have set November 15 as the date to finish the last 16 miles of the Indiana Turnpike. The 16-mile stretch connects the turnpike with Chicago.

The Indiana Turnpike is an important addition to our country's roads. Its completion means the completion of a superhighway between Chicago and New York.

Superhighways Are Speedy

A superhighway between Chicago and New York means an almost nonstop ride between the two cities. There are no traffic lights to stop a driver. The four-lane road goes over or under railroad crossings and highway intersections. Cars going in opposite directions have separate lanes. On the Indiana Turnpike, the east and west lanes are 56 feet apart.

Motorists will make stops for gasoline and food and rest, of course. The only other stops will be at toll stations at state lines. Each state charges a toll from trucks and passenger cars using its turnpike. Thus, in time the road pays for itself.

Toll Charges

A motorist driving a passenger car will pay a total of about ten dollars in tolls to travel the distance between New York and Chicago. However, by using the turnpikes instead of regular roads, he will save nine hours driving time between the two cities.

The New York-Chicago superhighway has been in the making for over 20 years. The superhighway has been put together link by link as the different states built turnpikes.

Workmen put a finishing touch to a section of the Indiana Turnpike. They are sealing cracks to keep moisture out of cement. ➡

Pennsylvania Turnpike Oldest

The Pennsylvania Turnpike is the oldest. It was finished over 20 years ago. The Ohio Turnpike was finished a year ago, and the New Jersey Turnpike about four years ago. The Indiana Turnpike completes the New York-Chicago superhighway. A trip along the superhighway will take the tourist through fertile farm lands and across mountains. The superhighways will take tourists around big cities, too.

Russia Crushes Hungary

A SICKENING tragedy has taken place in Hungary. In Poland, leaders won more freedom from the Soviet Union (Russia). These leaders demanded that Russian tanks leave. The tanks left.

"If Poland can win more freedom, why can't we?" people in Hungary began saying.

Freedom Fighters

Suddenly, groups of freedom fighters rose up all over Hungary. Workingmen, farmers, teen-agers, and women fought with whatever weapons they could find. Tens of thousands of soldiers of the Hungarian army joined the fight against Russia.

Budapest became a shattered city as Russian tanks pounded at rebel strongholds. The Communist government tried to stop the fighting by making promises of freedom. The secret radio stations kept repeating these words: "We won't stop fighting until the Russians leave."

The Russians agreed to leave. Their tanks rumbled out of Budapest.

Alas, the retreat was a trick. Without warning, a quarter of a million fresh Russian soldiers and some 4,500 tanks poured into Hungary. Russia began a savage, all-out attack to crush the gallant freedom fighters.

Finally, the last signal of the last Hungarian Freedom Station reached the outside world: "Civilized people of the world. . . . Help us. . . . Save us. SOS—SOS. . . . The light vanishes. The shadows grow darker from hour to hour. Listen to our cry. . . . God be with you and with us." Silence!

U.N. Brands Russia

The world watched in horror. The U.N. branded Russia's attack as a violation of the U.N. Charter and a move to make Hungary a slave state. Russia said, "Keep out of Hungary!" But U.N. delegates voted to send observers into Hungary.

Thousands of refugees fled for their lives. President Eisenhower said the U.S. would take 5,000 of them. Other nations offered help.

This one picture of battle-scarred Budapest is worth ten thousand words.

International

Mystery Carved in Stone

American Museum of Natural History (James Chapin)

SCIENCE IN THE NEWS It was Easter Sunday, 1722, when a Dutch ship dropped anchor off an island in the South Pacific. A strange sight greeted the crew. Lining the cliffs of the island were huge stone heads.

Ever since the discovery of Easter Island, the stone heads have remained a mystery. Who were the ancient people who carved the heads? How did they get to the island?

New clues to the mystery of Easter Island have recently been uncovered by a Norwegian explorer, Thor Heyerdahl.

In the past, it was thought that Easter Island had been the home of just one kind of ancient people. The Heyerdahl expedition found the remains of three different civilizations. "The gigantic stone statues," says Mr. Heyerdahl, "belong to the second of these three epochs.

"Our excavations uncovered a number of large and small stone statues of other material and of a very different style from the stone heads of the second epoch. A number of these earliest statues showed striking similarities to prehistoric statues on the nearest shores of South America."

Was Easter Island, then, first settled by people from South America? Mr. Heyerdahl will spend two years studying the findings of his expedition.

Smokey Bear Wants Your Help

Smokey Bear is growing up. A few years ago, Smokey was a little bear cub. He had lost his mother in a big forest fire.

Today, Smokey is a large bear. He lives in a cage at the zoo in Washington, D.C.

Smokey is busy helping the U.S. Forest Service. Smokey's picture is seen in many places. He asks us to remember to keep forest fires from starting.

Smokey knows you are old enough to help him. You keep away from matches. You tell people not to be careless with fire. You can help smaller children learn fire safety, too.

Smokey looks at his poster picture.

U.S. Forest Service

Smokey wants your help. Will you help him?

Postman uses "Lolli-Pups" to make friends.

Postmen Give "Lolli-Pups"

"Lolli-Pups" are candy. The postman has them in his pocket. He gives them to unfriendly dogs along his route. The "Lolli-Pups" may help make the dogs more friendly.

Last year, many postmen were bitten by unfriendly dogs.

The United States Post Office Department hopes the "Lolli-Pups" will help keep the postmen safe.

Does your postman carry "Lolli-Pups" in his pocket? The next time you see the postman, ask him about "Lolli-Pups."

Do you know any unfriendly dogs in your neighborhood that might need a "Lolli-Pup"?

News Report

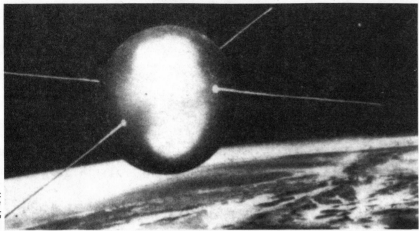

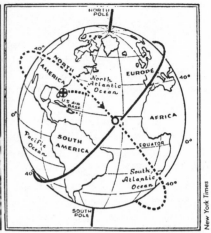

United Press

New York Times

A U.S. satellite, a model of which is shown above, will be launched from Florida. Its path, or orbit, is shown by the broken line on the map. The solid line is one of the early orbits of the Russian satellite.

Man Launches Space Craft Number One

October 4, 1957, and September 20, 1519, are two dates that belong together. (See the box at the lower right.) In September 1519, man's first ocean craft started around the earth. In October 1957, man's first space craft started around the earth.

The Russian sputnik (spo͞ot′-nĭk), or satellite, really is a space craft. It is a "ship" without a crew, but traveling with a load. The sputnik's load is radio equipment.

Other craft of many kinds will follow the sputnik into space.

U.S. Space Craft

U.S. scientists are planning to send up small test satellites in the next few weeks. Larger U.S. satellites will be launched next spring. A satellite carrier is being tested.

By the time you read this, an American rocket may be farther out in space than anything man

Our satellite carrier is a three-stage rocket. The picture shows the second stage being positioned for test firing. The launching tower is at Cape Canaveral, Florida.

has made before. This rocket is ready to be launched at Eniwetok (ĕn′ĭ-wē′tŏk), a Pacific island.

Elevator to Space

The Eniwetok rocket will have a head start. A giant balloon will lift it 20 miles. The rocket is planned to blast off from the balloon and go about 4,000 miles higher. It may reach the moon.

Some scientists say that by the time you finish high school, space craft will be carrying passengers. Man has sent his first craft into space. Soon, man may go, too. All aboard for Out There!

United Press

Around Our World . . . Faster and Faster

1522 First Ship Around the World   3 Years
Ferdinand Magellan's ship *Victoria:* Left Spain September 20, 1519; returned September 8, 1522.

1929 First Airship Around the World   20 Days, 4 Hours
German dirigible *Graf Zeppelin:* Friedrichshafen, Germany, and return via Tokyo, Los Angeles, Lakehurst (N.J.) —21,700 miles.

1949 First Nonstop Airplane Around the World 94 Hours, 1 Minute
Air Force Boeing B-50 Superfortress *Lucky Lady II:* Fort Worth, Texas and return—23,452 miles.

1957 First Man-Made Satellite Around the World   96.2 Minutes
Russian 23-inch sphere *Sputnik;* launched October 4.

'Let's Get Together'
Six European Nations Set New Trade Plan

Shown in black are countries that have taken one step toward working together in a more united Europe.

WILL THERE ever be a "United States of Europe"? Many Europeans have long dreamed of such a union. They have seen United States grow strong together in America. "Why," they ask, "couldn't we Europeans also unite for greater strength?"

Six European nations have now taken an important step toward working more closely together. France, West Germany, Italy, Belgium, the Netherlands, and Luxembourg have signed a trade agreement. Within the next 15 years, these countries hope to set up a "common market" in Europe.

Too Many Markets

A market, as you know, is a place where things are sold. You can think of an entire country as a market. So the six nations are like six separate markets.

Today, a German car costs more in the Italian market than in the German market. Why? Italy also makes cars. Naturally, she wants to sell as many of her own cars as possible. So she puts a tax, or *tariff* (tăr'ĭf) on cars sent to Italy from other countries. The tariff raises the price of German or British or American cars sold in Italy.

Tariffs are like walls around a country. They do not stop trade entirely. But they do keep goods from moving freely from one country to another.

Now—a Common Market

Little by little, the six European nations hope to break down their tariff walls. Instead of six separate markets, they plan to become one common market. Then a German car could be sold in Italy without having its price raised by a tariff.

The new trade agreement includes other plans. In time, workmen will be allowed to move freely from one country to another, to go wherever they are needed. The six nations will share their discoveries and resources for atomic power. A "European bank" will loan money to help new industries get started.

What Lies Ahead?

The trade agreement must now be approved by the parliaments of the six nations. It will take about 15 years for all the plans to be completely worked out.

If these plans succeed, what is the next step? It could be closer political ties. It could be a "United States of Europe."

"Welcome, neighbor," is the title of the cartoon above. "History repeats?" is the question asked by the cartoonist who (below) recalls the beginning of the U.S.A.

WHAT'S COOKING IN THE U.S.A.?

A LOOK of surprise passed over Mrs. Stone's face when her young son walked into the house.

"Why, Phil! I thought you had planned to have dinner at Jim's house."

Phil looked sheepish. "I was mistaken, Mother. I'm not expected until tomorrow night."

"Oh, dear," said Mrs. Stone. "Your father and I have to leave in a few minutes for that dinner party. I won't have time to fix your dinner."

"Don't worry about me, Mother. I'll just get a meal out of the freezer."

Half an hour later, Phil sat before the TV set eating a hot, ready-made platter of chicken, mashed potatoes, and peas. At the dinner party, his mother buttered a fluffy biscuit.

"I wish I could bake biscuits like these," she said.

Smiling, her hostess replied, "But I didn't make them. I bought them ready to bake at the store.

To tell you another secret, that soup you liked so much came frozen in a can."

Thirty years ago, Mrs. Stone's mother spent five to six hours a day cooking meals. Today, Mrs. Stone spends less than half that time. She buys much of her food already prepared—bread, baby foods, cake mixes, canned fruits and vegetables, and frozen foods of all kinds.

Sixteen years ago, the average supermarket handled about 3,000 items. Today's housewife can choose among some 6,000 items. Americans are eating a more varied and healthful diet than ever before.

Thanks to Science

Our changing food habits owe much to the modern, scientific ways of canning and freezing food. Science has also given us new ways to market food.

Several supermarkets have set up vending machines outside the

The "automatic dairy" sells milk in quart and half-gallon cartons.

store. After closing hours, customers can still buy for themselves dairy products, canned goods, pastry, eggs, meat, and frozen food.

Scientists are now working on better ways to sell complete, hot meals through vending machines. New ideas, as well as new foods, are "cooking" in this country.

The Mountain That Is Being Changed Into a Statue

Hi there, Girls and Boys,

Did you use to enjoy modeling figures out of clay? Perhaps you still do. Then, what do you think of a sculptor who is modeling a figure with dynamite?

The sculptor is Korczak Ziolkowski who is blasting a giant figure of the Sioux chief, Crazy Horse, out of the granite in the Black Hills of South Dakota. Since 1949, the sculptor has blasted several hundred thousand tons of granite.

Sculptor Korczak Ziolkowski is shown here with model of Crazy Horse statue he is blasting out of granite mountain in the Black Hills.

He still has several million tons to go. However, when he has finished, a giant 563-foot figure of Crazy Horse on a horse will stand where there is now an arched granite mountain.

Visiting the place where the statue is being made prompted me to go on across the border to Montana. I wanted to see the place where the famous Battle of the Little Bighorn took place. There, on June 25, 1876, as you know, Custer and his band of 241 men were wiped out by Indians led by Crazy Horse and Sitting Bull.

The Indians won the battle. However, they didn't win back the *Paha Sapa* (the Indian name for the Black Hills). They had gone on the warpath because settlers had moved into their Paha Sapa hunting grounds. Now Crazy Horse is coming back to Paha Sapa under the skillful hands of an artist.

Almost any place is a fine hunting ground for Wee Brucie.

Your friend,

Tom Trott

Keeping Clean With Machines

Harold M. Lambert

Keeping clean is a big job.
Everything needs cleaning at times.
Streets, buildings, machines, cars!
Machines make some cleaning easier.
Some machines clean
other machines!

One big machine helps
to clean cars.
It makes quick work of getting
the dirt off a car.

Rub, rub! Swish, swish!
Men rub off the dirt.
Then, the machine sprays water
over all the car at one time.

J. Fred Muggs Changes Jobs

J. Fred Muggs is leaving a television show. He is a chimpanzee. Have you ever seen him on television?

On the television show, J. Fred was dressed in many different clothes. He did funny tricks. He made people laugh. Many people liked him. These people sent him fan letters.

Now, J. Fred will travel to many places. He will make more people laugh.

J. Fred has two owners. He lives with them in New Jersey.

International

J. Fred's funny tricks make people laugh.

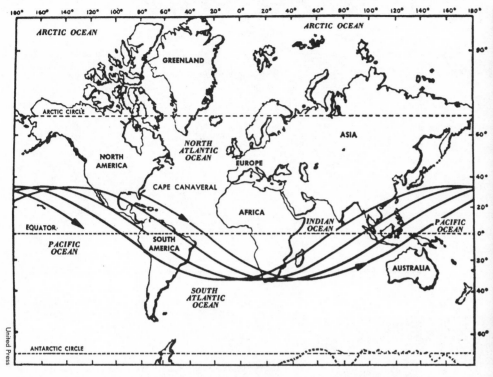

Our first satellite circles the earth in a zone extending about 2,000 miles on either side of the equator. Right—The satellite itself is above the top dark ring. ➡

Our First Satellite Reports from Space

Our first satellite is a singing traveler. The 1958 Alpha (also called "Explorer") is humming messages as it speeds through space.

The satellite is crammed with 11 pounds of instruments. The satellite can "feel" and "hear" as it travels.

A Voice from Space

Alpha has a voice with which to report what it feels and hears. The voice comes from two tiny radio stations inside Alpha. Alpha hums its report.

You may have heard Alpha humming from space on radio or television. The hum is actually a many-part song. Each part is one kind of information being sent by Alpha. Stations on earth separate the blended hum into its different parts.

Alpha is heard singing around the earth. About 12 *minitrack* stations have special "ears" listening to the far-off singer. These ears are so sensitive that they could hear a traveler 20 times as far away as Alpha.

Travel Information

Alpha reports its own temperature, inside and out. The outside temperature is above 100 degrees (Fahrenheit). The inside temperature is a little more than 80 degrees.

The satellite reports that space is not completely empty. Alpha occasionally is struck by a bit of dust.

Alpha goes through rain, too. It is not the earth's kind of wet rain, but space rain of mysterious cosmic rays. They seem to be electrical rays. Some cosmic rays reach the earth.

Alpha's reports are full of information you will need when you sail out on the space ocean.

News Report

Supermarkets Spread Around the World

Supermarkets are on the move. They're spreading all over the world. They're also growing in number and size in our country.

Supermarkets are even going to fairs. Last year, Uncle Sam took one to a fair in Yugoslavia (yoo′gō-slä′vĭ-à). The year be-

Above: Follow the arrows to new supermarkets! You will find yourself going to four countries and a city in southeast Asia.

Wide World

Left: Here is a view of the new supermarket in Singapore. Can you read the language used there?

fore, a supermarket was displayed at a fair in Italy.

Fair Visitors Liked Supermarkets

Until the supermarkets were shown at these fairs, most people in the two countries had never even heard of a supermarket. They were surprised by what they saw: the packaged foods (especially the meats and vegetables), the carts, the check-out counters.

Now, both Yugoslavia and Italy have their first supermarkets. Within the past month, supermarkets were opened in other distant places. One was in the city of Singapore in southeastern Asia. The other was in Israel. (See map.) The first one in France is to open soon.

These supermarkets are not the first in foreign countries. There are some in South America, for example. The new stores, however, point up how an American product is being widely accepted. In countries where there are only one or two, more are planned and are being built.

Those persons who build the first supermarket in a foreign country can't be sure that the store will be a success. They think that housewives may want to keep to the old way of going to one store for meat and to many other shops for other things.

The owner of Italy's first supermarket, for example, thought that he was making the store too big. On opening day, he was surprised. The shelves were cleaned out by customers before they could be restocked. He now says that he needs a larger store.

Supermarkets Change in U.S.

Meantime, supermarkets are changing in our country. Bigger stores with bigger parking lots are being built. More nonfood items are being sold. Changes are being made to make shopping easier and faster.

Sub Blazes Trail Under the Arctic Ice

The *Nautilus* prepares to leave a Hawaiian Navy base at the start of the voyage.

Trace the route of the *Nautilus* with a pencil.

A sub found a new way of getting through the ice-filled waters of the Arctic Ocean. It went under the ice. The sub was the *Nautilus*. It blazed a new trail between the Atlantic and Pacific oceans.

The *Nautilus* started its exciting voyage from the Hawaiian Islands. It ended the voyage 21 days later in England (see map).

During the 8,000-mile trip, the crew saw few sights. The sub was under water most of the time. It surfaced only a few times. One time was at Point Barrow, Alaska, as the sub was about to begin its undersea trip across the top of the world.

The sub surfaced again after the *Nautilus* had finished its trip under the ice. The Captain was flown to Washington. He was given a medal by the President. At the same time, the President gave out the big news. The *Nautilus* had sailed from the Pacific to the Atlantic under the ice of the Arctic Ocean.

The trip under the Arctic ice took four days. The crew didn't have to be told that there was ice overhead. They could see it! The *Nautilus* has its own television system. The men saw the ice on the television screen.

The sub was under the ice, but the men knew where they were at all times. For example, they knew the exact moment they were under the North Pole.

As the *Nautilus* neared the Pole, the Captain asked the men to be quiet. The seconds were counted off. At the exact second, the Captain said, "This is it. We're under the Pole." To celebrate, the crew had a steak dinner followed by "North Pole cake."

The event was worth celebrating. The *Nautilus* had blazed a new path through the sea. Someday, giant cargo subs may use this road to carry goods.

News From Inside the Earth

News. An H-bomb was exploded deep inside the earth recently. Scientists say that the test proved the earth's core is a thick fluid ball. This core is surrounded by millions of pounds of rock.

An A-bomb explosion showed that the Sierra Nevada Mountains are nine times bigger below the earth's surface than above it.

Science. Scientists can cause earthquakes by exploding powerful bombs under the earth's surface. They learn many secrets about the inside of the earth.

The man-made earthquakes shocked the earth as if it had been pounded by giant hammers. The earth shook and sent out waves just as a stone thrown in a pond does. The waves traveled for thousands of miles through the crust of the earth.

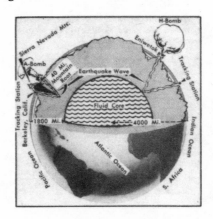

Meet Beaver's Brother

I guess just about everybody knows "the Beaver." He is Beaver Theodore Cleaver on the "Leave It to Beaver" TV show and, in real life, 10-year-old Jerry Mathers.

If you watch the show, you also know Beaver's older brother, Wally. Wally is played by Tony Dow. Together, Beaver and Wally get into more scrapes than some boys could think of in a whole year. It all adds up to an hilarious half hour and one of my TV favorites. I bet it's one of your favorite shows, too.

Much has been written about Jerry Mathers (Beaver) but little about his costar Tony Dow (Wally). Tall, blond, blue-eyed Tony is the kind of boy I thought you might like to meet.

Only 13, he has a busy program both on and off the set. While filming the TV series, he still has to go to school. He attends the studio school with Jerry Mathers. Since the start of the series last year, the two have become close buddies.

Tony also finds time for sports and hobbies. He likes just about any sport you can name. Besides being a skilled swimmer and an expert at volleyball, he is talented at acrobatics. He spends many of his free hours on the trampoline keeping in condition.

Tony's hobbies include playing chess and building model planes. He plays both the piano and the accordion and has mastered several styles of dancing.

His plan for the future is to continue acting. I hope he does.

Jerry Mathers (left) and Tony Dow have fun together as "Beaver" and "Wally" on "Leave It to Beaver" TV show.

Don't you?

What scrape will Wally and "the Beaver" get into on their next show? I'll "leave that to Beaver!"

The children are having fun whirling their hoops.

Hula Hoops Are Whirling

American children have a new toy. It is the hula hoop.

Children play with hoops in different ways. They whirl the hoops around their waists. They roll the hoops on the ground. Children do many kinds of tricks with the hoops.

Hula hoops are made of plastic. They are a good kind of toy. Whirling hoops is good exercise for children.

Zip A Really Real Story

(Left) In Red China, children and adults alike are ordered to take part in a daily exercise program. (Right) At Red China's "Number One automobile plant" in Changchun (between Harbin and Mukden), a new truck is said to roll off the assembly lines every four minutes.

RED CHINA--Its 'Great Leap Forward'

Last fall Kao Chung helped his parents and friends tear down their homes. He helped build large barracks in their place. His parents now live in these barracks.

Chung lives at a boarding school nearby. He spends half his day studying, the other half working in a steel mill. He is 12 years old.

Chung may see his parents for a short while on week ends. They often work 14 hours a day in the fields or in ditches digging canals.

The Kao family belongs to a "people's commune." These communes were set up last year in Red China by the Communists, led by Mao Tse-tung (mä′o dzŭ′dōong′).

"People's Communes." The communes are units about the size of a United States county in which thousands of people live and work together. The people do not own anything. They have given up their homes, garden plots, and cattle.

The communes are organized like an army. They are broken down into "production brigades." Each brigade has its own dining hall, nursery, and "tailoring team." Members work both on farms and in factories.

The Red Chinese call the communes "steppingstones to pure communism." The world looks upon the experiment with horror. It is not human. It breaks up families and destroys all family life.

"Great Leap Forward." Mao Tse-tung wants Red China to be a giant among nations. He plans to make it a modern industrial state. The communes are part of a production drive he calls the "great leap forward."

The communes increase Red China's work force. Women work in the fields instead of in homes. Communes give leaders more control over grain production.

Mao has forced the people to enter communes. Red Chinese must work harder, he says, to produce more food and goods.

Leap, and Then What? Production under Mao's plan has taken a great leap. Food production for 1958 may be double that of 1957. Steel output may be more than double.

However, there is a limit to people's strength. People in Red China have been used like machines. They are tired. They miss their homes. Will Mao be able to push them into another leap?

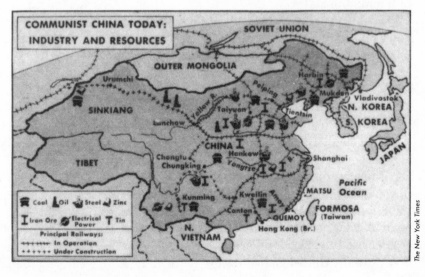

COMMUNIST CHINA TODAY: INDUSTRY AND RESOURCES

OUR COUNTRY CHANGES

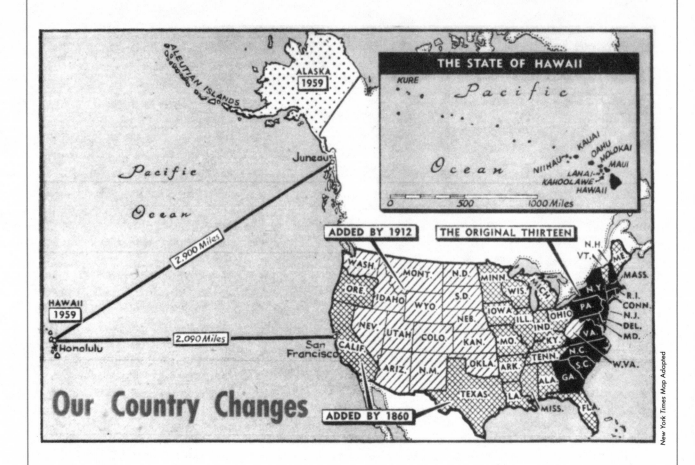

Our Country Changes

Get ready! Get Set! Stretch—your mind! Stretch your mind to the far north and westward over the Pacific Ocean to picture the new United States. This new United States came into being this year with the addition of Alaska and Hawaii as our 49th and 50th states.

The old 48-state United States extended for 3,000 miles from coast to coast and 1,600 miles from border to border. Now, the 50-state United States reaches up to the Arctic Ocean and stretches out into the middle of the Pacific. Its scenery includes the tundra of the Arctic and the lush, tropical plant life of Hawaii.

In fact, with Hawaii a state, our country now reaches beyond North America. The distance from San Francisco to Honolulu is about 2,100 miles. Beyond that, our new island state stretches for 1,600 miles northwestward across the Pacific toward Asia. There are eight main islands and a dozen or so tiny islands and coral reefs.

A 50-state United States means more than a change in the size of our country. It means a change in facts about the United States.

● As you already know, Alaska is now our biggest state. It is also the state with the smallest population, replacing Nevada. In size, Hawaii is the fourth smallest, replacing New Jersey. Its population of over 600,000 is, however, bigger than that of many states.

● The highest mountain in the United States is now Mt. McKinley in Alaska. The title used to be held by Mt. Whitney in California.

● Mount Lassen in California used to be famous as the only active volcano in the United States. Now we have many. There are 34 active volcanoes in Alaska and two in Hawaii.

● The wettest place in the United States now is Mount Waialeah (wī'ä-lä'å) on the island of Kauai (kou'ī). The average yearly rainfall there is 400 inches. The wettest place in the old United States was northwest Washington where the yearly rainfall sometimes reaches 120 inches.

President Takes a Trip

Reporters crowded into the news conference room at the White House. They had heard reports that President Eisenhower was planning to make a trip. They were expecting some announcement. The President entered. A hush fell over the room.

"Please sit down," the President said.

"In order to confirm some of the things that you have been reading in the papers, I want to give you an announcement. I am planning to leave Washington on December 3 for a two-and-a-half-weeks trip which will take me to ten countries."

Trip Will Make History

The trip will be the longest ever taken by a United States President. It will cover about 20,000 miles and will touch on three continents—Europe, Africa, and Asia. The visit to Asia will be the first ever made there by a President in office.

The President leaves this week on a trip to three continents. He will be accompanied by his son, Major John Eisenhower, his son's wife, Barbara, aides, secretaries, and secret service men. The President will make most of the trip in his new jet plane.

Men Study The Ocean

A Frenchman will use his diving saucer to study the ocean.

Men from many countries are studying the ocean.
Little submarines help the men.
They take men down to the floor of the ocean.

The floor of the ocean is not flat.

There are big hills on the floor.
There are cracks in the floor.

Men take pictures in the ocean.
They take pictures of fish.
Many kinds of fish live in the ocean.

My **WEEKLY READER**

1960-1969

There was the charm of the youngest-ever president, of tiny tots at home in the White House. There was the wonder of space, of U.S. astronauts putting footprints on the moon. There was the high courage of Martin Luther King, Jr., and his followers battling for their vision of racial justice.

In bloody counterpoint marched war, riot, and murder. Like a fire bell in the night, the Kennedy assassination in 1963 warned of things to come. By 1966, U.S. armed forces, 500,000 strong, were deeply mired in Vietnam and, at home, anti-war protests were mounting.

At the same time, there was strife of another sort. Frustrated by continued racism and lack of economic betterment, angry blacks torched whole blocks of stores and homes in the decayed heart of many large U.S. cities. The national anguish continued in 1968 when both Martin Luther King and Robert Kennedy fell victims of assassination.

Weekly Reader's pages mirrored the decade's shifting mien. In 1963, school children sorrowed over a fallen president with help from a special memorial issue; in 1969, children rejoiced in wonder over a photo of the first lunar footprint.

Weekly Reader also reflected the shadow of Vietnam that hung over the late '60s. Its pages carried none of the patriotic mobilization efforts evident in the wartime '40s. On the other hand, news of the increasing anti-war protest was also muted. Like the rest of the country, *Weekly Reader* had a difficult time realizing that America might have made a mistake. And like the rest of the country, it ended the decade unsure of its direction.

U.S. Has Two Space 'Firsts'

"Hello, this is Bill Jakes calling. Are you reading me out there?" The man spoke into a phone at Holmdel, N.J.

"Yes, we're reading you loud and clear," came the answer from a man in Goldstone, California.

First Satellite Phone Call

The words spoken were not important. The way the call was made, however, made the phone call an important "first." The words spoken in New Jersey were sent by radio signal to a satellite 1,000 miles in the sky. The signals bounced off the satellite and were picked up at Goldstone.

The phone call was the first ever to be made by way of a satellite. It marked the beginning of a new era of communication.

The satellite is named Echo I. It is 10 stories high and made of a very thin plastic film.

Echo I is a big step forward in the use of satellites to link the world. Satellites will be used for sending telephone and television signals around the world. Then, television can be tuned in "live" from different parts of the world.

The telephone company already has a plan for communicating by way of satellites. The plan calls for 50 satellites. The satellites would circle the earth in a north-south orbit. They would be at a height of 3,000 miles.

Capsule Caught

The Air Force took a giant step toward space travel. A big plane caught a falling nose cone or capsule in mid-air. The catch was made 200 miles northwest of Hawaii. A trapeze, fitted with hooks, hanging down from the plane caught hold of the capsule's parachute. The capsule is gold-plated.

The capsule had been the nose cone of Discoverer XIV, a rocket fired from Vandenberg Air Force Base in California. The rocket was fired into a north-south orbit. The capsule was designed to separate from the rocket as Discoverer XIV made its 17th trip around the earth.

When Discoverer XIV swung southward over Alaska, gas jets pointed the rocket toward the earth. The capsule freed itself from the rest of the rocket. It slowed down. A parachute tied to the capsule opened to lower it slowly.

The capsule's fall was first followed by the radio signals it sent out. Then it was spotted on radar screens of ships and planes. The big plane passed over the capsule and snagged it on the third try.

The mid-air catch was made eight days after a similar nose cone was fished out of the Pacific. The capsules are the first man-made objects to be recovered after circling the earth.

A huge, shiny ball like the one shown here (right) was used in the first attempt to link the world by satellites. The drawing below shows how the satellite was used.

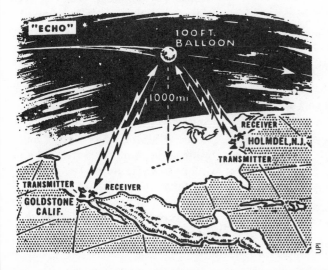

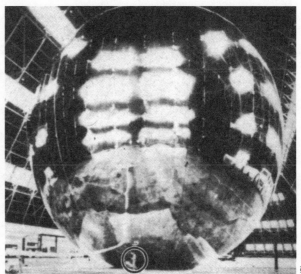

'Storm' Warnings Echo from Cuba

Cubans stand in long lines outside U.S. Embassy in Havana. They hope to obtain visas to go to the United States.

Fidel Castro marched victoriously into Havana. He had overthrown Cuban Dictator Fulgencio Batista. "Fidel has arrived," the people sang. "Now we Cubans are freed from the claws of the tyrant."

That scene took place in January 1959. At that time, Castro made many promises. Few of them have been kept.

Echoes of Promises

Castro promised the people freedom. "Power does not interest me," he said. "I will not take it."

Today, there is no sign of the promised freedom. No elections have been held. No one dares speak out against the government for fear of arrest or death. All power is in the hands of Castro and his Communist friends.

Castro promised the peasants (small farmers) a better life. He promised land to those without land, jobs to those without jobs.

Under Batista, the wealth of Cuba had been in the hands of a few large land owners. The peasants had no land and no real jobs. For three months of the year, they cut sugar cane. The rest of the year, they were idle and penniless.

Castro planned to change this condition. He would break up the large plantations into small plots and give them to the peasants.

Castro began seizing large properties—oil refineries, sugar plantations, cattle ranches. Many of these were owned by U.S. companies. As yet, these companies have not been paid for their property.

Castro has not turned this land over to the peasants as he promised. Instead, he has turned it into giant farms owned and run by the government.

Today, most of Cuba's peasants are no better off than they were before. They are still without land. Many are without jobs. Pay is low. . . . Taxes are high. . . . Food is scarce.

Echoes of Discontent

Discontent with Castro's government is growing. People resent the rising prices, political arrests, and the spread of Communism.

Some Cubans have fled to freedom in the United States. Some have taken to the hills to fight against the government.

Echoes of 'Hate America'

Castro is afraid of this opposition. To keep the masses behind him, he started a "hate-America" campaign. He spread rumors that the U.S. planned to invade Cuba.

Castro's campaign became so heated that the U.S. Government decided to stop buying sugar from Cuba. The U.S. was Cuba's biggest customer. The cut is costing Cuba about 100 million dollars in income. The U.S. also stopped sending supplies to Cuba with the exception of food and medicines.

Castro already has signed one trade agreement with the Soviet Union. Now, he hopes the Soviets will take more sugar in exchange for the machines, oil, arms, and other supplies Cuba needs. Without them, Castro's government may fall.

The United States has a naval base at Guántanamo Bay, Cuba. Control of the base was given to the United States under past treaties with Cuba.

The long, hard campaign trail led Sen. and Mrs. John F. Kennedy to the White House.

New President Gets Ready

On January 20, Senator John F. Kennedy will start to work at the "hardest job in the world." On that date, as you know, the youngest man ever to be elected President of the United States will be inaugurated.

The Presidency is one of the most important jobs in the world. There are many things a new President has to do before he takes office. In times past, a President could take time getting used to the office, but not any more. Today, he has to "hit the ground running" on January 20.

Choosing the people who will work with him is the first task of the new President. Some of the helpers he selects are those who will work with him in the White House. Others are those who will head the different departments of the Government. Mr. Kennedy has already named many of his helpers.

The Inauguration Day speech is always an important one. In the weeks to come, Mr. Kennedy will work on it.

The new President will have to be ready to suggest laws to Congress. Mr. Kennedy is now working on the program he will suggest.

More Roads for North America

A blast of dynamite echoes in Ontario along the north shore of Lake Superior. What had been a hard bed of granite is now a heap of rock rubble. Power shovels move in to clear the rubble away. Graders and paving machines will follow.

This scene will be repeated time and again from now on through the summer, as Canada's road builders work to finish "The Gap." The Gap is one of the two remaining stretches of the Trans-Canada Highway to be completed (see map). The hard rock has made The Gap one of the toughest road jobs Canada's engineers have faced.

U.S. Road Builders' Problems

U.S. road builders have problems, too. They don't have many wilderness areas to cut with roads. Their job is to build new roads around and in settled areas. To lay out routes where there are homes, farms, and businesses is difficult.

Laying a route through a forest or swampland also raises problems. A bird or animal refuge may be destroyed by the road. People ask whether it is necessary to destroy a forest or swampland to make a new road.

Despite difficulties, road building goes on. Road builders will be busier than ever this year. More money than ever before will be spent on highways. Our country will spend over 11 billion dollars, Canada over a billion.

Road-Building Projects

Canada wants to finish its Trans-Canada Highway. The highway runs from St. Johns in eastern Newfoundland to Victoria in British Columbia. This highway will speed up travel across Canada. It will make wilderness areas easy to reach.

U.S. builders want to add more miles of superhighways to our network of interstate highways. The "interstate" is a 41,000-mile network of superhighways to connect the bigger cities of the 48 states. Over 4,000 of the 41,000 miles have been built. Thousands of miles of other roads have also been built.

Road builders are working for more and better roads for travelers and truckers today. They are also building for the future. The superhighways built today will mean fewer traffic tie-ups when *you* are ready to drive.

Below: Broken lines mark the two stretches of the Trans-Canada Highway still to be completed.

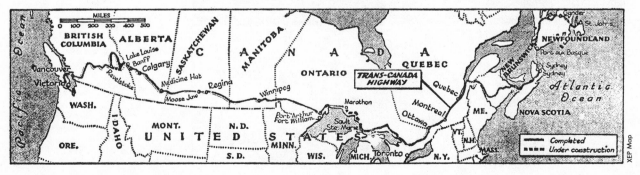

News of the Week

In this cottage lived the owner of the world's most famous cupboard.

Wide World

Mother Hubbard's Cottage

"Old Mother Hubbard" was a real person. Her cottage still stands in Plympton, England.

The cottage will go on standing. People have decided to make some badly needed repairs to the walls and roof.

Mother Hubbard lived 150 years ago. She was housekeeper for a woman named Sarah Martin, who wrote the poem about Mother Hubbard and her bare cupboard.

The cottage was about to be torn down last summer. Officials decided to keep the cottage for tourists to visit.

Hays from Monkmeyer

Machines help teachers and children. Many different kinds of machines are used in classrooms. These machines help children to learn.

One machine is a tape recorder. Children talk into this machine. It plays back the children's voices. The children listen to hear whether they are speaking correctly. They can hear the mistakes they might make.

PEANUT AND JOCKO — By Schomaker

Wow! That building is tall!

How many stories does it have? Ha, ha, ha!

Stories? It is a building not a book! Ha, ha, ha!

Wise Old Owl Says

MY WEEKLY READER is your newspaper. Read the news every week. Look at the news pictures. Talk about MY WEEKLY READER at home.

Communists Threaten Southeast Asia

South Vietnam's President—Ngo Dinh Diem (nō dǐn zǐm)

Street Scene in Saigon, Capital of South Vietnam

The Communists came in the middle of the night. They came screaming and shooting. They searched the village, house by house, taking food and weapons. They left just before dawn. Behind them were the smoldering ruins of seven government buildings and the bodies of five government guards.

Multiply this scene by forty or fifty. You will have a picture of what goes on each night all up and down the countryside of South Vietnam, from the forested highlands to the swampy rice lands of the Mekong River delta.

The Red Tide. The Communist movement is like a tide sweeping the country. The movement is led and armed by Communist North Vietnam. North Vietnam moves in supplies over the border and through the Communist-held area in Laos. The North Vietnamese aim is to overthrow the free government in South Vietnam and set up a Communist government in its

place. Then North Vietnam would have more rice land for its people.

On paper, the Communist attempt to take over South Vietnam would appear to have little chance of success. Government soldiers are better armed. They outnumber the Communist rebels ten to one.

The rebels, however, are fighting a kind of war well suited to the jungle, mountain, and swampland of South Vietnam. The Communists hide in the jungle. They fight only when they think they can win.

Also, the Communists are getting help from many South Vietnamese villagers. Some villagers help the enemy out of fear; others, because they believe the Communist promises of a better life.

The Communist tactics seem to be working. The rebels have spread over half of South Vietnam. The South Vietnamese government has been unable to stop them.

The Flood Tide. To add to the government's problems, a natural disaster recently hit South Vietnam. The Mekong River overflowed its banks. The flood water turned 2,500 square miles of rice-growing land into a sea. The flood washed away homes, ruined farm machines, drowned pigs, poultry, and buffalo, and destroyed the entire rice surplus for next year.

Stemming the Tides. The South Vietnamese government called on the U.S. for help. The U.S.—which has already spent two billion dollars on aid for South Vietnam—sent more aid. The U.S. rushed food, clothing, and medicines to relieve victims of the flood tide. It sent more military advisers, weapons, and troop-carrying helicopters to help push back the Red tide.

The U.S. wants South Vietnam to remain free. If South Vietnam stems the Communist tide, so may the rest of Southeast Asia.

A Vietnamese farmer follows behind his water buffaloes while plowing his rice field near Saigon. Recent floods have damaged rice fields over a wide area in the south.

SHOOTING FOR THE MOON

SHOOTING FOR THE MOON

President Kennedy, in a report before the United States Congress, said, "I believe that this nation should commit itself to achieving the goal, before this decade is out, of landing a man on the moon and returning him safely to the earth. No single space project in this period will be more impressive to mankind or more important for the long-range exploration of space."

President Kennedy stated that the project would cost taxpayers billions of dollars. The project will also take much time and work by many scientists and engineers.

Satellites of different kinds will be used for world-wide communications and for world-wide weather observations. Some satellites (see photo) may be used as space stations for rocket ships.

Peace Corps Goes Into Action

The telephones are ringing. The switchboards are jammed. The mail is making mountains on office desks. The place is the headquarters of the Peace Corps in Washington, D. C. The calls and letters are from young people asking about the Corps.

What is the Peace Corps? The Peace Corps was set up by order of President Kennedy on March 1. The President defined the Corps as "a pool of trained American men and women sent overseas to help foreign countries."

Who will be in the Corps? The Peace Corps will be made up mostly of young people just out of college. Membership, however, is open to all Americans who are over 18 and are qualified. People trained in mechanical skills are as welcome as college graduates.

Where will members go? Peace Corpsmen will be sent to places in Africa, Asia, and Latin America where a need for help is great. They will go only to countries where they are invited. They will stay for two or three years.

What will the Peace Corps do? The main job will be to help people in backward countries help themselves. The Corpsmen will teach people to read and write. They will show people how to build roads and schools. They will open health centers. They will introduce new ways of farming.

What training will Corpsmen get? Before they are sent overseas, they will get three to six months of training. They will be taught the history, customs, and language of the country in which they will work. They also will be trained in the skill or subject they will teach.

What will life in the Corps be like? "Life in the Peace Corps will not be easy," said the President.

Corpsmen will be expected to live alongside the people they are to help—doing the same work, eating the same food, talking the same language. Corpsmen will receive only enough money to take care of food, clothing, health, and housing needs. Their reward will be the satisfaction of having helped to build a better world.

What are people saying about the Corps? Some people are saying that the Peace Corps could do more harm than good. They fear that foreigners will resent the youth and inexperience of the Americans. Most people, however, are in favor of the Corps. They are saying that it will win many new friends for the United States.

Sargent Shriver, head of Peace Corps, points to an area of Africa where members may be sent. ➡

Taking the Salt out of Sea Water

Science News   Uncle Sam has tackled a big problem — providing more water for the people of the United States. The United States uses 32 billion gallons of water a day. As the population increases, water usage will, of course, also go up. The need for finding new sources of water is great. With oceans washing three sides of our country, sea water is looked upon as a possible source.

The main interest is in finding a cheap way of taking the salt out of sea water (at a cost of about 50 cents for a thousand gallons). There is also an interest, however, in taking salt out of brackish underground water.

The Government is building five big plants for changing salt water to fresh water. Three of the plants will be built on the seacoasts and two will be inland—at Webster, S. D., and Roswell, N. M.

Various ways of taking the salt out of sea water have been tried, and many are already in use. On Navy ships, for example, fresh water is made by boiling sea water. The fresh water evaporates as steam, leaving the brine. The steam is cooled to produce water. This method is too costly, however, where much water is needed.

Several ways of desalting sea water by freezing have been worked out. One way is to flash-freeze the water. The ice crystals are then washed free of salt. During the freezing, part of the water turns to vapor. The vapor is also turned to pure water. In another method, certain kinds of gas that don't mix with water are used to freeze sea water. The pure ice is washed free of salt and then melted into water.

Science News: Spiders Spin for Man

The Texas State Highway Department has a black widow spider on its payroll. The spider's pay is an occasional fly and a little water. In return, the spider spins threads of silk on racks. When it has been fed, the black widow spider can spin out $100 worth of silk at one time. The workmen are careful not to get bitten. The black widow's bite can cause death.

The threads are used by the Highway Department as cross hairs on surveying instruments. Cross hairs are used in the eyepiece to help the viewer sight more accurately.

This black widow spider is hard at work for the Texas State Highway Department, spinning thread on a rack.

The thread of black widow spiders is preferred because it is always even in diameter. The silk of other spiders looks knotty.

Spiders aid mankind in another way, too. They are a big help in man's battle against insects. For this reason, spiders are welcome in some homes in hot climates. They keep the homes free of insect pests.

As you probably know, the spider is an arachnid (a-rak-nid), not an insect. Spiders have four pairs of legs to insects' three. Spiders have no wings, while insects usually have two pairs. There are other differences, too.

Here are some facts about spiders you may not know:

● Some spiders can make sounds by rubbing together two parts of the body as locusts do. The sound they make, however, is not as shrill as that made by locusts.

● The young of spiders are called spiderlings.

● Spiders live almost everywhere on earth. They have been found 22,000 feet up on Mt. Everest.

Helge Ingstad points to the spot on the map where he discovered ruins.

Discovery Made in the North

A Norwegian explorer has discovered buried ruins on the northern tip of Newfoundland. The ruins may be pieces of houses almost a thousand years old. One large building had five rooms and a hall. The houses may have been built by the Vikings.

The Vikings lived long ago. Their homes were in countries we now call Norway, Sweden, and Denmark. The Vikings sailed the seas and often explored faraway places. They are believed to have landed in North America 500 years before Christopher Columbus.

Buddy Good Citizen

Dear Girls and Boys,

I was not careful.

I ran into the fence.

Love,

Buddy

Desert Rat 'Hits the Trail'

A new machine bounces along the desert. Soft sands and sharp rocks cannot stop it. This machine is called a *Desert Rat*. It is used to travel quickly across rough areas.

The *Desert Rat* can carry two people. A steering wheel can be controlled by either person. At full speed, the *Desert Rat* can move along at 20 miles an hour.

The *Desert Rat* is like a two-seater mule.

We can split the atom . . . We can fly faster than sound . . . We can launch earth satellites . . . We can guide missiles . . . . . . BUT . . .

The Problem of Disarmament

Disarmament means doing away with the instruments of waging war. Disarmament has been man's dream for more than fifty years. Yet all of man's attempts to control, cut down, or outlaw weapons have failed. Mistrust among nations and unsettled world problems have led to a buildup of arms instead.

The need for finding a way to disarm nations has become more pressing since the beginning of the atomic age. Today's armaments include weapons that could destroy the whole world.

The U.S. Plan

President Kennedy is well aware of the danger of atomic war, by accident or design, so long as the arms race goes on. For this reason, he has challenged the Soviet Union "not to an arms race but to a peace race."

The President has backed up his challenge with a new plan for world disarmament. The plan will be taken up at the disarmament meeting in Geneva this week.

The final goals of the plan are:
✔ to do away with all national armies.
✔ to destroy all atomic weapons and other arms of mass destruction.
✔ to depend on the United Nations to keep the peace through a U.N. Peace Force.

The goals are to be reached in three stages. The first stage calls for a stop to the testing of atomic weapons and a start on the reduction of arms and armies.

Each stage of disarmament is to be accompanied by inspection. Inspection is necessary to make sure that all nations are disarming; that no nation is cheating.

The Soviet Reaction

The Soviet Union agrees with the U.S. on the goal of the new disarmament plan. It disagrees on the matter of inspection. The U.S. and other Western nations want close inspection from the start. The Soviet Union wants close inspection only after complete disarmament is reached.

The West sees a possible trap in this Soviet stand. The Soviet Union is saying to the West: "You disarm and depend on our good faith to do so too."

But the Soviet Union has broken faith with the West before. In 1958, the U.S., Britain, and the Soviet Union agreed to stop testing atomic weapons for three years while they tried to work out a test-ban treaty. The U.S. and Britain lived up to the agreement in word and deed. The Soviet Union did not. It used the time to prepare for the big series of tests that began last September.

The West learned from this experience that the Soviets could not be trusted. The experience strengthened Western demands for inspection at all stages of disarmament.

The Outlook

Disarmament talks have bogged down over the question of inspection in the past. Chances are they will again. Both the Soviet Union and the West agree, however, that the problem cannot be dropped. Talks must continue until some agreement on disarmament is reached.

THE PROBLEM: HOW D'YOU MAKE SURE THE OTHER FELLOW WILL LOWER HIS GUN WHEN YOU DO?

I'VE GOT TO KEEP TRYING —

Cartoons Review News of the Year

What kind of year has it been? The cartoons on these two pages comment on the year's news. Let's see what the cartoons say.

"Just Throw Your Weight Around." The Soviet Union is a strong military and industrial power. Its announced intention is to spread Communism throughout the world. Its tactics are to make trouble first in one country, then in another, in the hope of weakening the free world's defenses.

• In Laos and South Vietnam, the Soviet Union has encouraged Communist rebels in their attempts to overthrow pro-West governments.

• In Berlin, the Soviet Union has tried to force out the Western powers by sealing off the city and tampering with its supply routes.

The cartoon at the top of the page comments on these Soviet tactics. It pictures Soviet leader, Nikita Khrushchev, as a teacher in the art of tumbling. The world is his trampoline. His pupil is Chinese Communist leader, Mao Tse-tung. "It's easy," says teacher Khrushchev, "just throw your weight around."

"Put 'Er There, Pal." The U.S. has met Communist actions with counter-actions. In South Vietnam, the U.S. has gone to the aid of the pro-West government. The U.S. has sent more than 5,000 soldiers to Vietnam to help train the South Vietnamese army.

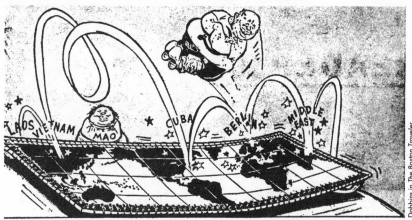

"It's easy, just throw your weight around."

Dobbins in *The Boston Traveler*

The U.S. is also helping the South Vietnamese government move scattered country dwellers from their homes. These people are being resettled in protected villages where the Communists cannot use them to secure food and intelligence.

The cartoon, "Put 'er there," comments on the U.S. aid. The aid is keeping South Vietnam from sinking under Communist attack. (The hammer and sickle—Soviet emblem—is a symbol for Communism.)

"You always insist on holding me to the book."
Pelley in *The Christian Science Monitor*

Pelley in *The Christian Science Monitor*

"You Always Insist on Holding Me to the Book." The U.S. has answered Soviet demands that the West get out of Berlin by saying: "The West will not be forced out of West Berlin. The West will fight if necessary to protect the freedom of that city's people." The West also insists that it has the right of free

travel to the city through Communist East Germany. The West says this right was understood in the agreement that divided Germany and its capital among the four big powers at the end of World War II.

The cartoon, "You always insist on holding me to the book," likens the East-West struggle over Berlin to the folk tale about Little Red Riding Hood. Little Red Riding Hood is on her way from West Germany to Grandma's house in West Berlin. On her way through Communist territory, she meets the Soviet wolf. He tries to stop her. She uses both gun and agreement to force him to keep his word and let her pass.

"Flying High." Not all news this year has been grim. The morale of the United States was lifted by a great success in space. On February 20, Colonel John Glenn orbited the earth three times and came

"Put 'er there, pal."

Reprinted by permission of Newspaper Enterprise Assoc., Inc.

"Flying high!"

Rosen in *The Albany Times-Union*

back to earth a national hero. In the cartoon, he is shown with the U.S. Capitol dome over his head.

"Cutting the Bonds." Thanks to a new U.S. aid program, construction began this year on new homes and schools in some Latin Amer-

Crook in Newsday (L.I.)

"Cutting the bonds."

ican countries. The aid program is called the Alliance for Progress. Under the Alliance, the U.S. has agreed to give more than a billion dollars a year in aid to Latin American countries. In return, Latin America must carry out certain reforms needed to make sure the aid reaches all its people, not just a privileged few.

Latin America needs aid. About half its people are without enough food. Two out of every five cannot read or write. The average person earns only about $350 a year. The cartoon below shows the new aid program cutting these bonds of poverty.

"A Better Kind of War." The U.S. during the past year sent about 1,000 Peace Corpsmen to 14 countries. There, says the cartoon below, Corpsmen waged "a better kind of war." They fought hunger and inexperience with picks, shovels, and technical skills. They

showed people in underdeveloped countries how to help themselves.

The Corps' first year was so successful that Congress recently voted to increase the number of Peace Corpsmen to nearly 10,000 by autumn of 1963.

Cormack in The Christian Science Monitor

"To wage a better kind of war"

Orbit Bound

Any day now, an Atlas rocket will roar off its launching pad, climb above Cape Canaveral, and arc toward the northeast. It will curve into orbit about 100 miles up and eject a Mercury capsule. Inside the capsule will be America's first orbital spaceman. That man is to be Marine Lt. Colonel John Glenn.

Colonel Glenn will orbit the earth three times at a speed of about 18,000 miles an hour. He will use the same route used last November by the chimpanzee Enos. Glenn's flight will last 4½ hours. For four hours of that time, he will be weightless.

Colonel Glenn is the "old man" of the seven-member astronaut team. He is 40 years old. He is married and has two children—Carolyn, 14, and David, 15. The Colonel is a veteran pilot and has won medals for his service in both World War II and the Korean War. He has been training for the orbital flight with the other astronauts for almost three years.

Should Glenn be unable to make the trip for any reason, his back-up pilot, Lt. Commander Scott Carpenter, will take his place.

But Glenn is prepared and ready. He says he is not afraid. He has confidence in the mission, in the people involved, and in himself. He also has a deep religious faith.

UPI

Astronaut Glenn will be first in orbit for the U.S.

In the December 8 issue of *Life* magazine, he wrote: "I think that people who are always afraid of what will happen to them whenever they attempt to do something new will seldom do or dare very much—or take the risks which are necessary to bring on progress."

News Shorts

Wide World

Two Russian spacemen made big space news. They circled the earth at the same time.

Each man rode in a separate space capsule. One man circled the earth 64 times. The other circled the earth 48 times.

Man-Made Snow Shoots from Machines

UPI

This snow-making machine looks much like a fireman's hose.

Skiers don't have to look to the sky for snow. New snow-making machines can make snow for ski areas.

One kind of snow-maker has twin pipes. They carry water and air to the machine. There the water and air are changed to a spray. The machine shoots out a mist. If the air is below freezing, the mist turns to snow.

Much snow is needed for skiing. Snow-making machines go to work when there is not enough real snow.

Some skiers think that the man-made snow is better than real snow. Man-made snow is fine and packs tight. It stands up under heavy use. It doesn't melt quickly. It lasts three times as long as real snow.

UNCLE FUNNY BUNNY   **By Schomaker**

Stop eating candy! You won't eat any dinner.

Yes, I will. I will even make the dinner.

Mmm. What kind of soup is this?

Chocolate soup!

John Kennedy—the young athlete

Lieutenant Kennedy—a Navy hero

Senator Kennedy on campaign trail

President Kennedy, a world figure

. . . a proud and devoted father

. . . and a man with heavy burdens

John F. Kennedy . . . Courageous Leader Killed

John Fitzgerald Kennedy, our 35th President, was born into a family of wealth. His life might have been a quiet and easy one. Instead he chose the path of action and struggle.

Like all political leaders, he was a controversial figure. Many people agreed with his policies. Many did not. Yet even his political enemies acknowledged his qualities of character. High on this list of qualities were courage, energy, leadership, a deep love of family, and a scholarly, perceptive mind.

He was born May 29, 1917, in Brookline, Mass., one of nine children of Rose and Joseph P. Kennedy. His father, a financier, became one of the wealthiest men in America. Joseph Kennedy also served in the Administration of Franklin D. Roosevelt and became U.S. Ambassador to England before World War II.

The future President attended Choate School in Connecticut before entering Harvard University. He traveled in Europe during summer vacations. During his senior year at Harvard, he wrote a thesis about the Nazi menace. It was published as a book under the title *Why England Slept* and became a best-seller.

His deeds in World War II as a Navy PT boat commander have become a model of wartime courage. After his boat was cut in half by a Japanese destroyer, young Kennedy towed an injured shipmate through the water for five hours with a strap clenched in his teeth. Mr. Kennedy's back was seriously injured in the collision.

He entered politics after the war, being elected to the House of Representatives in 1946 and to the Senate in 1952. He faced death twice during serious operations on his injured spine. During his recovery, he wrote *Profiles in Courage*, which won the Pulitzer prize.

John F. Kennedy continued to display courage and devotion to duty after his election to the Presidency in 1960. He accepted the blame for the ill-fated Cuban invasion in 1961. He forced Soviet Premier Khrushchev to order the withdrawal of Soviet missiles from Cuba in 1962. Again he stood firm in the recent crisis on the Berlin autobahn.

Despite the long hours he spent at his desk and in traveling to many parts of the world, Mr. Kennedy found time to be with his family. He showed deep sadness at the death of his infant son last summer, but courageously continued his search for peace and a better world.

Lyndon Johnson Is 36th President

"I will do my best. That is all I can do. I ask for your help—and God's."

These words were part of the first message President Lyndon Johnson spoke to the people of the United States as President. He spoke them at the airfield on landing in Washington on the evening of November 22.

An hour and 39 minutes after the death of President John Kennedy, Mr. Johnson took the oath of office. He was sworn in as 36th President on the Presidential jetliner at Dallas.

Despite the grief and shock that wrapped the country on news of the death of President Kennedy, the office of President passed smoothly and quickly to Mr. Johnson. The change was made without chaos because our Founding Fathers wrote a strong Constitution and established a strong Government.

Mr. Johnson will fill out the late Mr. Kennedy's term of office. The office of Vice President will remain vacant. The next in line to the Presidency is the Speaker of the House of Representatives, John W. McCormack of Massachusetts. Next November, elections for President and Vice President will be held. The persons elected will begin serving a four-year term on January 20, 1965.

Mr. Kennedy served as President for two years and ten months. He believed strongly in human rights. Among the hundreds of tributes were these words from Sir Winston Churchill: "The loss to the United States and to the world is incalculable. Those who come after Mr. Kennedy must strive the more to achieve the ideals of world peace and human happiness and dignity to which his Presidency was dedicated."

The Late President Kennedy and the New President Johnson.

Ham, the Chimponaut, Retires

Our first space flyer has been retired by the Air Force. The Government is giving him a comfortable home, food, and medical care for the rest of his life. His new home is the National Zoological Park in Washington, D.C.

The flyer is Ham, the chimpanzee. Ham made headlines on **January 31, 1961.** He was launched from Cape Canaveral, Florida, in a test flight of the Mercury spacecraft. Ham showed the way for U.S. Astronauts.

Ham had his pre-flight training at Holloman Air Force Base, New Mexico. (Ham's name is from **H**olloman **A**eromedical Laboratory.) He learned to wear a space suit, to push and pull levers, and to work by himself.

On the morning of his flight, Ham had a hearty breakfast—cooking oil, raw egg, baby cereal,

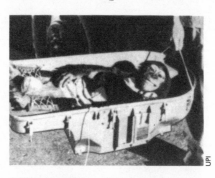

BEFORE AND AFTER: Ham is carried from the van to the launching pad. After his flight, he reaches for a treat.

condensed milk, and gelatin. He was driven to the launching pad in the same van that later carried Shepard, Glenn, Grissom, Carpenter, and Cooper. Ham took his sky ride in the same kind of Mercury capsule the Astronauts used later.

A Redstone rocket boosted Ham 155 miles into the sky. He reached a speed of 5,800 miles an hour (more than a mile and a half per second). He splashed into the Atlantic after a 414-mile trip lasting 18 minutes.

Ham was rescued by a helicopter, which lifted his capsule out of the water. His first food after the flight was one of his favorite treats—a juicy, red apple.

Ham had no ill effects from his flight. Ham has retired from flying, but not from eating red apples.

Israel Works To Make the Desert Bloom

Israel is a country with a dream. The dream is to make its desert "blossom as the rose." To help make the dream come true, Israel is building a giant pipeline. The pipeline will carry Jordan River water from the Sea of Galilee to the Negev (nĕ'gĕv) desert—a distance of about 150 miles. (See map on page 186.) The water will turn the desert sands into fertile soil.

Israel already has begun to lay the pipeline to the Negev. It hopes to finish the job by the end of 1964.

Israel Needs Jordan River Water. The need for water in Israel is great. In area, the country is not much larger than the state of New Jersey, and two-thirds of this area is desert. The desert is called "Negev," a Hebrew word meaning "dry." Skies over the Negev are cloudless most of the year, and a blazing sun bakes the earth.

Only in the northern and central parts of Israel is there enough rainfall and underground water to support life. This area is not large enough to hold Israel's fast-growing population.

When the nation of Israel was set up by the United Nations in 1948, it opened its doors to Jewish refugees from all over the world. Since then, refugees have been arriving in Israel by the thousands. Today, the population of Israel is about two million. By 1970, it is expected to reach three million.

To make room for the newcomers, Israel must develop its desert region. Already, Israel has built some farm settlements in the northern Negev and has been piping in water for irrigation. But now water resources, other than the Jordan, have been used almost to the danger point. Further development of the desert depends upon the Jordan-Negev project.

Arab Neighbors Oppose Project. Israel's plan for using the Jordan's water is opposed by its Arab neighbors, however. These nations threaten to stop Israel. They say that, if necessary, they will build a dam in Syria to keep the Jordan's water from reaching Israel. The dam would divert the water into new channels in Jordan and Syria, causing the Sea of Galilee and the whole Jordan Valley to dry up.

The Arab nations are against Israel's plan because they fear development of the Negev would make Israel too strong a nation. They also fear that diversion of the Jordan by Israel would endanger their own plans to use the Jordan River for irrigation. The country of Jordan especially needs this river's water. (See page 187.)

Israel claims that its project would take only about half the Jordan's water. The country of Jordan, Israel says, would continue to receive all the water it could use.

Israel, therefore, is going ahead with its project. For Israel, a pipeline bringing water to the desert is the answer to a dream. It is also a lifeline to the future.

(Below) With water from the Jordan, Israel can grow more olive groves like this one on the hillsides of the Negev desert.

This pipe is nine feet in diameter. It is so big a jeep could drive through it.

ABC-TV

UPI

Science News: Voiceprints

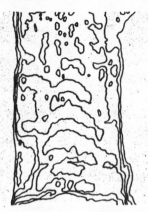

Voiceprints, like fingerprints, show a different pattern for each person.

News: People speak into a new machine. It changes their words to voiceprints. Each voiceprint is different.

Science: Most of us can tell a friend's voice. People are identified by their voices.

Many voice sounds are made in your voice box. It is inside your throat.

Two vocal cords are in your voice box. Sounds are made when the cords move back and forth.

Most men have long, heavy vocal cords. Men's voices usually have low pitches. Most women have short, thin cords. Women's voices usually have higher pitches.

An Unusual Camera

A new camera is being tested. It has a six-foot-long tube. The camera looks like a snake.

The new camera can take pictures around corners. It can take pictures even after it is tied in a knot.

A New Stamp for the New Year

Early this month, postal rates in the U.S. were raised. A few days later, a new five-cent stamp went on sale.

The U.S. flag on the stamp is red, white, and blue. The White House is outlined in blue. The words *United States* and *Postage* are not on the stamp.

President Johnson tells Congress that one out of every five Americans is "Still . . . ill-housed, ill-clothed, ill-fed."

Flannery in *The Baltimore Evening Sun*

POVERTY

President Declares 'War on Poverty' in U.S.

The United States is the richest nation in the world. It is a land of two-car families, ranch-style homes, and overflowing grocery carts. Yet, in the midst of all this plenty, there are about 35 million Americans—one fifth of the total population—who live in poverty. These Americans do not have decent homes. They do not have proper food. They do not have enough clothes.

It is these Americans that President Johnson had in mind when he said in a recent speech to Congress: "This Administration today, here and now, declares war on poverty in America. . . . It will not be a short or easy struggle, but we shall not rest until that war is won."

Causes of Poverty. The President's aim is not only to relieve poverty by handing out food and clothing but to prevent poverty by attacking its causes. These causes include poor health, poor schooling, lack of training in useful skills, and lack of jobs.

Weapons Against Poverty. The President's chief weapons in the attack on poverty are:

✔ better health. He would build more hospitals and health centers, train more nurses.

✔ better homes. He would clean up slums, put up low-cost housing.

✔ better schools. He would build new schools, hire new teachers.

✔ better training. He would train men now without work in skills needed to get jobs.

✔ better job opportunities. He would give loans to industries so that they could build more factories and hire more workers.

To pay for these weapons, President Johnson is asking Congress for about one billion dollars. Much of this money would be spent in the big pockets of poverty—city slums, backwoods areas, mountain valleys.

These pockets of poverty will be the battlegrounds in the new war.

Alaskans Face Giant Task

Streets of homes in Seward were turned to rubble.

A teacher in Anchorage takes a picture of the school where she had taught.

Wrecked fishing boats are aground at Kodiak.

"I haven't found anyone yet who isn't going to rebuild. It will be a better town than before." These words were spoken by the mayor of Anchorage. They show how Alaskans have faced a giant disaster. One of the most powerful earthquakes in history hit the state. The damage is estimated at 750 million dollars.

Many Kinds of Damage

The damage was large because the quake hit the most heavily populated part of Alaska. A large part of the downtown section of Anchorage was destroyed. Hundreds of homes in Anchorage and coastal towns were destroyed and many more damaged. Schools were destroyed.

The state's transportation system was badly hurt. The control tower at the Anchorage airport was wrecked. Long stretches of highway were destroyed. About 17 bridges went down. Railroad tracks were twisted. Many waterways were blocked.

One of the state's main industries, fishing, was hit hard. About one-fourth of the fishing boats were destroyed and others damaged. Docks and canneries were wrecked.

A New Alaska To Rise

Now Alaska is in a hurry to get on with its giant rebuilding task. The job of tearing down ruined buildings has begun. Lumber has been shipped from the Pacific Northwest for new homes and the repair of damaged ones. Companies whose big buildings in Anchorage were wrecked have promised to rebuild. Studies of the ground will be made to find the best places.

Many fishermen feel that the earthquake may in the long run prove a benefit to them. They will now get the modern boats and equipment they have needed to improve Alaska's fishing industry.

Faced with disaster, Alaskans have shown hope and courage. The feeling is that a new Alaska will rise from the ruins. No one speaks of leaving the state. Instead, Alaskans say, "We'll rebuild Alaska."

Names in the News

Honor for American

Dr. Martin Luther King is being honored with a great international award. It is the Nobel (no-BELL) Peace Prize.

The prize is awarded to people or groups of any nationality working for peace and friendship. Money for the prizes was left many years ago by Alfred Nobel, a Swedish chemist who invented dynamite.

Dr. King's award has been given for his work in gaining rights for Negroes by peaceful means. Dr. King is the youngest man ever to receive the Nobel Peace Prize.

Dr. Martin Luther King and family

STARR Gazing At the Beatles

My readers write me that the Beatles are "interesting people," "the newest singing sensation," and "the nicest, best, cleanest, most talented group in the world."

Well, I want you to know that I think the Beatles are *gear*, too. (In case you don't know what *gear* means, it's native Beatle-ese for *fab, really great.*)

● I like the four-four beat of Ringo Starr's drum.

● I like the long hair (though I wouldn't want to see it on my friends).

● And I like the fact that the Beatles never take themselves too seriously. They stomp, stamp, jump for joy and seem to be having so much fun that it's contagious. The Beatles admit that they're having a great laugh. What they want to get across, Paul says, is "that we enjoy it

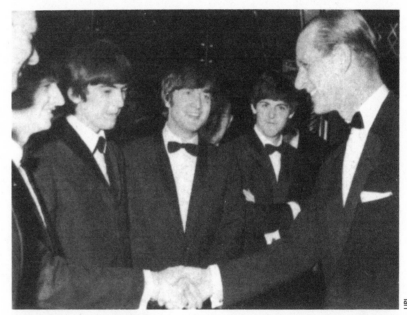

Prince Philip, a confirmed Beatle fan, shakes hands with drummer Ringo Starr while other Beatles (l. to r.) George Harrison, John Lennon and Paul McCartney look on.

and want everybody to have a good time."

As you probably know, the Beatles are from Liverpool, England. Most of their songs are written by Paul and John, and the name Beatle was invented by John, too. The name is supposed to suggest the steady pounding beat of the rhythms of rock.

Last February, the Beatles decided to invade the United States. They came and in ten days they conquered many American teenagers. They're coming back in August, so any of you who haven't been taken in by the Beatles, beware! You may find yourself joining in yet with a *yeah, yeah, yeah!*

Beauty Is Around You

Someday, you might notice birds flying in the sky, a leaf falling from a tree, or a flowering bush. The birds will be doing what they do each day. The leaf will be one of many that fall from trees. The bush will have had flowers for a long time.

And yet, at the moment you notice them, you will see beauty. That's the way it is with beauty. It is all around you. But you cannot enjoy it until you notice it.

Canadian Gov't. Travel Bureau

Happy

New TV Camera Is Light and Mobile

A new portable TV camera brought you those close-up action pictures of the Winter Olympics. Smaller than most portable home TV sets, the camera needs no outside power. Together with a pack, it weighs less than 30 pounds. The pack has transmitters and a rechargeable battery. The cameraman carries the pack on his back.

Sylvania Electric Products Inc.

This new camera was used to film skiing events in Austria.

Cubans Seek Refuge in U.S.

The announcement came on October 3 from Cuban leader Fidel Castro: *All those wishing to leave Cuba may do so.**

No sooner had Castro spoken than thousands of Cubans began making their way to Camarioca, the port of departure. There, they lined the shore waiting for boats to take them across the Florida Straits to the United States and freedom.

These people were voting with their feet against Fidel Castro's rule. They felt that Castro had let them down.

Promises and Realities of Castro Regime. Most Cubans had expected much of Fidel Castro when he seized power in January 1959. Castro had overthrown a hated dictator. He had marched triumphantly into Havana, the

---
*Castro's offer did not include young people of military age (14 to 27).

The Shark V carried some 34 Cubans from Camarioca to Florida. Each could bring only one suitcase. Other possessions were seized by Castro.

capital, with promises of freedom and democracy. "Power does not interest me," he had said. "I will not take it."

At that time, Castro had also promised the people a better life. He would break up large sugar plantations into small plots. He would give these plots to people without land. He would start new industries, making jobs for people without jobs.

But Castro did not keep these promises. Instead of freedom, he gave the people police rule. Instead of democracy, he set up a Communist government with close ties to the Soviet Union. He

Young Cubans enjoy snack at refugee center in Miami. Their parents said that they left Cuba to escape a Castro campaign to make every child a Communist.

XEP Map

allowed no elections to be held. He imprisoned or killed those who spoke out against his rule.

Castro did seize the property of large landowners. But he did not divide the land among the poor farmers. He turned it into giant farms, owned and run by the government. The farmers became hired workers.

The new farm system was less efficient. Management was poor. Production of sugar—Cuba's chief money-earner—fell from over six million tons in 1961 to less than four million tons in 1963. Only a great cane-cutting effort by the Cuban people last year brought sugar output back to pre-Castro levels.

Mistakes in farming were repeated in industry. Castro put up new factories, but he did not have money to buy needed raw materials. He did not have trained managers. Many factories had to shut down.

Conditions in Cuba Today. Chiefly because of Castro's mis-

(Continued on next page)

CUBA (Cont.)

takes and poor planning, living conditions in Cuba today are in many ways worse than they were when he came to power. Almost everything that is eaten, worn, or used is in short supply. In Havana, many foods are rationed. Shoes are limited to one pair per person a year.

Reason for the Open Door. Poor living conditions and lack of freedom are believed to have caused unrest in Cuba. Some U.S.

Fidel Castro talks on TV to Cuban people.

officials suggest that this unrest may have been the reason for Castro's recent decision to let Cubans leave. Castro, they said, was getting rid of unhappy people who might one day rise up against his rule. He also was reducing the demand for Cuba's limited supplies of food and clothing.

Whatever Castro's reason for opening the exit door, Cubans who passed through were delighted. They said upon reaching the United States: "It is like a wonderful new world."

Rescue of Abu Simbel Temples Is Under Way

The giant statues, temples, and pyramids that the Egyptians built in ancient times were looked on as wonders of the world. Another engineering feat is now under way on the west bank of the Nile at Abu Simbel in southern Egypt. The Great Temple of Rameses II and a smaller one honoring his queen are being cut up into huge blocks. The blocks are lifted to the top of the cliff. There, the statues and temples will be put together again to look as they did when the Nile flowed past them.

The temples are being moved to save them

from being covered by the waters of a reservoir. The waters piling up behind the new Aswan High Dam would in time cover the temples. The reservoir will stretch for 300 miles behind the dam. About 14 small temples were moved earlier.

At Abu Simbel, workmen have already cut up and removed the row of baboons carved out of the rock above the entrance. Next month, the task of cutting up the giant statues of Rameses II is expected to begin. The statues will be sawed into 20- and 30-ton blocks of stone.

Sixty-six-foot-high statues of Rameses II and the temple behind them will be cut up and lifted to the top of the cliff. The rebuilt temple will stand 225 feet above its present location. A smaller temple, located 300 feet downstream, is also being saved the same way.

Baboon frieze already cut up lies in chunks on top of cliff.

World 'Looks' at Mars

This summer marked a great advance in space science. The photo at the bottom of this page is one of the pictures of Mars taken by Mariner 4 on July 14. The pictures give people on earth their first close look at another planet.

Mariner 4 is a 575-pound spacecraft with arms like a windmill. It was shot up into space on November 28. The spacecraft used sun power on its long journey to Mars to provide the power for its special equipment. The long arms were covered with cells to gather the sunlight. An electric eye in Mariner was kept on the star Canopus to help steer the spacecraft to Mars.

Long-Distance Photography

As Mariner 4 neared Mars, excitement rose. Would the spacecraft's camera and other instruments work after the long journey? Then came signals showing that everything was working fine. Mariner took 21 pictures and part of a 22d as it flew past Mars. The pictures were taken when Mariner was about 7,000 to 10,000 miles above the surface of Mars.

The pictures were stored on a tape recorder and radioed to earth. The signals for each picture took more than eight hours to reach the earth from Mariner. The distance was 134 million miles.

Knowledge from Photos

The photos showed that Mars is marked with craters. The large number of craters in the pictures leads scientists to believe that Mars may have thousands of them. The earth has about 116 craters. Most of them are too small to be seen from a distance of thousands of miles.

The Martian land looks dead in the photos. Scientists could find no mountain chains or oceans. The land looks to scientists as if Mars has been dry for a very long time. Many scientists believe, therefore, that there is no life on the planet. Other scientists think that life in some form may be found there, even though the planet has no water.

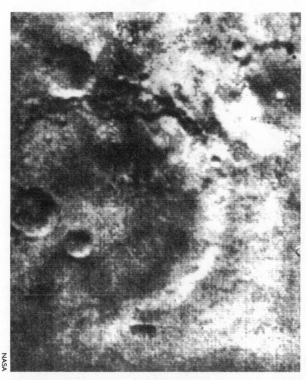

NASA

Mariner 4 sped across millions of miles to photograph Mars.

NASA

This photo was the 11th taken by Mariner 4. Scientists call it one of the most remarkable scientific photos of the age.

News Shorts

Does Elvar Want To Talk?

Dr. John C. Lilly of Miami, Florida, thinks that Elvar, his trained porpoise, wants to talk. Dr. Lilly has done laboratory tests with this porpoise for four years. The porpoise, or dolphin, repeats sounds made by Dr. Lilly.

Sometimes when Elvar is waiting for Dr. Lilly to begin a test, he makes sounds as if he were trying to say, "All right, let's go." Dr. Lilly and his scientists think that the animal understands the words.

Other scientists do not believe that Elvar is trying to talk. These scientists think that Elvar just copies certain sounds, as a parrot does.

Elvar has spent four of his eight years in a tank.

The 85-pound Early Bird satellite was scheduled to be on the air for the first time Monday. Plans called for American TV viewers to see the Huntley-Brinkley program live from London, England. Chet Huntley (left) was in London, England. David Brinkley (right) was in Washington, D.C. Early Bird is in a permanent orbit about 22,000 miles above the equator near Brazil. The satellite will bring Americans regular live TV programs from other countries. Mostly, however, Early Bird will be used to relay overseas telephone calls.

New kind of moon machine has been designed.

Moon Lab Designed

A lab for two men to live in on the moon for two weeks has been designed by Bendix Corporation of Ann Arbor, Michigan. The new machine would be used by astronauts who have landed on the moon as a part of Project Apollo. The machine would be used as the astronauts' home and lab. Astronauts will collect soil and rock samples from the moon's surface. Experiments on these samples can be done in the moon lab.

Inside Red China: The Struggle for Power*

Wide World

Red Guards put up news bulletins in Canton, Red China. Wall posters are used by both sides in the struggle for power in Red China.

- *Street Fighting in the Cities*
- *Bloody Battles in the Country*
- *Suicides Among Leaders*

These are some of the news flashes coming out of Communist China today. The sources of the reports are Chinese newspapers and wall posters, Chinese refugees, and travelers returning from China.

Some of the reports are believed to be true. Others are thought to be rumor. All are being studied by U.S. experts for clues to what is happening in Communist China.

So far, only one thing is clear. Communist China, the world's most populous nation, is undergoing a great struggle for power.

Who Is Opposing Whom? The struggle is between two groups of Communist leaders. On one side are party boss Mao Tse-tung (mow dzuh-doong) and his followers. They are trying to press a strict form of communism on the Chinese people. They would do away with private farm plots and with pay raises in factories. They would offer people only hard work and sacrifice.

The Maoists have gathered to their side millions of teen-agers. These teen-agers, called Red Guards, are roaming the countryside spreading Mao's "thoughts."

On the other side in the struggle is a group of leaders who believe in a different kind of communism—one that would offer the Chinese people some comforts and rewards for their work. These leaders are said to have millions of China's workers on their side. Reports tell of workers fighting Red Guards in all parts of the country.

Who Is Winning? China-watchers are not yet sure which side is winning the struggle in China. One day Mao is reported to hold most of the country. The next day his enemies are said to be in control.

Most China-watchers believe that the struggle will not be decided until China's army chooses sides. Mao has called on the army for help, but its loyalty to Mao is uncertain.

What Is the Struggle Doing to China? Whatever the outcome of the struggle in China, the country will be feeling its harmful effects for years. The struggle has brought to a halt all higher education. Mao has closed high schools and colleges to free students for Red Guard duty.

The struggle also has slowed work on farms and in factories. Output of food and factory goods is down. A drop in exports is expected to follow. Gains made in China in the past 17 years are being wiped out.

What Does the Struggle Mean for the Rest of the World? The setbacks and disorder in China make some China-watchers feel that China is no longer a threat to the outside world. China, they say, might even have to stop its aid to the Communist forces in Vietnam. North Vietnam might then be free to seek a peace agreement.

Other China-watchers disagree. They warn that present or future leaders of China might try to unite the country by setting out on a foreign adventure. They might step into the Vietnam war with force. There is no slowdown, these China-watchers point out, in China's plans to make atomic weapons. **China, they say, must be watched as carefully tomorrow as it is today.**

*This story actually appeared in a 1967 issue of **Weekly Reader**. However, because of the importance of the topic, and to accommodate other major 1967 stories, it is included here.

War in Vietnam

Wide World

U.S. helicopters lift GI's out of a rubber plantation in enemy-controlled territory north of Saigon. Men were searching for Vietcong.

- *U.S. Air Strikes Smash Oil Depots at Hanoi*
- *GI's Scatter Foe After Hard Fight in Highlands*
- *Enemy Forces in South Put at 282,000*
- *Units of Fourth U.S. Infantry Division Land at Quinhon (kwee-nyon)*

These were some of the newspaper headlines this summer. They tell of a war that is being fought in Vietnam. They raise the questions: What is the war about? Why is the U.S.—a country half a world away—taking such an active part?

Fight Against Communists. The war in Vietnam is between Communist rebels (called Vietcong) and the government of South Vietnam. The Vietcong are trying to overthrow the government and replace it with Communist rule. The Vietcong are being helped by Communist North Vietnam. They are being backed by Communist China.

These Communist countries are interested in South Vietnam for two possible reasons: South Vietnam has rich rice land which the Communists could use for their fast-growing populations. Control of South Vietnam could give the Communists a base for taking the rest of Southeast Asia.

Communist Methods. The Vietcong know that they would have trouble taking South Vietnam in face-to-face battle. They are outnumbered about two to one by government forces. For that reason, the Vietcong are fighting a hit-and-run war. They strike when they think they can win, then hide in the jungle.

The Vietcong also get help from some of the South Vietnamese people. These people live in out-of-the-way villages. They are poor, with little or no schooling. Some are won over with promises of a better life. Others are frightened into helping with threats of torture and death.

These methods work well for the Communists.

Today, they control a large part of the South Vietnamese countryside.

Government Methods. The government of South Vietnam is trying to stop the Communists by beating them at their own game. The government is using helicopters to find the enemy and to carry soldiers into enemy territory for surprise attack.

The government also is carrying on a campaign to win the loyalty of its people. It is trying to give more protection from Communist terrorists. It is helping build schools and health centers.

U.S. Aid. Left to its own resources, the government of South Vietnam could not fight a war against the Communists and at the same time build a better life for its people. It has had to depend on the U.S. and a few other countries for help.

U.S. aid to South Vietnam at first was limited to money, supplies, and advisers. But about two years ago, North Vietnam began pouring more men and supplies into South Vietnam. The U.S. realized that if South Vietnam were to be saved, more direct help was needed. So, in February 1965, President Johnson ordered U.S. planes to begin bombing bases and supply centers in North Vietnam. The next month, he began sending U.S. soldiers to South Vietnam. Today, U.S. fighting strength in Vietnam is about 300,000 men.

"Hawks" and "Doves" in U.S. Not everyone in the U.S. goes along with the President's plans on Vietnam. Some people say that the U.S. is not doing enough in Vietnam, that it should send more men, step up its bombing of the North, and try for a quick victory. These people are called "hawks."

Others in the U.S. are against direct U.S. participation in the war. They fear that by being in Vietnam the U.S. is taking the chance of widening the war, possibly bringing in Communist China. They would like the U.S. to pull its forces out of Vietnam. These people are called "doves."

President Johnson's answer to both "hawks" and "doves" is this: The U.S. does not want to conquer North Vietnam. It wants North Vietnam to "let its neighbor alone." Once North Vietnam agrees to this, he says, U.S. soldiers can come home.

South Vietnam "Geografacts"

AREA: 65,000 square miles—about that of Missouri

CLIMATE: Tropical with two seasons—hot and dry and hot and rainy

TERRAIN: Thick jungle, mountains, and swampland over much of country

CHIEF RESOURCE: Fertile soil in Mekong River Delta for rice-growing

CHIEF PRODUCTS: Rice, rubber, tea, coffee, quinine, timber.

Those Fantastic Lasers
Bright Future for 'Controlled' Light

Recently, Russian scientists reported that they had used a special kind of light beam to carry telephone messages from one place to another. The beam took the place of telephone wires.

These scientists were making use of one of the most exciting inventions of modern times. The invention is called a laser (LAY-zer). It was discovered seven or eight years ago by U.S. scientists.

Laser beams are so powerful that they can cut instantly through metals, or even through the hardest substance known to man—diamonds. Scientists think that a light beam of such power holds great promise for the future. Like most inventions, however, many years of work lie ahead before lasers will be in common use. Lasers are already used or will soon be used in such fields as:

● **Communications.** In theory, a single laser beam could carry all the telephone, TV, and radio signals now used in the world. Lasers could thus eliminate costly wire and cable installations.

● **Medicine.** Laser devices have already been used to "weld" torn retinas in the human eye. Some skin cancers and tumors have been destroyed. Microscopic laser beams may someday do delicate surgery deep inside the human brain. Dental drills probably will be replaced by the painless rays of the laser beam.

● **Range Finding.** Distances to objects can be computed by measuring the time it takes for a laser beam to travel to and from the object. Satellites have been located and tracked. Aerial bombers and artillery spotters use laser range finders to calculate distances to military targets.

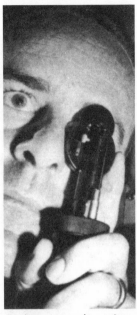

Honeywell, Inc.

Eye doctors can mend torn retinas by firing a tiny hot beam of light into the injury, welding it together.

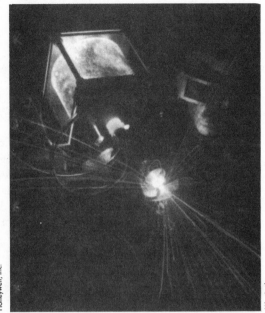

Westinghouse

In industry, lasers are used to cut and weld metals. The worker above is wearing goggles to prevent injury to the eyes from the intense light of the laser beam.

Bell Telephone Laboratories

Message-carrying laser beams, left, are being reflected between mirrors. Explorer 22 satellite, below, was tracked by laser beams.

How Lasers Work

A laser makes use of light in a very special way. Light rays from ordinary light bulbs or from the sun scatter in all directions at once. These rays are diffuse, or out of step with one another. A laser derives its power by causing rays of light to travel together in a very narrow beam. In other words, the rays are tightly controlled; they radiate in step like a squad of soldiers in column formation.

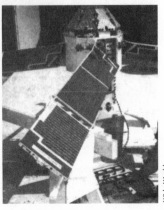

Wide World

STARR Gazing at the 'Splendid Splinter'

"I can't tell you how pleased I am," Ted Williams said. "This is a wonderful day for me." The former Boston Red Sox outfielder had just been informed of his election last month to baseball's Hall of Fame in Cooperstown, New York.

Williams was named to the Hall of Fame by members of the Baseball Writers' Association in his first year of eligibility. (A player must be retired five years to be eligible.) He was the only one of 71 candidates chosen and he was elected by a landslide vote.

There is little question that Ted Williams deserved the honor. He was one of the most feared sluggers of all time. In 19 seasons with the Red Sox, he hit 521 homers to rank behind only Babe Ruth (714) and Jimmy Foxx (534). He had a lifetime batting average of .344 and he was the last man to bat over .400 (.406 in 1941).

The Red Sox thought so much of their "Splendid Splinter"* that they asked him to stay on after he retired from playing in 1960. Williams today, at 47, is a vice president of the club.

———
*Called that because he was tall and lanky.

Ted Williams looks back over his career in baseball. A fine sense of timing, a whiplash swing, exceptional eyesight, and quick wrist action made him one of the best hitters of all time.

UPI

Wide World

Judy Doesn't Like Pigeons

Judy is an elephant in a zoo. She has trouble with pigeons. They take peanuts that people toss to Judy.

A pigeon flies to the ground. Judy snorts and goes after it.

She flaps her ears. She stamps her feet. She whips her trunk in the air.

The pigeon flies off, and Judy seems to say, "Don't come back!" But soon, more pigeons come.

After The Six Day War

Israeli soldiers stand beneath their flag on east bank of Suez Canal. Israel took east bank from Egypt in recent war.

Winning the war against Arab nations was easy. It took Israel just six days last June to knock out the Arab armies and overrun parts of Jordan, Egypt, and Syria.

Winning the peace is more difficult. For almost four months, Israel has been trying to get Arab leaders to sit down and talk about a settlement. But Arab hatred for Israel is so deep that not even crushing defeat can make Arabs come to the peace table.

Why is there such hatred for Israel among Arab nations? Will real peace between Arabs and Israelis ever be possible?

Cause of Hatred. The answer to the first question is simply this: The Arabs hate the Israelis because the Israeli nation occupies part of what was once Palestine. The Arabs look upon Palestine as Arab land.

True, the Arabs say, the Jews lived in Palestine in ancient times. But the Jews were driven out by the Romans about A.D. 70. In the years that followed, the Arabs settled there and came to think of the land as their home. So when the Israeli nation was created by the U.N. in 1948 as a home for the Jewish people, the Palestinian Arabs were resentful. Joined by Arabs from neighboring countries, they attacked the new nation. But the Arabs were defeated by the Israelis and many Arabs fled from Israel.

Then—as now—the Arabs would not agree to a peace settlement. Fighting along Israel's borders continued off and on for years. In 1956 and again last June, the fighting turned into all-out war.

Chances for Peace. This repeated warfare has hurt the Arab nations. The most recent war resulted in two serious losses for Egypt. One loss is the Sinai (SIGH nigh) Peninsula with its oil fields.

These fields had provided half of Egypt's fuel oil. The other loss is millions of dollars in income from Suez Canal tolls. The fighting blocked the canal, closing it to traffic.

The country of Jordan suffered even greater loss. Israel took from Jordan the land on the west bank of the Jordan River. This land had provided half of Jordan's food supply.

Israel hopes that in time the need for these lost territories will force the Arabs to accept a peace settlement. In return for any Arab territory, however, Israel will demand (1) Arab agreement that Israel has a right to exist, (2) borders that are safe from Arab attack, and (3) use by Israeli ships of the Suez Canal and Gulf of Aqaba (AKH uh buh), which has been denied Israel in the past.

Most Arabs say that they would find it hard to agree to these demands. Some Arabs say that they never could. These Arabs say that they would rather let Israel stay in Arab territory until Arab nations can rearm and retake it by force.

Will there be peace in the Middle East? Most observers say no—at least not for a long time. As one Arab newsman puts it: "Only a miracle will prevent a return to the battlefield."

Many countries beyond the borders of the Middle East are hoping that the miracle will come to pass. The Middle East is important as a land bridge to three continents, as a waterway for shipping goods between Europe and Asia, and as a producer of about one-fourth of the world's oil. While the Middle East remains under the threat of war, progress both in the Middle East and in other parts of the world is slowed.

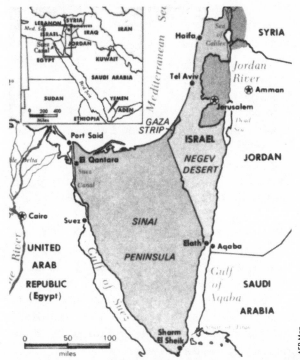

Darker areas are Arab lands taken by Israel in June 1967.

Pollution Cleanup Ahead

Dirty rivers and dirty lakes—the words sum up one of the biggest problems the U.S. faces. They sum up the careless way Americans treated valuable waters for more than 300 years.

Factories built next to rivers poured their wastes into them. Cities released sewage into the water. People threw garbage and trash into the rivers. The Great Lakes were also used for dumping wastes.

As industries, cities, and population increased, more and more wastes were dumped into rivers, streams, and lakes. America's waters turned into open sewers. A river that sparkles in the sun is, at close hand, brown and thick, with junk floating on the surface. Mighty rivers such as the Mississippi and Hudson are highly polluted. Lake Erie is the most polluted of the Great Lakes, with Lake Michigan second.

Pollution of the waters killed fish and other water life. The dirty waters came to be recognized as a danger to health.

Cleanup Ahead. Now a big job faces the U.S. The first aim is to keep the waters from getting more polluted. The second aim is to clean the waters. The cost will run to many billions of dollars.

Cleanup Action. The 50 states have agreed to set up rules to prevent more pollution. Cities and industries will be limited as to the amount of wastes they can release into interstate waters. The states must send their plans by June 30 to the Federal Water Pollution Control Administration.

Last year Congress passed a bill to give cities close to three and a half billion dollars for new sewage-treatment plants. The plants will be built during the next four years.

Many industries are already acting to cut down on pollution of nearby waters. They are building treatment plants to clean wastes before they are released.

Filters will be put to use on Lake Erie. Lumps of coal will be used in the filters to separate lumps of sewage from water before it flows into the lake. The first will be built near Cleveland.

Lake Tahoe a "Lab." Lake Tahoe, high in the Sierra Nevadas on the California-Nevada border, is known for its beautiful, clear water. With more people living on it, the lake began to get polluted. Pipelines have been laid to carry sewage across the mountain. The lake will be a water pollution laboratory. It will be studied to see how other pollutants—fertilizers, refuse from building projects, water running off streets—change the lake.

Pollutants destroy oxygen in a body of water causing fish to die, as in this Ohio lake.

Scientists at this Purdue University lab are doing research on ways of preventing water and air pollution.

Fifth-Graders Solve Problems By Computer

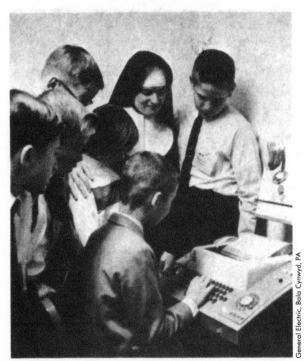

Student shows his classmates and teacher how to work with a computer at an information processing center.

The fifth-grader had a farm problem. His farm needed a certain number of tool kits and milking machines. How much would they cost?

The fifth-grader was "programming" (giving needed information to) a distant computer. His program gave the cost of each item and the computer gave the student the total cost.

Several fifth-graders in a Baltimore, Maryland, school have learned how to solve math problems by computer. They and their classmates in a modern math class have discovered that using computers can be fun.

The class recently visited an information processing center in Washington, D.C. They were there for a lesson in the use of computers to solve difficult problems quickly and easily. Some of their classmates were their teachers.

Computers aren't going to take over all math problems for the class. The children are learning how computers solve business problems today. Teacher believes they may be using computers in their homes someday.

Thurgood Marshall is chosen as Justice.

Judge To Join Court

Next Monday, October 2, the U.S. Supreme Court begins hearing cases. The Supreme Court is the highest court in the land. When the nine black-robed justices walk into the courtroom, among them will be the first Negro judge in the court. He is Thurgood Marshall. He was named to the Supreme Court by President Johnson this past June.

Mr. Marshall's law career began in 1933 when he finished law school. He finished at the top of his class. He used his knowledge of the law to help Negroes fight for equal rights. For many years he served as a leader in the National Association for the Advancement of Colored People (NAACP).

In 1935 Mr. Marshall won an important court victory. The court ruled that the University of Maryland must accept a Negro student. In 1954 he gained his biggest court victory. He brought a school case before the Supreme Court. The Supreme Court ruled that to refuse equal rights to Negroes in public schools was against the U.S. Constitution.

Before being named to the Supreme Court, Mr. Marshall was in the Justice Department. He was Solicitor General.

Professor Glaser with his dog Butch reads from Brailler.

'Brailler' To Help Blind

A new machine can now quickly change English to Braille. This machine, the "Brailler," gives the blind more materials to read.

First the lesson is typed on a typewriter. A telephone links this typewriter to a computer that changes the typed words into Braille. Finally these Braille words are flashed to the Brailler where they are printed out. Even people who cannot read Braille can prepare the lesson. Large amounts of printed matter can be changed to Braille in a short time.

Braille is a reading plan for the blind. The letters in our alphabet are changed to raised dots that can be read with the fingers.

Were Two Continents Once Together?

South America—Africa as they may have been.

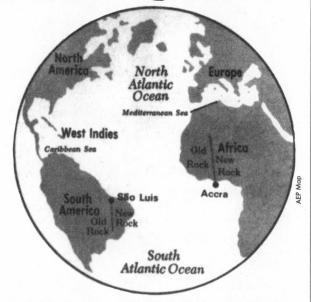

South America and Africa as they are today.

Look at a globe of the world. The continents of Africa and South America are separated by an ocean. Could they ever have been joined together in one supercontinent that broke in two and drifted apart?

In West Africa, scientists have found a very clear line that separates two areas of rock. The rock on one side of the line is about 550 million years old. The rock on the other side tests out at 2,000 million years old.

Recently, scientists have found the same kind of line, dividing rocks of the very same age, near São Luis, Brazil. The line is just where it would be if Africa and South America had once been joined. This makes some people think that the continents are slowly wandering apart.

Is Paper Clothing Here To Stay?

Paper clothing may be a passing fancy, or it may make up a large part of tomorrow's wardrobe. Soft, strong paper is now being used for the throw-away clothing. The paper clothing is not supposed to be washed or dry-cleaned. The material is treated so that it will not fall apart when wet. It sews and feels like cloth. The clothing is colorful and costs little.

Paper dresses sell for as little as $1.29 or as much as $15.00

The Big Question

Richard Nixon

"I believe in the American dream," said Richard Nixon. "I have seen it come true in my own life." The Republican candidate was talking to reporters after winning his second nomination for President of the United States.

Mr. Nixon thought back to his boyhood days in Yorba Linda, California. He had worked as a clerk in his father's grocery store. Little had he known then that by the time he was 55, he would have been nominated twice for the highest office in the land.

The first nomination came in 1960. Nixon by then had left the grocery store, put himself through law school, and served his country as a congressman, a senator, and as Vice-President. He had earned a reputation as a hard campaigner and a fighter against communism.

Nixon's experience and reputation were not quite enough, however, to win him the Presidency. He was defeated in a close race by John F. Kennedy. Nixon went back to California and in 1962 ran for governor. He was defeated again. He left his home state, moved to New York, and took up the practice of law. No one—not even Nixon—thought that he would ever run for high office again.

But Nixon continued to work for the Republican party. He helped elect many Republicans to office in 1966. Last month, these Republicans gave Mr. Nixon another chance at the Presidency.

This time, Mr. Nixon believes that he will win. A majority of Americans, he feels, are unhappy with the old leadership. They are tired, he says, of big Government spending programs and tired of violence at home and abroad. To these people, Mr. Nixon and his running mate, Spiro Agnew, are promising economy in Government, a crackdown on lawlessness, and an "honorable end to the war in Vietnam."

"Nixon's the One," said Republicans on August 7 at Miami Beach. They chose him to be their candidate for President.

"Unite With Humphrey," said the Democrats three weeks later at Chicago. They named him to carry their banner into the Presidential campaign.

That campaign is now under way. Candidates Nixon and Humphrey are stumping the country for votes. They have until Election Day, November 5, to make themselves and their views known to the voters.

A look at the candidates and their campaign promises is presented here.

Hubert Humphrey

Hubert Humphrey, called by many the "Happy Warrior," has seldom been happier than he was on August 28. On that day—as Richard Nixon had before him—he saw the American dream come true. The son of a struggling druggist in Wallace, South Dakota, he had grown up to be nominated, at 57, for the highest office in the land.

The journey from his father's drugstore to the nomination was a long one for Hubert Humphrey. It took him to the University of Minnesota to study government and to teach, to Minneapolis, Minnesota, to be mayor, and to the U.S. Congress to be a senator. Then, in 1960, Humphrey's journey took him along the presidential campaign trail in a bid for the Democratic nomination. Mr. Humphrey lost out in that year to John F. Kennedy. He went on, however, to be President Johnson's vice-presidential running mate in 1964, and then Vice-President.

As a senator, Mr. Humphrey had earned a reputation as a champion of the workingman, of the poor, and of world peace. But in the last four years, this reputation has changed somewhat because of Mr. Humphrey's strong defense of President Johnson's Vietnam war policy. This defense of the war has cost Mr. Humphrey the backing of many Democrats. His nomination for President has left his party badly divided.

Mr. Humphrey's first job as candidate will be to try to reunite the party. His next job will be to try to win the election. Mr. Humphrey believes that, with the help of vice-presidential running mate Edmund Muskie, he can do both. He is campaigning partly on the Johnson-Humphrey record but also on promises of "order with justice," more help to the cities, and a search for new ways to end the war in Vietnam.

Summer Riots...

Milwaukee homes burn in 1967 riot.

Wide World

- *What actually happened in the 1967 riots?*
- *Why did it happen?*
- *What can be done to keep it from happening again?*

Those were the questions that President Johnson asked of his Commission on Civil Disorders. The Commission was set up last July, following the summer riots.

The Commission worked for seven months. It visited the riot cities; heard witnesses, sought the advice of experts. By March 3, the Commission was ready with the answers.

What Happened and Why? The Commission found that the press had exaggerated the extent of the riots. Of the 164 reported, only 8 turned out to be major; 33, serious. In most cases, the riots involved Negroes acting against white authority and white property in Negro neighborhoods.

As to the causes of the riots, the Commission found no sign that they were planned by any organization or group. Chief blame for the riots, the Commission says, lies with white Americans.

For years, the Commission says, whites have discriminated against Negroes in schooling, hiring, and housing. As a result, most Negroes have had fewer years of schooling than whites. They are twice as likely as whites to be out of work, three times as likely to be in low-paying unskilled jobs. They are more than twice as likely to be living in poverty.

What's more, the Commission says, white people have left the city Negroes to their plight. As more Negroes have moved into the cities, white people have moved out. The way things are going, the Commission says, "Our nation is moving toward two societies, one black, one white—separate and unequal."

What Can Be Done? To end riots and keep the nation from splitting into two societies, the Commission recommends:
- Creation of 2 million new jobs in three years;
- Building of 6 million low-rent housing units in five years;
- Passage of laws that would permit Negroes to buy or rent homes in any neighborhood;
- Steps to give each family a yearly income at least as high as the poverty level of $3,335;
- An all-out effort to improve schooling in poor neighborhoods.

Response to Findings. The Commission's report was met with mixed response across the nation. Most Negro leaders have praised it. Roy Wilkins, a Commission member, has called it "exceedingly honest." Martin Luther King has called it "timely."

Among white Americans, there has been objection to the charge that race prejudice caused the riots. Lawlessness, some white Americans say, was as much—if not more—to blame. The report, they feel, should have called for a "crackdown" on rioters.

From Congress, there have been complaints that the programs called for in the report are too costly. The price tag could run into hundreds of billions of dollars.

Other congressmen, however, agree with the Commission on the need for action.

Los Angeles County sheriff inspects "rescue vehicle" to be used if riots recur in southern California this summer.

Gov. Otto Kerner of Illinois (left), Negro leader Roy Wilkins, and Sen. Harris of Oklahoma discuss their report.

Martin Luther King—Rights Crusader

"It may get me crucified. I may even die. But I want it said even if I die in the struggle that 'He died to make men free.'" Martin Luther King, 1962

When Dr. Martin Luther King was struck down by a sniper's bullet in Memphis, people wondered if his fight for equality would continue.

The fact that Dr. Ralph Abernathy was named to take Dr. King's place reassured his followers. Dr. Abernathy is now leader of the Southern Christian Leadership Conference. He will continue Dr. King's teaching that violence is wrong.

Dr. King went to Memphis to support the garbage collectors' strike for higher wages and better work conditions. After Dr. King's death, the strikers won.

"I have a dream that one day this nation will rise up and live out the true meaning of its creed. . . ." Martin Luther King, March on Washington.

Dr. King matched his dream with action. As pastor of a Baptist church in Montgomery, Alabama, he began speaking for equal rights. Dr. King became a leader of the Negroes

Dr. King spoke of his dream to crowds after March on Washington, 1963.

Dr. King, before he was shot, stands on balcony with Dr. Abernathy (right).

in a bus boycott in Montgomery. Negroes refused to ride buses in which they had to give up their seats to whites. The Negroes won. In November 1956, the Supreme Court called the Alabama segregation laws unconstitutional. Dr. King became a hero. In 1964, he was honored for his work. He won the Nobel Peace Prize.

Senator Edward Brooke has asked Congress to set aside January 15, Dr. King's birthday, as Martin Luther King Day to honor the civil rights leader.

Civil Rights Bill Becomes Law

The *Civil Rights Act of 1968* was passed by Congress and signed by President Johnson last month. The White House ceremony was solemn with the memory of the slaying of Dr. Martin Luther King. President Johnson said, "Now with this bill, the voice of justice speaks again. It proclaims that fair housing for all—all human beings who live in this country—is now a part of the American way of life." The bill opens the sale and rental of four-fifths of the country's homes and apartments to all races and religions. The President would like to see Congress pass other programs such as more low-cost housing, job training, health programs, and education for the poor.

Soviet Tanks Crush a Dream

Czechs jeer at a Soviet tank in Prague, Czechoslovak capital, during Soviet invasion.

August 20 was a sad day for the people of Czechoslovakia. On that day, the Soviet Union invaded their country.

The people of Czechoslovakia wept. They screamed at the Soviet soldiers to go home. They hurled stones at the Soviet tanks. But it was no use. The Soviets had the power. They stayed, and they forced the Czechoslovak government to carry out Soviet orders.

The Soviets say that they entered Czechoslovakia because Czech officials had asked them to come to save communism. Western experts do not believe that any Czech invited the Soviets. They do believe, however, that the invasion was to save communism.

A new Czech leader named Alexander Dubcek (DOOB-chek) had been carrying out an experiment in Czechoslovakia. He had been trying to combine communism with democracy. He had given the Czechoslovakian people new freedoms. He had allowed them to speak out against the Communist government, to print the news freely, and to travel anywhere they wished.

The Soviets, Western experts say, feared that a desire for these freedoms would spread to other Communist nations in Eastern Europe, even to the Soviet Union itself. To the Soviets, these freedoms were a threat to the Communist system.

AEP photo by Nils Lommerin

A New House Moves
A new house moves.
It goes around and around.

Push Hour

The railroad stations in Tokyo, Japan, hire many *oshiya* or "pushing boys." These are young men hired to shove people into the trains.

Most Japanese who work in Tokyo live outside the city. They travel to work by train or bus. The trains are so crowded during the morning and evening rush hours that passengers lose buttons and even shoes. Never a day passes without torn clothes and scratches.

Wide World

Pushing boys shove Japanese into trains at rush hours.

Footsteps on Another World

"This is the greatest week in the history of the world since the Creation," said President Nixon. He was speaking of the week this summer in which two U.S. astronauts landed on the moon and returned safely to Earth. The astronauts were Neil Armstrong and Edwin Aldrin.

Lunar Landing. The great week began for the astronauts on Sunday, July 20. That was the day their craft touched down on the moon's Sea of Tranquility. Touchdown time was 4:17 p.m. EDT.

About seven hours after the landing, the astronauts opened the lunar module hatch. Neil Armstrong backed out. He climbed down a ladder and placed the first human foot on lunar soil. Taking the first step on the new world, he said: "That's one small step for a man, one giant leap for mankind."

Armstrong was followed to the lunar surface by Astronaut Aldrin. Together, the two men began a historic two-hour tour. They bounded about in the moon's weak gravity. They set up experiments. They snapped pictures. They scooped up rocks. And, all the while, they radioed their feelings and findings back to Earth.

Lunar Tour. How did the moon look to the astronauts? "It has a stark beauty all its own," said Armstrong. "It's like much of the high desert of the United States. It's different, but it's very pretty."

"Beautiful! Beautiful!" said his companion. "Magnificent desolation."

Armstrong described the lunar soil. It is "fine and powdery," he said, and sticky. He told how it clung to his boots and gloves.

Aldrin looked at lunar rocks. He found some that were purple. Others had small holes, suggesting that they might have been thrown out by volcanoes.

The astronauts gathered samples of the rocks to bring home for more study. They loaded the rocks into the lunar module along with bags of lunar soil and dust. Then, the astronauts reboarded. They ate and slept. The next day, they took off to rejoin Michael Collins in the Apollo command ship. It was waiting for them

View of moon (left photo) was taken through astronomer's telescope. Edwin Aldrin (right) got a much closer view.

in lunar orbit. The astronauts docked with the ship, then headed for Earth and a splashdown in the Pacific.

Future Apollos. The Apollo 11 astronauts were no sooner back from the moon than space officials began talking about a return trip. The next flight—Apollo 12—is planned for November 14. It will take astronauts Charles Conrad and Alan Bean to a landing on the moon's Sea of Storms.

After Apollo 12 will come eight more lunar flights. These will take men to still other parts of the moon for still longer exploration times.

Importance of Lunar Flights. Scientists are counting on the Apollo flights and their cargoes of moon rock to unlock lunar secrets. For hundreds of years, man has wondered: *What is the moon made of? How old is the moon? Where did it*

come from? Was it torn from Earth, or was it a planet captured by the Earth's gravity when it wandered too close? Did the moon ever have air or water? Did it ever have life?

Next Step: Mars? Once man has learned what he wants to know about the moon, where will his curiosity take him next? Will it be to Mars, as some scientists say?

This question is now being studied by a group named by the President to set up new U.S. goals in space. The group is headed by Vice-President Agnew. Mr. Agnew favors a landing on Mars. He would like to see U.S. astronauts land there by 1999. If President Nixon accepts such a goal for the nation, Neil Armstrong's historic step onto the moon could become man's first step toward the planets.

HERE MEN FROM THE PLANET EARTH
FIRST SET FOOT UPON THE MOON
JULY 1969, A. D.
WE CAME IN PEACE FOR ALL MANKIND

NEIL A. ARMSTRONG
ASTRONAUT

MICHAEL COLLINS
ASTRONAUT

EDWIN E. ALDRIN, JR.
ASTRONAUT

RICHARD NIXON
PRESIDENT, UNITED STATES OF AMERICA

Plaque remains on moon to say earthmen were there and came in peace.

Apollo 11 astronauts talk with their wives from quarantine trailer in Hawaii. Trailer was en route from recovery ship to Lunar Receiving Lab in Houston, Texas. Astronauts had to remain in quarantine for about three weeks to make sure they carried no moon germs that could be harmful to man.

Hunger in U.S. Is Big Problem

The Senator opened a refrigerator door in a shack at a camp for migrant farm workers in Florida. Inside, he saw a plate of green beans, corn bread, and a piece of pork fat. He found the same small quantity of food in other shacks. "Simply shocking," the Senator said later.

The Senator was George S. McGovern. He heads a Senate committee studying hunger in the U.S. The committee plans to visit at least 12 states. One aim of the committee is to bring hunger in the U.S. to the attention of the American public. Senator Ernest F. Hollings of South Carolina proved an attention-getter when he told the committee, "There is hunger in South Carolina." The state's lawmakers ordered a study of the problem.

Millions of Hungry People

No one knows the exact number of hungry people in the U.S., but most estimates put the figure at ten million. Among them are people of different races and nationalities all over the country, in rural areas and in cities.

Hunger means that children and adults have very little to eat, often having to skip meals. Meal after meal may be the same, such as beans or grits. The meals are, therefore, not nutritious; they lack vitamins or other food substances needed for good health. The result is that the hungry get sick easily, and cannot easily be cured.

Food Programs

Ways of helping the hungry have been worked out by the Federal Government. These include free lunches at school and food stamps that are used to buy food at stores. Families pay for the stamps, with the poorest paying least. The stamps are worth far more than they cost. Some families lack the money to pay even a few dollars for the stamps. Often the poor have not known of this kind of help, or the county in which they live has not wanted federal help.

The Government has been working on ways to improve the food programs. One plan is to provide more food stamps. President Nixon will tell Congress what he would like done, but Congress will make the final decision.

New York Times Photo by Edward Hausner

Left: **South Carolina boy suffers from rickets, a bone disease caused by lack of vitamin D, of which milk is one source.**

A pesticide is sprayed from a plane over an orchard. DDT is applied to crops by spraying.

Cessna Aircraft Co.

Should Use of DDT Be Stopped?

Should people stop using DDT, a strong chemical that kills pests? This question is being asked around the world. DDT is used to kill pests that damage crops. It does its job well, but many people now say that it should be banned.

Why is DDT attacked? Studies have shown that DDT doesn't do its job and then disappear. DDT does not break down. Winds and rains carry DDT into rivers, lakes, and oceans. It gets into human tissue and into wildlife.

Scientists have, for example, found fish far out in the ocean with DDT in their flesh.

Other scientists have found that when trees are sprayed with DDT, many small birds die. Bald eagles lay eggs with very thin shells because of DDT. The shells break before the young eagles can grow in them and hatch.

How harmful DDT is to humans is not known. Some studies show that the effects may take many years to appear.

Other scientists say that substitute pesticides could make problems. A pesticide that lasts only a short time needs to be used more often. Many farmers want to continue to use DDT.

News Shorts

Bill Cosby Leads The Gang

Part of the old Cosby gang are Fat Albert and Cosby, Dumb Donald, and Weird Harold.

If you think Bill Cosby is funny today, you should have seen him as a boy. You will be able to see young Cosby on November 12 in his TV show, "Hey, Hey, Hey—It's Fat Albert." The show is about Cosby's boyhood in Philadelphia with his lively and funny gang of friends. Cosby wrote the show. He asked an artist to draw the gang in cartoon form.

A group of young boys helped

Bill Cosby directs boys in program about his pals.

NBC-TV

Cosby do the show. They taped the voices of the cartoon characters in a Hollywood studio. The boys felt like stars. They played it "cool." But they were too cool for Cosby. In Cosby's gang no one acted really cool. So Cosby swung into action.

Cosby put on an act for the voice dubbers. The group was soon shouting and laughing. That was the sound Cosby wanted. The taping began. No one stood in front of a microphone. When Cosby wanted shouts for an arm wrestling scene, the boys acted out the real thing. When Cosby wanted cheers for Fat Albert's winning touchdown, he crashed around the studio. The shouts that followed him were just what Cosby needed.

When the tape was played back, Cosby was happy with the "street" gang. For the gang, it was a hard day's work. But all of them say it was cool (a lot of fun).

New U.S. Stamp

National Stamp Collecting Week is from November 17 to 23. During this week, collectors can get first-day cancellations of a new stamp from Columbus, Ohio. The 6-cent stamp will be issued by the U.S. Post Office Department on November 20.

The stamp draws attention to the work that is being done to cure crippling diseases and gives hope to those already crippled. The stamp shows a crippled boy. He is shown in a wheel chair, then rising, then almost standing, and finally stepping forward.

HOPE FOR THE CRIPPLED
U.S. POSTAGE 6 CENTS

U.S. Post Office

Citizens In Action

On the night of October 15, thousands of people marched to the White House. Holding candles, they stood in silence in the street near the President's home. Earlier, they had a big meeting near the Washington Monument.

In other cities across the U.S., people marched, held meetings, or met for silent prayer. The number taking part is not known for certain, but it may have been in the millions.

All of these people were demonstrating against the Vietnam war. October 15 had been named Vietnam Moratorium Day. People were asked to observe the day to show President Nixon that many in the U.S. wanted the U.S. to get out of Vietnam soon.

Many people were against having the Moratorium Day. They said that the demonstration aided the enemy. They asked people to show support for the President by flying the U.S. flag and turning on car headlights.

In countries ruled by one man or a small group of men, people would not be allowed to demonstrate as Americans did on October 15.

How does Moratorium Day show the freedom of speech and action that the people of the U.S. enjoy? What can Americans do to keep their freedom of speech and action?

Weekly Reader EYE®

1970-1979

Successful peace efforts vied for headlines with war, revolution, and White House scandal in the troubled 1970s. Early in the decade, *Weekly Reader* told kids about Ping-Pong diplomacy—the surprise beginning of Chinese-American rapprochement after 25 years of hostility. A more somber story was the erratic winding down of the Vietnam War, which dragged on until 1975. Presidential politics took a dark turn with Watergate—a scandal that began with an attempted burglary in 1972 and peaked two years later with the first-ever resignation of a U.S. president.

Peace and violence continued their duel until the decade's end. In 1977, Egypt and Israel opened a peace process that led to a treaty in 1979. Also in 1979, bloody revolutions led to the ouster of the Shah in Iran and of strongman Somoza in Nicaragua. These upheavals had profound implications for the U.S. in the 1980s—as did the Soviet invasion of Afghanistan on the decade's final day.

For *Weekly Reader,* the 1970s were a difficult time. School enrollment was declining. Recession, brought on in large part by the 1973 Arab oil embargo, cut school funds. "The basics" were out of fashion. Circulation began to slip from a peak of 13 million. The decline became a hemorrhage as *Weekly Reader* backed away from its time-tested focus on hard news and even downplayed the *Weekly Reader* name itself. (The change in news emphasis is not readily apparent in this book's limited year-by-year selections.) By 1977, *Weekly Reader* had lost half its readership—a milestone that brought an abrupt rededication to the original *Weekly Reader* formula of news and skills. Circulation evened out, then rose by three million over the next decade to its present level of nine million.

Will they turn you on or will they turn on you

WHY DO YOU THINK THEY CALL IT DOPE?

SPEED KILLS

Don't blow it with drugs

Brother... don't pass it on

Don't "METH" around

DON'T COME UNGLUED

Slogans were taken from posters being used in antidrug campaigns across the country.

U.S. Tackles Drug Problem

- *Boy, 12, Found Dead from Heroin Overdose in Bathroom of City Tenement*
- *Girl, 12, Found Dazed and Sickened after Three-Day Spree of Drug Taking*
- *Child Addict Tells Lawmakers How He Stole To Support Drug Habit*
- *Eleven-Year-Old Is Arrested on Charges of Selling Heroin*
- *New York City Health Officials Report an Estimated 25,000 Teen-Age Heroin Addicts*
- *Number of Heroin-Caused Deaths among Teen-Agers in New York City Reaches 224 for 1969*

These recent headlines have produced concern in millions of American homes, including the White House. President Nixon has called the growing abuse of drugs by school-age youth "alarming." He has announced an all-out Government effort to deal with the problem.

Teaching Drug Facts. As part of its effort, the Government is planning a crash program in drug education. The program will train 150,000 teachers and 75,000 student and community leaders as drug information counselors, by the next school year. These counselors will then present facts about drugs to every school district in the country.

Warning of Drug Dangers. The Government will also make movies and TV spot announcements warning of drug dangers. The spot announcements will be something like those now being used to fight cigarette smoking. The President has asked television broadcasters to help the Government reach the public by running the antidrug messages in prime viewing time.

Shutting Off Drug Supply. Another part of the Government's effort to deal with the drug problem is a move to slow the flow of drugs coming into this country from Mexico and Turkey. These countries grow the opium poppies from which heroin (HEHR-uh-wuhn) is made. Mexico also grows hemp, which is the source of marijuana (mair-uh-WAHN-uh). The U.S. is offering help to both countries if they will destroy their poppy and hemp fields. Mexico already has agreed to do so.

The U.S. is also tightening border controls to prevent drug smuggling. Heroin and marijuana are being slipped into the U.S. in everything from cans labeled fish to hollowed-out ski poles. Customs inspectors have been told to search anything that could conceal drugs.

By making drugs harder to get and by giving teen-agers an understanding of the dangers of drugs, the Government is hoping to end, or at least to cut down, drug abuse.

A California health teacher takes up battle against drug abuse. He uses drug equipment and charts for his lectures.

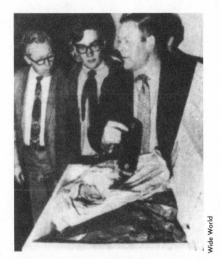

A U.S. agent shows reporters cake of hashish found in crates flown in from India. Hashish is a drug from hemp.

A Government official holds a brick of marijuana and a doll used to smuggle marijuana cigarettes into U.S.

What's What With Drugs?

What is a drug? A drug is any substance other than food that, when taken, produces a change in the body. Many drugs are valuable as medicines. If used properly and under a doctor's direction, they can help the body. If used improperly, drugs can harm the body.

What are the drugs most popular with young users and what are their effects? The most common drugs in use among young people today are heroin, marijuana, the amphetamines, or "up" drugs, and LSD.

• *Heroin* (also known as horse, junk, smack) is obtained from the juice of the poppy fruit. Once given as a pain-killer, the drug is now illegal in the U.S. Effect sought by heroin users is a feeling of physical warmth and peace. Drug damages judgment. Large doses can slow bodily functions enough to cause death. Drug is habit-forming. Users keep needing larger doses to achieve desired effect. Withdrawal is painful.

• *Marijuana* (pot, grass, hashish) is made from the dried leaves and flowers of the hemp plant. Drug has no known use in modern medicine. It is taken mainly for its intoxicating effects. Drug slows reflexes and clouds thinking. When taken in very large doses, it may cause hallucinations. Driving under the influence of marijuana is dangerous. To have, give, or sell the drug is against the law.

• *Amphetamines* (bennies, speed, wake-ups, pep pills) are man-made. Their medical use is to combat sleepiness and control appetite. Heavy doses can lead to malnutrition, exhaustion, and mental illness. If injected into a vein, large doses can cause abnormal heart rates and death. Amphetamines can be obtained legally only through a doctor.

• *LSD* (acid) is a powerful man-made chemical. Effects sought by users are insightful experiences and exhilaration. Dosage can cause serious mental changes and loss of the feeling of boundaries between the body and space. Sometimes users believe they can fly or float. Drug can also cause panic and violent and suicidal reactions. Possession of LSD is unlawful.

Why are some young people turning to drugs? Young users give many different reasons for starting on drugs. Some "turn on" to escape from problems. Some use drugs to rebel against their parents. Others try drugs out of curiosity or boredom or on a dare. Still others take drugs to be one of the crowd.

How can drug abuse be prevented? One way to prevent drug abuse is to make people aware of the possible dangers. Another way is to interest young people in other activities that will take up their time and bring them a sense of satisfaction. Such activities might be sports, volunteer work in playgrounds and parks, and antipollution efforts.

News Shorts News Shorts News Shorts

Lunar Rocks Hint at History

Some scientists believe that a great upheaval took place on the moon about 3½ billion years ago. The scientists got this idea after studying a moon "bead" that had undergone melting.

The scientists found the bead among samples from the moon. The samples were collected last July by the Apollo 11 astronauts.

Some scientists say the melting of the bead was caused by volcanic bursts inside the moon. Other scientists say that the melting may have been caused by falling objects that crashed on the moon. Others believe that very strong heat from the sun may have melted part of the moon. According to some scientists, such falling objects and solar heat may have also hit the Earth millions of years ago.

The scientists say that it is too early to reach any sure judgments about the moon. They will continue to study the moon samples for further facts.

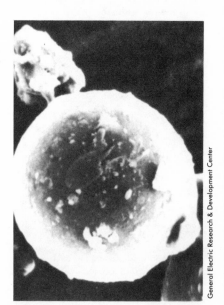

Scientists are studying this "bead" from moon. It is enlarged 6,600 times.

Science Sun's Rays Fire Solar Furnace

New York Times

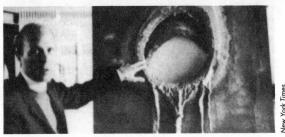

New York Times

The world's largest solar furnace will soon be ready for use in France. French scientists have built the furnace to harness the sun's power. The sun's heat will be used in experiments that need very high temperatures. The solar furnace was built on a hillside (top left) in a sunny region of the Pyrenees.

On the hillside there are 63 flat mirrors. These flat mirrors are tilted to catch rays of the sun. An electric-eye system directs the mirrors in following the sun. These flat mirrors reflect sunlight to a 9-story-high, bowl-shaped wall. Mounted on the bowl-shaped wall are 9,000 mirrors. The sun's rays are reflected from the wall to a hammerhead-shaped tower.

The focal point of the sun's rays is located within the tower. Experimental materials are placed at this bull's-eye (lower left) in the tower. The heat at this point reaches about 7,000 degrees Fahrenheit.

With this great heat, researchers can find out what kinds of materials perform best at high temperatures.

How Do You Feel About New Uses of the Flag?

UPI

UPI

Demonstrator carries flag with "peace" sign.

Teen-ager wears flag as costume.

For nearly 200 years the U.S. flag has been used as a symbol of the whole country. It has stood for "one nation under God, indivisible, with liberty and justice for all." Now some Americans are using the flag to express feelings for and against the Vietnam war. Other Americans are wearing the flag as hats, ties, and vests. Still other Americans are using the flag as picnic cloths and some as seat covers.

These new uses of the flag have stirred up an angry debate. Some Americans approve of the new uses. Others disapprove.

Approve

People who approve of the new uses of the flag give several different arguments to back their stand. One argument goes like this:

"The flag belongs to all Americans—peace groups and war backers, students and construction workers, hippies and squares. If these Americans want to change the flag to make it stand for what they believe in, that should be their right. The Constitution gives every American freedom of speech, or expression.

"Therefore," continue those who approve of the new flag uses, "peace groups should be allowed to carry flags with peace signs in place of stars. The war's backers should be allowed to wave flags printed with the words 'America, love it or leave it.'"

A second argument heard in defense of the new flag uses is this:

"No object is sacred. The flag is only a piece of colored bunting. Using the flag for such things as trouser patches and minidresses may not be in good taste, but it cannot do the country any harm."

Disapprove

People who do not approve of what is being done to and with the flag give these reasons:

"The Stars and Stripes is a symbol of our nation. To use it as a banner of protest or to wear it as a costume shows disrespect for the nation. Such uses of the flag also dishonor the memory of the millions of Americans who have given their lives in the flag's defense."

Another point raised by those against the new flag uses is this:

"Such acts as writing or drawing on the flag, making changes in it, or cutting it up for clothing are against many state laws. People found guilty of these acts can be fined or sent to jail."

Flag "protectors" dismiss the argument that abuse of the flag is allowed under the freedom of speech section of the Constitution. They say: "The free speech section may give Americans the right to attack the flag with words. It does not give Americans the right to abuse the flag itself."

New TV Show Enjoyed by All

Have you ever read a story or played with a toy meant for your little brother or sister and enjoyed it as much as they did? That's what might happen when you watch one of this season's biggest hits "Sesame (SES-a-me) Street."

The program is meant for children who are three to five years old. But it is being enjoyed by almost all who

Puppet and Puppeteer

Robert Fuhring for Children's Television Workshop

watch it—be they 3, 13, or 30.

Sesame Street is a lively place. Puppets and cartoon characters live there as well as humans who tell stories, sing, and dance.

The series of programs is designed to help prepare three-, four-, and five-year-old children for school. The program teaches letters, numbers, new words, and special skills. The use of lively cartoons and films makes the learning fun.

No one is too old to enjoy the songs, games, puppets, and cartoons on "Sesame Street."

Commission on Human Rights

White is beautiful.
Black is beautiful.
Yellow is beautiful.

<u>People</u> is beautiful.

Citizenship

A new poster is riding high on the sides of buses. It is deep down on subway walls. It is all around New York City.

The poster is written in slang. But it has a message for all people who read it. What do you think the poster means?

China 'Pongs' To U.S. 'Ping'

"I was quite a Ping-Pong player in my days at law school," President Nixon told his aides the other day. "I might say I was fairly good at it."

Ping-Pong is a favorite subject with the President now. He has been talking about the game since early April. That was when the Chinese Communists invited 15 American Ping-Pong players to visit the People's Republic of China. The players were the first American group to enter that country in more than 20 years.

The invitation surprised and delighted Mr. Nixon. He took it as a signal that leaders of the People's China wanted to improve relations with the United States.

Enemies for 22 Years. The two countries have been on unfriendly terms since 1949. In that year, the Chinese Communists seized the mainland of China and set up a Communist government there called the People's Republic. The U.S. refused to recognize the new government. The U.S. continued to recognize the old Nationalist government that had fled to the island of Taiwan (TIGH-wahn).

The U.S. also stopped all trade with mainland China. It discouraged Americans from traveling there. And it blocked entry of the country into the United Nations.

The Chinese Communists, for their part, closed their borders to Americans and started a "hate-America" campaign. Chinese children were taught from a very early age that Americans were "foreign devils."

Moves Toward Friendship. In recent years, U.S. leaders have talked about restoring friendship between the Chinese and American people. Two months ago President Nixon made a first move. He lifted a ban on U.S. travel to the Chinese mainland.

For a while the President thought the Chinese would not respond. Then came the Ping-Pong invitation. For the Chinese, it was a big move. Ping-Pong is their national game.

The American players were given

"Sure it's a hooky game... but at least he's wagging his tail."

Copyright, 1971, the Courier-Journal and Louisville Times Co. Reprinted by permission of Hugh Haynie.

a warm welcome in China. They were stuffed with such Chinese delicacies as smoked duck and hundred-year-old eggs. They were shown the Great Wall. They were taken on a tour of a factory, a school, and a farm. They were presented to Chou En-lai (joh en-ligh), one of Communist China's three top leaders.

Chou shook hands with each American player. He chatted for some time with long-haired Glenn Cowan about the hippie movement. Then Chou told the group: "You have opened a new page in the relations of the Chinese and American people."

What Next? Less than a day after Mr. Chou made his remark about a "new page," Americans began filling it in. The head of the U.S. Ping-Pong team invited the Chinese team to visit the United States. President Nixon announced that the U.S. was ready to start some trade with the People's Republic of China.

What else will be on the page? U.S. officials caution against expecting too much more too soon. Two problems, they say, are in the way of closer ties. One is America's continuing support of the Nationalist Chinese government on Taiwan. The other is the Vietnam war. The Americans and the Chinese Communists take different sides in that war.

Cartoonist shows U.S., represented by President Nixon, playing Ping-Pong with Communist China, a dragon with leader Mao Tse-tung's head. Net is Great Wall, built centuries ago to keep out China's enemies. Wall stretches more than 1,500 miles across northern China.

AEP Map by Joe Cornicelli

Map shows places visited by U.S. Ping-Pong team.

Wide World

American Ping-Pong player shakes hands with Premier Chou En-lai.

Nevertheless, there is a hopeful feeling in Washington about future Chinese-American relations. President Nixon is talking of visiting China one day. And crystal-ball gazers see American and Chinese leaders meeting at the Ping-Pong table.

Blacks Gain Public Offices

Kenneth Gibson was sworn in as mayor of Newark last summer.

Mayor Carl Stokes of Cleveland and Congressman Louis Stokes

Wilson Riles is new head of California school system.

Gwen Cherry is newly elected Florida lawmaker.

Senator Edward Brooke is only black in U.S. Senate.

IN MAYORS' offices, congressmen's offices, and other public offices changes are taking place. More blacks are running for office and winning. Thus, as the U.S. marks Negro History Week (February 7-13), many Negroes are adding to their history.

In the 1970 elections, three big-city offices were won by blacks. The cities of Dayton, Ohio; Wichita, Kansas; and Newark, New Jersey, elected black mayors. Altogether there are close to 50 black mayors in the U.S., including Carl Stokes of Cleveland and Walter Washington of Washington, D.C.

THE November elections added three black congressmen to the U.S. House of Representatives. There are now 12 Negroes in the House of Representatives, the largest number ever. The only black in the U.S. Senate is Edward Brooke of Massachusetts.

Negroes have also been elected to state legislatures, school boards, and various city offices. There are about 1,500 elected Negro officials—more than ever before.

Blacks running for office, helping in campaigns, or going out to vote do so in the belief that changes to better their lives can be brought about by law. This is called working within the American system.

SHIRLEY CHISHOLM, congresswoman from Brooklyn, said, "Once you're within the system, you have a chance to bring about certain changes." She is the first black woman member of the House of Representatives. She was reelected to a second term in November. "I'm here to help bring about change," she says. Having lived in the slum area she serves in Congress, Mrs. Chisholm knows the changes needed to better the lives of her people.

In Florida, Gwen Cherry became the first black woman elected to the Florida legislature. She has been a science teacher and a lawyer. Mrs. Cherry wants young people to believe that they too can achieve. Her own goal in life has been to do something important.

AN IMPORTANT office in California was won by a black, Dr. Wilson C. Riles. He was elected to head the state's school system, the largest in the U.S. One of Dr. Riles's goals is to find ways to get more money for schools. He is also much interested in the teaching of very young children.

Black leader Roy Wilkins recently summed up the 1970 elections. "They proved that millions of Negro Americans have chosen to work within the framework of the American system."

CONSUMERS ATTACK...

...UNSAFE CARS
UNCLEAN MEAT   UNSAFE MINES
UNSAFE TOYS
UNSAFE GAS PIPELINES...

Ralph Nader has been called a consumer champion. Why do we show him as a knight?

"This toy oven is dangerous. It gets too hot and could harm a child," a man told a judge.

"Nylon stockings don't last at all. They run as soon as they are put on," several women wrote to their congressmen in Washington.

"How can I tell whether this meat is fresh?" asked a shopper in a supermarket.

These are the voices of consumers. More and more consumers are making themselves heard across the land. Anyone who buys and uses a product or pays for services is a consumer. Consumers are complaining about many things, from poor products to poor repair work.

Powerful Voice. The strongest consumer voice among individuals is that of Ralph Nader, a lawyer. He first got interested in cars. He felt that many were not built for safe driving. He made a special study of one car, the Corvair. In 1965 he brought out a book about it, *Unsafe at Any Speed*. The book made him famous. The sales of Corvairs went down and the company stopped making them in 1969. Nader made speeches and appeared before Congress, talking about unsafe cars and tires. As a result, the Government set up stricter rules for making cars and tires safer.

Nader went on to attack unclean meat, unsafe natural gas pipelines, and unsafe mines. Laws aimed at correcting these conditions were passed by Congress. Nader is given a great deal of credit for making Congress see the need for these laws. He has also complained about fatty hot dogs and unclean fish.

Nader has been criticized by some businessmen for his work. His answer is that he is not against business but that he is for people.

Growth of Consumer Power. Nader's work has caused a growth of consumer power. More consumers are worried about health and safety and are asking for better goods and services.

Groups of young lawyers have joined Nader. Called Nader's Raiders, they have studied U.S. Government agencies. They try to find out whether the agencies are serving the people.

Members of Congress are aware of growing consumer power. They are thinking of setting up a consumer office that would be a strong voice in Government for the consumer.

One consumer claimed that loud toy guns and steel-tipped darts are dangerous.

Science

Chinese Use Needles To Deaden Pain

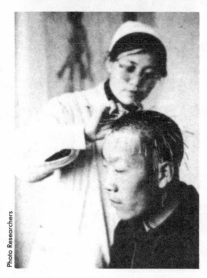

A number of thin, sharp needles are used in the ancient art of acupuncture.

Can needles that are stuck into a person's skin really kill pain? Some Chinese doctors use needles for killing all kinds of pain. The Chinese call this method *acupuncture*. It is a method that has been used in that country for more than 2,000 years.

Visitors Watch Operation

Recently some Canadians who visited the Chinese mainland had a chance to see acupuncture used during an operation. The operation was on a patient's heart. The heart patient was a middle-aged Chinese woman. To prepare her for the operation, needles were put into her wrists and forearms. The needles were the only form of pain-killer used during the operation.

Then the operation began. As the doctors operated on the woman, she remained awake and aware of the entire work being done. She was able to talk to the visitors who were watching the operation.

At one time during the operation, the woman asked for and received a glass of orange juice. She drank the juice without any difficulty. When the operation was over, the woman thanked the doctors. Then she turned to the visitors, said good-bye to them, and was taken directly to her hospital room.

Different persons have different ideas about how acupuncture works. But many Chinese doctors continue the practice of this ancient method in treating patients today.

Imagination Fun

Look at the picture, then have some fun using your imagination.

- Write a funny caption.
- Make up a "news" story.
- Make up a conversation. Tell what the mother and her pup are saying.
- Pretend you are the pup. Tell how you feel about this walk.

Red-Hot Vida Blue

Sports. A 22-year-old pitcher has become a sensation in the baseball world. His name is Vida Blue. Vida pitches for the Oakland Athletics and has won more than 20 games this year. His red-hot performance is one of the reasons the A's are having a winning season.

Vida came up to the American League about a year ago. He pitched several games for the A's in 1970. He even threw a no-hitter.

Baseball experts feel that Vida is one of the best fastballers in the league. His fast ball travels almost 100 miles an hour!

Van Bucher from Photo Researchers

Wide World

Japan Light Machinery Info. Center

UPI

Japanese Products Flood U.S.

Do you have a new television set at your house? If you do, check the back to see where it was made. Chances are one in three that it was made in Japan.

And what about your transistor radio, your camera, your brother's motorbike, your family's car? Figures show that nine out of every ten transistors sold in the U.S. are stamped "Made in Japan." So are two out of every three cameras, seven out of every ten motorbikes, and one out of every 15 cars.

The big sales of these and other Japanese products in the U.S. are a cause of growing concern. The Japanese sales mean a loss in sales and profits for some U.S. manufacturers. They also mean fewer jobs for U.S. workers.

Reasons for Japan's Booming Sales. Japanese salesmen do well in the U.S. because Japanese products are usually high in quality but low in price. In most cases, the price tag on a Japanese-made product is less than the price tag on a similar U.S.-made product.

The Japanese can charge less for products because their labor costs are lower. The average wage in Japan is about 90 cents an hour plus some added benefits. In the U.S. the average wage is $2.56 an hour.

Another reason for the booming Japanese trade here is the fact that in the past the U.S. has encouraged Japanese trade. It was one way of helping Japan recover from defeat in World War II (1941-45).

Complaints from U.S. Industry. The Japanese trade was all right with U.S. manufacturers so long as Japanese sales to the U.S. were less than U.S. sales to Japan. In 1964, however, Japan began selling more to the U.S. than it bought from the U.S. (see graph). By last year the trade difference in favor of Japan was about $3 billion. U.S. industry sounded an alarm. Businessmen and labor leaders began asking the U.S. Government to do something to even the trade exchange.

Ways of Dealing With Problem. According to business experts, there are several things the Government could do. It could protect U.S. industries by placing high taxes on all products coming into this country from Japan. The taxes would raise the prices of the Japanese products. Fewer Americans would buy them.

Or the U.S. could place limits on the amount of products that Japan could sell here.

Or the U.S. could let Japan have the market in products such as TV sets and cameras. U.S. manufacturers could then concentrate on things that Japan does not make or does not make as cheaply, such as jet planes and computers. In return, the Japanese could let these American specialties enter Japan. Japan now keeps out many U.S. products.

Action Taken by U.S. Government. So far the U.S. Government has chosen a middle course. It has

(cont. next page)

changed the value of the dollar so that foreign-made goods will cost more in this country. It has asked the Japanese to cut back their exports here. And it has asked the Japanese to make it easier for U.S. manufacturers to sell in Japan.

Japan has responded by limiting the amount of wool and man-made cloth it ships to the U.S. It also has begun letting in more of some U.S. products.

U.S. manufacturers welcome these moves by Japan. They do not believe, however, that the moves are coming fast enough or going far enough to solve the U.S. trade problem. Stronger action by the U.S. Government may be necessary, these manufacturers say.

Workers in Sony TV plant in Tokyo prepare sets for marketing.

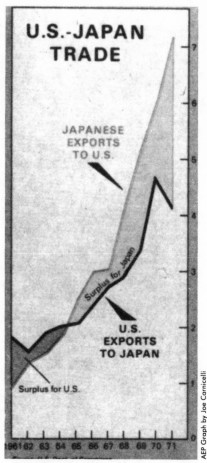

Present trade picture favors Japan.

Is Cable TV Coming to Your Home?

How would you like it

—if you could get 20 to 40 different channels on your TV set?

—if one of those channels continually broadcast time, news, and weather?

—if another showed a first-run Hollywood movie every night?

—if another brought live coverage of local events such as a high school game or a rock concert?

Well, all these things are possible with cable TV.

Cable TV is different from regular TV. It does not use rooftop antennas or "rabbit ears" to pull in signals from the air. Instead it uses a huge tower antenna. The tower is usually on a hilltop or in some other good reception area. The antenna collects TV signals from nearby and far away. These signals are then sent out to homes through cables, or wires.

The cost of hooking up to cable TV is around $15. On top of that there is a monthly service charge of $5 to $7.

These charges may turn some of you off cable TV. If you can get David Cassidy, Walter Cronkite, Flip Wilson, and the World Series on regular TV for free, you may ask: "Why should I hook to cable and pay?"

Cable TV salesmen give this answer: "Cable TV offers you more than regular TV. First of all, it gives you more channels. These allow a wider choice of programs. Second, it gives you special channels. These can be used free of charge by schools, the local government, and even you.

"And third," the salesmen say, "cable TV gives you better reception. Pictures are clearer. There is almost no snow or flutter. Cables are not affected by outside troublemakers such as mountains or storms."

A Woman President?

Shirley Chisholm wants to be President of the U.S. The U.S. has never had a woman President.

This year is an election year. Mrs. Chisholm may run for President.

Shirley Chisholm is now a member of Congress. Congress makes laws for the U.S. Mrs. Chisholm is the first black woman in Congress.

Citizens in Action

Sixth grader Randy Layton of Central Point, Oregon, gives a hoot about the environment. He wants other people to give a hoot too. That's the message he put on his prizewinning poster entered in the Oregon State Federation of Garden Clubs contest.

The U.S Forest Service is also using the slogan "Give a Hoot—Don't Pollute."

Antifreeze in Blood of Fish

Dr. DeVries studies a friendly fellow who may become part of his experiments on sea life in Antarctica.

A black perch is caught off the California coast and flown to Antarctica. There it is placed into the icy waters of McMurdo Sound. It freezes almost immediately. Yet, there in the same waters, thousands of other fish live. They stay alive even though the salt water is almost freezing at 28 degrees above zero.

Dr. Arthur DeVries, a scientist, has been trying to solve this mystery for the past six years. Part of this time has been spent in Antarctica studying fish, crabs, and other sea life. Now he thinks he has found the answer.

Dr. DeVries believes that fish living in the Antarctic waters have an antifreeze substance in their blood. The substance acts like the antifreeze in autos by lowering the freezing point of the blood. But he has also found that all fish do not have this antifreeze substance—or at least in equal amounts.

Scientists hope that the fishy antifreeze substance can be chemically made by man. Then it could be used to solve some of man's problems.

Airlines Check Travelers

Wide World

Airline workers check travelers at airports. The workers are watching out for hijackers. A hijacker takes over a plane. The pilot must fly wherever the hijacker wants to go.

One new checker is called Friskem. A worker holds Friskem in his hand. People walk by. Friskem lights up if a person is carrying a gun, a knife, or a bomb.

Here's Vicky

Hello, Friends,

If you are reading this then you are smart! You worked out how to read my letter.

My pals and I wanted to fool you. Look at the date. What special day is coming along? Are you getting ready to fool all your friends? How will you fool them? We're sure you'll think up some very funny ways.

April Fool! Vicky

Living things grow.

Mark the things that grow.

Scene of the Crime

Watergate Whodunit

Watergate is

_____ a. a group of apartment and office buildings

_____ b. the old location of the Democratic party headquarters

_____ c. the name of a bugging and burglary case

_____ d. a scandal that could damage the Republican party and the office of President.

If you checked all four answers, you are right. Watergate *is* an apartment-office complex in Washington, D.C. The Democrats *did* have an office there until last month. And on June 17, 1972, five men with ties to the Committee for the Reelection of the President were caught breaking into that office. The men had bugging equipment with them. It was reported that they were looking for information that might be used in the President's campaign against the Democrats.

The men were arrested along with two other conspirators. The seven were brought to trial and, in January, were convicted of burglary and wiretapping.

LATER DEVELOPMENTS

Throughout the investigation and trial of the Watergate seven, the word from the White House was that nobody there or in a top position on the Committee for Reelection knew about, or had anything to do with, the crime.

The President himself said on August 29: "Investigation indicates that no one in the White House staff, no one in this Administration, presently employed, was involved in this very bizarre incident."

But some newspapermen, some congressmen, and one of the trial judges thought that someone higher up was involved. They kept asking questions: "Who planned the break-in?" "Who hired the burglars?"

On March 19, one of the seven convicted men began giving some answers. He charged that:

● pressure was put on the seven to plead guilty and keep quiet.

● there was lying during the trial.

● others, including some close to the President, had known about and approved the bugging plan.

These charges troubled many Republican lawmakers. They began putting pressure on the President to do something to clear up the case. It was hurting the Republican party, they said.

On April 17, the President announced that he had done something. He had made a new investigation into the case. This investigation, he said, had uncovered facts that had not been known before. He hinted that some people in the White House might have been involved. If that is found to be true, he said, they will be fired.

The President followed that announcement with another on April 30. He had accepted the resignations of two top aides. He had asked for and accepted the resignation of another. All three men are rumored to have had something to do with Watergate. Court action, the President said, will determine whether or not any of the men are guilty of wrongdoing.

POSSIBLE EFFECTS

The President's announcements were greeted with some relief. Some people expressed fear, however, that even with this action, Watergate may have a long-lasting effect in damage to the Republican party and loss of trust in Government.

"Ouch!"

Hesse in St. Louis Globe-Democrat

Senior Report

Fuel Shortage Hits Parts of U.S.

• In Denver, Colorado, 23 schools were closed for a week because there was no gas to heat them.

• In Brainard, Nebraska, more than 100,000 bushels of wet corn were piled on the streets because farmers couldn't get fuel to dry the harvested crop.

• In Des Moines, Iowa, employees at one factory were told to come to work dressed for the outdoors. The thermostat was being turned down to 45 degrees.

And that's only part of the story. In many other cities and towns in the Midwest this month, there were closings of schools and factories and lowered temperatures because of a shortage of natural gas fuel.

Blame the Weather! The gas shortage is being blamed chiefly on the weather. A wet fall and an unusually cold winter have brought more demands for gas fuel than companies can meet.

The head of one gas supply company explains: "We can get only so much gas a day. We don't have enough to go around."

Homeowners have first call on the gas and are still getting deliveries. Gas companies have had to cut off service, however, to many schools, grain dryers, and factories.

Most of these buildings have equipment to switch over to oil heat in an emergency. In the past, that is what they have done. But this winter, supplies of heating oil are tight too. The reason, says U.S. emergency planner George Lincoln, is that refineries haven't been making extra heating oil. Instead they've been making more gasoline to meet a rising demand for that fuel.

The gasoline demand is up, Lincoln explains, because more cars are on the road, and new cars with their anti-pollution devices use more gas.

Imports to the Rescue. The Government is concerned about the present fuel shortage and has taken steps to ease it. Imports of heating oil have been increased. Shipments are now on the way to the U.S. from the Virgin Islands and the Soviet Union.

In addition, a campaign has been started to get Americans to save fuel. People are being asked to lower thermostat settings by 2 or 3 degrees, to keep shades pulled, and to shut off heat in unused rooms.

Long-Term Answers. Besides these short-term relief measures, the Government is making plans to meet future fuel needs. It is encouraging oilmen to build more refineries and to search for new deposits of oil and gas. Experts warn that present U.S. supplies of these fuels are fast being used up. Known supplies of U.S. natural gas, they say, could run out in another 20 to 25 years.

The Government is also looking for a cheap way to turn coal into a clean-burning gas fuel. The U.S. has plenty of coal, but burned in its solid state, environmentalists say it is too dirty.

Experts doubt that these and other answers to the fuel problem will come in time to save the U.S. from more fuel-short winters. What Americans had better hope for, one expert says, is a ten-year spell of warmer weather.

Wide World

XEP Photo by Tom Keyes

(*Above*) Wet corn is piled on Midwest street awaiting fuel for drying equipment. (*Below*) Oil is delivered to home in Northeast. Supply is tight in many areas.

Right:
*Trudy Mitchell
is a roofer
in Utah. She says
that she might
like to learn plumb-
ing later.*
Below:
*Alane Vannater
is a cable TV in-
staller in Nevada.
She took the job
because she wanted
to work outdoors.*

Right below:
*Marsha Carlisle
put on a hard hat
and went to
work on a sewage treat-
ment plant in New
Hampshire.*
Center below:
*Emmie Peek
took truck driv-
er training
in New York. She now
drives her own
truck hauling cargo.*

Women Now Work In Many Kinds Of Jobs

"I don't want a desk job—I'm just one of those people who doesn't mind getting dirty," said Trudy Mitchell. She was answering a newsman's questions about her work as a roofer in Utah.

Marsha Carlisle was asked about her work as a laborer. She said, "I'm just trying to make some money."

Many Reasons. The answers suggest some of the reasons why many women are seeking jobs that in the past have usually been held by men. Some women like the jobs because they want to work outdoors or because they like working with tools. Better pay is another big reason. In Maryland, Liane Cammack and her daughter took a welding course. They had worked as clerks and said that the pay was too low. They like the high pay earned by welders.

A big change in the job picture is thus taking place in the U.S. Women work as house painters, electricians, telephone repairers, auto mechanics, and carpenters. A coming big work field for women is expected to be home appliance repair.

Part of the change also is in fields where women have held the same jobs as men. In such jobs women are trying to be treated equally with men for advancement to higher paying jobs. Many companies are now looking for women

to fill top jobs. Women may become managers of banks or top officers in big industries.

Many top jobs in industries take special training. Women in colleges are taking courses that will open up new kinds of jobs for them. For example, twice as many women as in the past are now studying to be engineers.

Government Help. Moving into men's jobs has not been easy for women. Women who have been trying to get such jobs are now getting help from the Government.

The Government has set up rules against job discrimination. Under the rules, all jobs should be open to women. A woman cannot, for example, be barred from a job that requires lifting loads. An equal pay law also requires that women get the same pay as men for the same kind of work.

Wide World

Olga Is Tops

Olga Korbut is the girl athlete of the year. She won the award in New York.

Olga is only 4 feet 10 inches tall. But she does flips, handstands, and great moves on a balance beam.

The gymnast is from Russia. She and five other Russian gymnasts traveled the U.S. They visited many cities and put on shows.

Olga made a hit with many Americans. In Chicago they had "Olga Korbut Day."

'Come Get Your Din-Din, Morris'

Morris is TV's most famous cat. He stars in cat food commercials. Morris acts finicky. He "tells" other cats, "You have to act finicky to keep your human under control."

A man found Morris at an animal shelter in Chicago. He took Morris to a commercial tryout. Many cats had tried out before. But when Morris walked in, he got the job on the spot.

9-Lives

Wide World

Roberto Clemente, Superstar

Wide World

"Roberto was the greatest ballplayer I ever saw." "Roberto died serving his fellowman." People said these things about Roberto Clemente.

Roberto Clemente was a baseball superstar from Puerto Rico. He played right field for the Pittsburgh Pirates. He won several baseball awards.

Roberto died in a plane crash. He was on his way to Nicaragua. There had been an earthquake in that country. Thousands of survivors had no food or homes. Roberto was taking food and money to them. His plane crashed on takeoff from San Juan, Puerto Rico.

What Can U.S. Do To Help Feed World's Hungry?

Dibo is 11 years old. He lives in West Africa, south of the Sahara. And he is hungry.

Dibo will tell you that he hasn't had a meal in as many days as he can remember. He has lived, he says, on leaves and grass.

A visitor can see that Dibo is suffering from a lack of proper food. The child shows all the signs of malnutrition. His stomach is swollen. His arms and legs are matchstick thin. And his eyes are sunken and staring.

Dibo isn't alone in his suffering. There are millions like him in the world today. According to a U.N. report, one of every four people may be suffering from hunger and its consequences.

Why So Much Hunger?

Why is there so much hunger in the world? Experts say it's because growing populations are eating up food faster than the world's farmers can produce it.

This year the world is expected to produce 942 million tons of grain, not counting rice. That's 27 million tons less than the world consumed last year.

Part of the reason for the shortfall, experts say, is bad weather. Droughts and floods have hurt crops in some of the world's main food-growing regions. Some of these are places where food is most needed.

Nations that have been particularly hard hit are India and Bangladesh. Millions there may starve before the year is out.

In Africa below the Sahara—another hard-hit region—drought burned up almost all the crops seven years in a row. The loss of food has caused the deaths of at least 200,000 people.

Another reason experts give for the present food crisis is a shortage of fertilizer. Fertilizer can double crop yield but its price is high now because of the shortage. Those nations most needing it can't afford it.

What Can the U.S. Do?

In the past, most hungry nations have turned to the U.S. for food. The U.S. is the leading exporter of grain and one of the world's few food-surplus nations. Now, however, even the U.S. supplies are dwindling.

If the U.S. is to go on sharing its resources, says Dr. Lester Brown of the Overseas Development Council, "Americans will have to do the food equivalent of turning thermostats down 6 degrees—that is, skip one meal a week."

Other public officials have suggested that Americans give up one hamburger a week. Beef cattle eat huge amounts of grain. If the U.S. raised less beef, there would be more grain available to ship abroad.

Another thing the U.S. might ship abroad, says Senator Hubert Humphrey, is the 3 million tons of fertilizer it spreads on lawns and golf courses.

These conservation measures may help in the short run. For long-run help, some experts suggest that the U.S. and other food-rich countries put a part of each year's crop into a world grain bank for use when needed.

The U.S. could also encourage its farmers to grow more, experts say. And it could help farmers in other lands grow more by teaching them modern farming methods.

If the U.S. doesn't share its resources and knowledge, Mr. Brown says, a year from now Americans may "see people starve to death on the TV news."

Hungry child in India awaits day's only nutritious meal from UNICEF.

Some Win And Some Lose In Energy Crisis

Tony Costa is a winner. He cleans chimneys for a living. He decided to be a chimney sweep when he was in high school. He got the idea, he said, from the chimney sweeps in the Mary Poppins movie.

For years, Costa's business was pretty slow. He got maybe one or two jobs a week. Then the Arabs cut off oil shipments. Natural gas suppliers ran short. And suddenly everybody wanted to use fireplaces. "Bingo!" said Tony. "I started getting more calls than I could take care of. If they added five days to every week, I still wouldn't be able to keep up."

Energy crisis keeps oil-lamp makers busy.

. . . brings orders to insulation firm.

Sam Lewis is a loser. He owns a plastic toy factory. In the good old days of 1971 and 1972, he was doing several million dollars worth of business a year. He had 90 people working for him.

Now he can't get enough raw materials for his plastics. They're made from oil. His business has been cut in half and he's had to lay off 32 people. "If the oil shortage gets any worse," he said, "I'll have to close down."

There are other winners and losers in the energy crisis. On the winning side are makers of things that keep people and places warm. That includes makers of heavy winter clothing, storm windows, and wood-burning stoves.

On the losing side are those who need oil for power, those who need it for products—such as plastics, drugs, nylon—and those who depend on other people having it. The last group includes most of the recreation industries.

Some Big Losers. Some of the losers are really hurting. Large automakers, for example, are stuck with big cars they can't sell. The cars are gas-guzzlers and many people don't want them. The companies have had to cut their big-car production. That has meant temporary shutdowns and layoffs. General Motors closed down 16 plants for a while, idling 105,000 workers.

Small-plane makers are having their troubles, too. President Nixon has ordered a big cut in fuel for pleasure and business flying. Industry officials say the cut could throw 150,000 people out of work in a matter of six months. Cessna Aircraft in Witchita, Kansas, has already laid off 2,400 of its 11,400 workers.

The ski industry could also suffer. The President of Ski Industries America says fuel shortages and the Sunday closing of gas stations threatens 750,000 jobs and $2 billion in business.

Outlook for '74. The Government is trying to keep the en-

ergy crisis from causing even greater hardship for U.S. industries. The President has asked for a cutback in the use of oil in homes and office buildings so that industries will have more. He has also asked for lower clean-air standards so some factories and power plants can burn coal instead of oil.

If these oil-saving measures are carried out, if the winter is mild, if the Arabs start shipping us oil again, the outlook for 1974 is not too grim. According to a top White House official, the crisis should not cause too many more people to lose their jobs.

On the other hand, if people don't conserve energy, if the winter is cold, if the Arabs continue to refuse to sell us oil, some experts are predicting a very bad year. Prices for fuel, they say could go out of sight. Many businesses could be forced to close down. As many as 14 million of the 84 million people now working could be out of jobs.

Energy crisis hurts plastic makers.

. . . hits Vermont's ski industry.

Robinson Is Named the First Black Manager

UPI

FRANK ROBINSON has become the first black manager in major-league baseball history.

He also will be the highest paid manager. The Cleveland Indians set his salary at $173,000 per year.

"I've wanted this for a long time," said Robinson after being told of his new job.

But he will be more than just a manager. Robinson will be one of the few playing managers. He is the Indians' designated hitter.

Some baseball people are against managers also playing ball. They argue that just being manager takes up most of a person's time. But the Indians don't feel that way. They seem to like having a man who is both manager and a designated hitter and has more home runs than anybody except Henry Aaron, Babe Ruth, and Willie Mays.

The role of manager will not be new to Robinson. He managed the Puerto Rican League Santurce Club for five years.

"I managed them because I wanted to be ready if a major-league job opened," he said. "I wanted to learn what it's like to handle 25 personalities."

What will Robinson be like as a major-league manager?

He has said, "I am an uncomplicated, single-minded guy. My single-mindedness involves baseball. I'm not out to win friends. Just ball games."

eye on news

Writing Aid

Becky Schroeder's invention helps people write in the dark. The 12-year-old came up with the idea of coating a heavy sheet of paper with phosphorescent paint. When the sheet is put under writing paper, it glows in the dark for as long as two hours. Becky got the idea while trying to do her homework one evening while waiting in her mom's car.

The U.S. Patent Office gave Becky's invention Patent No. 3,832,556. Becky is now one of the youngest patent holders in the U.S.

Wide World

Becky had a "bright" idea!

Senior Spinoff

Women on the Beat?

Editor: I don't think that there should be policewomen on the force because they don't know how to run and they are too scared to shoot a gun and they are reckless drivers.
—*Steve Rackley   Easley, S.C.*

Editor: I think there should be women on the force, because there would be more people on the force and less people getting away. There might be men who would quit, but there would be lots of women trying. Men might be stronger, but women are supposed to be smarter.
—*Jeff McClure   Easley, S.C.*

Editor: I think there should not be any female cops. I think the women's place is in a home and the men's place is on the beat.
—*David Clifford   Syracuse, N.Y.*

Editor: I think that 50 percent should be women police because I think women should have equal rights.
—*Ronald Howell   Hartshorn, Mo.*

Science News

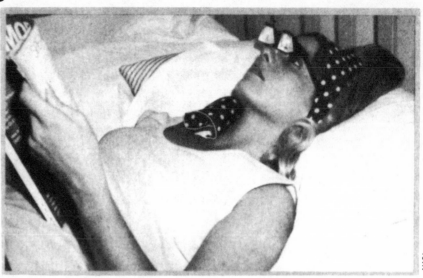

NASA

Women Given Space Tests

The nurse reads without raising her head.

How will women do on long space trips? In California, space scientists gave 12 flight nurses some tests to find out.

Some of the tests checked to see how the women might feel without *gravity*. Gravity is a special kind of pull. It keeps people and things from floating off into space.

One of the tests made the nurses feel the same weightlessness spacemen feel in space.

The nurses lay on beds. They kept very still. The women were fed and bathed. Some nurses passed the time by reading books. They didn't lift their heads. The nurses used special eyeglasses.

Scientists found some women could do as well as men on long space flights. Maybe the first Space Shuttle flight will have women scientists on board.

The Sun Helps Heat a School

Many places are using the sun to help heat buildings these days. Boxes made of glass are set up to trap the heat from the sun. Behind these glass boxes are metal pipes filled with water. They are painted black because dark colors help to hold heat. The warm water is then pumped through more pipes to heat the building.

The school in the photo at right has 180 glass panels on the roof to help catch the heat from the sun. The sunlight heats about 150,000 gallons of water. This hot water is then pumped through special pipes to help heat some of the classrooms in the school.

Your class might like to try a simple experiment to find out how the sun can help heat buildings. The materials you will need and the directions are given in the Teacher's Edition.

UPI

The Timonium Elementary School, Maryland, was the first school in the U.S. to be heated by solar energy.

New World Greets Viet Orphans

Nurse plays with South Vietnamese orphan after her arrival in U.S.

Lua blinked back tears as she was carried off the huge jet at the Los Angeles airport.

The four-year-old heard an airline official call out her name. Then a strange man and woman ran toward her.

The little girl looked frightened. But the man took her in his arms and hugged her. The woman hugged her too. Lua gazed at them both. Then she smiled.

A few minutes later, Lua was tottering out of the airport, her hands in the hands of her new parents.

Lua was one of 2,000 war orphans flown to the U.S. recently from South Vietnam. The orphans ranged in age from two months to 12 years. Most, like Lua, had adoptive parents waiting for them.

Orphan Airlift. The airlift of the orphans was the idea of Ed Daly, president of World Airways. Daly was in Saigon, the South Vietnamese capital, when fighting began to close in around the city. He became concerned for the safety of the children in Saigon's orphanages.

Daly arranged to have the first group of children flown out in one of his own planes. Then the U.S. Government took over the job.

The first Government flight ended in tragedy. The jet crashed, killing many of the children and adults on board. But the tragedy did not stop the airlift. It continued, and the rest of the children arrived safely in the United States.

The arrival of the orphans brought an outpouring of offers to adopt them. When people were told that most of the 2,000 already had been spoken for, they pleaded that more orphans be flown here. An estimated 25,000 remain in Vietnamese orphanages.

How Good for the Children? Not everyone in the U.S. feels that continuing the airlift is a good idea. Some believe it is bad for the children to be taken from their homeland to a country where sounds, foods, and faces are different.

"We're ripping them right out of their culture, their community," said an American doctor. "I don't think we understand the value of those things."

The orphan airlift is also opposed by many Vietnamese. They accuse the U.S. of "robbing" their country of its children. They say all Vietnamese —Communists as well as non-Communists—love children. The orphans will be cared for, whoever is in power.

Americans in favor of the airlift answer this argument by saying that left in Vietnam, the orphans face a bleak future. Their country has been torn apart by war. No matter how much the Vietnamese love children, they do not have the means to care for all those who are homeless. The orphans will be better off in loving homes in the U.S., these Americans say.

Some Americans also feel a special responsibility for the children. "Our participation in the war helped make these children orphans. It is our duty to care for them," one said.

President Ford said, "This is the least we can do."

Orphans from South Vietnam rest aboard World Airways jet during refueling stop in Japan. Children were on their way to new homes in the United States. Trip was planned and paid for by World Airways president Edward Daly

Citizen Lee Once Again

"It's an excellent thing for Congress to do, particularly at this time of our Bicentennial," said Robert E. Lee IV. Congress had just voted to make his great-grandfather a citizen once again.

The first Robert E. Lee was commander of the Confederate Army during the Civil War. He lost his citizenship by leading troops against the U.S. Government.

At the war's end, Gen. Lee asked President Andrew Johnson for a pardon. This would have given Lee back his citizenship. The pardon was never granted. The reason may have been the absence of a required oath of loyalty to the U.S. Lee had signed an oath, but for some reason it never reached the President.

The oath was found in 1970, buried among old papers in the National Archives—the building where Government records are kept. Following the discovery, a bill was introduced in Congress to give Lee full citizenship. The bill passed this year.

Statue of Lee stands in Richmond, Va.

Message to Outer Space: 'Is Anyone There?'

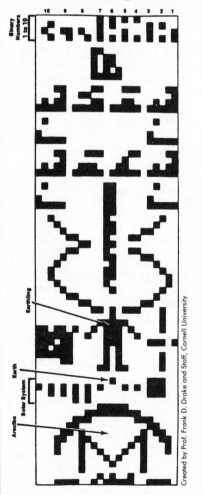

Created by Prof. Frank D. Drake and Staff, Cornell University

"Ark," said Zark, sitting in an observatory on a planet of Messier 13, a cluster of 300,000 stars near the edge of the Milky Way. "I think I am getting a message from outer space."

His colleagues ran rapidly to see what message their huge radio antenna was picking up.

"It's in binary code—a signal system used by primitive computers," said Zing, head of the observatory.

"It must be from an intelligent civilization," said Zark. "Look, the top section is the binary code for a number system based on 10."

"Yes," said Zing. "And there, below it, is what must be a representation of the creature sending the message."

"And below that is a diagram of a nine-planet solar system. The message must be coming from the star's third planet," Zark said.

"But what is that symbol below?" asked Zing.

"It looks like a primitive radio antenna. That must be the instrument used to transmit this signal," replied Zark.

"I've located the source of the signal," said assistant Xanc. "It is very close. The radio message probably took only 24,000 years to reach us."

"Good," Zing replied. "We must answer the message immediately. I hope the people there have a long life span. It will be 48,000 years from the time they sent their message to the time they receive our reply."

The imaginary dialogue above might take place on some distant planet many years from now, if there are any people out there.

The message was sent by the world's largest radio antenna at the Arecibo Observatory in Puerto Rico. The message, which took three minutes to broadcast, was the first attempt by humans to communicate with another planet by radio.

But no one connected with the experiment will know if the message is received and a reply sent. It takes 24,000 years for the signal to reach the Messier 13 star cluster. A reply, if sent the same way, will not reach earth till the year 49974.

NEW PARTS FOR PEOPLE

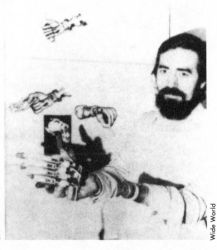

Accident victims show manufactured arms and hands. Fingers on hand at right are moved by a motor.

Kenny B. Fixt is going back to the body shop. The metal plate he had installed last month is working fine. But now he wants to get a radial head *for a joint that's out of whack. He may even have a couple of arteries checked out. Dacron or Teflon replacements might be nice, he thinks.*

Don't be fooled by what you've just read. The gentleman isn't going to an auto repair shop. The parts he wants replaced are in his own body.

The metal plate is in his head. The radial head is for his elbow. And the artificial arteries will replace the worn-out blood carriers in his leg.

The day is coming when more and more people will make plans like those of Kenny's. They will go to a hospital to replace worn-out body parts.

Anyone interested in replacement parts today can find large supplies of body parts on medical shelves. A person can get about 30 important parts of his body replaced if needed.

Why Replace Body Parts?

Bodies need new parts for a number of reasons. Parts come in handy if an accident has happened. A youngster who lost a hand in a bike accident is one example. He got a mechanical hand for about $2,200. He controls the hand with muscles in his lower arm.

Disease is another reason body parts are replaced. Such was the case of a woman who suffered with arthritis in her hip. She got a steel and plastic hip joint for about $1,300. Now, for the first time in years, she can tie a shoe without feeling pain.

New parts can correct birth defects too. A young man born without an outer ear went to a doctor for help. He was fitted with a silicone ear. His own skin grew over the artificial ear. The cost? About $1,500.

How Good Are the New Parts?

How do the manufactured parts measure up to the original equipment we were born with? Very well, reports show.

People with new parts go back to doing such things as dancing, running, and playing golf, tennis, and baseball. A number of hip replacements showed no signs of wear after ten years of use. One new hip was so strong it wasn't even damaged in a skiing accident, even though the skier broke a leg.

Man speaks with artificial larynx after diseased voice box was removed. Above is a joint for thumb.

'Peanuts' Has a Birthday

Charlie Brown is 25 years old this year. Lucy and Linus are too. They were "born" in a cartoon strip in 1950. Charles Schulz first drew the strip that year.

Charles Schulz has done better than the Charlie he draws. Mr. Schulz earned $90 a month when he started the strip. Today "Peanuts" appears in more than a thousand U.S. newspapers. Charles Schulz has earned millions of dollars.

What made "Peanuts" a success? Mr. Schulz thinks that a fun-loving dog named Snoopy did it. What do you think?

Jewish Families Celebrate Holiday

Jewish people around the world are celebrating a holiday this week. It's called Hanukkah (HAH-nə-kə). Another name for this holiday is the Festival of Lights. The festival this year began on November 29. It ends on December 6.

During the festival, Jewish people celebrate a great event in their history. More than 2,000 years ago they were repairing their temple for worship. They didn't think they had enough oil for the lamp in the temple. But the lamp burned brightly for eight days.

Each night of Hanukkah Jewish families light a candle. They eat special festival foods and exchange gifts. Hanukkah is a happy time for Jewish families.

A Jewish boy lights one of the eight candles of a *menorah*.

FUNNYBUNNY   by Don Robison

I'll take fifty hot dogs.

Are they all for you?

No. Pansy Panda will eat one of them.

200

ARE NUCLEAR PLANTS SAFE?

No! Nuclear plants are unsafe, say some scientists and environmentalists. Here demonstrators protest plan to build nuclear plant near foot of volcano in Washington State.

Yes! Nuclear power is safe power, say plant owners, many workers, and some Government scientists. Here, workers protest move by environmentalists to close a plant in New York.

Wide World

New York Times/Paul Hosefros

• *Senior* readers Rhys Evans and John Compton live in Grover City, California. Their homes are about 8 miles from the nearly completed Diablo Canyon nuclear power plant. The plant sits almost on top of a fault that some scientists think may have caused a 1927 earthquake.

Does it bother the boys that this plant may soon go into operation? Are they afraid of an earthquake breaking the plant apart, letting deadly radioactive material escape into the air?

"No," Rhys told *Senior.* "There hasn't been an earthquake there for a long time."

"Well, maybe a little if you think of it," said John. "But Diablo is built real strong. If there is an earthquake, it would probably stand."

• Pam Cavender and George Woodruff live in Huntsville, Alabama, midway between two nuclear plants—Brown's Ferry and Bel Fonte. There was a fire at the Brown's Ferry plant last spring. It could have caused a serious accident. Did that thought frighten these sixth graders?

Pam said: "Yes, I think it was very dangerous. If an accident had occurred, radio-active material might have gotten out into the environment and could have harmed man." But George wasn't bothered too much. "I don't feel there is too much danger from that plant," he told *Senior.*

These sixth graders are taking part in the present debate over nuclear power plants. Are they safe?

Experts Disagree. Some scientists claim that the plants are not safe. Four engineers at nuclear plants recently quit their jobs. Their reason: Nuclear plants are poorly designed and unsafe, they said. One engineer called his plant "an accident waiting to happen."

These scientists want more protection for power plant reactors. A reactor "burns" highly radioactive atomic fuel to produce heat. The heat, in turn, changes water into steam to run generators that produce electric power.

To work safely, a reactor needs a continuous supply of cooling water. If an accident cut off the water supply, the rods holding the atomic fuel could become so hot they would melt. This molten mass might burn a hole through the bottom of the reactor container. Radioactive gases could escape, killing many people.

Power company officials and many nuclear experts say that the chances of such a thing happening are very slight. Reactors, they say, are safe. They have been built with millions of dollars of safety features, including extra water supplies and different sets of pipes to bring the water in.

"Atomic power plants are probably the safest buildings around," claims an official of the Nuclear Regulatory Commission.

A recent Government study of nuclear power plant safety seems to back up this statement. The study showed that the risk of a person's dying in a nuclear power plant accident was one chance in 300 million a year. That is about 120 times smaller than the chance that a person would die in a hurricane.

Supporters of nuclear power think this risk is worth taking. They argue that nuclear plants produce electricity more cheaply than plants run by coal or oil. In addition, nuclear plants do not pollute the air.

How close do you live to the site of a present or future nuclear power plant?

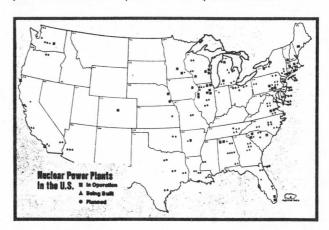

Nuclear Power Plants in the U.S. ▪ In Operation ▲ Being Built ● Planned

Kids Create Bicentennial Art

American Revolution Bicentennial 1776-1976

This likeness of Abe Lincoln is actually a hooked rug made by 13-year-old Annette Dunbebin. Annette is an eighth grader in Takoma Park, Md.

This painting was created by David Huff of Kettering, Ohio. David is a nine-year-old in the fourth grade.

"Ringing Out Liberty" is the name of this pastel drawing created by 13-year-old Tom O'Neil of Kettering, Ohio.

Tom is an eighth grade student. His drawing captures the spirit of freedom in the U.S.

What kind of art best represents America?

That's the question many students in art classes across the U.S. wrestled with recently.

The students came up with their own answers. Some students painted pictures about America. Other students sketched drawings and molded clay figures to show the Bicentennial spirit.

Their artistic efforts were part of a program called "America—Heritage, Festival, and Horizons."

Sixty works of art were finally chosen to represent how kids feel about the U.S. in this Bicentennial year.

Marilee Boland made this sneaker out of clay. Marilee calls her creation "America Size 4½." Marilee is 16 years old and goes to Fairmont West High School in Kettering, Ohio.

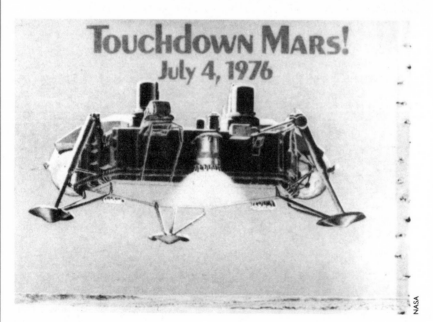

NASA

Hello Mars!... Hello Mars!... Get ready for a visit from earthlings on July 4... Over...

Is there anything on Mars to receive the message?

Scientists are ready and waiting to find out.

They are tuned in to two Viking spacecraft that are journeying 460 million miles from Earth to Mars. The spacecraft will send two landers to the Martian surface. One lander is due to land there July 4, America's birthday. The other is scheduled to land September 4.

Scientists hope the landers will help to answer the age-old question: Is there life on Mars?

Scientists don't expect to find hairy monsters or huge plants as some science fiction writers have dreamed up. But they do hope to find tiny life (microorganisms) that can only be seen with a microscope.

The scientists will look for Martian life in the soil. Digging arms on the landers will scoop up soil and put it in the small labs inside the landers sitting on the Martian surface.

Scientists in California will control the lab experiments by radio. They'll read the information as it comes from Mars.

What are the chances of finding life on the dry, windswept surface of Mars? Scientists have their guesses. What are yours?

Special Olympics

Everyone needs to feel special. Mentally retarded children often face day after day of failure and frustration. The Special Olympics help to give the mentally retarded child a chance to find improvement and self-esteem—to feel special.

The Special Olympics offer youngsters a chance to belong, to make a contribution. They learn skills and team play. "The games offer vital experiences in winning and losing—but most of all in trying," said Eunice Kennedy Shriver, president of Special Olympics, Inc. "As Special Olympics athletes say in the oath that opens the games: 'Let me win, but if I cannot win, let me be brave in the attempt.' "

The Special Olympics give a special kind of joy to those who take part in the activities, whether they win an event or not. They also provide a very special joy to those who watch as the youngsters strive to do their best . . . and a little bit better.

The child below does her thing on the balance beam in a Special Olympics meet. If you've ever tried balancing, you probably know how difficult it is. This youngster's patience and practice paid off!

These girls ran in one of the many events in the International Special Olympics. Their enthusiasm is evident as they strain to do their best and give every ounce of effort to win—or "to be brave in the attempt."

Many of the mentally retarded children have been told that they couldn't compete. They've been told, "You just can't do it!" But the people who work with the youngsters in the Special Olympics programs tell the children, "You can do it, all you need is a chance to try!" With a chance, love, and help, the kids make it!

HAMILL HAIRCUT. Dorothy Hamill made more than sports history when she skated for her Olympic gold medal at Innsbruck. She made hair history. Thousands of girls looked at her short swinging hairdo and wanted the same cut. Now you see it everywhere.

eye on news

Coretta King, president of the King Center, sits by husband's picture.

Celebrations Honor King

Many boys and girls in the United States are planning a party for January 15. They will celebrate the birthday of the slain civil rights leader, Martin Luther King, Jr. Children will sing songs, make posters, and put on plays.

In a few U.S. cities and states, officials have declared January 15 *Martin Luther King Day.*

Celebrations will also be held at The Martin Luther King, Jr. Center for Social Change in Atlanta, Ga.

People who work at the center are trying to carry out Dr. King's dream. His dream was that all people be treated equally and with respect.

'Now Hear This!'

"It's time for you zoo visitors to get smart," squawked Ozzie Ostrich. "You're all watching the wrong animals. Look at you crowding around the seals. So what if they can catch fish out of the air? They can't run and kick."

Ozzie kept on squawking. "I'm the main animal at this zoo. Come on, you other animals! What's so great about you? What? What?"

"Well, I'll tell you why I'm the greatest," said _____ . "I . . . .

TIME OUT FOR HEALTH

New Choking Rescue Method

A two-year-old boy swallows a penny and begins choking. He can't breathe, and his face turns blue. Would you know how to help him? Anna Matos of Hartford, Conn., did.

She stood behind him and grabbed just below his rib cage. She made a fist with one hand and covered it with her other hand. Then she gave a quick, upward push with her hands. Air was forced out of the boy's lungs. The penny popped out of his mouth.

This new rescue method was invented by Dr. Henry Heimlich. It has saved hundreds of people from choking to death. It will soon be taught by the American Red Cross.

(Above) Anna Marie Matos shows classmates the Heimlich method.
(Left) The *back blow* is another choking rescue method.

BIG CITIES CRY 'HELP'

Carlos Sanchez lives in New York City. A few weeks ago a gang of teenagers jumped him. They took off with his bike and school lunch money.

"You were lucky," his friends told him. "You only got robbed. You didn't get beat up."

• Norma Brown lives in Detroit. She's been working as a secretary for a large company. But now the company is planning to move out of Detroit to avoid the high city taxes. Norma will be joining the thousands of Detroiters who are unemployed.

• Donald Friedman lives in St. Louis. He may not live there much longer though. The smoke and chemical fumes are aggravating a lung condition. Some days he can hardly breathe. Doctors tell him to move out of the city.

Crime, unemployment, air pollution are some of the troubles big-city dwellers face today. Other troubles are traffic jams, breakdowns in public transportation, crumbling buildings, poor schools, littered playgrounds, heavy property taxes, and high living costs.

Flight to Suburbs. These troubles are causing thousands of businesses and well-to-do families to flee to the suburbs. Census Bureau figures show that the populations of 37 of the nation's 58 largest cities have fallen since 1970.

When businesses and well-to-do families leave, conditions in the cities grow worse. When businesses go, so do jobs. And when the well-to-do go, so do spending dollars and tax money. The well-to-do are the ones who pay the taxes that pay for the public services.

The loss of tax dollars is forcing the layoff of many city workers. In some cities, libraries have had to close.

Things are especially bad in New York City. Millions of dollars have been borrowed just to keep the gar-

New York City children play in lot next to abandoned building.

bage collected, police on the streets, and teachers in the schools. Now city officials are wondering where they'll get the money to pay back the loans. They hesitate to raise taxes any higher for fear of losing more taxpayers.

Hope for Federal Rescue. The mayors of the troubled cities are counting on the Federal Government to come to the rescue. They have asked President Carter for help.

The President has said that the cities are a top concern. He is planning a program to create thousands of new jobs for city people. He is also planning to channel more money into cities for use in restoring decaying neighborhoods.

On the whole, the mayors are pleased with the President's plan. Some wish he would do more. But most agree with New York City's mayor, Abraham Beame: "It's a good beginning—it's going to be helpful."

Discuss: "A nation without cities is unthinkable," said the president of the National League of Cities. Do you agree or disagree? Why? What suggestions do you have for making cities better places to live?

'SOS' Sounded For Harp Seals

Wide World

UPI

A seal hunter goes after white harp seal pup on floating ice pack off coast of Newfoundland. Hunter kills white-coated pup with a crushing blow to skull. Hunter uses regulation hardwood club as killing instrument.

Save our seals!" the demonstrators chant. "Stop the slaughter!"

The demonstrators parade in front of the Canadian and Norwegian embassies in Washington, D.C.

Over a thousand miles to the north, on the pack ice off Newfoundland, other demonstrators chant similar slogans and shake their fists at men wielding clubs.

The demonstrators are concerned about baby harp seals. Within a few weeks hunters will kill up to 170,000 of these white furry pups to provide fur trim for coats for human beings.

The seal hunt takes place off Canada's northeast coast every March. March is when the seal pups are born.

Hunters like to get the pups before they are ten days old. After that time the pups begin to shed their white coats for dark gray pelts. The dark pelts are not as valuable.

Way of Making a Living. Canadian and Norwegian hunters claim that the yearly hunt is necessary. "It's our only way of making a living," they say.

The hunters are backed by the Canadian government. The government allows them to take a certain number of baby seals each year. This year the number is 170,000.

The government maintains that in addition to providing hunters with a livelihood, the hunt helps to control the harp seal population. Seals are big fish eaters. Each harp seal eats 1.5 tons of fish a year. If seal numbers were allowed to grow, the seals could reduce the catch of fishermen.

Humane or Cruel? The government does not see anything inhumane about the seal hunt. Law requires that the baby seals be killed by a blow to the skull with a hardwood club. Death from such a blow is quick and painless, officials say.

Protesters disagree. Observers report that some hunters do not swing their clubs hard enough. Sometimes it takes seven or eight blows to kill an infant seal.

Protesters are also concerned about the mothers of the baby seals. Sometimes a mother will throw herself across her pup to try to protect it. Later she will nuzzle the dead pup's body. "You can tell she is grieving," says one observer.

Protesters also disagree with the Canadian government's claim that the harp seal population needs control. A count now being taken from the air suggests that the number of harp seals is dwindling.

Once, 10 million harp seals played in the surf off Newfoundland. Today there may be fewer than a million, conservationists say. They fear the breed will be extinct by 1985 if the present rate of killing goes on.

Save Seals Campaign. Conservation groups are trying to get the Canadian government to halt the killing. In return for a ban on the hunt, Swiss conservationist Franz Weber has offered Canada $400,000. The money is for use in retraining hunters for other jobs. Weber also says he will provide Newfoundland with machines that can make a fake fur much like the baby seal pelts. "And it's washable too," he adds.

So far, the Canadian government has not accepted Weber's offer. Nor has it answered the SOS from conservation groups trying to save the seals. Instead, the government has warned that any interference with the hunt will be dealt with severely.

Conservation groups aren't backing off, however. "We will continue to protest the slaughter of baby harp seals until it stops," they say.

Wide World

Animal protection group marches through Montreal in support of ban on seal hunting.

THE BERMUDA TRIANGLE

... A WATERY GRAVE

There is something strange going on in the Atlantic Ocean. Is that something dark, mysterious, and unexplained?

For years, ships and planes have gone to watery graves beneath the deep waters near Bermuda, Puerto Rico, and Florida.

A line connecting these three locations makes a triangle. (See map.) Sometimes this watery area is called the *Bermuda Triangle.* Sometimes it is called the *Devil's Triangle.*

During the last 100 years, at least 40 ships and 20 airplanes have disappeared in the Triangle. In every case except one, no wreckage was ever found. There were no survivors to tell what had happened in the mysterious waters.

Although strange things have been happening in the Bermuda Triangle for more than a century, it wasn't until December 5, 1945, that a disappearance made big news. Then, five U.S. Navy torpedo bombers flew a mission that took them over the Triangle. The five planes never came back.

Only a mixed-up radio message from one of the pilots was received. "Cannot see land. . . . We seem to be off course . . . ," he said.

After that message, nothing was ever heard from the planes.

When U.S. Navy officials found out the planes were missing, they sent a large rescue airplane to the Bermuda Triangle. This plane was also lost.

"We're not even able to make a guess as to what happened," said a Navy officer, commenting on the six missing planes.

Some people believe there are reasonable explanations for the strange events in the Bermuda Triangle. Lawrence D. Kusche is one of these people.

In his book about the Triangle, Kusche writes that the pilots of the five Navy bombers were new on the job. He believes they simply got lost and crashed. He also writes that leaking gas fumes may have caused the search plane to explode without a trace.

Other experts disagree with the reasonable explanations by Kusche and others.

In a book about the Bermuda Triangle, John Wallace Spencer says he believes the strange events in the Triangle were caused by creatures operating UFO's.

What do you think? Is the Bermuda Triangle a strange, mysterious place? Or is it just an ordinary place in the ocean?

How would you feel if you were a passenger on a plane or ship traveling in the Triangle?

Map shows where some strange disappearances took place in the Bermuda Triangle.

The Bermuda Triangle

XEP Map by Joe Carnicelli

FLORIDA

1963 (U.S. Ship)

1973 (Norwegian Ship)

1956 (U.S. Seaplane)

1945 (5 U.S.N. Planes)

1945 (U.S. Search Plane)

1967 (U.S. Cabin Cruiser)

1948 (U.S. Airliner)

BAHAMA ISLANDS

1965 (U.S.A.F. Plane)

CUBA

PUERTO RICO

1840 (French Ship)

1948 (British Airliner)

1947 (U.S.A.F. Bomber)

BERMUDA

1949 (British Airliner)

1955 (U.S. Yacht)

1918 (U.S. Ship)

(U.S.A.F. KB-50)

Atlantic Ocean

I can swim circles around this triangle.

PLAYGROUND FOR HANDICAPPED

A wheelchair won't keep a youngster from having fun in a new playground being planned for New York City. The playground is being designed for handicapped as well as for normal kids. Building will start in 1978.

The New York City Planning Commission held a contest for designs of games and play areas. Among the winning entries were a double tire swing, an air mattress for jumping on, a horse-drawn wagon, a floating platform, and a steam shovel that picks up and transports sand.

In Animal Race kids move animals to finish line by squeezing air balls.

President Carter Hears What You Think

XEP Photo by Frank Torsitano

Students meet with President Carter in Washington, D.C.

Six students talked with President Carter. They told him what *Weekly Reader* readers think about crime, pollution, and other problems.

The President listened. He told the kids some of his ideas. Then he said, "I'm proud of you." He is glad kids care about their country.

King Tut Draws American Crowds

A huge gold mask, jeweled chests, and animal-shaped chairs are drawing big crowds in the U.S. These objects are part of a special show. The show is a collection of treasures of an Egyptian king.

King Tut was crowned when he was nine years old. He died when he was 18 or 19. His body was placed in a solid gold coffin. He and his treasures were hidden for 3,000 years. Now the treasures are on show in the U.S.

Wide World

An Egyptian museum official inspects King Tut's famous gold mask after its arrival from Egypt.

Special Suit Protects Juan

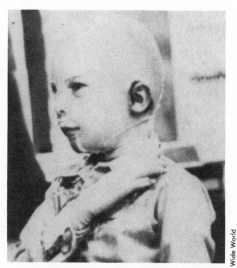

Wide World

Juan Salazar was burned in an explosion.

Thanks to a special suit, Juan and his two friends are back in school. Over a year ago the three boys were badly burned. They spent many months in the hospital. Doctors feared that the boys would be out of school for a long, long time.

With the suits, the boys were able to go back to school after about ten months. The suits cover the entire body. They have holes for eyes, ears, nose, mouth, and fingertips. The suits will protect the burns until they are completely healed.

NICARAGUA:
Putting Down a Bloody Uprising

Armed rebel youth fights for Masaya.

Wide World

Machine guns chatter nearby. Homemade rebel fire-bombs explode in the night. Ambulance sirens wail through the streets.

The Nicaraguan city of Masaya (mə-SAH-yə) is in flames. Nicaragua is at war—with itself.

The Nicaraguan army, called the National Guard, is fighting rebel groups trying to overthrow the government.

The rebels' faces—reddened by Guard-set blazes—aren't those of old, hardened fighters. They are the faces of teenagers. Villagers call them *los muchachos*—"the boys." Most are 14 or 15 years old. A few are only 12.

"The young are fighting for us because the men don't have the nerve," says a tired old woman the next morning.

Suddenly shots shatter the air. Several families have been forced from their homes by the army. Men and boys 15 years and older are lined against a wall—and shot.

"Somoza is trying to destroy us—destroy us all," cries an old woman as she weeps over her dead grandson.

She is referring to Anastasio Somoza—Nicaragua's President. Many people claim he is a cruel dictator.

Somoza is the latest member of his family to rule this Central American country. With U.S. support the family seized control of Nicaragua 42 years ago.

Many Nicaraguans claim that the Somozas have stolen huge fortunes from the country and killed all opponents.

The U.S. is blamed for supporting Somoza. Many Nicaraguans say that only U.S. aid has kept him in power.

But now Somoza's power may be ending.

Most of the country's 2.6 million people are against him.

Various armed groups have tried to overthrow Somoza and his loyal army. The best known are the *Sandinistas*. They launched a major attack a few months ago. They seized key cities including Masaya, León, and the capital of Managua.

Then the army retook each city. And the Sandinistas fled to the mountains or across the border to Costa Rica.

But the fighting in Nicaragua isn't over. The Sandinistas will return, says a Somoza opponent. "And thousands of men and boys will rush to fight beside them. All Nicaraguans fight for one goal—to overthrow Somoza."

However, they aren't united on Somoza's replacement.

Sandinistas boast that they get help from Communist Cuba—a U.S. enemy. The Sandinistas claim they admire Cuba and want to copy its Communist government.

But most Nicaraguans want a democratic form of government like that of the U.S. Many Nicaraguans fear the Sandinistas almost as much as they hate the Somozans.

All sides have asked the U.S. for help. The U.S. must decide whom to support: its old ally, Somoza; the Communist Sandinistas; or the poorly organized democratic groups.

DISCUSS: Who do you think the U.S. should support?

The map at right indicates major cities attacked by Nicaraguan rebels in their efforts to overthrow Somoza. All the cities were retaken by the army. Hundreds of civilians died in the civil war.

XEP Map by Joe Carnicelli

How Safe Is Our Drinking Water?

The 4,300 people living in Gray, Maine, are happy. Why? Recently, the residents of this small southwestern Maine community were told by health officials that their water is once again safe to drink.

For one week the people of Gray were cautioned to stay away from the drinking water. Health officials found significant traces of chemical pollution in the town's water supply. The chemicals, the officials claimed, could possibly cause cancer.

Water Worries Not Just in Maine

Gray, Maine, is not the only town in the U.S. keeping a close watch for chemicals being dumped into its water system. The Environmental Protection Agency (EPA) reports that hundreds of thousands of people in many of our nation's cities and towns may be drinking water containing suspected cancer-causing chemicals. Many of these chemicals are coming from industrial wastes, says EPA.

"The chemical poisoning of water systems is a rapidly growing area of concern," says an EPA spokesperson. "And as we [EPA] start taking a closer look at more water systems, we're going to discover more water contamination."

Scientist Jerimiah Murphy tests water to discover how much pollution the sample contains.

Fighting Dirty Water

Fighting water pollution in our nation's 240,000 water systems is not an easy task for EPA officials. To ensure safer drinking water, the EPA has enlisted the help of local water officials. The local officials—under the threat of a stiff fine—must report any pollution problems to the EPA.

Other ways the EPA is combating water pollution are by:

- Placing heavy fines—$10,000 a day—against industries that are polluting rivers and streams
- Forcing water officials to tell the public about contaminated drinking water through the news media
- Having all water systems tested on a regular basis
- Encouraging citizens to sue local, state, and federal water officials if contaminated drinking water is not corrected.

More Safety Standards Needed?

Not everyone is pleased with EPA's handling of our drinking water problem. Dr. Robert H. Harris of the Environmental Defense Fund says, "The new rules don't adequately tell how and where water samples will be taken. Water samples are usually taken in some public place like a firehouse.

"But," added Harris, "EPA should pick some houses having both old and new plumbing. Then it could get an idea of the water quality."

Harris also feels the EPA is not doing enough in alerting the public to the harm that can be caused by drinking contaminated water.

"We are dealing with a time bomb with a 25 year fuse," said Harris. "Exposing people to cancer-causing substances might not show up on a population for 25 years or so after the exposure."

What Do You Think?

Would you like to see more done to combat water pollution? If so, what would you suggest?

Jim Stives, a water engineer, mans a computerized water purification and distribution center.

News UPDATE

Women Astronauts Train for Space

They zoom down 45-foot towers into mosquito-infested water. They ride in tiny rafts in choppy seas. They slide under open parachutes and get lifted up by a helicopter hoist. And sometimes they admit asking themselves, "What am I doing here?"

They're the six women scientists in the newest class of astronaut candidates. They're undergoing a crash course in survival training. If they pass the course, they're another step nearer to a seat on the space shuttle when it starts its regular missions in 1980.

So far, from all reports, the women are doing well. They are experts in their fields of engineering, physics, and medicine and have had little trouble in the classroom.

As for the physical part of their training—NASA officials say the women are getting no special treatment. They're expected to do everything the men do, and they're doing it. A fellow astronaut praises the women this way, "I've got to hand it to these gals. They've got a lot of guts."

Trainee Margaret Seddon waits turn.

John Paul II waves from St. Peter's.

New Pope Is Polish

For the second time in a little over two months the Roman Catholic Church has a new Pope. He is Karol Cardinal Wojtyla (voy-TEE-wah), 58, of Poland.

Cardinal Wojtyla was elected Pope following the death of John Paul I who died after only 34 days in office. The new Pope has chosen the name John Paul II.

John Paul II is the first non-Italian Pope in 455 years. He is also the first Pope from a Communist country.

According to a Polish government spokesman, John Paul II is "a man who in his biography has everything."

In school he was an excellent student. He was best in languages and speaks at least five besides his native Polish.

He was a young adult in Poland during the Nazi occupation and had to study for the priesthood in secret. During that time he worked in a chemical factory, so he knows manual labor.

He is a man of action. He is an enthusiastic mountain climber and skier. He has performed on the stage, playing Shakespeare's *Hamlet*. And he is said to have a fine voice for folk songs.

John Paul II is also an author and a poet. He has published more than 300 books, poems, and articles.

And he is a defender of the poor and oppressed. For 14 years as an archbishop, he spoke out for more religious freedom in Poland. He also championed workers who demanded higher pay and better working conditions.

Those close to the new Pope expect him to continue his defense of human rights in his new office. They look to him to be not only a strong leader of the world's 700 million Roman Catholics but also a force for good among all the peoples of the world.

Space Suit Frees 'Bubble Boy'

David is six years old. He lives in a large bubble. Until recently he had never left that bubble to walk around or be hugged.

When David was born, doctors learned his body couldn't fight diseases. So he was raised alone in a large plastic bubble.

But now David can leave that bubble for short times. He can walk around; he can be hugged. David can do these things because of a special space suit like the ones that astronauts wear. The suit protects him outside his bubble.

David wears his new space suit and walks with his family for the first time.

Tass from Sovfoto

Scientists plan to spend six months studying the baby mammoth.

XEP Art by Joe Carnicelli

Scientists Study Baby Mammoth

Scientists were excited. A bulldozer operator in Siberia had discovered the frozen body of a baby mammoth. It was the first complete baby mammoth ever found.

Mammoths were huge animals of the past. They were much like elephants of today. Mammoths became extinct about 10,000 years ago.

Scientists learned much from studying the baby mammoth. They say the mammoth was six months old when it died. It was chestnut-colored. It was 45 inches long and 41 inches high. The mammoth had a 22-inch trunk and tiny ears. And it looked like the mammoths pictured in Stone-Age cave paintings.

Zip And Nip

Language Purposes: To introduce a new friend, Nip; to help children learn to observe visual clues and describe details in logical order.

Shah's Iran Engulfed by
The Flames of Revolution

The Shah of Iran, weeping for the kingdom he may have lost, boarded the royal jet in Tehran, his capital. With his empress at his side, he piloted the jet for a last look at the country he had ruled for 37 years.

The Shah, or king, was flying into exile, said many people. He may never be allowed to return home again.

"Shah raft! Shah raft! (The Shah is gone!)," shouted joyful crowds, celebrating in the streets below.

The year of rioting that had seen 2,000 people killed had finally driven the Shah from Iran's throne. Iran's 2,500-year history of royal rule was ending, said observers.

Elsewhere, Iranians wept. The Shah was gone. They had called him "King of Kings," "Shadow of the Almighty," "Protector of the Weak." They loved him. And now he was gone.

Shah of Iran

Caught in the center of Iran's raging flames of revolution had been one man—Shah Mohammed Riza Pahlavi (moh-HAHM-əd rih-ZAH PAH-lə-vee).

The Shah was considered a U.S. friend. But future Iranian governments might not be friendly. That worries the U.S.

The Shah has warned U.S. leaders that without him controlling Iran, World War III might begin.

Iran is important to the U.S. and other Western nations for two reasons, says the Shah. First, Iran is the world's second largest oil exporter. It sells oil to the U.S. and its allies.

Second, Iran is important because of its location (see map). Much of the oil from Mideast countries must be shipped past Iran. Over half the oil used by Japan and Western Europe passes through the Iranian-controlled Persian Gulf.

The Shah says he protected Iranian oil and the Gulf for the U.S. Without him, he says, this protection will end.

Iran could be torn apart by civil war. The Soviet army could sweep across Iran's border. Soviet troops could seize Iran's oil and the Persian Gulf, the Shah says.

By controlling Iran and the Gulf, the Soviets would have the U.S. and its allies by the throat, warn U.S. experts. The Soviets could cut off oil to Western nations. Then the U.S. might have to go to war over Iran, experts say.

President Carter has warned the Soviets to stay out of Iranian affairs. And he has ordered a Navy task force to stand by to defend Iran from outsiders.

People Against the Shah

The Shah's troubles began because he modernized Iran, say his friends. When he was crowned, the Shah said: "It is no joy to be king of a nation of beggars." So he worked to make Iran an oil-rich world power. In 20 years he modernized the way Iranians work, live, dress, and eat, say his backers.

But modernization created two groups of enemies. One group is the middle class. That group hates the Shah because he didn't modernize fast enough, say his backers.

The Shah's other enemies are Iran's Muslim religious leaders. They oppose all modernization, says the Shah.

The most important Muslim leader is 78-year-old Ayatolluh Ruhollah Khomeini. He is the *mullah*, or priest, who led the people opposed to the Shah.

Khomeini says he wants to replace the Shah with a Muslim state. In such a nation Muslim religious laws would replace the nation's present laws. The religious laws would forbid alcohol, close banks, and end women's rights, says the Shah.

But many Iranians say the Shah misunderstands his enemies. "We didn't oppose the Shah because we are religious hotheads or because we are greedy," an Iranian student told *Senior*. "We were against the Shah because he was bad. He stole money. He stole land. He took lives," the student said. "There isn't a family in Iran that hasn't had a friend or relative jailed, tortured, or killed by the Shah's secret police," he said.

Final Royal Acts

In the end, the Shah's throne could not be saved by the people who loved him, the fiercely loyal military group that backed him, or the U.S. that considered him a friend.

The Shah appointed a new government leader. He is Shahpur Bakhtiar. Then the Shah left for safety in the U.S.

Trouble began as soon as the Shah left. People who united to bring down the Shah started fighting with each other. Students wanted new freedoms. Businesses demanded law and order. And Khomeini demanded Bakhtiar's resignation.

Meanwhile, the military sat quietly. "We wait for the civil war," said one soldier. "Iran has had a king for 2,500 years. Without a Shah, Iranians will tear the country apart. Only the Shah can save Iran. He will—he must—return someday."

Wide World photos

Demonstrators march through Tehran (left) demanding that Americans go home and the Shah be overthrown. Demonstrators support Khomeini (above). Iran is considered vital to U.S. because of its location.

XEP Map by Joe Carnicelli

Egypt, Israel Peace Comes...

Peace has come!" said a smiling Jimmy Carter as he was joined on the White House lawn by Egyptian President Anwar Sadat (sə-DAHT) and Israeli Prime Minister Menachem Begin (BAY-gən).

The men had gathered to sign Arabic, Hebrew, and English copies of a peace treaty. The treaty ended nearly 31 years of conflict that four times had broken into war between Egypt and Israel.

"No more war," Begin told Sadat. "No more bloodshed. Peace unto you. *Shalom, salaam,* forever." (*Shalom* means "peace" in Hebrew. *Salaam* is "peace" in Arabic.)

"No more bloodshed," agreed Sadat.

But even as the men signed the peace treaty, the Mideast was bracing for new bloodshed (see story below).

Long Struggle to Peace

The conflict between Egypt and Israel began in 1948—the year Israel was formed out of an area called Palestine. Arab Palestinians—Muslims by faith—resented the creation of a Jewish nation where they lived.

The Palestinian Arabs asked Arab states for help. So Egypt and other Arab nations invaded Israel.

Israel defeated the Arab armies. And many Palestinians left the areas controlled by Israel for refugee camps along the Gaza Strip and the West Bank (see map). Gaza was ruled by Egypt, and the West Bank by Jordan.

Wars erupted again in 1956, 1967, and 1973. In 1967, Israel captured the Gaza Strip, West Bank, Golan Heights, Sinai, and Arab section of Jerusalem.

U.N. buffer zones were created after the 1973 war. But even with the buffer, a new Arab-Israeli war seemed assured.

Then, 16 months ago, Sadat unexpectedly flew to Israel to propose peace. Sadat's dramatic flight to Israel was followed last summer with a meeting in the U.S. There Sadat, Begin, and Carter began the work on a peace treaty.

About a month ago progress on the treaty seemed stalled. To rescue the peace effort, Carter flew to Israel and Egypt. It was Carter's trip, says Sadat, that saved the treaty.

Peace Agreement

Much of the peace treaty concerns Israeli-occupied lands captured in 1967. The two countries agreed to have Israel return the Sinai to Egypt within three

With flags waving behind them, Sadat, Carter, and Begin sign a treaty they hope wil bring peace to the Mideast.

years, with half the pullback completed in nine months.

However, there are still disagreements over Gaza, Jerusalem, and the West Bank. The treaty was left vague about these areas. Some experts fear continuing negotiations about these areas may destroy the effects of the treaty.

In the Israeli-occupied Gaza and West Bank, there are 1.1 million Palestinian Arabs. The treaty calls for Palestinian "self-rule" soon. But Egyptians, Palestinians, and Israelis disagree on

what *self-rule* means.

Palestinians say self-rule should lead to an independent Palestinian state.

But Begin argues such a Palestinian nation would be a threat to Israel. Begin wants to keep Israeli troops in Gaza and the West Bank indefinitely.

And Begin insists that Israel will never give up Jerusalem. But many Arabs, who—like the Jews—consider the city sacred, say the Arab section of Jerusalem should be returned to Arab rule, or the entire city made independent of Israel.

...As Mideast Troubles Grow

Even as Carter, Sadat, and Begin signed the treaty they hoped would bring peace to the Mideast, that region was the scene of new violence and bloodshed.

A border war ground on between Yemen and South Yemen.

The border war is considered important by the U.S. because of the effects on Saudi Arabia, Yemen's ally.

Saudi Arabia provides about 20 percent of U.S. oil imports. Until recently, Saudi Arabia has opposed Palestinian terrorist attacks and has worked to keep oil prices low.

But now the Saudis are under pressure from some Arab states to back terrorists, oppose the Egypt-Israel peace, and raise oil prices. The Saudis have agreed to raise oil prices.

Saudi leader Khalid reportedly no longer trusts the U.S. The U.S. can't protect the Shah of Iran, says Khalid, so how can the U.S. be counted on to help Saudi Arabia?

He's Still in Good Shape, Yet He Died at 18
Mystery of the Teenage Mummy

The scene was right out of the movie *Invasion of the Body Snatchers*. But it was all being done for science. The setting was Wesleyan University in Middletown, Conn. The time: last month.

A group of doctors and professors—four men and two women—had turned a university lab into an "operating room." Before the group lay a real Egyptian mummy.

Hours had been spent X-raying and unwrapping the corpse. Now it was time to "operate." The doctors were looking for the mummy's secret. Every mummy has a secret, it seems.

The first clue had shown up in the X rays. They revealed four cigar-shaped objects in the abdomen.

The study team guessed the objects might be either tubes containing the mummy's organs or scrolls. (Scrolls are a kind of rolled-up writing material.) The scrolls might reveal the mummy's name and facts about how he had lived.

Suspense mounted as one of the doctors leaned over the mummy and began to cut. The doctor had to use a surgeon's saw to cut through the tough leathery skin. Quickly, however, a flap in the abdomen was opened. Another doctor pulled out the cigar-shaped objects—one by one.

Masks protect doctors, TV crews from disease found in old mummy dust.

Last layer of linen wrapping is removed from mummy before "operating."

The mystery remained a mystery. The objects were tightly wrapped pieces of dark linen cloth. The study group could only guess at their purpose. (Mummy experts later said the cloth objects were probably symbolic replacements for the mummy's organs, which had been removed at burial.)

Cameramen from the TV networks left. Newsmen and TV reporters lingered to interview the doctors. Finally everyone left except the mummy.

The mummy study still continues, according to Dr. Stephen Dyson, the Wesleyan archeologist in charge of the project.

"The tissue is well-preserved. The bones are strong and well-formed. The teeth are in better shape than mine. There are no signs of broken bones, wounds, or crippling disease," Dr. Dyson said.

The obvious mystery remains, however. Why did this apparent model of physical fitness die at a young age? So far the mummy's keeping mum.

—John Maynard

Buddy Bear

Dear Girls and Boys,

I did something wrong.

I put my boots on the wrong feet.

Please don't laugh at me.

Everyone makes mistakes.

Love,

Buddy

Weekly Reader

1980-1988

Homelessness, drug abuse, and AIDS in the U.S.; war, assassination, and terror bombings abroad—these were prominent features of the news coverage of *Weekly Reader* in the 1980s.

The most persistent newsmaker of this tempestuous time was Iran's Khomeini. Throughout the '80s, the fanatic ayatollah waged bloody holy war against his Arab neighbors and the U.S. In a series of hostage-takings and lethal bombings, Iran's leader sought to bring the U.S. to its knees, at least symbolically. The plight of the hostages was one that children could easily understand, and they followed the story in *Weekly Reader* avidly. The greatest blow came in mid-decade, when Iran lured the White House into an arms-for-hostages deal. The deal miscarried, and news of this barter with an avowed enemy erupted into a political scandal almost as complex as Watergate.

From the decade's first day, U.S. relations with the Soviets soured over Afghanistan. Not until new Soviet leader Gorbachev suggested troop withdrawal did a diplomatic thaw occur. An encouraging result of this thaw was a nuclear arms reduction treaty signed in late 1987. Millions hoped the treaty would mean a greater sense of community and less calamity for the future.

Weekly Reader responded head-on to the stormy '80s. All grade levels carried more hard news and controversy than ever before. *Weekly Reader* concentrated especially on social problems at home and the steps being taken to solve them. In addition, it re-dedicated itself to balance in handling sensitive issues, a must for creating an informed citizenry for the year 2000—and beyond.

TRIBESMEN RESIST SOVIET INVADERS

Afghanistan is almost the size of Texas and home for 15 million to 18 million people.

An exact count of Afghans is hard to get for two reasons: Few Afghans read or write, and the people are scattered throughout the rugged land.

Half of Afghanistan has towering mountains so threatening that natives say even the birds must cross them on foot. Much of the other half of Afghanistan is arid desert, where few four-wheel drive vehicles make it through the sandbanks.

In between the mountains and desert are fertile valleys, where most Afghans farm and graze livestock.

The Afghan farming season is short, from March to May. Summer temperatures can climb to 120 degrees F. Winter temperatures may drop below zero. Nomads, who walk eight hours a day without rest, make sure they camp by sundown. When the sun sets, temperatures can swiftly drop from a warm 80 degrees F to below freezing.

War-Torn Land. Afghanistan is no stranger to conquering peoples.

In 328 B.C. Alexander the Great captured and ruled the land. He was followed by other conquerors—Scythians, White Huns, Turks, and Arabs, who brought with them a religion called *Islam.*

In 1223 Mongol chief Genghis Khan destroyed many proud cities.

In the 18th century the British and Russians clashed over Afghanistan. The British put their candidate on the throne. This ended the British clash with the Russians but not with the Afghans. Afghans slaughtered 16,500 British troops and followers and put an Afghan on the throne.

Today battles rage in Afghanistan as tribesmen fight the Soviets.

A Land of Variety. The armies that have pushed through Afghanistan for centuries left behind many cultures. Afghan's social groups and tribes keep these cultures alive.

An Afghan can be a Tajik in a business suit, an Uzbek wrapped in sheepskin, a Turkoman in high black boots and long, striped robe, or a Pathan in a knee-length shirt over baggy breeches.

Afghans speak any of 20 languages. Persian is the official language of Afghanistan.

Most Afghans are Muslims who take religion seriously. People are guided by old religious rules.

One such rule is hospitality. Travelers are welcomed into homes. An Afghan can be sure of safety even if he spends the night in an enemy's home. Afghans also follow the rules of repaying injury and never showing cowardice. Every man owns a gun, and, by Afghan belief, a boy becomes a man when he carries one.

Afghan Food. Afghans eat much bread and rice. They eat chunks of sheep meal called *mutton* and chicken, when available. Bowls of yogurt are served at meals, along with rounds of sweet tea.

Afghan Wildlife. The shy Marco Polo sheep, with huge spiral horns, live in the Afghan mountains, along with wild goats called *ibex.* Shaggy yaks carry goods and supply tribes with wool, milk, meat, and tough hides. The double-humped camel travels long distances in caravans.

Family Life. The family is important to Afghans. Relatives ranging from the very old to newborns live and travel together. Children are taught by family members since there are no schools outside cities.

The rugged land of Afghanistan is matched by its rugged people who hold strong to their customs. Because of this, experts say that Afghanistan may never step into the modern world.

Steve McCurry

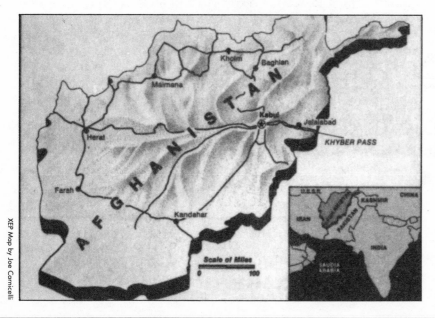

XEF Map by Joe Cornicelli

KHYBER PASS

Scale of Miles
0   100

Science News

Sleeping U.S. Volcano Perks to Life

Natural fireworks flared and boomed over the snows of southwestern Washington State recently. Clouds of smoke, ash, and burning gas appeared near the top of Mount Saint Helens, an old volcano in the Cascade Mountains.

Lightning arched across the craters of the volcano. One plume of smoke rose nearly 4 miles into the sky. Ash reached Spokane, Wash., 300 miles away.

Mount Saint Helens hasn't erupted since 1857, but on March 20 it showed signs that it was stirring to life. Scientists detected earthquakes under the mountain. The earthquakes increased in strength and frequency. By March 25 the quakes were being recorded at the rate of about four an hour.

Scientists watched the 9,677-foot-high mountain closely. Heat from the eruption melted snow on the peak and set off mud slides and avalanches. Officials ordered roadblocks set up to keep people away from the foot of the mountain.

Mount Saint Helens is located about 50 miles northeast of Portland, Oreg. Some geologists who have studied the peak say

Mount Saint Helens erupts. The mountain is one of several volcanoes in Cascades.

it is the most explosive U.S. mountain outside of Hawaii or Alaska.

Volcanoes can result from the eruption of molten lava, or *magma,* and hot gases. Pressure deep within the Earth forces magma up through cracks in the crust.

Lava cools and hardens into rock. If lava and ash build up continually, a volcano is formed. Cooled lava may plug the vent or chimney in the volcano through which the lava had flowed. Then the volcano becomes dormant. But the plug may cause the pressure to build up so much in the mountain that the volcano might blow its top.

Some experts say that the Cascades were formed by action along the American and Pacific plates (see poster). The western coast of North America is part of the "ring of fire" around the borders of the Pacific plate.

No one can predict when Mount Saint Helens might send out a dangerous lava flow. So scientists continue to watch the volcano. They say it may quiet down. Or it could remain active for years.

High Prices at the Supermarket May Go Even Higher

"Last year we had a nice Thanksgiving dinner for $30 or so," Chris said. "This year I expect that the food for the same nine people will cost me well over $40. I suppose I could cut out the extras like the nuts and the whipped cream for the pie . . .

or expect people to eat less!"

Economists warn Americans that they can expect today's food cost worries to stay around for many years. The U.S. Agriculture Department sees next year's food prices rising by as much as 15 percent, That

means shoppers would add $1.50 to every $10 grocery order they get at the supermarket.

Experts put the blame for the hike in food prices on (1) last summer's drought and heat, (2) U.S. farm exports to other countries, and (3) the overall inflation rate.

Restaurant owners are among the biggest buyers of food in the U.S. How do they manage with the high costs? Most try to avoid passing on their high food bills to their customers for fear of losing business. Some restaurant owners are cutting costs by using fewer flowers on the dining tables and butchering their own meat.

What can home cooks do to save the family dollars? Economists suggest they follow Chris's advice and skip the extras, buy specials, use cheaper foods in place of more expensive foods, and dig out recipes that make leftovers tasty.

CHINA WELCOMES U.S. IMPORTS

Don't be surprised if someday you're sipping on Great Wall orange juice, munching cereal from a lacquer-ware bowl, and padding around in Chinese straw slippers.

Youngsters in China need not be surprised either if they soon start snacking on popcorn and hot dogs and washing them down with a Coke.

People in the U.S. can expect to use more and more goods from China. And, in China, people can expect to use more and more goods from the U.S. Trade between the two countries is growing. The $2 billion the U.S. and China did in trade in 1979 is expected to double in 1980.

Trade shows will kick off the increase in trade between China and the U.S. A show of U.S.-made goods opens in China this month. At the show the Chinese will get a look at such things as U.S. fashions, frozen foods, and farm equipment.

A China show—the first official exhibit by the People's Republic of China in the U.S.—has brought 20,000 items to San Francisco and Chicago. Hundreds of thousands of Americans are seeing Chinese items

Shoppers in Peking may soon be eyeing U.S. clothing in shop windows.

XEP Map by Joe Carnicelli

ranging from plastic shoes to birds made by a Chinese glass blower. Next month the show will move to New York City.

U.S.-China Trade History

The U.S. and China exhibitions mark the rekindling of a friendship between the two nations that was interrupted 30 years ago.

When the Communists came to power in China in 1949, the U.S. stopped the trade of important goods to the People's Republic of China. In 1950 when the Chinese Communist Army entered Korea and attacked the United Nations forces, the U.S. stopped all trade and all contacts with the Chinese mainland.

It wasn't until the early 1970's that the U.S. and China made contact again. In 1971, Chinese officials invited the U.S. table tennis team to visit mainland China. The Chinese also began allowing news reporters, scientists, and students to visit the People's Republic of China.

Business Partners

In China today, tourism and tourist money are welcome. But most

of all, the Chinese welcome business.

The Chinese are showing U.S. oil men their offshore oil fields. They are showing their soybean crops to U.S. farmers who hope to find a strain that will be useful on U.S. farms.

American engineering companies are eyeing Chinese workers for projects in the Mideast. U.S. military equipment builders are talking about future sales to the Chinese. And U.S. farmers have heard the news that the Chinese recently agreed to buy about $1 billion worth of U.S. grain a year for four years, starting in 1981.

Although the outlook for trade with China looks good, U.S. leaders see some ruts ahead in the road to the China trade. One rut is China's lack of money to pay the bills for its imports. Another rut is trying to figure out what goods each country wants.

The Chinese have little use for such U.S. exports as face creams, aspirin, or milk. (Chinese don't drink milk.) And, few Chinese can afford a Coke that sells for 60 cents in China.

The V.P.'s
(Vocabulary Pals)

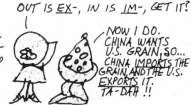

A Good Citizen Votes

Voters should listen to what the people who are running for President plan to do for the U.S. Voters should then vote for the person they think will do the best job. Use the ballot below to vote for the person you want to be President.

BALLOT FOR PRESIDENT	CARTER	REAGAN	ANDERSON	OTHER
	◯	◯	◯	◯

Knocked-Out Tooth Can Be Saved

Jeremy is playing shortstop for his team. A baseball flies directly at him and hits him in the mouth. Jeremy wipes the blood from his mouth and finds one of his upper front teeth in his hand. Now what is he going to do?

Jeremy's tooth is not a baby tooth. A new one won't grow in its place. But the dentist can replant this second-growth tooth—if Jeremy acts fast.

This is what he, or you, could do. *Don't* try to clean the tooth, even if it looks messy. Wrap the tooth in a wet cloth or place it in a glass of salted water. Have your parents take you and the tooth to the dentist's office immediately. The dentist can put the tooth back in and put wire around it to hold it in place.

HEALTH NEWS

Jeremy Miller has an empty place in his smile.

XEP photo by Dortha Cool

Peanut and Jocko

by Don Robison

Look at your socks!

What's wrong with them?

One sock is gray. The other one is blue.

I know it. I have another pair just like this at home!

MAIN NEWS

UPI

CAPTIVITY IN IRAN ENDS AFTER 444 DAYS

The 52 American hostages are home after 14 months of being held captive in Iran. This week they are greeting friends and families, sitting down to favorite meals, reading about their captivity in back copies of newspapers and magazines, and opening birthday and holiday presents that had been put aside for their return.

The release came after months of work to draw up an agreement acceptable to both the U.S. and Iran. The final agreement, as well as the release of the hostages, was arranged with the help of diplomats in Algeria, an Arab country in northwestern Africa.

The U.S. agreed to transfer to Algeria about $8 billion of Iranian money being held in U.S. banks. Once the airplane carrying the hostages out of Iran was airborne, the Algerians turned the money over to Iran.

The U.S.-Iran Crisis

The Americans were taken hostage on November 4, 1979, by Iranian militants who seized the U.S. embassy in Iran. The Iranians demanded that the Shah, a former ruler of Iran who was in a U.S. hospital for cancer treatment, be returned to Iran. The Iranians wanted the Shah to stand trial as a criminal.

Later the hostages became part of the dispute among leaders within the Iranian government. Diplomats reported then that no government official in Iran seemed to have the power to release the hostages.

In April 1980 the U.S. flew helicopters and planes into Iran to attempt to rescue the hostages. The attempt failed.

By September 1980 Iran was into a full-scale war with its neighbor Iraq. Iran began facing a serious need for money, arms, and friends to support its cause, diplomats reported.

Reasons for Hostage Release

Observers point to the continuing Iran-Iraq war as one reason Iran decided the time had come to release the hostages. Observers also say that Iranian leaders wanted the hostages released by Inauguration Day. Observers say the Iranians did not want to deal with the incoming Reagan Administration.

People throughout the world are rejoicing with Americans that the hostage ordeal is over.

EVENTS IN U.S.–IRAN CRISIS

Jan. 16, 1979—Iranians force Shah to leave. He goes to Egypt.
Feb. 1, 1979—Khomeini, exiled from Iran for 15 years, returns to become Iran's leader.
Oct. 22, 1979—Shah comes secretly to U.S. for cancer treatment.
Nov. 4, 1979—Iranian militants seize U.S. embassy and seize 66 Americans.
Nov. 19-20, 1979—Thirteen American hostages are released.
Jan. 29, 1980—Canadians spirit out of Iran six Americans hiding in Canadian embassy.
April 25, 1980—U.S. gives up rescue of hostages in Iran.
July 10, 1980—Hostage Richard Queen is released because of illness.
July 27, 1980—Shah dies in Egypt.
Dec. 21, 1980—Iran demands $24 billion as a guarantee that Shah's wealth and Iran's money held in U.S. banks will be returned. Demand called "unreasonable" by U.S. Negotiations continue.
Jan. 16, 1981—World bankers help work out money agreement in Algeria.
Jan. 18, 1981—U.S. and Iran reach agreement on release of hostages.

NEWS/SPECIAL

Protecting The President Is a Tough Problem

Wide World

A look of shock came over President Reagan's face. Gunfire had sounded from a crowd gathered to see the President as he left a meeting in a hotel in Washington, D.C., last week. One bullet struck the President in his chest.

Secret Service agents pushed the President into his car. The car sped to a hospital, where doctors worked for two hours to remove the bullet from the President's chest. Hospital officials reported the President to be in "good" condition.

At the same time the President was shot, a Secret Service agent, a D.C. policeman, and the President's press secretary were also shot. The men had been struck by bullets reported to have been fired by the gunman.

At the scene of the attack police arrested 25-year-old John Hinckley from Colorado. One of the things they charged him with was attempting to kill a U.S. President.

Presidents in Danger

Americans, thankful Mr. Reagan survived the shooting, are shocked over the latest violence directed at the nation's leader.

In the last 100 years one out of every three Presidents has either been assassinated or faced near *assassination* (the murder of a politically important person).

"Violence is very much abroad in the U.S. today," said one law officer after the March 30 shooting of President Reagan.

How Much Protection?

The attempted assassination of Mr. Reagan again raises the question: *How much protection should the U.S. President have against citizens?*

"Total protection would mean turning the White House into a fortress and forcing the President to stay inside," say security experts.

Under total protection, the experts add, a President would appear to be living in fear of his own people.

Abraham Lincoln, before his death at the hand of an assassin in 1865, faced the security problem with familiar wry humor. He said:

"Though it would be safer for a President to live in a cage, it would interfere with his business."

Heavy protection for a President would mean a police-state image for the U.S. Too little protection for the country's leader may lead to tragedy.

Americans last experienced such a tragedy in 1963 when President John F. Kennedy was killed. Kennedy was the first President to be killed in office in 62 years.

Is Tighter Security the Answer?

After Mr. Kennedy's death security for Presidents, Vice-Presidents, and even presidential candidates was strengthened. The number of Secret Service agents—the people who guard the President's life— had been increased from about 400 to 1,600. The money spent to protect top U.S. leaders has risen from $5½ million in 1963 to more than $100 million today.

Yet presidential security failed to keep Mr. Reagan from harm last week.

"Assassins have surprise on their side," said a security expert last week. "You never know when and where they will strike.

"That gives assassins an edge— especially in a country where the top leader is expected to meet the public every chance he can."

UPI

Secret Service agent Tim McCarthy is helped onto stretcher by agents and police after he was wounded in recent attempt on President Reagan's life.

President Names Woman To Highest Court

UPI

"If elected, I will appoint a woman to the U.S. Supreme Court," promised Ronald Reagan last year when he was running for President.

This summer, he kept his word.

One of the justices of the nation's highest Court retired, and the President named Sandra Day O'Connor, a 51-year-old Arizona judge, to take his place.

Next month, O'Connor will become the first woman to serve on the U.S. Supreme Court in that Court's 191-year-history. She will bring to the job 29 years of experience as a lawyer, state lawmaker, trial and appeals court judge.

O'Connor will also bring to the Court her own brand of horse sense. As a child, she spent summers riding horses on her family's 162,000-acre ranch, the Lazy B, on the Arizona-New Mexico border. "I didn't do all the things boys did," she recalls, "but I roped steer, fixed windmills, and repaired fences."

O'Connor went to private and public schools in Texas. She graduated from high school at age 16 and went on to Stanford University in California, where she studied law and ranked in the top ten of her class.

Married to another lawyer, O'Connor is the mother of three sons. When not in court, she enjoys cooking Mexican dishes, golfing, swimming, and tennis.

SPACE SHUTTLE

Its Work May Change Your Future

The space shuttle is again getting off the ground. Its second launch is set for September 30.

In the coming decades, scientists expect to hear praise from people who have used the shuttle—manufacturers, national security planners, communications companies, space travelers, maybe even you.

Defense Worker

Military leaders say the shuttle could launch satellites in space. Some of these satellites could warn of space attacks. Other satellites, armed with lasers, could fire back at attackers. Experts see a fleet of shuttles protecting the U.S. against space warfare.

Space Message Centers

Scientists are counting on the shuttle to put communications satellites into space. These would beam many telephone, radio, and TV signals right into homes, cars, businesses and even to receivers worn on wrists. Now signals from satellites must be beamed to switching stations that then send the signals by wire to receivers.

Eyes of the world will be on the second lift-off of the shuttle from Florida. On board *Columbia* will be the crew, Joe Engle (left) and Richard Truly.

UPI

Technology Station

Scientists are counting on the shuttle to carry small factories into space, where goods could be made under weightless and germ-free conditions. Such goods might include combinations of metals that do not mix evenly on Earth, superclear crystals, and very pure medicines.

Payoffs for You

Space experts are counting on the shuttle to bring many pluses into peoples' lives. For example, satellites launched from the shuttle could keep watch over city streets, which would perhaps help make streets safer; could warn pilots that their air route was not a safe one; could allow two-way talks over wrist radios; and could increase TV signals from far-off countries.

Sound amazing? Certainly. And keep in mind these are space scientists talking—not Buck Rogers!

Minnesota Teenager Survives Deep Freeze

Jean Hilliard (in photo below) still has some frostbite on her legs and feet; but, other than that, she says she's "feeling real good." And that, her doctors say, is a miracle.

Back in December the Minnesota teenager was driving home one night when her car went off the road. She spent the night in temperatures 22 degrees below zero.

When she was found the next day, doctors say, "her body was frozen solid like a cordwood stick." They couldn't even puncture her skin with a needle. Her temperature was too low to register on thermometers. Her heart was beating at less than one-fifth the normal rate.

The doctors wrapped the frozen girl in warm, moist pads. Slowly her body thawed, and her temperature began to climb.

How did she survive the freezing?

Doctors don't really know, but say there have been cases when people have survived body temperatures as low as 68 degrees.

The human body, doctors say, reacts to extreme cold much as the body of a hibernating animal does. The body's functions are slowed, which reduces the cells' need for oxygen from the blood. In that slow-motion state even brain cells can live many minutes after the heart has stopped.

Wide World

How Much Is a Million? a Trillion?

Students at the Glenbrook School in Pulaski, Wis., don't have to try to imagine what a million of anything looks like. All they have to do is look at the huge pile of 1 million bottle caps heaped in one room of the school. (See photo above.) Students collected the caps after a math teacher decided such a project would help them understand what a million really is.

Wide World

The pile of bottle caps might even help students understand the size of the U.S. Government's debt. President Reagan recently said the debt would reach a trillion dollars. To picture how much that is, Glenbrook students just have to imagine a million piles of a million bottle caps.

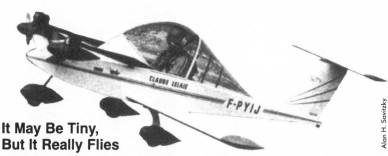

Alan H. Savitzky

It May Be Tiny, But It Really Flies

This little plane wowed the audience at a recent airplane show in Oshkosh, Wis. The plane was designed in France and is called Cri-Cri (KREE-KREE), which means "cricket" in French. Only 12 feet long, *Cri-* *Cri* is one of the smallest planes in the world. But it flies like much bigger planes. The one-person plane takes off fast with both tiny engines roaring. It zooms along at up to 110 miles an hour.

Who Owns Sunlight?

Many city and state officials in the U.S. are making laws against some tall buildings—those that block sunlight from neighbors' solar collectors.

More and more people are using solar energy in their homes and businesses. Many scientists say the sun could supply one-sixth to one-third of the energy needed in the U.S. by the end of the century—just 19 years from now.

So, many lawmakers are looking for ways to encourage the use of solar collectors. Lawmakers are also looking for ways to make sure that those solar collectors get plenty of sun.

A few states already have "right to light" laws. In New Mexico whoever sets up a solar collector is guaranteed the right to sunlight over a planned skyscraper. In California people are not allowed to grow plants and trees that cast shadows across a neighbor's solar collector.

Art by John Jones

Eleanor Smeal (left) leads the National Organization for Women (NOW). She is one of the leaders in the fight for passage of ERA.

UPI

The Equal Rights Amendment —
STOP OR GO?

"ERA ... all the way ..." shout paraders marching through a small Illinois town.

Bill and his sister, both too young to vote, are marching with their parents in support of the ERA—the Equal Rights Amendment.

"Stop ERA ... Protect American families and homes," shout a group of people along the parade route. Melissa, one of Bill's classmates, is in this group.

Bill and Melissa are both presenting their views on a proposed *amendment* [change] to the U.S. Constitution. That amendment could affect the rest of their lives.

Across the country, other people are parading and demonstrating this winter over the same issue—the ERA. And there is a growing sense of urgency among ERA supporters. That is because the deadline for passing the ERA—June 30—is fast approaching.

What's the ERA?

The ERA is sort of an antidiscrimination bill for women. It was designed to ensure that women receive equal treatment with men. The ERA says: "Equality of rights under the law shall not be denied or abridged [lessened] by the United States or by any state on account of sex."

The ERA was passed by Congress in 1972. But before it can become part of the Constitution, it must be *ratified*—or approved—by three-fourths (38) of the 50 states. So far, only 35 states have approved the amendment.

Three more of the remaining 15 states (see map) are needed for passage of the ERA. But most experts doubt that any of these remaining states will approve the ERA by the deadline. The last state to approve the ERA was Indiana, back in 1977. And one state, Oklahoma, defeated the ERA last month.

Even if 38 states do approve the ERA, there will still be problems: (1) Five of the 35 states that originally approved it have withdrawn their approval, which may or may not be legal. (2) In 1979, Congress extended the original deadline for passage of the ERA from that year to 1982. That act was ruled illegal by an Idaho court. Higher courts may disagree.

DISCUSS: Do you think men and women should be treated as equals? Why or why not? Do you think ERA would change the way women are treated? If so, how? Do you support ERA? Why or why not?

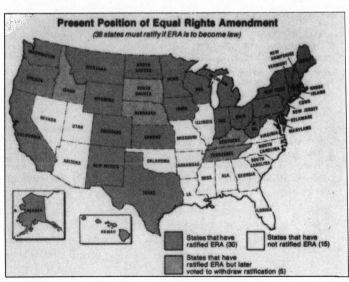

Present Position of Equal Rights Amendment
(38 states must ratify if ERA is to become law)

States that have ratified ERA (30)

States that have not ratified ERA (15)

States that have ratified ERA but later voted to withdraw ratification (5)

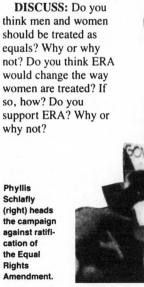

Phyllis Schlafly (right) heads the campaign against ratification of the Equal Rights Amendment.

UPI

UNEMPLOYMENT

Over 11 Million U.S. Workers Are Unemployed

The percentage of the U.S. work force without jobs reached a record high in September, according to U.S. Government figures. The percentage was 10.1 percent—slightly more than one out of every ten U.S. workers.

Not since 1940 had the percentage of unemployed been greater. That was the last year of the Great Depression.

Help for the Jobless

Where do unemployed workers find help? Here are some sources:

Unemployed insurance payments. Millions of today's jobless people collect these payments for 26 weeks—sometimes longer. The amount of unemployment pay varies from state to state, but an

Jobless office worker advertises his need for work. In what other ways can a person try to find a job?

average weekly payment is about $100. The money comes from a Government fund to which employers contribute.

Direct Government aid. The U.S. Government aids millions of jobless workers and their families by providing welfare payments and food stamps.

Private aid. Churches, the Red Cross, and similar volunteer organizations provide families with clothes, food, and even money for heating fuel.

Almost all jobless people agree that being out of work is a nasty experience.

"It's like death, but you go on breathing," says one jobless worker.

Troubled Times in POLAND

Polish-Americans in U.S. show support for the Poles and their opposition to communism.

For the people of Poland, the Christmas holidays and the weeks that followed were bleak.

On December 13, martial law went into effect.

The head of the Polish Communist party and the Polish government, General Jaruzelski, had ordered the armed forces to seize power in Poland. He wanted to end the demands being made by members of the trade union Solidarity. They had been demanding more

freedom and better living conditions for all the people of Poland.

Martial law has taken away the little freedom the Poles had won. In addition, Poles now face worsening economic conditions.

Supplies of food, clothing, and fuel have run out or have become costly. Some shoppers wait up to 16 hours in long lines for food for one family meal.

What's Ahead?

People throughout the world are waiting to see what will happen now in Poland. They wonder if the Poles will ever get back the freedoms they gained and lost. They question whether the Polish government will get workers to produce more. They wonder if the leaders of Solidarity and the Polish government will ever work together.

MISSING CHILDREN

Thousands of Searches Are Held Yearly to Find Missing Youngsters

Five-year-old Timmy White and his mother (on the cover) are as happy as any people can be. The photo was taken in 1980 when Timmy returned safely to his home in Ukiah, Calif., after being kidnapped.

Timmy White disappeared while walking to his baby-sitter's home after school. For 17 days, no one knew where Timmy was or whether he was even alive.

The story of Timmy White ended happily. But many other kidnapped youngsters and their parents are not so lucky as the Whites.

Hundreds of thousands of youngsters disappear in the U.S. every year. About nine out of ten of these children return within two weeks. The whereabouts of the others remains a mystery.

Missing Children—What's Being Done?

Parents, police officers, including the FBI, and youngsters themselves are helping to ease the problem of missing children.

The FBI now helps trace missing youngsters. Under a new law, parents can have their missing child's name placed on the FBI's computerized list of missing persons and fugitives. This FBI help will enable officials to

---

Many parents try to find their missing child on their own. Often they travel far in their search.

---

trace missing children in every state—and perhaps save their lives.

If police officers in a community can't find a missing child, they usually pass on information to police in other communities.

Many parents try to find their missing child on their own. They send information and photos to all parts of the U.S. Often they travel far in their search.

Several citizen groups, such as Find-Me, Inc. and SEARCH, aid parents who have a missing child. Some groups have toll-free phone numbers so parents can give information and ask for help.

How Children Can Help

Youngsters can do their part by following safety

Policeman puts another child's photo on missing-persons bulletin board in New York City.

rules set by their parents, school, or police department.

In Atlanta, Ga., recently the police and fire departments passed out these rules to children:

Children should **ALWAYS**
• tell a police officer when a "friendly stranger" tries to join their play group or talks to them in a public place.
• write down the license number of a driver who offers them a ride or bothers them in any way. Children without a pencil can write the number in the dirt with a stick.
• tell someone—teacher, police officer, mail carrier, or parents—if they see a stranger or a car hanging around their school, playground, or any other place where children gather.
• go with friends when going to movies, theaters, or other public places.

Children should **NEVER**
• get in a car with a stranger who asks directions or offers payment for a chore.
• be alone in alleys, empty buildings, or other secluded places.
• take money, candy, or other treats from any stranger.
• let strangers touch them.

The V.P.'s (Vocabulary Pals)

IS KIDNAPPING A CHILD SLEEPING?

NO SILLY. IT'S THE TAKING AWAY OF A PERSON BY FORCE. IT'S A SERIOUS CRIME.

AND FUGITIVE?

A FUGITIVE IS A PERSON WHO'S RUNNING AWAY AND MOVING FROM PLACE TO PLACE.

HOW ABOUT FBI?

THE INITIALS FBI STAND FOR FEDERAL BUREAU OF INVESTIGATION. IT'S A NATIONAL LAW-ENFORCEMENT AGENCY.

Weekly Reader Got Him Started

THE WORLD OF SPORTS

Some people said that it couldn't be done. But last month Peter Snell (right) of New Zealand did it. He broke the world record for the one-mile run.

Courtesy Benji Durden Photo by Bill Baptist

Benji Durden winning the 1982 Houston-Tenneco Marathon (above). At left, the *Weekly Reader* article that inspired Durden to try running.

Benji Durden is one of the top three marathon runners in the U.S. today. The Georgia runner has already won two marathons (26-mile races) this year, and he hopes to be one of the three U.S. runners in the 1984 Olympic marathon.

Ask Benji what got him started in running, and he'll tell you it was *Weekly Reader.*

"I was 11 years old when I read in *Weekly Reader* that New Zealand's Peter Snell had set a new world's record for the mile," says Durden. "At first, the story didn't say much to me. But then another kid in the class started saying that what Snell did was no big deal. That got me interested."

For Fact Finders

What were George Washington's famous false teeth made of?

Last week's answer: *Tin cans were developed between 1820 and 1839.*

UPI

Workman Putties Lincoln's Nose

President Abraham Lincoln looks sad, but you would, too, if you were having your nose puttied.

The patching job takes place every fall at Mount Rushmore National Memorial in South Dakota.

An employee of the National Park Service repairs the granite sculpture of four U.S. Presidents. As the worker is lowered down each face, he places special putty in any small cracks he finds. The putty keeps water from settling in the cracks and damaging the faces.

Besides Lincoln, the Presidents staring out across the Black Hills are George Washington, Thomas Jefferson, and Theodore Roosevelt. Each face is five stories high. Lincoln's nose is 1½ stories long.

How many 🐟 ? ___ How many 🐠 ? ___ How many ⭐ ? ___

HOMELESS IN AMERICA

Homeless People Roam U.S. in Search of Work

Rick Morgan, his wife, Susan, and their two young children are seeing a lot of the U.S. these days. Since summer, they've been to Atlanta, Ga., New Orleans, La., Kansas City, Mo., and Denver, Colo.

The Morgans are not on vacation. Rick has been looking for work for himself and a home for his family. By last month, he hadn't found either.

The Morgans have had a great deal of company in their search. Hundreds of thousands of people are homeless in America today, and their number is growing.

"This is a national emergency," says one official who helps the homeless.

Why Are So Many Homeless?

Even in good times, the U.S. has thousands of homeless people. Until recently, many of these people were drifters, alcoholics, and former mental patients out on their own.

Today, with hard times, charity workers talk about the "new poor"—families like the Morgans. These new poor people are victims of job layoffs taking place in the U.S.—especially in the Northeast and Midwest.

Many homeless families owned homes and lived comfortably some months back. Then unemployment came. The families kept going for a while on money from their savings and unemployment benefits. When this money gave out, many could no longer make mortgage payments on their homes. They lost their homes or were forced to sell them. Finally, they took to the road to find work and a new place to live.

Many headed for California or for states in the South and Southwest, where jobs were thought to be plentiful. A few of the travelers found jobs, but many found nothing and ended up stranded in cities or towns far from their hometowns.

Today, homeless people, including the new poor, can be found throughout the U.S. They live under highway

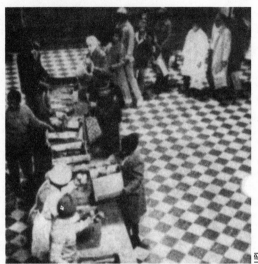

Needy people, including the homeless, line up for food at a Washington, D.C. church. About 300 people a day are fed.

bridges (see cover), in tent cities beside highways, or even in cardboard boxes on big-city streets.

The homeless battle to survive, but they risk illness from hunger and fatigue. They even risk death from wintertime exposure and violent crime.

What's Being Done To Help?

Some city governments such as New York, N.Y., and Phoenix, Ariz., provide limited shelter for those who need it. Officials in Phoenix and Houston, Tex., try to discourage the homeless from coming in search of jobs. The officials say jobs don't exist.

Church groups and other private charities in many U.S. cities and towns do their best to help. In both Phoenix and Detroit, Mich., these groups have joined together to work more effectively. A joint group in Detroit is planning a 1,000-bed shelter that is expected to be full soon after it opens.

Many private charities agree that the job is too big for them. But they are cheered by the thought that some help may be on the way.

The U.S. Congress is considering a $50-million emergency food and shelter program for the homeless. If the program is approved, it will be good news for homeless people from Maryland to California.

Man-Made Heart

First of Many?

The Jarvik-7 man-made heart is constructed of plastic and aluminum.

Dr. Jarvik invented a man-made heart and tested it in a calf.

The man was dying. His heart was failing faster than expected. Soon it would stop.

No drugs, no corrective surgery could save the man, 61-year-old Barney Clark.

He had only one hope—hope in something never tried before. Clark would need a permanent, man-made heart.

Surgeons at the University of Utah hospital moved swiftly that night. During seven and a half hours of surgery, doctors cut open Clark's chest and removed his natural heart. Then they put in a gleaming aluminum and plastic pump—a man-made heart. The man-made heart was called a Jarvik-7 after its inventor, Dr. Robert Jarvik.

Two six-foot-long hoses were inserted through Clark's chest to connect the pump to a nearby 375-pound air compressor. The large air compressor would power the man-made heart in Clark's chest.

The next morning, the plastic and aluminum Jarvik-7 was whirring softly inside Clark's chest, pumping blood throughout his body. The surgery and the Jarvik-7 were successes, said doctors.

Clark had become the first person in history to receive a permanent, man-made heart.

New Hope for Many

The history-making surgery performed on Clark last month offers new hope to thousands of Americans. Nearly 50,000 Americans a year might be aided by man-made hearts, say doctors.

These new hearts might give patients a few extra days of life, or even five or more extra years, say experts. They point out that in an experiment on a calf, a Jarvik-7 heart kept that animal alive for 268 days.

However, doctors warn, the surgery and the man-made heart might cause problems for some people. There could be life-threatening complications caused by the surgery. Or a patient's body might react poorly to the pumping power of the new, man-made heart. And, say doctors, the tubes connecting the heart to the air compressor might allow infections to enter the body.

The mental strain of living with an artificial heart is another problem patients will have to face, say doctors. Some patients will not be able to live with the thought that they are being kept alive by a plastic and aluminum pump connected to an air compressor. That is why patients with man-made hearts will receive—as Clark did—a key they can use to turn off the life-supporting air compressor if they wish.

Improvements Ahead

Researchers like Dr. Jarvik are already working on ways to improve the Jarvik-7 and to reduce its $16,450 price tag.

Within a few years the researchers hope to replace the bulky air compressor used to power the Jarvik-7 with a suitcase-sized, battery-powered unit. This smaller unit would give people with Jarvik-7 hearts more freedom to move around.

But to be truly useful, says Dr. Jarvik, a man-made heart "must be forgettable." In the future, a tiny pump, powered by batteries on the patient's belt, may make that possible, Jarvik says.

Soviets Shoot Down Unarmed Plane

This is an artist's idea of what happened to the passenger airliner.

On August 31, a Soviet fighter plane shot down an unarmed South Korean passenger jet. The passenger plane was on its way from New York City to Seoul, South Korea, by way of Alaska. The plane was hit by a Soviet missile after it went off course over Soviet territory. All of the plane's 269 passengers were killed in the attack. Among those who died were many Americans, including a U.S. congressman.

For some reason, the plane flew over a Soviet island in the Sea of Japan. Then several Soviet fighter planes followed the airliner for over two hours. U.S. officials say the Soviet fighter gave no warning before it fired at the unarmed passenger plane.

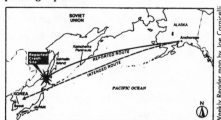

Drugs and Drinking Survey Results

Sixth-Graders Say the Main Reason Kids Their Age Use Marijuana Is...

① TO FEEL OLDER 16%

② TO HAVE A GOOD TIME 17%

③ TO GET OVER FEELING BAD 13%

④ TO FIT IN WITH OTHER KIDS 46%

Weekly Reader art by Dave Morrell

See pages 4-5

Do you feel pressure from others your age to try alcohol or drugs?

In your town, how big a problem do you think there is with alcohol and drug abuse among people your age?

You and 3.7 million other students in grades 4 through 12 were asked these and other questions earlier this year as part of the *Weekly Reader* Drugs and Drinking Survey.

Nearly half a million students responded. Here is how those of you in the sixth grade responded:

• The dangers of drugs and drinking are learned about equally from family, school, and TV and movies.

• The major sources of information that makes drugs and drinking seem like fun are other kids and TV and movies.

• The main reason kids your age start using marijuana and alcohol is to fit in with other kids.

• Four of every ten of you said there is at least some pressure from other kids your age to use alcohol; and one of three of you feels there is pressure to use marijuana.

• Most of you agree that there is at least some health risk in using alcohol and marijuana.

• More than a quarter of you say alcohol is a big problem with kids your age in your town; and more than a third say marijuana is a big problem.

• More than half of you think that at least some of the kids your age in your town have used marijuana, alcohol, glue or other chemicals, and uppers or downers.

Pioneer 10 Voyage to Stars

On June 13, a U.S. spacecraft will start a journey vastly different than any other in human history. Pioneer 10 will leave the solar system for flight into deep space. The spacecraft is to swing across the orbit of Neptune and out to the stars.

Launched in 1972, Pioneer has already traveled a total of 3.59 billion miles. It has radioed back exciting new information about the solar system.

for example, Pioneer 10 took the first closeup pictures of Jupiter.

Pioneer 10 continues radioing back information. Scientists expect to collect information from the spacecraft until it is over 5 billion miles from Earth.

Pioneer 10 also carries a special message on a metal plaque. The message is in the form of pictures.

The plaque is intended to explain Earth and Earth's people to any intelligent space beings who find the plaque. But no beings, if any exist, are likely to see the plaque for a long time. Even at a speed of over 30,000 miles an hour, Pioneer 10 will take at least 32,000 years to reach the nearest star on its

course. After that, Pioneer 10 will come near a star about once every million years.

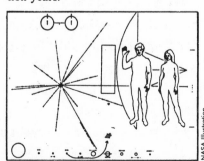

NASA Illustration

The metal plaque on Pioneer 10 (above) shows male and female humans. The plaque also illustrates scientific facts: a drawing of the solar system appears at the bottom, along with the path of Pioneer 10.

NEWS FEATURE

Help for Bald Eagles

These six-week-old eagles are living in Massachusetts.

Some people are bringing bald eagles to new places.

The people hope the eagles will make nests in the new places.

Understanding: American bald eagles are endangered in 43 states. Concerned groups are introducing eagle pairs in some states. The groups hope the eagles will help rebuild the eagle population.

Mask-Making Is Fun

In which movies did you see these characters?

Masks can make you laugh. Some masks are scary! Many masks are made for movies. There are masks of E.T., Yoda, and Darth Vader.

It takes a long time to make a mask. It takes many people too. Some people draw pictures that show how the mask must look. Others paint faces on the masks.

Which mask do you like best?

KIDS WRITE TO AUNT HELEN

Dear Aunt Helen,

My friend and I had a fight. Now she's turning all my other friends against me. Everyone's on her side. What should I do?

A.M.

Illinois

Dear A.M.,

I know it seems like everyone's ganging up on you. But try to cheer up. Read my suggestions. Maybe one of them will be helpful to you.

Love,

Aunt Helen

TALK IT OVER

Check the suggestions you think might work the best. Discuss your choice with the class.

☐ Make up with your friend. Talk about the problem that caused the fight. Try to settle your differences.

☐ Be patient. The children who are really your friends will realize it's not nice to gang up on you.

☐ Make some new friends.

Many Africans Go Hungry

Children Go Hungry In Africa

UPI

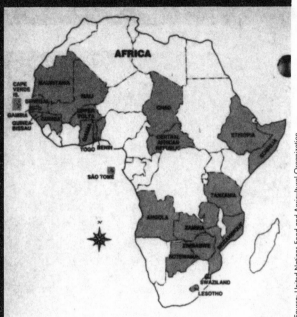

AFRICA

Countries in color face severe food shortages.

Source: United Nations Food and Agricultural Organization

● The young child waits patiently with a pail for a few spoonfuls of cereal. She is thin and frail due to extreme hunger. She has the face of an aged adult.

● A family sets fire to the brush near its home. The raging fire threatens nearby crops, but it also drives out rats that the family can kill and eat.

● An old woman—pained by arthritis—climbs slowly up a steep path to a road 1 mile from her home. A tank truck comes by and delivers a day's supply of water to her. The water fills a small jar.

These are familiar scenes in Africa today. At least 24 nations in the region face drought and possible famine. Four to five million people—including many children—are in danger of starvation.

Many people are dying each day. Others are barely staying alive by eating baked grass or devouring seed grain they would normally save for the next planting.

U.N. Asks for Help

The food crisis in Africa is the worst in this century, according to some food experts. Officials of the United Nations have asked other countries to give tons of food.

Early in 1984 the U.S. approved sending 217,000 tons of food. President Reagan has urged Congress to offer an additional 200,000 tons at a cost of $90 million.

Reasons for Famine

Why are so many Africans facing famine and death? Drought is the main reason. Harvests were poor last year because of a lack of rainfall. The harvests may be poor again this year, experts say.

Here are some other reasons for Africa's troubles, according to food experts.

—Population in Africa is growing faster than the food supply.

—Most African nations do not have the money for modern farm tools and farming research.

—Many regions in Africa lack good roads and trucks for delivering food to places where it is needed.

—Civil war and tribal unrest have upset life in some African regions. Refugees fleeing trouble often settle in areas where there is not enough farmland to provide them with food.

—Man-made damage to the land has worsened drought conditions. The cutting of tropical forests in recent years has brought erosion and turned the land into dry scrub or even desert.

The immediate need in Africa is for food to prevent starvation. But many African nations also need help to develop modern farming, industry, and education. With this long-range help, the nations could do a better job of coping with drought, food experts say.

U.S. War Against Drugs

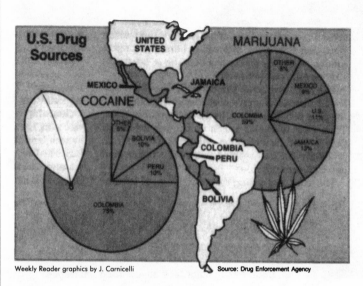

U.S. Drug Sources

Weekly Reader graphics by J. Carnicelli   Source: Drug Enforcement Agency

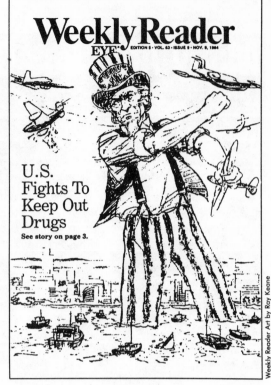

U.S. Fights To Keep Out Drugs

See story on page 3.

Weekly Reader Art by Roy Keane

The U.S. is waging a battle against drug suppliers. The battle has been going on for years and it has been tough. The U.S. has had some gains and some losses in the war.

On the plus side: Over the past year, law enforcers have seized more illegal drugs coming into the U.S. than ever before. They have seized cargoes of heroin, cocaine, marijuana and other drugs from vehicles that are hard to spot and even harder to catch. The agents have caught up with small, fast racing boats and with planes that fly so low radar can't spot them. They have found drugs hidden in shipments of flowers and in secret closets on boats and planes. Dogs have sniffed out drugs in baggage and cargo at airports and seaports.

The minus in the drug-traffic battle is the fact that more drugs are passing into the U.S. than are being seized. So far, drug arrests and seizures have only dented what has become the nation's largest business.

Reasons for Battle Losses

The problem of controlling drug traffic is giant-sized. The biggest reason for this is the huge profits that can be made selling drugs.

The large amounts of money in the drug trade lead to trouble. The money attracts crime groups. It can corrupt public officials.

For some nations drug trade is the main source of income. Some experts claim it is nearly impossible to get these nations to stop exporting drugs.

Drug traffic is also hard to control because of the large demand for drugs by people in the U.S.

Millions of Americans hand over billions of dollars each year to drug dealers. These users report that heroin, cocaine, and marijuana are easy to get.

U.S. Is in the Battle To Stay

To fight the invasion of drugs into the U.S., the U.S. Government has stepped up efforts to arrest and seize smugglers. The Government is also

● using the services of the nation's largest law enforcer, the FBI. Agents of the FBI track down major drug rings by tracing any large amounts of money that change hands.

● pushing for more and better searches at U.S. borders.

● talking nations that export illegal drugs into stopping the exports and turning over suspected dealers to the U.S.

● reducing the demand in the U.S. for drugs through drug education.

U.S. drug experts say that antidrug education pays off. Surveys show that young people nowadays are less likely to use drugs than were young people ten years ago.

Though people see little hope of curbing the flow of drugs into the U.S., one drug expert calls educating Americans about drugs, ". . . our one ray of hope."

EYE ON SCIENCE

Human Baby Receives Baboon's Heart

A newborn made medical history recently when doctors removed her imperfect heart and replaced it with the heart of a baboon. The operation took place at the Loma Linda University Medical Center near Riverside, Calif.

"Baby Fae" lived for 20 days with the walnut-sized heart beating in her chest.

She was born with an underdeveloped left ventricle—the main chamber of the heart for pumping blood through the body.

Baby Fae's last name has not been made public because her parents want to protect the family's privacy amid worldwide publicity given the operation.

Baby Fae was the 5th person in 20 years to receive the heart of a primate. None of the other patients lived longer than three and a half days with a primate heart.

Doctors at the medical center plan more experimental transplants of baboon hearts into human babies with heart diseases. If these transplants are helpful, doctors say, they will continue such animal-to-human transplants. This would ease the problem of too few human organs for transplants, doctors say. Many of the 70,000 Americans needing organ transplants may die because human organs are not available to save them.

If the demand for animal organs rises, more animals could be raised as a steady source of organs for transplantation, medical experts say.

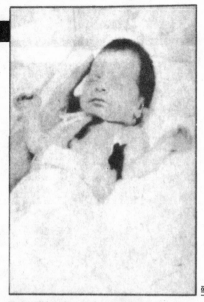

Baby Fae after her operation

Baby Fae's new heart came from a young baboon similar to this one.

Bodies Preserved For 138 Years

Use this story with the ear exercise on page 8.

The well-preserved bodies of two young British sailors have been found and examined on a tiny island in northern Canada. The bodies had been in graves in frozen ground for 138 years.

The sailors were members of an expedition that tried to navigate a water passage across North America from the Atlantic Ocean to the Pacific Ocean in the 1840's.

The expedition—138 men in two ships—never completed its voyage. The ships were trapped in Arctic ice for over a year. The men left the ships, but none survived in the cold Arctic wasteland.

Scientists took samples of tissue, organs, and bone from one of the sailors to find out how he had died. His name was John Torrington.

"There was no sign that he had had a painful death. His eyes were open and his face was a blank," one scientist said.

Map shows general area where preserved bodies were found.

Photo shows body of John Torrington preserved by frost in the ground.

Seiko

World's First TV Watch Is for Sale

What would you think of a TV with a screen only 1-inch wide? That's the size of a TV screen made by a company in Japan. The TV is part of a wristwatch. The screen is on the face of the watch. This watch has a radio too!

The TV watch hooks up to stereo headphones and a tiny channel selector that fits in a shirt pocket. The TV runs on two batteries. The batteries give five hours of viewing—or watching—on this watch.

Ostrich Guards Junkyard

Mr. Haynes says his workers are afraid of Oscar. Oscar chased one onto the top of a car.

UPI

Fletcher Haynes owns a car junkyard. He bought two dogs to guard it. But people often outsmarted the dogs and stole parts from the cars.

Mr. Haynes sold the dogs. Then he bought a mean ostrich called Oscar.

Now Oscar patrols the junkyard. No one has been able to outsmart him. When people come near, Oscar chases them and pecks them. Mr. Haynes says his junkyard hasn't been robbed since Oscar arrived.

Just for Fun!

Seven things in the picture are wrong. Put a ring around each of the seven things.

STAR WARS' DEFENSE-
CAN IT ASSURE PEACE?

Huge U.S. radar satellites silently orbit the planet. Suddenly they detect a Soviet missile launch . . . then another . . . and another. An attack has begun!

The launches are reported to a U.S. defense computer. The computer immediately activates tens of thousands of space-based and Earth-based weapons. It advises the President that the U.S. is under attack and that it is responding.

Space-based and Earth-based lasers blast away at enemy missiles, destroying them in blinding flashes of light. Long magnetic rail guns orbiting in space hurtle destructive objects at nuclear warheads, destroying them before they reach their targets in the U.S.

The sky seems ablaze with falling stars as pieces of destroyed missiles burn on reentering Earth's atmosphere.

Within 30 minutes the battle is over. Lasers power down. Rail guns are silent. Radars scan the planet.

This is the way President Ronald Reagan and some of his key advisers hope any future nuclear attack against the U.S. will turn out. Instead of the Soviet Union and the U.S. destroying each other in a hail of nuclear missiles, a space-based defense shield would protect the U.S.

The President called on the nation's top scientists and engineers to develop a way to defend the U.S. from nuclear attack. He called his plan the Strategic Defense Initiative. It has become known as the "Star Wars" defense plan.

Reasons for Star Wars Defense

The President's aim is to change the current basis of peace between the U.S. and the Soviet Union. The current basis of that peace is a theory called MAD—Mutually Assured Destruction. According to this theory, each superpower must have enough nuclear weapons to make sure that if it is attacked, it can respond with enough firepower to destroy the attacker.

Today, the Soviet Union has 8,700 usable nuclear warheads, and the U.S. has 11,000. "It is more than enough to blow both countries out of this world," says Reagan.

In place of Mutually Assured Destruction, the President wants *mutually assured defense*. Rather than hoping peace can be maintained by a threat of total destruction, the President wants to maintain peace with a foolproof defense shield. The President believes that both the U.S. and the Soviet Union will destroy their nuclear weapons when they realize they don't need them for defense.

Another reason given for the Star Wars defense plan is that the Soviets are working on similar weapons and defense plans. The U.S. can't afford to fall behind the Soviets in such important areas, say some people.

The Government plans to spend $21 billion over the next four years to develop Star Wars weapons. Already the U.S. has test-fired a laser beam that destroyed a rocket, and has shot down an orbiting satellite.

Some Oppose Star Wars Defense

First, critics say, it would be impossible to develop a computer that could control thousands of weapons in a struggle for survival that might last only 30 minutes. The system couldn't be made foolproof, say experts. At least some nuclear warheads would get through the defense shield, causing enormous destruction, they say.

Second, critics say, the Star Wars defense system would be too expensive even for the U.S. Some experts estimate that it could cost more than $1.2 trillion.

Third, critics say the Star Wars defense system might prompt the Soviets to attack the U.S. The Soviets might see the shield as a way for the U.S. to protect itself while attacking the Soviet Union. As a result, the Soviets might launch a nuclear attack on the U.S. before the defense shield has been completed.

In addition, say critics, there is the dark side of the Star Wars force. The same space weapons that could defend a nation could attack an enemy. The world might be replacing the threat of nuclear destruction with the threat of destruction from Star Wars weapons, they say.

Some people also fear the problems and costs of a Star Wars weapons race between the two superpowers. Soviet leader Mikhail Gorbachev, rather than see such a race, has even proposed a deep cut in the number of nuclear arms held by both nations. President Reagan, however, says his defense initiative is "too important to the world to give up in exchange for a different number of nuclear weapons."

Racial Conflict Tears South Africa Apart

Weekly Reader Art by Ray Keane

"NO!" screams the black South African. He has been badly beaten by other blacks and doused with gasoline. Someone strikes a match to set him ablaze.

"Stop!" shouts Bishop Desmond Tutu, the black religious leader who last year received the Nobel Peace Prize for his efforts to bring racial equality to South Africa.

"Freedom," Bishop Tutu tells the angry crowd, "*will* be ours. But freedom must come the right way—not like this," he says pointing to the gas-soaked man who had been accused of supporting white rule.

Bishop Tutu stands at the center of a conflict that threatens to tear his beloved country apart. The conflict pits the nation's well-armed ruling whites against the determined black majority that wants change and equal rights.

In the past 12 months more than 600 South Africans have been killed in the conflict. The country's president, P. W. Botha, has declared a state of emergency in the nation's most heavily populated areas.

Freedom Sought from Apartheid

The freedom Bishop Tutu promises his people is freedom from *apartheid* (ə-PAHR-tayt). In the Afrikaans language of South Africa, *apartheid* means "apartness." Apartheid is a system of laws designed to keep the nation's four racial groups separate and under white control.

There are about 5 million whites in this country of nearly 33 million people. There are about 3 million colored (people of mixed race), about 1 million Asians, and about 24 million blacks.

Most whites live well in South Africa, one of the world's richest nations. They generally go to better schools, are better paid, and have better jobs than blacks. A middle-class white family generally lives in a modern three-bedroom house in the suburbs with a small swimming pool and a live-in black maid. The whites control the national government.

Blacks cannot vote in national elections. Officially, blacks are not citizens of South Africa. Instead, they are considered citizens of one of the ten separate areas set aside for blacks within South Africa. The government calls these areas "tribal homelands."

Adult blacks outside their tribal homelands must carry passbooks stating their racial group, name, address, and occupation. Blacks usually live near large cities in shacks without running water, sewers, or paved roads.

Colored and Asians often live better than most blacks. They have a small voice in the government.

Blacks Demand Changes

Blacks are demanding changes in South Africa, the last white-ruled country on the African Continent. Blacks seek increases in pay, an end to passbooks, and representation in the nation's legislature. Some blacks demand "one man, one vote," which would give them control of the country.

Many whites recognize the need to give greater power to blacks but reject complete equality. Others oppose giving blacks any more power at all.

"One man, one vote would work one time," these whites say. Then, they say, black control would lead to a dictatorship just as it has in some other African nations. Whites would have no place to go, they say.

Bishop Desmond Tutu leads South African blacks in their struggle for racial equality.

U.S. Urges Change

Some Americans are staging demonstrations in the U.S. to protest conditions in South Africa. Some of the protesters demand that U.S. companies doing business in South Africa leave that country. They also demand that U.S. banks and other organizations stop loaning money to the government and companies of South Africa.

The U.S. Congress has protested conditions in South Africa by barring the sale of some South African products in the U.S. and the sale of some U.S. products to South Africa.

Other Americans, however, feel that reducing U.S. involvement in South Africa is the wrong thing to do. They say that most U.S. businesses there treat blacks and whites the same. This sets a good example for South African businesses to follow, these Americans say. These Americans also say that if U.S. loans to South Africa are stopped, it will be the blacks, not the whites, who will suffer.

William Perry: He's a Big Bear

The Chicago Bears are off to a good start in the National Football League. Playing no small part in their success is William Perry, a rookie (first year) lineman.

The Bears are known as the "Monsters of the Midway" because of their size. Biggest of the monsters is 22-year-old Perry—a former all-American at Clemson University.

At summer training camp, Perry weighed about 330 pounds. He found he was carrying too much weight. He was sluggish and not able to keep up with other players.

The Bears coach kept him away from the fries and the cheeseburgers and had him lift weights to build up his strength. Soon he was down to 318 pounds—and doing better on the field.

In college Perry was a star at sacking quarterbacks. He did it 25 times. In his senior year, he led the team in making tackles with 100.

Perry takes a kidding about his size. At Clemson he was known as "refrigerator" because of his size and love of food. But the kidding doesn't bother him. He comes from a family of 12 children—most of them big. At home

Being tackled by William Perry is an unforgettable experience.

he's not even the largest Perry. His brother Freddie tops him at 330 pounds.

Whale Returns to Sea

A humpback whale that lost its way on a migration from Alaska southward is believed safe at sea again.

The whale, named Humphrey, spent nearly a month splashing about the San Francisco (Calif.) Bay area. At one point the 40-foot whale was 70 miles from the sea, up the Sacramento River. Whale experts feared fresh water in the river might harm the animal.

Whale experts and volunteers herded the whale back down the river toward the Pacific Ocean by playing humpback whale sounds underwater and by banging on submerged pipes.

Some people called the whale E.T. because it was lost and couldn't call home.

Many people had good view of 45-ton wayward whale.

Soviet Union Names New Leader

Mikhail Gorbachev (gohr-bah-CHAWF) has been named as the new leader of the Soviet Union. He replaces Konstantin Chernenko, who died earlier this month after a long illness.

Gorbachev, at 54 years of age, is the youngest of the group of 10 Communist Party officials who rule the Soviet Union. He is an expert on farming, having studied agriculture as well as law in college. He also worked in his youth as a grain-harvester operator.

With this background, Gorbachev is expected to devote much of his time as leader to solving his country's farm problems. In recent years, the Soviet Union has not been able to grow enough grain to feed its 280 million people.

The U.S. is interested in what happens in the Soviet Union because the country ranks with the U.S. as one of the world's two superpowers. The Soviet Union is the largest nation in the world in land area and the third largest in population. Militarily, it is about equal to the United States.

The Soviet Union and the United States are currently engaged in arms control talks in Geneva, Switzerland. The big question in the minds of U.S. officials is—What effect will the change in leadership in the Soviet Union have on these talks?

🐾 World's Smallest Monkey

Use this story with the ear exercise on page 8.

UPI

The young pygmy marmoset in the photo may be larger than the toothbrush it is clinging to, but it's the smallest member of the monkey family.

You can find these tiny animals living in the South America rain forest—if you have sharp eyes. With their speckled brown coats, the marmosets blend right into the dark rain forest floor.

The animals live in small colonies. They gouge small holes in tree trunks and eat the sap. Insects and fruit also are part of their diet.

Another name for the animal is *leoncito*—Spanish for *little lion*.

Car Gets 4,010 Miles on a Gallon of Gas!

A car made in England has set a new world's record for gasoline use. In a contest held this summer, the car set a record of 4,010 miles on a gallon of gas. The car carries only one person, and its top speed is 15 miles an hour. Daniel Billington, an 11-year-old London (England) boy drove the car in the contest.

Times/Bandphoto

Whiskers: Citizenship

Dear Boys and Girls,

I walked home from school today. I was alone. A car started following me. I didn't know the people in the car.

I was scared. I ran home as fast as I could.

The car drove away. But I'm still scared. What should I have done? What would you do?

Your friend,

Whiskers

CRACK

Dangerous and Aimed at Kids

"I had just turned 13, and I thought I knew everything about drugs. So when some friends bought me crack (a smokable form of cocaine) as a birthday present, I was really excited," says Ted.

That was six months ago. Since then, Ted has become hooked on crack. To support his habit, he has sold drugs, stolen from his friends and family, and nearly killed a man he was trying to rob. He was kicked out of the house by his parents when he refused to seek drug treatment. Today, he is in a drug treatment program for young addicts.

"What I found out was that most of what I thought I knew about drugs was wrong," says Ted.

Among the mistaken ideas Ted had were that cocaine is only mildly addictive, that it is very expensive, and that it is almost harmless.

Extremely Addictive

What Ted learned in the six months after he first used crack was that cocaine in this form is extremely addictive. Experts say it is the most addictive drug known to man.

Crack—also called *rock*—is made by mixing cocaine with baking soda and water to form a paste that is 75 percent cocaine. After the paste dries, it is broken into little chips that resemble cracked pieces of soap or bits of white gravel. These chips are then sold cheap—for as little as $5 a chip. Users smoke the chips.

"Crack creates a tremendous high. As soon as you start to come down from it, you want more," says a drug enforcement agent. This desire for more soon becomes an *addiction*— an uncontrollable need for a drug.

"With crack, we're not talking about one or two years to create an addict," says the official. "About 95 percent of crack addicts became addicted to this form of cocaine in about two months. Some people—particularly kids—may develop an almost immediate need," he says.

And, warn experts, crack is physically very harmful. It can cause brain seizures, heart attacks, and lung damage.

Aimed at Kids

Crack was developed as a product by organized crime in much the same way a business develops a new shaving cream or perfume, says one drug enforcement official. A few years ago, some crime leaders realized that the market for high-priced cocaine and other drugs was getting too crowded for really high profits. They needed a fresh product that would be cheap, profitable, and create a lot of repeat sales. And they needed a new market.

Crack is the product. Kids are the market.

Cities across the U.S., but particularly large cities like New York and Los Angeles, are seeing rapid increases in the use of cocaine, especially crack, among teens. About 48 percent of all crack addicts are teenagers, say experts.

According to a recent survey, about 17 percent of high school seniors have tried cocaine. Of these seniors, an increasing number are trying cocaine for the first time as crack.

Efforts Made To Stop Drug Use

Many steps are being taken to stop the use of crack.

One step involves increased efforts by police and drug enforcement officials to catch drug sellers.

But cracking down on drug sales is hard to do, explain some police. Sometimes teenagers sell crack on streetcorners or on school grounds. And other times, crack is sold from crack "houses." A crack house is usually an apartment rented by criminals. The criminals put a heavy steel door on the apartment. A dealer sits inside the apartment taking money and slipping crack through a slot in the door. The door protects the sellers from police, giving the sellers time to throw away any drugs before police can break in.

And even when police do get inside, they don't find big criminals. Frequently they just find kids who have been hired to sell the drugs.

Other efforts to stop drug use involve trying to convince people that drugs aren't glamorous. Some TV, movie, and sports stars are giving anti-drug talks.

Still other people are alerting Americans—particularly school-age Americans—to the dangers of crack.

"The problem we face," says one official, "is that kids ignore scare tactics. They have heard scare stories about drugs before, and they don't want to listen anymore. Unfortunately, kids have stopped listening just when the most intensely addictive drug known to man has come on the market for them," he says.

WHAT COCAINE DOES TO THE BODY

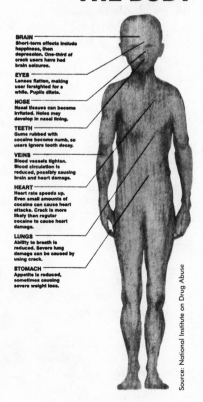

BRAIN
Short-term effects include happiness, then depression. One-third of crack users have had brain seizures.

EYES
Lenses flatten, making user farsighted for a while. Pupils dilate.

NOSE
Nasal tissues can become irritated. Holes may develop in nasal lining.

TEETH
Gums rubbed with cocaine become numb, so users ignore tooth decay.

VEINS
Blood vessels tighten. Blood circulation is reduced, possibly causing brain and heart damage.

HEART
Heart rate speeds up. Even small amounts of cocaine can cause heart attacks. Crack is more likely than regular cocaine to cause heart damage.

LUNGS
Ability to breath is reduced. Severe lung damage can be caused by using crack.

STOMACH
Appetite is reduced, sometimes causing severe weight loss.

Source: National Institute on Drug Abuse

Nuclear Energy

HOW MUCH RISK?

Thousands of Soviet children spent this summer away from home—but not by choice.

The children's homes were near the nuclear power plant at Chernobyl in the western Soviet Union. The plant's nuclear reactor exploded and burned last April.

Smoke from the fire sent dangerous radioactivity across the western Soviet Union and half of Europe.

By early summer 26 persons were dead and many others were expected to die from radiation sickness.

The children who lived in the area around Chernobyl were sent to camp to avoid further exposure to dangerous radioactivity. If radioactive levels remain high near Chernobyl, the children's return to their homes could be delayed indefinitely, nuclear experts say.

U.S. Plants: Are They Safer?

The Chernobyl explosion raises the question of whether similar accidents could happen in the U.S. The U.S. has 101 nuclear plants in operation.

U.S. Government rules require U.S. plants to meet tough safety standards to prevent the escape of radioactive material in case of an accident. These standards, many nuclear experts believe, are much tougher than those in the Soviet Union.

The U.S. standards require the use of thick concrete to surround almost all nuclear reactors—the devices in a nuclear plant that make electricity.

Most U.S. plants use water to control the activity of the nuclear reactor. Water is believed to reduce the risk of explosion and fire.

In spite of these and other safety measures, U.S. Government experts say that a nuclear accident could still happen in the United States.

Debate Over Nuclear Power

The risk of another nuclear accident has many people asking: Should nuclear power plants continue to operate?

Critics of nuclear power say the plants should be closed. After Chernobyl, protesters in the U.S. renewed their efforts to stop the building of more nuclear plants. In West Germany, a group marched with signs reading:

Some U.S. nuclear reactors have thick concrete domes for safety.

CHERNOBYL IS EVERYWHERE. The group believes that serious accidents can happen wherever a nuclear plant is operating.

Defenders of nuclear power say that outside the Soviet Union the safety record at nuclear plants has been good. Few people, if any, have been killed as a direct result of a nuclear accident, they say.

In addition, the defenders say that nuclear plants are a necessary source of electric power in the world. More than 300 nuclear plants are operating today in 26 countries. These plants provide about 15 percent of the world's electric power.

Scientists are studying the Chernobyl accident to find out what went wrong. Lessons they learn could lead to safer nuclear power plants in the Soviet Union and elsewhere in the world, including the U.S.

Nuclear reactor building at Chernobyl looks like this after accident.

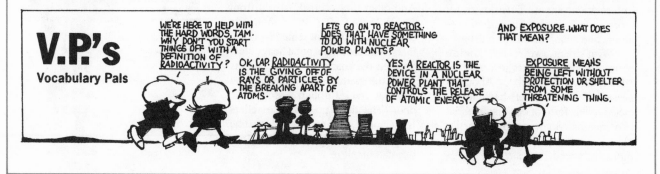

V.P.'s
Vocabulary Pals

WE'RE HERE TO HELP WITH THE HARD WORDS, TAM. WHY DON'T YOU START THINGS OFF WITH A DEFINITION OF RADIOACTIVITY?

OK, CAP. RADIOACTIVITY IS THE GIVING OFF OF RAYS OR PARTICLES BY THE BREAKING APART OF ATOMS.

LETS GO ON TO REACTOR. DOES THAT HAVE SOMETHING TO DO WITH NUCLEAR POWER PLANTS?

YES, A REACTOR IS THE DEVICE IN A NUCLEAR POWER PLANT THAT CONTROLS THE RELEASE OF ATOMIC ENERGY.

AND EXPOSURE. WHAT DOES THAT MEAN?

EXPOSURE MEANS BEING LEFT WITHOUT PROTECTION OR SHELTER FROM SOME THREATENING THING.

'We Mourn Seven Heroes'

'The future belongs to the brave.'

The space shuttle Challenger *exploded in a ball of fire about 74 seconds after launch Jan. 28, 1986. It was the worst disaster in U.S. space history. All seven astronauts aboard were killed. One of the astronauts was Christa McAuliffe, a schoolteacher who was to have been the first private citizen in space.*

President Ronald Reagan, in his speech to a grieving nation, expressed the sorrow and hopes of the country. Following is part of his address:

We mourn seven heroes: Michael Smith, Dick Scobee, Judith Resnik, Ronald McNair, Ellison Onizuka, Gregory Jarvis, and Christa McAuliffe. We mourn their loss as a nation, together. . . .

[The seven] were daring and brave and they had that special grace, that special spirit that says, "Give me a challenge and I'll meet it with joy." They had a hunger to explore the universe and discover its truths. They wished to serve and they did—they served all of us. . . .

And I want to say something to the schoolchildren of America who were watching the live coverage of the shuttle's takeoff. I know it's hard to understand that sometimes painful things like this happen. It's all part of the process of exploration and discovery, and it's all part of taking a chance and expanding man's horizons. The future doesn't belong to the fainthearted. It belongs to the brave. The *Challenger* crew was pulling us into the future and we'll continue to follow them. . . .

We'll continue our quest in space. There will be more shuttle flights and more shuttle crews and, yes, more volunteers, more civilians, more teachers in space. Nothing ends here. Our hopes and our journeys continue. . . .

STATUE OF LIBERTY
CELEBRATES 100TH BIRTHDAY

What may be the biggest, most exciting, most spectacular birthday celebration in U.S. history is scheduled for this summer.

The world's largest fireworks and laser show will light the sky. Tall sailing ships, 200 aircraft, nearly 40,000 boats, and more than 20,000 performers will take part.

This dazzling celebration is to mark the 100th birthday of the Statue of Liberty in New York Harbor. The celebration will also signal completion of nearly $40 million worth of restoration work on the famous U.S. symbol.

The giant celebration, being called Liberty Weekend, will begin July 3 with the official relighting of the statue.

Nearly 10 million visitors are expected to crowd into New York for the celebration, while millions more Americans will watch the birthday celebration on TV.

For two years, the Statue of Liberty stood surrounded by aluminum scaffolding as workers repaired the statue's framework and the 300 copper sheets—⅛ inch thick—that make up the statue's surface.

In addition, workers replaced the flame in the statue's torch, making the flame more like the one the famous French sculptor Frédéric-Auguste Bartholdi had planned when he designed the statue in 1874.

The torch now holds a new solid flame that is gold-plated to make it gleam in the sunlight. Brilliant quartz spotlights make the gold shine spectacularly at night.

All the work and effort is leading to the spectacular birthday celebration this Fourth of July weekend and to another 100 years, during which the statue will stand as a proud symbol of American freedoms.

Soviets Remember U.S. Schoolgirl With Stamp

A new Soviet stamp bears the likeness of Samantha Smith. The stamp is the Soviets' way of remembering the American schoolgirl who became their friend.

Samantha wrote the late Soviet leader Yuri Andropov in 1982, asking that the superpowers work for a more peaceful world. She later toured the Soviet Union as Andropov's guest.

Samantha died in a plane crash last August at the age of 13. She was re-

Soviet stamp worth five kopeks (about six cents) honors Samantha. Her name is in the Cyrillic letters of the Russian alphabet.

turning to her home in Maine from England. She had been there filming episodes of a new TV series that marked her first appearance as an actress.

The Soviets say they will never forget Samantha. They refer to her as "a little ambassador of peace."

In addition to the stamp, the Soviet Union has named a diamond, a flower, and a street in her honor. Soviet schoolchildren have formed an international friendship club and set up a museum in her memory. And students from more than a hundred Soviet schools recently competed for a chance to have their school renamed Samantha Smith.

Baby Killer Whale Survives in Captivity

David Butcher, director of animal behavior at Sea World, swims with Kandu, the killer whale, and her baby, Shamu.

A 700-pound baby was born recently in Orlando, Florida. The baby's name is Shamu. She's a killer whale calf at Sea World in Orlando. She's the first killer whale born in captivity to nurse from its mother long enough to survive.

If a mother killer whale is upset by being in captivity, she can't nurse her baby well. Shamu's mother, however, felt comfortable enough to take good care of Shamu.

Now, three-month-old Shamu is playful and curious. She imitates her mother by swimming on her back and making "spy hops" out of the water for a look at the world around her. She is even starting to make the high-pitched sounds all killer whales produce.

Peanut and Jocko® by Don Robison

AIDS

When Will A Cure Be Found?

Ryan White is 15 years old. Each night he folds his hands and prays: "Thank you, dear Lord, for another day."

When Ryan was 12, he caught AIDS as the result of a blood transfusion.

AIDS stands for *a*cquired *i*mmune *d*eficiency *s*yndrome. It is a disease that attacks and destroys the body's immune system—the system that fights diseases. A person with AIDS gets sick because his or her body is no longer able to defend itself against diseases. Even a cold can be fatal to an AIDS victim.

People in Ryan's town were afraid when they heard he had AIDS. They were afraid of AIDS—a disease they did not understand. And they were afraid of people like Ryan who had AIDS. So Ryan was barred from school. People slashed tires on his family's car. Someone shot a bullet through the living room window of his home.

After a year-long court battle, Ryan won the right to return to school. But by then he and his family had moved to another town. "I didn't want to die there," he says.

Today, Ryan weighs barely 60 pounds. Sometimes he can be seen wearing a sweater and a jacket with a blanket around him while standing in a hot kitchen. He holds his cold, blue hands over the red-hot coils of the kitchen stove. Ryan never seems to get warm anymore. And AIDS is allowing other diseases to destroy his body.

AIDS Spreading Rapidly in U.S.

AIDS has been spreading rapidly in the U.S. since the first case was discovered here in 1981. Today, there are 35,000 Americans who, like Ryan, are sick because of the disease. More than 20,000 Americans are reported to have died because of AIDS. In the next 24 hours, another 30 Americans will die because of AIDS. And this week, 374 more Americans may become infected.

The Centers for Disease Control estimates that there are about 1.5 million people in the U.S. now infected with the AIDS virus. Most of these people show no easily recognizable signs of the disease, yet many of them may become sick in time.

What Causes AIDS and How Does It Spread?

AIDS is caused by a virus named HIV. In infected people, the virus is present in body fluids such as blood and in fluids passed during sexual contact.

Most experts agree that people *cannot* catch AIDS from mosquito bites, food, toilet seats, eating utensils, sneezes, or the air. Additionally, people *cannot* catch AIDS through such normal daily contact as shaking

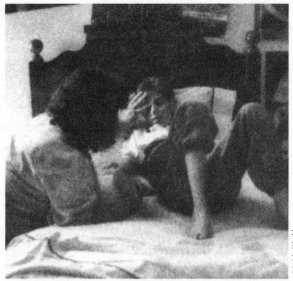

Ryan White caught AIDS from a blood transfusion. Every night he prays: "Thank you, dear Lord, for another day."

AP/Wide World

hands, playing, talking, or hugging an AIDS victim.

The AIDS virus is most often spread through sexual contact with an infected person. The disease is also often spread by drug users who share needles infected with the AIDS virus.

In addition, the disease has been spread from mothers to their unborn children during pregnancy. And in the past, some people have caught AIDS from blood transfusions. Now, however, all medical blood products are tested for AIDS before use. There is very little chance now of getting AIDS from blood transfusions.

How Can People Avoid AIDS?

The most effective way to avoid the risk of AIDS is to avoid all sexual contact and the sharing of needles with other people, say experts.

Some people, however, do not want to avoid all sexual contact. They are advised to know the health and previous behavior of their sexual partners and to take proper precautions.

Search for Cure

Today, medical researchers are investigating two ways to end the AIDS epidemic.

One way is to develop a vaccine to prevent people from catching AIDS. This month tests of a possible vaccine begin on volunteers. The vaccine contains dead parts of the AIDS virus. Doctors hope that the vaccine will cause the body's immune system to develop defenses against AIDS.

The other approach being investigated uses some drugs to stop the spread of the virus in infected people while using other drugs to rebuild the immune system.

Doctors warn, however, that it may take ten years or more before safe, effective drugs and vaccines are ready for the public. For large numbers of Americans who are, or will become, infected with AIDS, that will be too late.

IRAN-CONTRA DEAL IS INVESTIGATED

Ronald Reagan has begun his last two years as U.S. President amid great confusion. Last fall it was disclosed that the U.S. had sent secret shipments of weapons to Iran. Then it was reported that millions of dollars from the sale of the weapons had been given to rebels in Nicaragua called *Contras*.

The disclosures have raised stormy protests. Many Americans look upon Iran as an enemy. Iranian terrorism has included holding 52 Americans hostage for 444 days in 1979–1980. As for aid to Nicaragua, the U.S. Congress had forbidden it from 1984 to June 1986.

Last fall, Congress held hearings to find the facts behind the disclosures. They wanted to know if anyone in the White House had known about the operations.

Congress did not solve the puzzle then. Two key men in the puzzle, Poindexter and North, refused to tell what they knew.

Congress still asks *who did what?* and *who knows what?* Two special committees—one in the Senate, one in the House of Representatives—are continuing their investigations. In addition, an independent counsel has been named to investigate the case. This counsel, Lawrence E. Walsh, takes over the investigation from the U.S. Department of Justice.

Members of the investigating committees are seeking answers to these questions:

● **When did President Reagan approve the arms sale to Iran?**

A U.S. law forbid the sale of weapons to any country that supports terrorism. President Reagan has called Iran a terrorist country. Investigators want to know if the President approved an arms shipment to Iran at a time when it was against the law to do so.

● **Was there a profit made from the sale of arms to Iran; if so, what happened to it?**

Attorney General Edwin Meese, who heads the Department of Justice, said that the United States was repaid for the weapons. But, he said, a profit of "$10 million or $30 million" went into a bank account in Switzerland and money from that account found its way to the Contras.

If this did happen, investigators want to know who put the profit into the hands of the Contras. Some clues point to the Central Intelligence Agency (CIA). Other clues point to Lt. Col. North and his boss at the National Security Council (NSC), Vice Admiral Poindexter.

Americans want the questions about the Iran-Contra deal settled. They want to see the Government get on with the business of governing the country.

Lawrence Walsh heads investigation.

BEING HOMELESS *Fifth Grader Tells Her Story*

Jaime Brand, a homeless fifth grader, tells her story. Each day, she waits at the front door with her two younger sisters for the school buses. They wait inside. The neighborhood is dangerous.

The girls are not picked up at home. They do not have a home. They live at the Salvation Army shelter in Kansas City, Missouri, with their mom, dad, and a brother, Dusty, age 11.

Fifth grader Jaime misses the roomy three-bedroom apartment where the family once lived. The Brands were evicted after Mr. Brand got hurt on the job and was laid off. The family could not pay the rent.

Jaime also misses her old school. The new one bores her. "They just started division and haven't done fractions yet," she told *Weekly Reader*.

Before the buses come, Jaime reminds her sisters of the rules: Don't go anywhere after school because it's dangerous to walk to the shelter in the dark; don't let it bother you when kids call you "Salvation Army girl."

Jaime has lived at the shelter for three months and she is anxious to leave. The shelter is noisy and crowded. Sometimes 60 people are in the shelter. The Brand's room is very small and is made even more so when the girls' cots are set up at bedtime beside the three single beds.

Rules at the shelter bother Jaime. She really dislikes the 8:30 bedtime curfew for kids.

But things are looking up. Jaime told *Weekly Reader* that soon her family will be moving into a big house that the Salvation Army bought. They'll stay there until they save enough money for a place of their own.

There's lots of room, *clean* bathrooms with claw-foot tubs, even a piano that I hope I can learn to play," Jaime said.

Racial Conflict
On the Rise In U.S.?

• In Howard Beach, N.Y., 11 white youths attacked 3 black men as the men came out of a pizza parlor. One of the blacks was killed by a car while trying to flee his attackers.

• At the University of Massachusetts, white students brawled with black students after the last game of the 1986 World Series.

• In Cumming, Ga., about 50 persons, mostly blacks, began a walk for brotherhood. A crowd of 300 whites broke up the walk by throwing stones, bottles, and mud at the walkers. Four walkers were injured.

Such racial conflicts bother many people in the U.S., including President Reagan. In a recent TV address, Mr. Reagan told listeners "to be totally intolerant of racism anywhere around you." He was advising people to take a strong stand against racism.

Racism is the belief that certain races of people are by birth and nature superior to others. The word can also mean unfair treatment of certain races by members of another race.

Is Racism on the Rise?

Some leaders in the U.S. say racism is growing. They note that racist attacks reported in the U.S. have risen from 99 in 1980 to 276 last year.

Other leaders say racism is not growing. A U.S. Justice Department official says TV and newspapers are making racial tension in the U.S. seem worse than it really is.

Racism may not be rising, but it is still "very common" in the U.S., according to a recent poll of both blacks and whites.

What causes racism? The answer, according to many experts, is the fear people have of strangers or of anyone who looks or speaks differently.

"When differences are obvious—such as skin color, shape of eyes, or religious worship—the distrust becomes greater," says Thomas Pettigrew, a California psychologist.

What Can Be Done About Racism?

Many people who have studied the problem of racism say certain steps can be taken toward a solution. These steps include the following:

• *People can protest racial acts.* A few days after a crowd broke up a brotherhood walk in Cumming, Ga., both blacks and whites marched there to exercise their rights of free speech and peaceful assembly.

• *Whole communities can make a stand against organized racism.* When an armed group of Nazi-like racists moved to Coeur d'Alene, Idaho, trouble soon followed. The racists attempted bank robbery to finance racist schemes. Alarmed townspeople reacted. A human rights rally last summer drew 1,000 citizens. The citizens made it clear that the racist group was not welcome.

• *Young children can learn tolerance for people who are different in looks or speech.*

Tolerance, scholars say, is an obvious answer to the fear and hatred underlying racism.

photo by John Chiasson from Gamma-Liaison

People discuss racial tension in Howard Beach, N.Y.

VP's
Vocabulary Pals

RACISM- WHAT DOES THAT MEAN, CAP?

RACISM IS THE BELIEF THAT RACE ALONE MAKES ONE GROUP OF PEOPLE SUPERIOR TO ANOTHER.

WHAT ABOUT CIVIL RIGHTS?

CIVIL RIGHTS ARE FREEDOMS GUARANTEED TO U.S. CITIZENS BY THE U.S. CONSTITUTION AND BY CERTAIN ACTS OF CONGRESS.

HOW ABOUT TOLERANCE?

TOLERANCE IS SYMPATHY FOR BELIEFS OR PRACTICES DIFFERING OR CONFLICTING WITH ONE'S OWN.

Do Footprints Belong to 'Bigfoot'

For more than a hundred years reports have come from the northwestern United States of a strange apelike creature lurking in the forests. Those who claim to have seen the creature describe it as standing about 8 feet tall, weighing 800 pounds, and being covered with fur.

The Indians called the creature *Sasquatch*.

White settlers called it *Bigfoot*.

Until now, most scientists dismissed the reports of Bigfoot as products of the imagination, or as lies. Now some scientists are not so sure.

Recently some giant-size footprints were discovered that could have come from an 800-pound beast. The prints are 17 inches long. They have distinct skin ridges like those on fingers and toes and they show sweat pores and patterns of wear.

Fingerprint experts have examined casts of the prints. They generally agree that the prints are real.

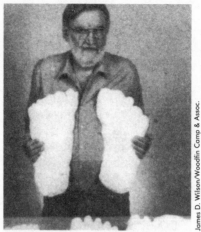

Grover Krantz holds plaster casts of prints that he believes belong to Bigfoot.

Photographer who took this picture in northern California claims creature is Bigfoot.

The prints have convinced at least one scientist—Grover Krantz of Washington State University—that Bigfoot exists. Krantz has a theory that Bigfoot is a hidden species of a subhuman creature that has survived for millions of years.

Krantz is planning a helicopter search for Bigfoot into the backcountry next spring. He hopes to win support for his theory by finding a specimen, either dead or alive.

Troublemaker in Space

A little monkey sent into space had a lot of Soviet scientists worried recently.

The monkey was strapped tightly into his spaceship seat. But, after five days, the monkey freed his left paw. He pushed and pulled happily at everything he could reach. He took out his feeding tube. He took the metal nameplate off his hat.

The monkey's name is Yerosha, which means "troublemaker" in Russian.

Soviet scientists thought Yerosha might harm the mission. The Soviets were testing the effects of weightlessness on animals.

But Yerosha was not able to reach the spaceship's controls. The flight ended safely.

Yerosha is strapped into spacecraft.

Peanut and Jocko

Reagan and Gorbachev Sign Arms Treaty

On December 8, 1987, Mikhail Gorbachev and Ronald Reagan sign the historic document reducing their nation's nuclear weapons.

What Does the Treaty Mean?

A few years ago, experts never would have predicted what actually happened in Washington, D.C., in December. The United States and the Soviet Union—enemies for 40 years—agreed to reduce weapons.

President Reagan and Soviet leader Gorbachev met to sign the most sweeping arms agreement in modern history.

The INF Treaty

The agreement is 56 typewritten pages plus 73 pages of facts and maps of where the weapons are kept. It deals with destroying *intermediate-range nuclear forces* (INF) belonging to the U.S. and the U.S.S.R.

Gorbachev agreed to get rid of Soviet land-based medium-range missiles. Reagan agreed to get rid of the same class of missiles belonging to the U.S.

The treaty is now before the U.S. Senate. It is believed likely that the lawmakers will approve the treaty when they vote on it in March or April.

The treaty calls for the Soviets to get rid of two missiles for every one the U.S. junks. A total of some 2,600 missiles will be destroyed.

Teams of inspectors from each country will be on hand to make sure the missiles are destroyed as stated in the INF treaty. That means Soviet inspectors will be at U.S. missile facilities such as the Redstone Arsenal in Alabama, and American inspectors will be at Soviet missile sites such as the Votkinsk Machine Plant in the Ural Mountains, which divide Europe and Asia.

This inspection of destroyed missiles is called *verification*. It is a check to make sure there is no cheating on the INF treaty.

What Is Ahead?

With the INF treaty in hand, Reagan and Gorbachev now are going after the hard part, an agreement to get rid of giant-sized nuclear weapons.

These are the long-range missiles and planes that experts call the heart of the nuclear forces. Long-range missiles launched from the U.S.S.R. could reach the U.S.; long-range missiles launched from the U.S. could reach the U.S.S.R. Both countries have as many as 12,000 of these nuclear missiles.

Reagan and Gorbachev are working on a treaty that would destroy half these weapons. This treaty is called the *Strategic Arms Reduction Treaty* (START).

The leaders face two big problems as they work on START. One problem is what to do about the proposed U.S. space-based defense system known as "Star Wars." Can it be developed and deployed under START?

The other problem is how to reduce the big missiles and still leave the two nations with protection. The leaders know that a nation under attack must have enough strength to strike back.

The two leaders would like to sign START at the next Reagan-Gorbachev summit, which may be held in Moscow in the late spring.

The Race Is On!

Next month, voters in Iowa and New Hampshire will pick candidates in special elections

DEMOCRATS. From left to right: Gary Hart, Albert Gore, Jr., Bruce Babbitt, Richard Gephardt, Paul Simon, Jesse Jackson, Michael Dukakis.

REPUBLICANS. From left to right: Alexander Haig, George Bush, Pierre du Pont, Jack Kemp, Robert Dole, Pat Robertson.

The election of the 41st President of United States is not until November 8—ten months away. But politics is already a big part of the winter news scene.

Seven Democrats and six Republicans have declared that they want the job of President. In recent months, these major candidates have been hard at work running their campaigns.

Citizens Vote Their Favorites

February is an important month for the presidential hopefuls. That's when they begin to find out what people really think of their ability to lead the nation.

On February 8, both Democratic and Republican voters in Iowa will cast their votes on the first major statewide test of Presidential Campaign '88. On February 16, the voters in New Hampshire will cast the second statewide votes of Presidential Campaign '88.

Over the next 18 weeks, other states will hold special elections. March 8 is called "Super Tuesday" because on that day millions of voters in 21 states will show which of the candidates they prefer.

These special state presidential elections are called *primaries* and *caucuses*. In these elections, the voters of the two major parties either pick a candidate or pick people who support a candidate. Either way, the voters show which candidate they like.

The presidential hopefuls will keep a sharp eye on the primary and caucus voting. They will learn who among them are the voters' favorites. It is likely that some candidates who do not do well in Iowa and New Hampshire will drop out of the presidential race.

Who Is the Leader?

The more votes each candidate gets, the more people he will have to support him at the national conventions. At the conventions, the candidates who will lead the Democratic and the Republican parties are decided.

The Democrats will hold their convention July 18 to 21 in Atlanta, Ga. The Republican convention will be held August 15 to 18 in New Orleans, La.

After the two candidates are picked, the campaign to win over the voters for the national election in November begins. The candidate who wins the national election becomes the next President of the United States.

Facts About the Candidates
Democrats

Bruce Babbitt—age 49 . . . former governor and attorney general of Arizona . . . lawyer . . . geologist . . . two children.

Michael Dukakis—age 54 . . . Massachusetts governor for a second term . . . lawyer . . . former state lawmaker . . . three children.

Richard Gephardt—age 46 . . . U.S. congressman from Missouri since 1981 . . . lawyer . . . lawmaker in St. Louis . . . three children.

Albert Gore, Jr.—age 39 . . . U.S. congressman and senator from Tennessee . . . former newspaper reporter and editor . . . four children.

Gary Hart—age 51 . . . former U.S. Senator from Colorado . . . lawyer . . . author . . . two children.

Jesse Jackson—age 46 . . .

Baptist minister and preacher from Illinois . . . aide to Rev. Martin Luther King, Jr. during 1960 civil rights struggle . . . five children.

Paul Simon—age 59 . . . U.S. congressman and senator from Illinois . . . former newspaper editor and publisher . . . author . . . teacher . . . two children.

Republicans

George Bush—age 64 . . . Vice President of the United States . . . former director of U.S. Central Intelligence Agency (CIA), U.S. ambassador to United Nations, U.S. envoy of China, and U.S. Congressman from Texas . . . five children.

Robert Dole—age 64 . . . U.S. Senator from Kansas . . . former U.S. congressman . . . majority leader in U.S. Senate, 1984 . . . U.S. Senate minority leader, 1987 . . . one child.

Pierre (Pete) du Pont—age 52 . . . former governor of Delaware . . . former U.S. congressman from Delaware . . . four children.

Alexander Haig—age 63 . . . former U.S. Secretary of State, assistant to President Nixon, NATO military commander . . . retired U.S. Army general . . . businessman . . . three children.

Jack Kemp—age 52 . . . U.S. congressman from New York . . . professional football player for 13 years . . . four children.

Pat Robertson—age 57 . . . Baptist minister from Virginia . . . television evangelist . . . founder of Christian Broadcast Network (CBN, cable) . . . four children.

A Daisy toy gun with markings to show it is not real

photo courtesy of Daisy Mfg. Co.

Toy Guns Are Under Fire

The city council of Los Angeles, Calif., recently took aim against toy guns. The members voted to ban the sale and manufacture of toy guns that look real.

Why? Several serious incidents involving toy guns have happened recently.

Last April, a 19-year-old man holding a toy gun was killed by a sheriff's deputy in California. The deputy thought the toy gun was real. The deputy fired in self-defense.

In two separate incidents last year, men with realistic-looking toy guns walked into TV studios in California, interrupting news broadcasts.

Some toy companies are trying to help. The Daisy Manufacturing Company is putting bright orange markings on its toy guns, so people can tell that the guns are not real.

But some police officers are worried that criminals will put the same markings on *real* guns. Seeing the markings, officers may hesitate before firing—and be fired on first.

The End of Three-Wheel Vehicle Sales

The sale of motorized tricycles known as ATV's (all-terrain vehicles) has been stopped. In December, a court banned future sales of the three-wheel ATV's for safety reasons. The court had been told that in the last five years, about 900 people were killed in ATV-accidents. Many victims were children.

Four-wheel models, said by safety experts to be nearly as dangerous, can still be sold.

Present ATV owners can continue using their outdoor toys. They will receive letters warning of their danger.

photo by American Honda Motors, Inc.

D.J.'s People
Super
Ice Skater:
Debi Thomas

Debi Thomas is a champion figure skater. She's absolutely dazzling on the ice. You should see her jump! Debi plans to compete in the 1988 Winter Olympics in Canada.

Here are some questions people ask about Debi Thomas.

Where does she live? Debi's home is in San Diego, California, but she trains in Boulder, Colorado.

How old is Debi? She's 20 years old.

What's her favorite food? Like a lot of people, Debi's crazy about pizza. She likes it covered with green peppers, mushrooms, and beef.

What are Debi's plans for the future? Someday Debi hopes to become a medical doctor; but right now, she has her eye set on an Olympic gold medal. She hopes to skate her way to the top in women's figure skating.

Kids Survive No-TV Week

Weekly Reader cartoon by D. Maccabe

Stacy Carter, 11, almost made it. But a few tempting TV programs—particularly "The Cosby Show"—did her in.

Stacy was one of 172 students and teachers at Hickory County School in Urbana, Mo., who tried to give up watching TV for a week.

The no-TV week in November was the idea of Jan Powell, the school's media director.

About 75 percent of the participants in no-TV week were successful, Powell says. Most of these participants kept diaries of what they did with their newfound spare time.

Jason Driskill, 10, made it through no-TV week. He said he read and played games with his brother and sister.

Jason and Stacy's fifth grade teacher, Audrey Green, made it through no-TV week too. She said her house was never cleaner!

Funnybunny

—Don Robison

INDEX

A

Abernathy, Ralph, 171
A-bomb, 131
Abu Simbel temples, 158
Acupuncture, 184
Addams, Jane, 21
Addiction, 241
Advertising, radio 59
"Aerobee" rocket, 97
Afghanistan, 217
Africa, 168
    Boer War, 118
    hunger, 233
    Peace Corps, 142
    WACS, 75
Agnew, Spiro, 173
Agriculture in Russia, 119
AIDS, 245
Airmail boy, 15
Airplane pilots, 92
Airplanes, 43, 45, 51, 57, 61, 62, 65, 224
    dogs, 72
    first nonstop flight, 125
    hijackers, 188
    Japan, 73
    jets, 100
    Korea, 230
    rockets, 97
    routes, 62
    speed, 17
Airports, 65
Airships, 57
Alaska, 70, 134, 218
    earthquake, 154
Alcohol, 231
Aldrin, Edwin, 173
Aleutians, 77
Alexander the Great, 217
Alliance for Progress, 147
Allison, Fran, 103
All-terrain vehicles, 251
Alpha satellite, 129
American Indians, 9, 19, 50, 127
    movies, 99
    Navajos, 93
    reservations, 93
American Nature Association, 14
American Printing House for the Blind, 62
American Red Cross, 23, 79, 204
Americans, new, 104
Amman, 110
Amphetamines, 178
Anchorage, 154
Anderson, Marian, 72
Andropov, Yuri, 244
Angie the Bookworm, 32
Animal library, 108
Antarctic, 14, 35, 187
Antifreeze, 187
Apartheid, 238
Apollo 11, 173
Apollo project, 160
April Fools Day, 188
Arab-Israeli War, 214
Arabs, 214
    Bunche, Ralph, 94
    energy crisis, 194
    Israel, 151
    Palestine, 89
Arctic Ocean, 62, 131, 235
Ark Royal aircraft carrier, 68
Armistice Day, 21, 50
Armstrong, Neil, 173
Army inventions, 70
Artificial body parts, 199
Assassinations, 222
Astronauts, 160, 173, 178, 243
    chimpanzee, 150
    women, 211
Astronomers, 19, 27

Aswan High Dam, 158
Atlas rocket, 147
Atomic power, 115, 201
Atomic weapons, 161
Auk, 32
Aunt Em, 100
Aunt Helen, 232
Australia, 66
Austria, 156
    before and after Hitler, 51
    Danube River, 90
    Rhine River, 41
Autogiro, 24, 40
Automobile, 61, 65, 114, 240
    cleaning machines, 128
    energy crisis, 194
    highways, 81, 117
    Japan, 185
    repair shops, 117
    Sabre, 103
    speed, 17

B

Babbitt, Bruce, 250
Baboon heart, 235
Baghdad, 110
Bakers, U.S. Army, 63
Bakhtiar, Shahpur, 213
Bald eagles, 14, 174, 232
Balloons, 48, 57
Ballot, 220
Baltic Sea, 53
Bartholdi, Frédéric-Auguste, 243
Baseball
    Blue, Vida, 184
    Clemente, Roberto, 192
    DiMaggio, Joe, 107
    Robinson, Frank, 195
    Ruth, Babe, 87
    Williams, Ted, 164
Batista, Fulgencio, 138
Beame, Abraham, 205
Bean, Alan, 173
Beatles, 155
Beauty, 156
Beavers, 18
Begin, Menachem, 214
Bel Fonte nuclear plant, 201
Bell, Alexander Graham, 46
Berlin, 119
    blockade, 89
    candy drop, 92
    crisis, 149
Bermuda Triangle, 207
Bernadotte, Count, 89
Bicentennial, 202
"Bigfoot," 248
Binary code, 198
Bismarck battleship, 68
Blackboards, 55
Blacks, 182, 186
    baseball, 195
    Bunche, Ralph, 94
    Carver, George Washington, 55
    Marshall, Thurgood, 167
    riots, 170
    school, 82
    World War II, 72
Black widow spiders, 143
Blimps, 57
Blind, 25
    children, 62
Blood transfusions, 187
    AIDS, 245
Blue, Vida, 184
Body parts, 199
Boer War, 118
Bottles, 14
Boy kings, 110
Boy Scout Cubs, 19
Boy Scouts of America, 19, 72
Boys Town, 91

Braille, 25, 62, 167
Bread, 63
Bridges
    George Washington, 39
    Golden Gate, 39
Brinkley, David, 160
Britain. *See* England, Great Britain.
British Broadcasting Company, 46
British Interplanetary Society, 102
Broadcasting, 59, 74
Brooke, Edward, 171
Brooklyn Bridge, 10
Brown's Ferry nuclear plant, 201
"Bubble" boy, 211
Bubblfil, 188
Budapest, 123
Buddy Bear, 144, 215
Bulganin, Nikolai, 119
Bunche, Ralph J., 94
Burma, 105, 114
Burns, protective suit for, 208
Bush, George, 251
Byrd, Admiral, 14, 35, 36, 40

C

California, 229
California Institute of Technology, 97
Cambodia, 114
Cameras, 152
    carrier pigeons, 28
    Japan, 185
    Land, 95
    Mars, 159
Canada, 62
    harp seals, 206
    roads, 138
Candy, Berlin lift, 92
Cape Canaveral, 147, 150
Carpenter, Scott, 147
Carrier pigeons, 28
Carrots, 64
Carter, Jimmy, 205, 208, 213, 214
Cartoons, 146
Carver, George Washington, 55
Casablanca, 77
Cascade Mountains, 218
Castor beans, 71
Castro, Fidel, 138, 157
Cellophane, 68
Chalk, 55
Challenger space shuttle, 243
Chamberlain, Neville, 51
Chernenko, Konstantin, 239
Chernobyl, 242
Chiang Kai-shek, General, 67
Chiang Kai-shek, Madame, 66
Chicago, 21, 65
    superhighway, 122
    trains, 61
Chicago World's Fair, 31
Child Health Day, 46
Child labor, 33
Child Labor Law, 33
Children
    blind, 62
    boy kings, 110
    labor, 33
    missing, 229
    Navajos, 93
    polio, 120
    Russia, 72
    Special Olympics, 203
    traffic safety, 52, 60
    United Nations, 101
    World War II, 53, 88
Chimpanzee in space, 150
China, 20, 67, 68, 94, 105
    acupuncture, 184
    Communist, 114, 133, 161
    imports, 219
    Japan, 45, 94

    pandas, 55
    Ping-Pong, 181
    wartime food, 71
Chinook, 14
Chisholm, Shirley, 182
Choking rescue method, 204
Chou En-lai, 181
Churchill, Winston, 118, 150
Circus, 52
Cities, 205
Citizenship, 180, 240
Civilian Conservation Camps (CCC), 34, 60
Civil Rights Bill, 171
Clark, Barney, 230
Cleaver, Theodore "Beaver," 132
Clemente, Roberto, 192
Coal
    India, 85
    Japan, 68
Coal miners, 42
Cocaine, 234, 241
Cockroaches, 114
Cod-liver oil, 10
Coffee, dandelion, 12
Collective farm (*kolkhoz*), 119
Collins, Michael, 173
Cologne (Germany), 41
Colorado, 93
Colorado River, 18
Columbus, Christopher, 144
Common Market, 126
Communes, 133
Communication satellite, 137, 142
Communism
    China, 133, 161, 183
    Cuba, 138, 157
    escape from, 113
    Indo-China, 114
    Nicaragua, 205
    Poland, 226
    Southeast Asia, 105, 141
    Vietnam, 162
Computers, 167, 198
Conrad, Frank, 59
Conservation, 50
Consumers, 183
Convoy system, 69
Cooks in Army, 63
Coolidge, Calvin, 11
Corregidor, 73
Corvair, 183
Cosby, Bill, 175
Cossack destroyer, 68
Costa Rica, 209
Cotton mills, 33
Crack, 241
Crazy Horse, 127
Cri-Cri, 224
Crime, 205, 208
Cuba, 138, 157–8
    Kennedy, John F., 149
    Nicaragua, 209
    sugar, 157
Czechoslovakia, 51, 113, 171

D

Dacron, 199
Dams
    Aswan High, 158
    Hoover, 18
    Joe Wheeler, 35
    Norris, 35
Damascus, 39
Dandelions, 12
Danny Doo and Loki, 64, 67
Danny Doo and Ranger Bill, 40
Danube River, 90
Danzig, 53
DDT, 174
Deaf, 25
Declaration of Independence, 87

de la Cierva, Juan, 24
Democratic Convention, 107, 250
Denmark, 144
Denver, 43, 190, 229
Department of the Interior, 93
Depression, The, 29, 34
Desert, 93
Desert Rat machine, 144
Destroyers, German, 69
Detroit, 15, 82, 205, 229
Diablo Canyon nuclear power plant,
   201
Diesel trains, 61
DiMaggio, Joe, 107
DiMaggio, Joe, Jr., 107
Dirigibles, 57
Disarmament, 145, 249
Discoverer XIV, 137
Disneyland, 120
Disney, Walt, 36, 67, 120
Displaced persons, 104
Dodo, 32
Dogs, 72, 114, 124, 184
   Chinook, 14
   electrical, 58
   German shepherd, 47
   seeing eye, 47
Dole, Robert, 251
Dolphins, 160
Dr. Carrot, 64
Dresden, 43
Drinking, 231
Drought, 42
Drugs, 177, 178, 231, 234, 241
Dubcek, Alexander, 171
Dukakis, Michael, 250
Du Pont, Pierre, 251
Durden, Benji, 228
Dust storms, 109

E

Eagles, 232
Earhart, Amelia, 40
Early Bird satellite, 160
Earthquakes
   Alaska, 154
   man-made, 131
Easter Island, 123
Echo I, 137
Ecuador, 102
Eden, Anthony, 118
Edison, Thomas A., 11, 115
Edward VIII, King of England, 42
   abdication, 47
Egypt, 121, 158, 165, 208
   Israel, 214
Einstein, Albert, 26
Eisenhower, Dwight, 75, 116, 135
Elections
   blacks, 182
   Presidential, 169, 250–1
Elektro and Sparko, 58
Elephant, 164
Electrical dog, 58
Electrical man, 58
Electrical power
   dams, 19
   Pakistan, 85
Electrical railway, 11
Electricity, 35
   —atomic power, 115
Electric light bulb, 11
Elizabeth II, Queen of England, 47,
   106, 118
Elsie the cow, 88
Elvar the porpoise, 160
Empire State Building, 22
Energy crisis, 194
England. *See also* Great Britain.
   Hitler, 51
   WACS, 75
   wartime food, 71
Environment, 187
Environmental Defense Fund, 210
Environmental Protection Agency
   (EPA), 210
Equal Rights Amendment (ERA), 225

Erosion, 37
Eskimo curlew, 32
Ethiopia, 38
Europa ocean liner, 17
Europe, 126
   post-war food, 78
   refugees, 79
"Explorer" satellite, 129
Expressways, 82
Extinction, 32

F

"Fabricating" factories, 83
Factories
   child labor, 33
   U.S., 29, 65, 70
Famine, 233
Far East, 68
Farming
   Russia, 119
   victory gardens, 72
Fat Albert, 175
Federal Bureau of Investigation, 234
Feisal II of Iraq, 39, 110
Fertilizer, 79, 193
Figure skating, 252
Fish, 187, 228
Flag, 116, 179
Flanagan, Father E. J., 91
Food
   China, 133
   high prices, 218
   supermarkets, 130
Ford, Gerald, 197
Forest fires, 124
Fort Knox, 43
France, 41, 126, 179
   Hitler, 51
   Indo-China, 114
   Joan of Arc, 15
   Suez Canal, 121
Franklin, Benjamin, 31
Freedom fighters, 123
Freedom Train, 87
Freight trains, 61
"Friskem," 188
Frostbite, 224
Frozen food, 127
Fuel shortage, 190
Funnybunny, 252

G

Galilee, 89
Gandhi, Mahatma, 23, 85
Gas masks, 51
Gasoline
   automobiles, 103
   rationing, 82
   shortage, 190
Gaza Strip, 214
General Motors, 103
Geneva peace talks, 114, 239
George V, King of England, 42
George VI, King of England, 47
George Washington Bridge, 39
Gephardt, Richard, 250
German Army carrier pigeons, 28
Germany, 41, 126
   Berlin, 119
   Einstein, Albert, 27
   industrial recovery, 118
   Nazi persecution, 49
   submarines, 69
Gibson, Kenneth, 182
Glass houses, 48
Glenn, John, 147
Golan Heights, 214
Gold, 43
Golden Gate Bridge, 39
Golden Gate Fair, 58
Gorbachev, Mikhail, 237, 239, 249
   arms treaty, 249
Gore, Albert, 250
Graf Zeppelin airship, 125
Grain, 193

Russia, 119
U.S., 37
Gravity, 196
Great Britain, 66. *See also* England.
   Afghanistan, 217
   atomic power, 115
   disarmament, 145
   Edward VIII, 42, 47
   Elizabeth II, 47
   George VI, 42, 47
   Suez, 121
Great Lakes, 166
Great Wall of China, 50
Greece, 102
   ancient, 38
Greenland, 62, 70
Gulf of Aqaba, 165
Gum, 95
Guns, 65
   toy, 251
Gymnasts, 192

H

Haig, Alexander, 251
Hamill, Dorothy, 203
Ham, the Chimponaut, 150
Handicapped, 207
Hanukkah, 200
Happy, 156
Harding, Warren, 59
Harp seals, 206
Harris, Robert H., 210
Harrison, George, 155
Hart, Gary, 250
Havana, 138, 157
Hawaii, 77, 84, 134, 218
   49th state, 110
H-bomb, 131
Heart
   baboon, 235
   Jarvik-7, 230
   man-made, 230
Heath hen, 32
Heimlich, Henry, 204
Heimlich method, 204
Helicopters, 110
Heroin, 177, 178, 234
Heyerdahl, Thor, 123
Highways, 82, 139
Hijackers, 188
Hillary, Edmund, 112
Hinckley, John, 222
Hindus, 85
Hitler, Adolph, 49, 51, 69
   Poland, 53
   Rhineland, 41
Hollings, Ernest F., 174
Holloman Air Force Base, 150
Homeless, 229, 246
Homes in U.S., 82
   "war on poverty," 153
Honolulu, 86
Hoover Dam, 18
Hoover, Herbert, 9, 20, 22, 24, 27
Hopkins, Harry, 34
Hops, 116
Howard Beach, 247
Hudson River, 39
Hula hoops, 132
Hull House, 21
Hull, Secretary of State, 54
Humpback whales, 239
Humphrey, Hubert H., 169, 193
Hungary
   Russia, 123
   U.S., 23, 193
Huntley, Chet, 160
Hussar, 44
Hussein I, King of Jordan, 110

I

Ibex, 217
India, 105, 114
   Gandhi, Mahatma, 21
   independence, 85

King Edward VIII, 42
Indiana turnpike, 122
Indo-China, 105, 114
Indonesia, 105, 114
Infantile paralysis, 77
Inflation, 218
Interstate highways, 139
Inventions, 70
Iran, 213
   U.S. hostages, 221
Iran-Contra deal, 246
Iraq, 39, 110
"Iron Curtain," 90
Islam, 217
Israel, 89, 149
   Egypt, 214
   Six-Day War, 165
Italy, 126
   Ethiopia, 39
   Hitler, 57
   supermarkets, 130
   WACS, 75

J

Jackson, Jesse, 250–1
Japan, 20, 66
   China, 45
   Diet, 94
   election, 94
   Philippines, 73
   products, 185–6
   trains, 172
   World War II, 94
Jarvik, Robert, 230
Jarvik-7 heart, 230
Jarvis, Gregory, 243
Jefferson, Thomas, 26, 228
Jerusalem, 214
Jet airplanes, 100
Jews and Judaism, 214
   Bunche, Ralph, 94
   Germany, 49
   Hanukkah, 200
   Israel, 165
   Palestine, 89
Jinnah, Ali, 85
Joan of Arc, 15
Jobs
   women, 191
   riots, 170
   "war on poverty," 153
Johnson, Lyndon, 150, 153, 170
Jordan, 110, 151, 165, 214

K

Kalinin, Mikhail, 30
Karachi, 85
KDKA, 59
Keller, Helen, 25
Kemp, Jack, 251
Kennedy, John F., 139, 145, 149, 150,
   169, 222
   moon shot, 142
Kennedy, Mrs. John F., 139
Kennedy, Joseph P., 149
Kennedy, Rose, 149
Kerner, Otto, 170
Khomeini, Ayatolluh Ruhollah, 213
Khrushchev, Nikita, 146
Kilroy, 84
King, Coretta, 203
King, Martin Luther, Jr., 155, 170,
   171, 203
Korbut, Olga, 192
Korea, 68, 102, 105, 230
Kukla, 103
Kukla, Fran, and Ollie, 111

L

Labrador duck, 32
Lake Superior, 139
Lake Tahoe, 166

Land camera, 95
Land, Edwin H., 95
Laos, 114, 141, 146
Lasers, 163
Latin America, 147
    Peace Corps, 142
Lava, 218
Lawrence of Arabia, 39
League of Nations, 36
    Italy-Ethiopia conflict, 38
"Leave It to Beaver," 132
Lee, Robert E., 198
Lee, Robert E. IV, 198
Lennon, John, 155
León, 209
Letters to the Editor, 195
Library, pet, 108
Lifeboats, 68
Limes line, 50
Lincoln, Abraham, 26, 222, 228
Lindbergh, Charles, 54
Linz, 90
Little America, 35
Litvinoff, Maxim, 30
Liverpool, 155
"Lolli-Pups," 124
Loma Linda University Medical Center, 235
London, 23, 86, 121
London Zoo, 55
Los Angeles riots, 170
Lowell Observatory, 19
LSD, 178
Lunar rock, 178
Luzon, 73

M

MacArthur, Dwight, 73, 94, 99
Machines
    cleaning, 128
    children and teachers, 140
    snow-making, 156
Magellan, Ferdinand, 125
Maginot Line, 50
Magma, 218
Magna Carta, 87
Malaya, 105, 114
Malenkov, Georgi, 109
Mammoth, 212
Managua, 209
Manchuria, 45
Manila, 73
Mao Tse-Tung, 133, 161
Marathon, 228
Marconi, Guglielmo, 31
Marijuana, 177, 178, 231, 234
Mariner 4, 159
Mars, 159, 173, 202
Marshall, Thurgood, 167
Martin Luther King Day, 203
Masaya, 209
McAuliffe, Christa, 243
McCarthy, Charlie, 50
McCartney, Paul, 155
McCormack, John W., 150
McGovern, George S., 174
McMurdo Sound, 187
McNair, Ronald, 243
Mekong River Delta, 162
Menorah, 200
Methyl alcohol, 103
Michael, King of Rumania, 13
Michigan, 95
Mickey Mouse, 35
Middle East, 201
Milk bottles, 14
Milkweed floss, 76
Milne, A. A., 36
Milwaukee riots, 170
Mindanao, 73
Missing children, 229
Monkeys, 240
    space, 248
Moon, 142
    lab, 160
    landing, 173
    man-made, 102

rocks, 178
Morris the cat, 192
Morse, Samuel, 46
Moscow, 109
Moslems, 85
Mother Hubbard, 140
Motorbikes, 185
Mountbattan, Earl, 85
Mount Everest, 112, 143
Mount McKinley, 98
Mount Rushmore, 27, 228
Mount Saint Helens, 218
Mount Waialeah, 134
Mount Whitney, 134
Mount Wilson Observatory, 27
Movies, 11
    Rin-Tin-Tin, 28
    seats, 88
Mr. Grumpy and Mr. Sprite, 11
Muggs, J. Fred, 128
Mullah, 213
Mummy, 215
Music
    appreciation, 22
    typewriter, 43
Muskie, Edmund, 169
Muslims, 213, 214
    Afghanistan, 217
Mutton, 217

N

NAACP, 167
Nader, Ralph, 183
Nader's Raiders, 183
Nassar, Gamal Abdel, 121
National bird, 14
National Child Labor Committee, 33
National flower, 14
Nautilus submarine, 130
Navajos, 93
Nazi persecution, 49
Negev desert, 151
Negroes. See Blacks.
Nehru, Jawaharlal, 85
Nepal, 112
Netherlands Indies, 68
Neutrality Act, 54
New Delhi, 85
Newfoundland, 144, 206
New Jersey turnpike, 122
New Mexico, 224
    Navajos, 93
Newsboys, 28
New York
    gold, 43
    turnpike, 122
New York City, 9-10, 22, 44, 86, 97, 180, 205, 229
    blackboards, 55
    expressways, 82
    refugees, 113
New York World's Fair, 58
New Zealand, 112
Nicaragua, 209
Nile River, 158
Nippon (Land of the Rising Sun), 45
Nixon, Richard, 169, 177, 181, 189, 194
Nobel Peace Prize, 155, 238
Norkay, Tensing, 112
Norris Dam, 35
North Pole, 131
NRA, 29, 32, 33
Nuclear Arms Control Treaty, 249
Nuclear energy, 242
Nuclear missiles, 237
Nuclear plant safety, 201
Nuclear Regulatory Commission, 201

O

Ocean liners, 17
O'Connor, Sandra Day, 223
Ohio turnpike, 122
Oil
    China, 219

Cuba, 138
    energy crisis, 194
    India, 85
    Southeast Asia, 105
    U.S. shortage, 190
Oklahoma, 225
Ollie, 103
Olympics, 156, 203
Onizuka, Ellison, 243
Orlando (Florida), 244
Orphans, 200
Oscar, 68, 71, 75, 80
Oshiya (pushing boys), 172
Ostriches, 204, 236
Otters, 114

P

Pacific Ocean, 73
Pahlavi, Shah Mohammed Riza, 213
Pakistan
    independence, 85
    water power, 85
Palestine, 89, 213
    Bunche, Ralph, 94
Panama Canal, 27, 54
Panda, 54, 67
Paper clothing, 168
Paris, 15, 53
Passenger pigeons, 32
Passenger trains, 61
Patents, 195
Peace
    Addams, Jane, 21
    atomic power, 115
    Egypt-Israel, 214
    Ethiopia-Italy, 38
    Gandhi, Mahatma, 23
    Joan of Arc, 15
    Lawrence of Arabia, 39
    Smith, Samantha, 244
    U.S. and Russia, 249
Peace Corps, 141, 147
Peanut and Jocko, 140, 180, 220, 244, 248
Peanuts, 54, 83
Pearl Harbor, 94
Peek the Brownie, 76
Penguins, 40
Pennsylvania turnpike, 82, 122
Peppermint hay, 95
Perkins Institution, 62
Perry, William "The Refrigerator," 239
Pesticides, 174
Pet library, 108
Philippine Islands, 73, 84, 99, 105, 114
Phonograph, 11
Pigeons, 28
Piney Woods School, 82
Ping-Pong, 181
Piñon nuts, 93
Pioneer 10, 231
Pip, 24
Pirates, 20
Planets, 112
Plastics, 83
    hula hoops, 132
Playground for handicapped, 207
Pledge of Allegiance, 116
Poland, 53, 123, 226
    escape to freedom, 113
Police, 10
Polio, 120
Pollution, 166, 205, 208, 210
Pony, 15
Pope John Paul I, 211
Pope John Paul II, 211
Porpoise, 160
Poverty
    Great Britain, 42
    U.S., 21, 29, 34, 153
Prague, 171
Preserved bodies, 235
Presidential election, 169, 250
Presidential protection, 222

Prince Charles of England, 106
Prince of Wales, 42
Prince Philip of England, 106, 155
Profiles in Courage, 149
Puerto Rico, 192, 198
Puppets
    "Sesame Street," 180
    television, 103
Puzzles, 36, 44
Pygmy marmoset, 240

Q

Quakers, 9
Quebec, 77

R

Racial conflict
    Africa, 238
    U.S., 170, 247
Radio, 51, 59, 65, 74
    advertising, 59
    Japan, 185
    Marconi, 31
    overseas, 86
    two-way, 70
Radioactivity, 242
Radiophone, 86
Radio transmitters, 59
Radio tubes, 74
Railroads, 64, 77, 78
    Japan, 172
Rationing, 78, 82
    sugar, 84
RCA-Victor, 46
Reading and writing
    Navajos, 93
    U.S., 91
Rebus, 31
Red Guards, 161
Reagan, Ronald, 222, 226, 233, 237, 243, 246
    racial conflict, 247
    Soviet arms treaty, 249
Red Sea, 121
Refugees
    Cuba, 157
    Europe, 79
    German, 49
Regensburg, 90
Relief, 34
Republican Convention, 107, 248
Resnick, Judith, 243
Retarded children, 203
Rhine River, 42
Rice, 105, 193
    Japan, 45
    Vietnam, 141
Rickets, 174
Right-to-light laws, 224
Ringling Brothers and Barnum and Bailey Circus, 52
Rin-Tin-Tin, 28
Riots, 170
Roads, 139
Robertson, Pat, 251
Robinson, Frank, 195
Rockets, 147, 150
Rocketships, 97
"Roof of the World," 62
Roosevelt, Eleanor, 27
Roosevelt, Franklin D., 27, 29, 52, 77, 149
    Nazi persecution, 49
    neutrality, 54
    relief, 34
    Russia, 30
    Tennessee Valley project, 35
    unemployment, 29
Roosevelt, Theodore, 27, 228
Rubber, 105
    U.S., 92
Rumania, 13, 90
Russia, 30, 62, 109, 119. See also
Soviet Union.

Afghanistan, 217
airplane record, 43
children, 72
Hungary, 123
Indo-China, 114
Iron Curtain, 90
Korbut, Olga, 192
lasers, 163
Southeast Asia, 105
spacemen, 148
Sputnik, 125
wartime food, 71
Russian Revolution, 30
Ruth, Babe, 87

S

Sabre automobile, 103
Sadat, Anwar, 214
Safety
nuclear plant, 201
traffic, 10
Safety Sallies, 52
Saigon, 141, 197
Salazar, Juan, 208
Salk, Jonas, 120
Salt, 143
Samson, Ralph, 98
Sandinistas, 209
San Francisco, 39, 43, 97, 110
Santa Fe Railroad, 61
Satellites, 125, 142, 160
telephone, 137
U.S., 129
Schools
blind children, 25
reading and writing, 91
solar heat, 196
war countries, 88
"war on poverty," 153
Scientific theory, 27
Scobee, Dick, 243
Sea cows, 40
Sea lions, 114
Sea of Galilee, 151
Sea water, 143
Sea World, 244
"Sealcone," 14
Seals, 206
Seashore, 24
Secret Service, 222
Seeing eye dogs, 47
"Sesame Street," 180
Shah of Iran, 213, 221
Shamu the whale, 244
Shepard, Alan, 243
Ships, 54, 65
Hussar, 44
Shipyards, 64
Shriver, Eunice Kennedy, 203
Shriver, Sargent, 142
Silk, 68
Silver Bullet automobile, 17
Simon, Paul, 251
Sinai Desert, 214
Singapore, 130
Six-Day War, 165
Ski industry, 194
Slums, 81
Smeal, Eleanor, 225
Smith, Alfred, 9–10
Smith, Margaret Chase, 91
Smith, Michael, 243
Smith, Samantha, 244
Smokey Bear, 124
Snell, Peter, 228
Sno-Blo, 106
Snow, 106
Snow-making machines, 148
Solar furnaces, 179
Solar heat, 196
Somoza, Anastasio, 209
South Africa, 238
South America, 168
supermarkets, 130
South Dakota, 27, 228
Southeast Asia, 105, 114
South Pacific, 123
South Pole, 14

Soviet Union, 30, 190, 244. See also
Russia.
Cuba, 138
Czechoslovakia, 171
disarmament, 145, 249
Korean jet, 230
nuclear energy, 242
Soybeans, 71, 83
Space
capsule, 138
crafts, 231
Mars, 159
message, 198
monkey, 248
Russia, 148
shuttle, 223, 243
tests for women, 196
Special Olympics, 203
Speed, 17, 61
Spiders, 143
Stalin, Joseph, 109, 119
Stamps, 32, 152, 175, 244
Starr, Ringo, 155
"Star Wars" defense, 237
Statehood, 110
Statue of Liberty, 243
Steel, 133
"Stern gang," 89
Stokes, Carl, 182
Submarines, 131, 135
German, 69
treasure search, 44
Suburbs, 205
Suez Canal, 121, 165
Sugar
Cuba, 138, 157
Hawaii, 110
rationing, 84
Sunflower seeds, 71
Sunlight, 224
Superhighways, 118, 139
Supermarkets, 127, 130, 218
Supreme Court, 167
Sweden, 144
Sweet potatoes, 55
Syria, 151, 201

T

Taiwan, 181
Tanks, 65
Tape recorder, 140
Teeth, 220
Teflon, 199
Teheran, also Tehran, 77, 213
Telegram, 11
Telephone, 11, 46, 51, 163
long distance dialing, 101
manners, 101
overseas, 86
satellite, 137
Teleprinter, 86
Telescopes, 27
Television, 47, 59, 74, 98, 180
cable, 186
color, 111
Japan, 145
Kukla, Fran, and Ollie, 103
Marconi, 31
mobile, 156
Morris the cat, 192
Muggs, J. Fred, 128
no-TV week, 252
political elections, 107
rules, 102
watch, 236
Ten-cent stores, 58
Tennessee River, 35
Texas, 143
Thailand, 105, 114
Thanksgiving Day Parade, 35
Thomas, Debi, 252
Tibet, 112
Tickle Box, 108
Tokyo, 99, 172
Tom Trott, 87, 127
Torpedoes, 69
Toy guns, 251
Trade

Common Market, 126
U.S.-China, 119
U.S.-Russia, 30
Traffic
policemen, 10
safety, 10, 52, 60
Trailer homes, 64
Trains, 17
Trans-Canada Highway, 139
Trappers, 62
Treasure ship, 44
Tree belt, 37
Truman, Harry S., 77, 81
Turnpikes, 122
Tuskegee Institute, 55
Tut, King, 208
Tutu, Desmond, 238
Typewriter for music, 43

U

Uncle Ben, 20, 104
Uncle Funny Bunny, 148
and Chumpy, 84
Underground cities, 50
Unemployment, 29, 205, 226
UNICEF, 193
United Nations, 69, 102, 151
African food crisis, 233
Bunche, Ralph, 94
disarmament, 145
Hungary, 123
Indo-China War, 114
Palestine, 89
United Nations Relief and Rehabilitation Administration (UNRRA), 79
United States. See also specific events, people, and places.
Army, 63
bicentennial, 202
budget, 34
China, 181, 219
cities, 205
Constitution, 110, 150
Cuba, 138, 157
debt, 224
disarmament, 145, 249
displaced persons, 104
drug problems, 177
election, 9–10, 188, 250–1
farmers, 78
flag, 179
fuel shortage, 192
growth, 134
homes, 81
hunger, 174
Iran, 213, 221
Japan-China relations, 45
Japanese products, 185–6
lunar landing, 173
Nicaragua, 209
nuclear energy, 201, 242
poverty, 153
riots, 170
Russia, 30
roads, 139
satellite, 125, 129, 137
supermarkets, 130
television, 98
unemployment, 226
Vietnam, 142, 197
war bonds, 76
warplanes, 65
world hunger, 193
United States Census Bureau, 91
United States Forest Service, 124, 187
United States Patent Office, 195
United States Post Office Department, 124
University of Massachusetts, 247
Unsafe at Any Speed, 183
Untouchables, 43

V

V-E Day, 78
Verdun, 50
Vietnam, 114, 141, 146, 161, 169

orphans, 197
war, 162, 181
Vietnam Moratorium Day, 175
Vikings, 144
Viking spacecraft, 202
Virgin Islands, 190
Vocabulary Pals, 219, 227, 242, 247
Voiceprints, 152
Volcanoes, 134
Volkswagen, 118
Voters, 220

W

WACS, 75
Wainwright, General, 80
Walesa, Lech, 226
Walkie-talkies, 70, 99
War inventions, 70
"War on poverty," 153
Warm Springs, 77
Washington, D.C., 80, 142, 167, 182, 189, 249
Washington, George, 27, 228
Washington, Walter, 182
Wasp carrier, 67
Water, 210
Israel, 151
salt, 143
Watergate, 189
Weathermen, 75
Weather stations, 62
Wesleyan University, 215
West Africa, 193
West Bank, 214
Westinghouse Company, 59
Whales, 239, 244
Wheat, 37
Whiskers, 240
White House, 24, 135, 139, 152, 177
fire, 20
March, 139
Watergate, 189
Whooping crane, 108
Why England Slept, 149
Wilkins, Roy, 170, 182
Williams, Ted, 164
Willie Wonders, 32, 36
Willy Quack, 95
Wilmington (North Carolina), 64
Winnie the Pooh, 36
Wise Owl, 28, 40
WJZ, 59
Wolves of the sea (submarines), 69
Women
astronauts, 211
Presidential candidates, 188
space tests, 196
Supreme Court justice, 223
World War I, 21, 30, 37, 38, 41, 50
debt, 45
Lawrence of Arabia, 39
Poland, 53
World War II, 90, 94, 185.
See also specific people and places.
displaced persons, 104
Kennedy, John F., 149
Navajos, 93
World's Fair, 58
Writing aid, 195
WWJ, 59

Y

Yaks, 112
Yalta, 77
Yankee Clipper
DiMaggio, Joe, 107
ship, 17
train, 17
Yugloslavia, 102, 130

Z

Ziolkowski, Korczak, 127
Zip, 132, 212
Zoos, 40, 204
London, 55